THE NON-ALIGNED MOVEMENT

The Non-Aligned Movement

The Origins of a Third World Alliance

Peter Willetts

Frances Pinter Ltd., London

First published in Great Britain in 1978 by
Frances Pinter (Publishers) Limited
5 Dryden Street, London WC2E 9NW

Reprinted 1982

ISBN 0 903804 33 6 Hardback
ISBN 0 86187 210 X Paperback

Printed in Great Britain by
Redwood Burn Limited, Trowbridge, Wiltshire
and bound by Pegasus Bookbinding, Melksham, Wiltshire

Contents

List of Tables

List of Figures

Foreword

Professor Ali Mazrui

No principle of foreign policy in the second half of the twentieth century has had a greater impact on relations between small countries and Big Powers than non-alignment. The concept has changed in meaning and operational implications since its inception in the 1950s, but it continues to affect significantly the diplomatic orientation of a majority of states in the developing world.

Peter Willetts is justified in distinguishing between non-alignment as a principle of foreign policy in individual countries and the Non-Aligned as a collective Movement in world politics. This study pays special attention to the latter aspect of non-alignment—a solidarity of the less powerful in global affairs.

But what kind of Movement has it been? It is possible to identify in non-alignment a solidarity of protest, a Movement for moderation in East-West relations, and a commitment to global reform in North-South relations. The solidarity of protest is a continuing theme. But historically there has been a change of focus from a preoccupation with reducing the level of conflict in East-West relations to a more pronounced emphasis on transforming the basis of North-South relations.

An examination of the issues that have preoccupied the Non-Aligned states over the years reveal anti-colonialism as a persistent theme of *protest*. In the days of Jawaharlal Nehru non-alignment was also anxious to *moderate* the tensions of the Cold War and prevent too sharp a polarization of the world. But the 1970s especially have witnessed in non-alignment a clearer focus on a basic *restructuring of the global system* in the direction of greater equity in North-South relations.

Willetts' study does indicate that protest, moderation and reform were all present all along in the Movement, but the change of focus is also discernible on closer analysis of aims, purposes and changing rhetoric.

Non-alignment in the 1960s began to subsume some of the protest of Afro-Asian solidarity. Non-alignment in the 1970s has subsumed some of the reformist zeal of the Group of Seventy-Seven and the Movement has taken the lead in the struggle for a New International Economic Order.

Although the Non-Aligned still predominantly consist of African and Asian states, two countries outside those two continents have played a significant role in the history of the Movement. The two countries are Yugoslavia and Cuba. Peter Willetts in concentrating on the origins of non-alignment focuses especially on Yugoslavia, not least because Marshal Tito was among the founders. Tito's friendship with Nehru and Nasser, coupled with the leadership of Kwawe Nkrumah in Africa, all helped to lay the foundations of the Movement.

Peter Willetts goes through some of the reasons which influenced specific leaders to declare themselves to be Non-Aligned in those early days. In the case of Tito the reasons were connected with his break with Moscow in 1948, and his subsequent reluctance to embrace the West on the rebound. Non-alignment provided a third way for Tito, an opportunity to retain independence from both Moscow and the Western alliance.

It is partly from this point of view that Tito's Yugoslavia can be compared with Castro's Cuba. Just as Tito had rebelled against the hegemony of Moscow, so Castro came to rebel against the hegemony of Washington. Just as Yugoslavia had for so long been in 'splendid isolation' in Eastern Europe in the shadow of regional ostracism, so too was Cuba isolated in the Americas in the shadow of more elaborate hemispheric sanctions. Just as Tito subsequently found a sense of mission in greater participation in the politics of the Third World, so too did Castro find such a sense of mission in his own distinctively revolutionary way. Just as Tito had laid the foundations that made possible the later development of 'Eurocommunism' and challenged the Moscow doctrine of 'proletarian internationalism', so had Castro innovated with a Marxist state in the Americas—and challenged Washington's right to keep communism out of the hemisphere.

But there were differences, as well as similarities, between Tito's Yugoslavia and Castro's Cuba. Whereas Yugoslavia more clearly asserted her independence from both the West and the East, Cuba under Castro was forced to be excessively dependent upon the Soviet Union. And yet, even this dependence was important for non-alignment in the crises of 1962. China's conflict with India in

1962 was indeed a major crisis for non-alignment. Could a country like India keep out of alliances—and still be safe? The West rallied to India's support in 1962 morally and to some extent materially. And yet the Western Press at the same time seemed to rejoice in Nehru's discomfiture and embarrassment. Had Nehru underestimated the danger of 'communist aggression'? In view of China's humiliation of India had non-alignment lost its validity?

It was the other crisis of 1962—the Cuban missile crisis—which reasserted the validity of non-alignment as a doctrine of minimising military entanglement with either bloc. Castro's Cuba had permitted the establishment of a missile base on its soil by the Soviet Union, aimed at the United States. The Non-Aligned were suspicious of military bases controlled by super powers in small countries. Castro had violated a basic precept of non-alignment. The world has thus been taken to the brink of nuclear war when Washington demanded the dismantling of the missiles. To make matters worse Castro himself was humiliated when Moscow agreed to the dismantling of the missiles virtually without consulting Havana on the subject. The Super Powers, having reached a tense confrontation (eye-ball to eye-ball) later reached an understanding between themselves in almost complete disregard of whether the government of Cuba agreed or not. If Nehru's humiliation that year at the hands of China had challenged the *raison d'être* of non-alignment, Cuba's humiliation over the missile crisis re-established the validity of the policy. If India had suffered partly because it was not part of a military alliance, Cuba had suffered by the reverse reason of drifting into a *de facto* alliance with the Soviet Union. The two crises of 1962 cancelled each other out from the point of view of non-alignment.

Now the sixth summit meeting of the Non-Aligned Movement is scheduled to take place in Havana in 1979. Yet the issue of whether Cuba is 'truly non-aligned' in view of its close links with the Soviet Union remains alive and controversial within the Movement. It was an issue which provoked much passion and acrimony at the Belgrade Ministerial Conference of July 1978—not least because of Cuba's military involvement in African conflicts. The setting was symbolic. Belgrade was listening to debates about the Non-Aligned credentials of Havana. Yet, from the point of view of non-alignment, those two capitals were the most important historically outside the heartland of Asia and Africa. Tito was a hero in terms of East-West relations. Castro was a hero in terms of North-South relations. Tito's non-alignment had combined a solidarity of protest with a commitment to moderation in East-West relations. Castro's non-alignment had tended to define the protest in terms of opposition to imperialism in North-South relations. Taken together, these two non-Africans and non-Asians—Tito and Castro—had captured the changing focus of non-alignment from the old days of the Cold War to the current groping for a new global economic order.

Dr. Willetts' study adds concreteness to this story. To some extent this book is a biography of the origins of a Movement and a profile of a non-military alliance. I cannot say that I agree with every aspect of this biography. Nor is the profile quite what I would have drawn. But my own interpretation of non-alignment will never be the same again after reading Willetts' account. This is a book which has enriched my understanding of one of the most important movements in the politics of the twentieth century.

September 1978

Preface

It is hoped that this book will appeal to three audiences: primarily to those with an interest in non-alignment, but in addition to researchers involved in the problems of data collection and to specialists in cluster-analysis. For the first group, with a substantive interest in the international relations of the Third World, it represents a contribution to an area of study that has been much neglected. The static, outmoded connotations that the word 'non-alignment' carries for most Westerners has led us to ignore the dynamic growth of an ideology and new institutions in the Third World. The growth has occurred explicitly in the name of non-alignment, and is examined in an outline diplomatic history in Chapter One. Chapters Two to Five are devoted to seeing whether or not the countries that formed the Non-Aligned Movement in the 1960s had a distinct form of foreign policy behaviour. They are compared to four other groups of countries. The last chapter summarises the relationships between the different dimensions of behaviour and discusses whether the theory of neo-colonialism helps to explain the results.

The book breaks new ground, both in being the first study to examine the diplomatic origins and the development of new institutions for the Movement and in being the first attempt to present a systematic profile of all the membership of the Non-Aligned. The extent of the neglect of the subject is shown in that it is believed to be the first time that the simple distinction has been made between membership and non-membership of the Movement in the Third World. The Non-Aligned and the Non-Bloc countries form two separate groups to be compared with each other. However, most readers will feel that much of this vast subject has not received attention. In particular the concern with development, culminating in the Algiers summit's initiative in calling the Sixth

Special Session of the General Assembly on the establishment of a New International Economic Order, and the concern with the arms race, culminating in the Colombo initiative for the Tenth Special Session on disarmament, are both dealt with in a brief manner. The relationship between non-alignment and the problems of development and of disarmament would each merit a book on their own. They are given less attention in the current work because they are seen as being less central to identifying the main features of the Non-Aligned Movement.

Chapters Two to Six all are based on the quantitative analysis of a wide range of data. The attempt has been made to present all these results in a way that is understandable to those who have an interest in the substantive material, but no methodological training. Only the ability to feel at ease with numbers, particularly as percentages, is essential. Sections which discuss how the data was created, its validity and its reliability are not difficult, but may be omitted by the non-specialist reader and are marked D*. Statistical sections that are not essential or are more difficult in the statistics they use are marked S*. Where such sections occur they may be omitted and are followed by a verbal, non-statistical summary. An elementary understanding of analysis of variance, correlation and regression is sufficient for all the main text. At times a few technical terms, such as 'the proportion of the variation that is explained', are used outside the S* sections because in their context a commonsense interpretation of the words gives a good idea of their technical meaning. One of the functions of Chapter Three is to provide an explanation of how voting blocs in the United Nations may be identified. The more detailed results are given on East-West issues and on colonial issues in Chapters Four and Five, and Chapter Three could be omitted. The aim of this style of writing is to bridge the gap between the traditional scholars and the behaviouralists. The anti-behaviouralists cannot ignore the important substantive conclusions that the Non-Aligned are different in the 1970s from the 1960s; that they are still a coherent group; and that East-West relations is not a relevant dimension to identify them.

One methodological point does need explanation for the more general reader. The distinction between the following levels of measurement for different types of data should be understood.

(a) *Nominal variables* represent no more than the naming of distinct categories. For example, this occurs when we label countries by their geographical region as African, Asian, European, etc.

(b) *Ordinal variables* are formed from categories that may be arranged in an order, according to some property. Thus the ordered categories (i) high Western arms trade, (ii) moderate Western arms trade, (iii) no arms trade, (iv) modern Eastern arms trade and (v) high Eastern arms trade used on page 133 give an Index of Military Alignment, which is an ordinal variable.

(c) *Interval variables* are obtained when the ordering can be based on genuine numerical data. Thus the number of people in a U.N. delegation is used as an interval measure of participation.

The distinction between the levels of measurement is important, because correlation and regression is only valid between two interval variables. However it is common social science practice to treat some ordinal variables as if they really were interval variables. The readers must attempt to judge for themselves whether this represents a reasonable relaxation to enable more interesting analysis to proceed or is an unjustified distortion of the data.

The second audience for this book is among those who are interested in the practical problems of quantitative work. Special care has been taken to discuss the strengths and weaknesses of each source of data. This is important to ensure replicability and is part of building a scientific subject in which results can be compared and accumulated. Too often so little is written about data that the reader has no basis to assess the validity of the results obtained. Thus the sections marked D* in this book should be of particular interest to those teaching about quantitative methods or to postgraduate students just starting on their own research.

A third audience consists of those people in any scientific discipline who are interested in cluster-analysis. The methods outlined in Chapter Three to answer the question 'What states vote together as a distinct group in the U.N.?' could be used to answer 'In what way do states form groups that trade together?' or 'What patterns may be found in the friendship choices of a group of schoolchildren?' or 'Which archaeological sites belong to the same cultural period?' A non-technical explanation is given in Chapter Three and a full technical explanation in Appendices Five and Six.

Some points of terminology are worth mentioning. Just as one may refer to conservatism with a small c and use capital letters when referring to the Conservative Party, so the convention has been adopted in this study of distinguishing between non-alignment as a set of ideas and the Non-Aligned as a specific group of states. Whenever Non-Aligned is written in capitals, reference is being made to the states that attended the relevant Conference of Heads of State or Government of Non-Aligned States. Secondly, the word 'state' has been used to describe the territorial units that are actors in the international system and the common practice of using the word 'nation' as a synonym has been rejected. However, to avoid repetition 'country' has been used instead at times. When mention is made of actions or decisions of a state, this should of course be taken as a shorthand reference to the actions or decisions of the appropriate member of the government of the state. Thirdly, it has at times been found convenient to use 'Third World' to mean all the states of Latin America, the Caribbean, Africa and Asia with the addition of Yugoslavia, but excluding South Africa, Australia, New Zealand, the Soviet Union and China. Lastly, as several of the indicators are derived from data on activity in the United Nations, states that are not members of the U.N. have been excluded completely from this study, as units of analysis. If any statement does relate to non-members, then specific mention is made of them.

Thanks are due to many people for the support and assistance they gave to this research. Special mention should be made of Helge Hveem, now at the Peace Research Institute Oslo, who sparked the whole project off, by suggesting that we prepare jointly a paper for the Universities of East Africa Social Science Conference at Dar es Salaam in December 1970. The staff and students of the Department of Political Science and Public Administration, Makerere University, presented an exciting and stimulating intellectual environment. In particular, Professor Ali Mazrui, then the head of the department and now at the University of Michigan, and Professor Maurice East, now at the University of Kentucky, provided great encouragement to continue with the work. Both in the staff seminars and in the undergraduate Methods of Social Investigation class, Makerere offered a challenge that is too rarely available to those engaged in quantitative work. The sterile debate between 'traditionalists' and 'scientists' was submerged in a catholic tolerance, and the demand was for exploration of the substantive implications rather than the technical features of methodological decisions. It is hoped that this challenge has been met, to some extent at least, in the attempt to give a more detailed explanation than is usual of the decisions taken in the gathering and the coding of the data. Later, the Department of Government, Essex University, were very generous in providing both a base and computer facilities for six months. Then Strathclyde University's Social Statistics Laboratory, provided an environment in which data analysis was free from the administrative and technical obstacles that normally frustrate computer work. Mark Franklin made it possible for the work to continue in yet another move to City University, London, by generously providing a copy of the DAEDAL computer package.

The data on voting in the United Nations was obtained on a

magnetic tape from the Inter-University Consortium for Political and Social Research at the University of Michigan and their assistance is gratefully acknowledged. The *American Political Science Review* is thanked for permission to reprint as Appendix Five an article, which originally appeared in their June 1972 issue.

The extension of the work on U.N. voting to produce the bloc diagrams in Chapters Three, Four and Five was only possible through the assistance given by Dr. John Ford of the University of Essex. He translated my requirements into a matrix algebra problem and provided a working Fortran version of the algorithm for incorporation in my computer programme. Thus Appendix Six is predominantly his work. Barbara Farbey, a Research Fellow at City University, took the main data and produced most interesting results using the techniques of pattern recognition, but unfortunately it was not possible to include those results in this work.

Thanks are also due for documents and verbal information provided by the Ministry of Foreign Affairs in Kampala, the Ministry of Information in Dar es Salaam, the O.A.U. Secretariat in Addis Ababa, the Ministry of Information in Cairo and L. Mates, Director of the Institute of International Politics and Economics in Belgrade. David Johns, now at the University of California, was particularly helpful in obtaining documents of the Cairo Conference. Margaret McAfee, Anne Marie Paterson and Prudence Pinsent of the United Nations Library in London provided patient and thorough assistance in chasing many obscure points of detailed information. Pamela Child and Dinah Hilton are thanked for accurate typing from a messy manuscript, as is Martyn Jones of the Centre for Educational Technology at the City University for artwork on the diagrams. The study would not have been possible without the support of all these institutions and individuals, but any errors of fact, judgement and interpretation remain the responsibility of the author.

CHAPTER ONE

Diplomacy, Ideology and Institutionalisation

The concept of non-alignment came into general currency in the early 1960s. To many it seemed as if the Non-Aligned might only be of temporary significance, because with the waning of the Cold War non-alignment would soon become irrelevant. But in practice the diplomats of the Third World have shown no sign of calling a halt to holding conferences of Non-Aligned States. The following list shows that, on the contrary, the frequency of meetings has tended to increase.

TABLE 1.1   THE MAIN MEETINGS OF THE NON-ALIGNED*

Place and Level of Representation	Date	Number of Members
1. Cairo Preparatory Meeting	5th–12th June 1961	20
2. Belgrade First Summit	1st–6th September 1961	25
3. Colombo Preparatory Meeting	23rd–28th March 1964	23
4. Cairo Ministerial Meeting	2nd October 1964	—
5. Cairo Second Summit	5th–10th October 1964	47
6. Belgrade Consultative Meeting	8th–12th July 1969	44
7. New York Consultative Meeting	27th September 1969	53
8. Dar es Salaam Preparatory Meeting	13th–17th April 1970	51
9. Lusaka Ministerial Meeting	6th–7th September 1970	—
10. Lusaka Third Summit	8th–10th September 1970	53
11. New York Consultative Meeting	30th September 1971	55
12. Georgetown Ministerial Conference	8th–12th August 1972	59
13. Algiers Ministerial Meeting	1st–4th September 1973	—
14. Algiers Fourth Summit	5th–9th September 1973	75
15. Lima Ministerial Conference	25th–30th August 1975	81
16. Colombo Ministerial Meeting	11th–14th August 1976	—
17. Colombo Fifth Summit	16th–19th August 1976	85
18. Belgrade Ministerial Conference	24th–30th July 1978	—
19. Havana Sixth Summit	Due late 1979	

*See also Table 1.2.

It is the purpose of this study to examine why the Non-Aligned do continue to meet together. First of all we will consider what ideas have been put forward under the name of non-alignment and then we will see whether foreign policy decisions match up to these ideas.

The approach used to study non-alignment

John Burton, writing in the period immediately after the 1961 summit conference, said:

> So far nonalignment has been studied primarily in a national context; nonalignment in Burma, Ceylon, Egypt, India. . . . Alone these national studies are not satisfactory, for they do not distinguish those national influences which are unique to nonalignment, from others which are common to aligned and to nonaligned alike.[1]

Many years later, Burton's comment is as valid as when it was first written. There are now more than eighty states that have declared themselves to be Non-Aligned, by attending one of the recent meetings. In order to make valid statements about non-alignment, one must take into account the policies and the actions of all the members of this group. At times, comparisons with other groups of states will be called for. Particular comparisons, such as between India and Pakistan or between Egypt and Turkey, are not sufficient, as we cannot know whether such comparisons are typical for all the Non-Aligned and all the other states. Therefore wherever possible data will be gathered on all the independent states.

Because of the large number of states involved and the wide range of information that is available on their foreign policy decisions, many of the statements about the Non-Aligned must be quantitative ones. It is only by the use of quantitative methods that one can summarise such a large volume of information. It is probably true to say that a majority of those interested in the international relations of the Third World are hostile to the use of quantitative methods: John Burton certainly is.[2] Thus there have been several works that engage in a general discussion of non-alignment, but there has been no systematic empirical study of the Non-Aligned.[3] The present study attempts to fill this gap.

The founders of non-alignment

Many writers trace the origins of non-alignment back as far as the late 1940s. While it is almost impossible to trace the evolution of ideas with any precision, it is too facile to accept the judgement of the Non-Aligned politicians, some of whom seek to add legitimacy by giving the ideas a long history. We will see below that it was not until the late 1950s that Yugoslavia, Egypt and India began to work together and develop a common approach. Their contribution to non-alignment does not go any further back. When they first came to power Tito, Nasser and Nehru did not consider that their countries would lead a new movement in the Third World. Only after non-alignment had been developed as a coherent ideology did they seek to reinterpret the past to claim that they had always been Non-Aligned.

One of the more frequent ways in which non-alignment is given false roots is by referring back to the 'Asian African Conference', which was held in the Indonesian city of Bandung in 1955. This conference brought together all the independent countries of Asia and Africa, except Korea and Israel. The 29 states attending ranged from the communists (China and North Vietnam) on the one hand to the Western allies (Turkey, the Philippines and South Vietnam) on the other hand. The debates reflected the Cold-War attitudes of the time. The problem of colonialism in Asia and Africa could not be discussed without counter-reference to Soviet domination in Eastern Europe. The Ten Principles for relations between states, adopted in the final declaration, included an endorsement of military pacts while they omitted the desire of some states to proclaim 'peaceful co-existence'.[4] In the states that attended, in the tone of the debates and in the resulting decisions, Bandung was not a forerunner of the Non-Aligned conferences. The importance of Bandung was that for the first time a group of former colonial territories had met together without any of the European powers, and to all those taking part this was an assertion of their independence.

Non-alignment was not widely recognised as a coherent set of ideas, that was the basic justification for the foreign policy of particular states, until those states came together and articulated their common interests and similarity of outlook in the 1961 Belgrade Conference. This summit originated from the increasingly close co-operation between Tito, Nasser and Nehru since 1956. Thus, if there is any point at which non-alignment was conceived, it was in the 1956 Suez-Hungary crisis, the greatest confrontation between radical nationalism and the major powers to occur in the first twenty years of the post-war era. This double crisis brought the three countries, Yugoslavia, Egypt and India, close together.

When the nationalisation of the Suez Canal led to the invasion of Egypt by Israel, Britain and France, India supported Egypt for obvious reasons of sympathy, but also had a close strategic interest in the Suez Canal, which was crucial for her trade routes. Furthermore, India greatly benefited from forming a close alliance with Egypt which for many years prevented her rival Pakistan being able to rally support by an appeal to Moslem solidarity.[5] Equally it was only to be expected that Yugoslavia, like the other communist countries, would support Egypt against the two Western powers. But in addition Yugoslavia felt seriously threatened by the Soviet invasion of Hungary, which occurred in the same month as the Suez invasion. Yugoslavia felt close to Egypt, as both were small states threatened by the narrow interests of the Great Powers. A further factor was that, by one of the accidents of history, Yugoslavia was on the Security Council in 1956 and was able to propose the 'Uniting for Peace' resolution that circumvented British and French vetoes and took the Suez crisis to the General Assembly. The resulting Emergency Special Session of the General Assembly was of critical importance in rallying support for Egypt, and the U.N. Emergency Force provided a convenient diplomatic handle to lever the British and French troops out of Egypt again.[6] In later visits to Yugoslavia and India, President Nasser laid special stress on expressing thanks for the 'unselfish assistance' and 'great support' that Egypt received in 1956, when it was 'confronted by aggression'.[7]

Yugoslavia

The three founders of non-alignment were very different from each other in their perspectives on the world. Tito was the leader of a country that had in 1948 successfully survived a confrontation with one of the Great Powers and has ever since felt the need to guard against possible intervention by the Soviet Union. It is interesting to note that in the early 1950s Yugoslavia sought to deal with this situation by an approach that was the opposite of non-alignment, that is by adopting a pro-Western alignment in the Cold War. In February 1953 the Balkan Treaty was signed with Greece and Turkey. In March 1953 Tito visited Britain and was told by Churchill 'we are your allies'.[8] In 1954 Tito visited Turkey and then later while he was in Greece it was announced that it had been agreed to convert the Balkan Treaty into a formal military alliance. Popovich the Yugoslavian Foreign Minister was quoted as having 'no neutralist illusions'.[9]

With the major changes in the Soviet Union after the death of Stalin leading to the 1955 rapprochement between Tito and Khrushchev, the Balkan alliance was soon forgotten. Tito then saw that the best long-term hope for Yugoslavia's security lay in easing the ideological confrontation between the United States and the Soviet Union. Tito became a communist ideologue arguing for Krushchev's new policy of co-existence. The 1956 Hungarian crisis strained relations between Yugoslavia and the Soviet Union, but did not diminish the desire to influence ideology in the Soviet Union. Thus until 1961 the key concept in Yugoslavia's foreign policy was not non-alignment but 'peaceful and active co-existence'. In 1961 it was simple to weld 'co-existence' together with the ideas of other leaders so that it formed a part of 'non-alignment'. The two sets of ideas are not contradictory. As may be seen by comparing Tito's definition of 'co-existence' in 1955[10] with Section II of the Belgrade Declaration and Section IV of the Cairo Programme for Peace,[11] there is a clear continuity in the ideas.

India

Unlike Egypt and Yugoslavia, India's independence has never seriously been threatened. Her only major clash with a Great Power came in a border war with China after the Belgrade Conference, when India merely lost some of her prestige. To many, non-alignment is based on India and the attempts to trace non-alignment back to the 1940s are usually based on attempts to read non-alignment into the foreign policy of India, immediately after independence. Some writers talk as if 'non-alignment' has been the declared policy of India since independence.[12] Others such as Devdutt admit that the term was not used at first,

The term 'independent policy' was more frequently employed during the period 1946–50; the term 'peace area approach' was preferred during the period 1950–58 and the term 'non-alignment' came more into vogue after 1958.[13]

but maintain that the change in terminology does not reflect any change in policy.

However, non-alignment of the 1960s is primarily a policy for the Third World, a defensive policy for small states. India's emphasis has been quite different. There is a strong case for maintaining that India's policy, in practice, has from independence and all through the 1950s been in conformity with non-alignment. But if so, it must be classified as a variation *sui generis*. India's approach is not to be wary and antagonistic towards the Great Powers but to assert that it *is* a Great Power. Certainly not a Great Power of the first rank, but a Great Power that relies not so much on economic and military might as on the prestige of an independent, moral, foreign policy. Thus India's emphasis on independence is very different from that of Burma or Nepal or, in more recent times, Burundi or Congo (Brazzaville).

Even the much-quoted phrases, from Nehru's early speeches, which are taken to typify 'non-alignment', often have an aggressive tone to them that does not fit with subsequent ideas of non-alignment. In December 1947 Nehru said:

> We have proclaimed during this past year that we will not attach ourselves to any particular group. That has nothing to do with neutrality. . . . We are not going to join a war if we can help it: and *we are going to join the side which is to our interest* when the time comes to make the choice.[14]

A year later he rejected

> . . . trying to align ourselves with this great power or that and becoming its camp-followers in the hope that some crumbs might fall from their table.[15]

But in 1948 the policy had not become a foreign policy ideology because (amongst other reasons) it was not generalised beyond India. There was no sense of solidarity, when he said:

> I can understand some of the smaller countries of Europe or some of the smaller countries of Asia being forced by circumstances to bow down before some of the greater powers, because they cannot help it.[16]

That did not apply to India as

> We are not citizens of a weak or mean country [*sic*] and I think it is foolish for us to get frightened, even from a military point of view, of the greatest of the powers today.[17]

The clearest indication that India is playing a different game from the other small powers is when Nehru said:

> If we had been some odd little nation [*sic*] somewhere in Asia or Europe, it (our independent policy) would not have mattered much. But because we count. . . . Everything we do becomes a matter for comment . . . we are potentially a great nation and a big Power.[18]

India's independent policy, deciding issues on their merits alone, while being a component of non-alignment is adopted mainly because it conforms to India's role of being a special type of Great Power.

> . . . we have to plough a lonely furrow in the United Nations. . . . Nonetheless . . . I am quite sure that by adopting that position, we shall ultimately gain in national and international prestige . . . fairly soon . . . a large number of the small nations . . . will probably look to India more than to other countries for a lead.[19]

Thus India's independent, moralistic policy had a sound political foundation. It was a non-partisan foreign policy for a country that has a very broad spectrum in its internal policies, ranging from the communists to the Jan Sangh;[20] it conforms to both the nationalist and the Ghandian moralist traditions in Indian politics; and it also compensates for military weakness by creating prestige and influence in line with India's desire to be a Great Power.

In 1954 India's attempt to project her moral approach became a sustained propaganda offensive with the *Five Principles* or *Panchsheel* being offered as a solution to the world's problems. They were first launched in a trade and communications agreement for Tibet, between India and China. The preamble said that the two countries

Have resolved to enter into the present agreement based on the following principles:
(1) Mutual respect for each other's territorial integrity and sovereignty;
(2) Mutual non-aggression;
(3) Mutual non-interference in each other's internal affairs;
(4) Equality and mutual benefit; and
(5) Peaceful co-existence.[21]

The *Panchsheel* are so general that it is difficult to give them precise meaning in terms of foreign policy behaviour, for example they do not preclude either bilateral or multilateral military alliances (which are always claimed to be defensive rather than aggressive). Thus the *Panchsheel* were able to receive the explicit endorsement of the Soviet Union, only one month after the Warsaw Pact had been signed.[22] Coming ten years after the Second World War the *Panchsheel* are the modern equivalent of the Kellog-Briand Pact signed ten years after the First World War. Within three years, 18 countries from all parts of the world, with the exception of the major Western powers, had endorsed the *Panchsheel* in Joint Communiqués or Joint Statements with various Indian leaders.[23] The *Panchsheel* were also partially incorporated in the *Ten Principles* enunciated at Bandung and after cursory and acrimonious discussion in the last three days of the session were partially endorsed in a United Nations resolution in December 1957.[24]

The fact that both Yugoslavia and India were launching the idea of peaceful co-existence at about the same time must have helped to promote the friendship between the two countries. But when we come to the first Non-Aligned Conference it is the more carefully elaborated ideas of Tito that are included in the Belgrade Declaration and there is no mention, either explicitly or implicitly, of the *Panchsheel*.

However, to say that India's simple moralistic approach has not made a useful contribution to international affairs is not to deny that India's actual role on many *specific* issues has been extremely valuable. In the early 1950s, India's warnings on the consequences of American troops entering North Korea; her assistance in achieving a Korean armistice; her role in the Neutral Nations Repatriation Commission; her contribution to the Geneva Settlement on Indo-China; her chairmanship of the International Commissions on Cambodia, Laos and Vietnam; her persistent lobbying in the U.N. for progress in disarmament talks; these are but the highlights of India's early foreign policy that consistently matched well in practice to the later development of the ideology of non-alignment. But the fact that the *Panchsheel* were only a tool of Indian diplomacy and not the basis of policy, that the real basis of policy was the claim to be a special type of Great Power, makes the more belligerent foreign policy of the 1960s seem less like a dramatic change. Thus the Goa invasion,[25] intransigence over Kashmir, hostility to international concern for the Nagas, a bellicose response to the border dispute with China, refusal to sign the Nuclear Non-Proliferation Treaty[26] and the invasion of East Pakistan are all events that have led to accusations of hypocrisy and have dented India's claim to assert moral leadership, but equally they are all typical examples of Great Power behaviour.

Egypt

While both Yugoslavia and India are in the paradoxical position of being amongst the founders of non-alignment yet being atypical of the movement as a whole, Egypt is both a founder and a more typical member of the movement. Nasser's claim to fame was as one of the great nationalists of the 20th century and we will see that radical nationalism brought the Non-Aligned together.

When Nasser first defined Egypt's role, in 'The Philosophy of the Revolution', a short while after he had taken power, he saw Egypt as the centre of three circles, the 'Arab circle', the 'African Continent circle' and 'the circle of our brethren-in-Islam'.

There is no doubt that the Arab circle is the most important of all these circles and the circle most closely connected with us.[27]

In those early days of 1954, the significance of the Second Circle had not been clearly thought out. Africa received little mention and there was even an imperialist assertion that

We certainly cannot, under any conditions, relinquish our responsibility to help spread the light of knowledge and civilisation up to the very depth of the virgin jungles of the Continent.[28]

The Third Circle offered a romantic vision to Nasser of 'hundreds of millions of Moslems, all united by the same Faith'.[29] It inspired what may well be, for the Third World, the first suggestion on record of modern 'conference diplomacy'. As Nasser 'stood before the Qaaba' he decided that 'The Pilgrimage should have a potential political power'. There should be 'a periodical political conference . . . (of) the heads of all Islamic States'.[30]

Despite Nasser's claim to the contrary, it is clear that he sees Egypt being the leader in each of these circles. Indeed the very idea of circles implies a centre on which they all depend. Nasser said, 'I always imagine that in this region there is a role wandering aimlessly about in search of an actor to play it' and 'The Philosophy of the Revolution' ends with the assertion 'it is we, and we alone, in virtue of our position, who can play the part'.[31]

Throughout the 1950s the First Circle of the Arab world continued to be of prime importance for Egypt. There was a series of crises to absorb Egypt's attention. Egypt vigorously opposed the Baghdad Pact, which attempted to bring Arab states into military alliance with the West. She supported the Algerian F.L.N. fighting for independence from France and nationalised the Suez Canal, with the result that she suffered the tripartite invasion. Then the formation of the United Arab Republic by the merger of Egypt and Syria was followed by revolution in Iraq and British and American troops being moved into Jordan and the Lebanon. It was only in 1960 that friendship with Nkrumah and the Congo crisis led Nasser to play an active role in the African Second Circle. Nasser never paid serious attention to the Third Circle of Islam and indeed when Saudi Arabia and Iran took the lead, in late 1965 and early 1966, in promoting international Moslem political co-operation Nasser was even antagonistic to the idea, fearing that it would be a conservative force.[32]

Professor Mazrui has suggested that Egypt gains great strength in being at the centre of these different circles and that she gains support in one area by making it relevant to the others. For example, the major enemy of the Arab Circle, Israel, is made relevant to the African Circle by branding it a neo-colonialist state. Mazrui has also characterised non-alignment as Egypt's Fourth Circle.[33]

In some ways non-alignment does fit well with the other three circles. Arab nationalism is the origin of Egypt's interest in non-alignment. Egypt wanted to break away from Western domination. Yet, in accepting communist military and economic aid and in facing a strong communist party at home, Egypt wanted to make it clear that she would not in any way become a Russian satellite. All the various crises that caused so much concern to Egypt in the 1950s were seen as being the result of Great Power interference in Arab affairs. The Arab First Circle and the Non-Aligned Fourth Circle had considerable overlap and only differed in their centres of interest and emphasis. The anti-Big Power and anti-colonial sentiment of non-alignment also fitted well with the African Circle. Finally, with its emphasis on the state as an independent unit, non-alignment to an extent fitted with the attempt to modernise and secularise Islam (though it did not fit so well with Pan-Islamic sentiment, which transcends states).

However, in a more fundamental way, in the early years, the Fourth Circle was an alternative to the first three circles and cut across them. Thus when Nasser dispatched invitations to the first Non-Aligned Preparatory Conference in Cairo in June 1961, five Arab states (Jordan, Lebanon, Libya, Tunisia and Yemen) were left out. Non-alignment was also a reflection of and helped to perpetuate divisions in the African Circle between the radicals and the conservatives. And in the Circle of Islam non-alignment involved the rejection of Pakistan and Malaya in favour of their enemies India and Indonesia. Later on the contradictions were removed and by 1964 Egypt was able to play host, first, to the Arab League Heads of State, then the O.A.U. annual Assembly and finally the second Non-Aligned Conference to which all the Arabs and Africans were invited *by virtue* of being members of the League and/or the O.A.U. Only Pakistan and Malaya remained outside the fold.

The first Non-Aligned Summit Conference

Why was the first Non-Aligned Summit Conference held in 1961 rather than earlier or later? The conference was the product of three factors: the close relations between Yugoslavia, Egypt and India; the dramatic impact of the African states on world affairs in 1960; and a sudden increase in tension after hopes had been raised for an easing in the Cold War.

Yugoslavia first clearly showed its interest in developing strong relations with the Third World countries when Tito went to Asia from 1st December 1954 to 5th February 1955, an exceptionally long period for any Head of State to be away from home. The trip included three weeks stay in India and on the way back Nasser had his first meeting with Tito. A few days later Nehru also came to Egypt and met Nasser for the first time. From this point in early 1955 bilateral meetings among the three men became particularly frequent. Their potential for leadership was recognised when all three came together at Brione, Yugoslavia, in July 1956. Much to the irritation of Nehru the press focused attention on this tripartite summit and asked whether a new Third World bloc was being formed. While the three did not undertake any formal commitments to each other that would justify describing them as a bloc, they did cement close personal relationships. In biographical sketches of Nasser a leading Egyptian journalist, Heikal, has testified how, in addition to their meetings, Nasser was in regular correspondence with Tito and Nehru, consulting them on all the major problems of those times.[34]

The second factor in bringing the Non-Aligned together was the importance attached to African issues in 1960. Sixteen new African states became independent and joined the U.N. in that year. At the same time awareness of the problem of *apartheid* was heightened by the South African police shooting at a peaceful crowd, killing sixty-seven and wounding nearly two hundred Africans on the 21st March at Sharpeville. The Algerian guerrilla war against the French, which was already of great concern at the Brione meeting, continued with increasing ferocity. In the Congo (now Zaïre), the breakdown of the government, within a few weeks of indepen- dence, led to other countries taking sides with the factions, thus threatening to bring the Cold War into the heart of Africa. The issues were all a challenge to radical African nationalism, yet the new ex-French states on joining the U.N. offered obsequious praise both to De Gaulle and to France[35] and even refused to give strong support to Algerian independence.

The twenty-six African states, that were then independent, split sharply. Twelve of the ex-French colonies banded together to form the Brazzaville Group. They felt specifically threatened by Morocco's claim to the territory of Mauritania, one of their number, and generally were afraid that Nkrumah's campaign for Pan-African union would lead to Ghanaian domination. In the Congo they supported the more conservative leader, President Kasavubu. On the other hand Ghana, Guinea, Mali, Morocco and the United Arab Republic formed a rival Casablanca Group, which included the Algerian Provisional Government as a full participant. They were radical nationalists, Pan-African and in the Congo supported the Prime Minister, Lumumba, against Kasavubu. None of the Brazzaville Group were at the first Non-Aligned summit, whereas all of the Casablanca Group, including the Algerians, were there.

The third factor that contributed to the calling of the Belgrade summit was an increase in Cold-War tensions. In 1959 Chairman Khrushchev of the Soviet Union had visited President Eisenhower in America and hopes were raised by the cordial 'spirit of Camp David'. A summit conference, to negotiate a solution to problems in Europe, with the British and the French included, was planned for May 1960 in Paris. Just before it was due to start an American U2 spy-plane was shot down in the Soviet Union and the resulting furore brought about the collapse of the summit. This was followed by friction over access from West Berlin to East Berlin. The Congo crisis in the summer led to denunciations by the Soviet Union of the West and of the U.N. Secretary-General. When Khrushchev addressed the 15th Session of the General Assembly, he tried to rally support from the Third World in an angry speech, in which he emphasised points by thumping on the rostrum with his shoe.

In response to the general increase in tension the Yugoslavs called a meeting, at their permanent mission to the United Nations in New York, of Tito, Nasser, Nehru, Nkrumah and Sukarno. Both the Egyptians and the Yugoslavs have referred to this get-together, at the General Assembly's 15th Session in September 1960, as being the first Non-Aligned meeting.[36] The five leaders agreed to sponsor jointly a simple resolution calling for the American President and the Soviet Chairman 'to renew their contacts interrupted recently'.[37] The resolution failed to get communist support and met with Western obstruction. Argentina obtained a separate vote on the references to 'the President' and 'the Chairman of the Council of Ministers' and these words were deleted through lack of a two-thirds majority, leaving the resolution simply calling for America and the Soviet Union to renew their contacts. Nehru then withdrew the resolution, as it no longer had much meaning or usefulness.

It is likely that the idea of a Heads of State Meeting of the Third World was tentatively discussed amongst these five leaders at the U.N., but without getting strong support. Nehru would have been reluctant to step onto any podium smaller than the world stage; Nkrumah was primarily interested in Pan-African politics and eagerly accepted Morocco's initiative for the January 1961 Casablanca Conference; while Sukarno wished to regain the limelight that had shone on the Bandung Conference and in March 1961 sent out letters calling for a second Afro-Asian Conference. The idea of an Afro-Asian Conference had two disadvantages: it would exclude Yugoslavia and it would not produce a united group of states. Given the large number of aligned states in Asia and conservative states in Africa, the radicals would even have found themselves in the minority.

The crucial initiative came from Tito who undertook a long tour of Africa, from 13th February to 23rd April 1961, visiting nine countries, Ghana, Togo, Liberia, Guinea, Mali, Morocco, Tunisia, Sudan and the United Arab Republic, to promote the idea of a conference of like-minded, radical nationalist states. The Indians were opposed to a gathering that might concentrate on anti-colonialism for, as Nehru later said, 'the era of classic colonialism is gone and dead'.[38]

But on his tour Tito found enough support that, ignoring Indian opposition, he and Nasser decided to go ahead on their own and on the 26th April invited to Cairo a small group of 17 other states (the actual invitations were never made public, but it is unlikely at this early stage in the movement that there were any refusals). Following this *fait accompli* the Indians had to support the idea and they asked that their name should be joined to those of the original sponsors.[39]

The twenty states that met for the preparatory meeting in Cairo in June 1961, to discuss the idea of holding a summit, consisted of the six Casablanca states and three other African states which were among the closest to them in the U.N. 15th Session;[40] seven central and east Asian states, which were not militarily aligned;[41] Iraq, which had recently left the Baghdad Pact; Saudi Arabia, which was temporarily on good terms with Egypt; Cuba, which had just successfully defeated the Bay of Pigs attack and Yugoslavia.

At the Cairo meeting India argued against the Non-Aligned being a relatively small coherent exclusive group and proposed that many more countries should be invited to the full summit conference.[42] It proved impossible to reach agreement on this issue and so the matter was left to a Committee of Ambassadors to resolve. The decision appears to have been a compromise that produced invitations for Cyprus, Lebanon, Nigeria, Togo, Upper Volta and three Latin American states.[43] Of these eight new candidates only Cyprus and Lebanon subsequently attended as full participants in September 1961 at the Belgrade summit. After the Committee finished its work, Tunisia established its nationalist credentials by fighting with the French at Bizerta and so received a late invitation. The Congolese were able to come because Adoula and Gizenga formed a coalition government, and out of the vicissitudes of its relations with Egypt the Yemen found its way to Belgrade as well, making a total of 25 states at the first summit.

Six years of close political co-operation between Egypt, India and Yugoslavia showed how three states from different continents and with very different political systems could nevertheless have similar foreign policies. This provided a nucleus around which other Third World states could gather. The conflict between the Casablanca and the Brazzaville Groups showed that a broadly based Afro-Asian meeting would not be successful. Finally these African disputes and the general increase in tension made some of the Afro-Asians feel that they must band together to avoid being involved in the Cold

War. The result was a summit conference, including less than half of the Afro-Asians, under the name of non-alignment, at Belgrade in September 1961.

The perpetuation of non-alignment

While I maintain non-alignment was not born until 1961 as a coherent group of ideas propounded by a group of relatively like-minded states, it has also been maintained by other people that non-alignment did not live beyond 1961: that the second conference in Cairo in 1964 was an Afro-Asian and not a non-aligned conference.[44] We have already noted that in 1961 part of the reason for the Belgrade Conference being held was to head off the idea of a second Bandung. This conflict between non-alignment and 'Afro-Asianism' became even more pronounced when competition developed from the middle of 1963 between Sukarno wanting a second Bandung and Tito wanting a second Belgrade.

By this time the need to assert non-alignment did not seem so pressing and an Afro-Asian conference appeared to have much more chance of success. The international political climate had greatly improved. After the earlier setback of the Cuba missile crisis in October 1962, there followed the nuclear test-ban treaty, the establishment between Washington and Moscow of a 'hot-line' telecommunications link and the beginnings of a general *détente* between the Super Powers. Just as important for the future of non-alignment was a concurrent *détente* between the rival African groups, when the issues that divided them were resolved or shelved. Algeria became independent in a negotiated settlement with France, and joined the U.N. In the Congo U.N. troops brought to an end Tshombe's provincial secessionist regime, thus removing one of the most bitter points of conflict. Mauritania's admission to the U.N. in October 1961, after a Soviet veto had imposed a year's delay, meant Morocco's hopes of gaining control were no longer a serious threat. Similarly Nkrumah's plans for Pan-African government ceased to be an issue because he gained so little support from the other African states. The decline in conflict within Africa made it possible to disband the Casablanca and the Brazzaville Groups and form the Organisation of African Unity in May 1963.

As a result of the relaxation of tension in Africa a second Non-Aligned meeting would be larger and less exclusive than the first one. Therefore the actual differences in composition between a new Belgrade and a new Bandung conference could have been minimal. One of these differences was of major importance: Communist China would attend an Afro-Asian and not a Non-Aligned meeting.

As the depth of the split between China and the Soviet Union became more public, China increasingly sought to portray herself as a Third World country opposed to the hegemony of both the United States and the Soviet Union. The drive for a second Bandung was part of China's drive for influence in the Third World at this time. Indonesia had taken the initiative because she wanted to regain the prestige that she obtained in 1955 as a result of the first Afro-Asian Conference. Pakistan also was an enthusiastic supporter of China her enemy's enemy, and in any case would be left out of a second Belgrade.

Almost identical factors were at work on the other side. Mrs. Bandaranaike hoped for a prestige boost in bringing a Non-Aligned conference to Ceylon; India could restore her position, after the 1962 war with China, by once again appearing as a leader of the Non-Aligned; and Yugoslavia did not want to be left out of an Afro-Asian meeting, especially if the result would be an increase in Chinese influence. The issue was decided in October 1963 when Mrs. Bandaranaike visited Cairo and Nasser joined her in a joint communiqué calling for a Non-Aligned conference.[45] After much diplomatic activity, a Preparatory Meeting of Ambassadors was held in Colombo in March 1964 and the second full Non-Aligned Conference was held in Cairo in October 1964.

Preparations also went ahead for the second Bandung and a preliminary meeting was held in Djakarta in April 1964, but of the 60 or so eligible states only 22 turned up and even 12 of the original 29 Bandung countries were absent. Then with Nasser's support for the Non-Aligned Conference and his refusal to attend yet another summit in 1964,[46] the full Afro-Asian Conference had to be postponed until March 1965. In the event the Afro-Asian Foreign Ministers met in June and then again in October 1965. India successfully sought to counter-balance Chinese influence by obtaining a consensus that Russia should be invited. China in anticipation of defeat stayed away from the October meeting but she was saved from complete humiliation by the decision of the others not to go ahead with the Afro-Asian summit.[47]

Thus, Afro-Asianism is now officially dead, and it even appears that in more recent years the Afro-Asian caucus group in the United Nations has ceased to operate.[48] However, in another sense Afro-Asianism is not dead, and has instead merged with non-alignment. There was an important change in the issuing of invitations to the Cairo summit as compared to the Belgrade summit. In 1961 Africa and the Arab world were deeply divided and the invitations were to an exclusive grouping mainly of radical nationalist states. By 1964 these divisions had been overcome, at least for the time being. The most important change had been the formation of the O.A.U. Although this is essentially an organisation formed by the conservative African states, one of the few concessions made to the radicals was to include among the 'Principles' of the O.A.U. an 'affirmation of a policy of non-alignment with regard to all blocs'.[49] Thus all African states were invited to the second Non-Aligned summit, despite the fact that some did not claim to be non-aligned. Equally, all the Arabs, and all but the most obviously aligned of the Asians were invited.[50] The official list was:

(a) The 25 which had taken part in the First Conference held in Belgrade in 1961;
(b) All those which subscribed to the Charter of the Organisation of African Unity;
(c) All Arab countries which had taken part in the Cairo Heads of Arab States Conference in January 1964;
(d) Malawi, Laos, Jamaica, Trinidad and Tobago, Argentine, Bolivia, Brazil, Chile, Mexico, Uruguay, Venezuela, Austria, Finland and Sweden;
(e) Zambia and British Guiana, if their independence was proclaimed before October;
(f) —Also as full participants—the Provisional Government of Angola headed by Holden Roberto and any other provisional government formed in Africa between March and October 1964 and recognised by the Organisation of African Unity.[51]

The result is that Pan-Africanism, Pan-Arab nationalism and to an extent the weak Pan-Asian sentiment have been merged into non-alignment.

The second Non-Aligned summit in Cairo did not come at a time when international tension was high. Indeed, as the final document points out, there had been a general improvement in the international situation. To some this means that the conference had little point.[52] But it must not be forgotten that the very fact of holding the conference forestalled a second Bandung and thereby contributed to its collapse. This was an important victory for non-alignment in Afro-Asia. In as much as it is general ideology, non-alignment must apply to the relations of the small states with China, just as much as to their relations with America and the Soviet Union. Therefore it was a victory that China's drive to assert itself as the leader of the coloured peoples was thwarted. Future Chinese involvement in Afro-Asia was more likely, as a consequence, to be on the basis of equal state-to-state relations (as in the Tanzam railway project), than through close involvement in a country's internal politics (as for example in Burundi or Indonesia in the mid-1960s).

In the preparations for the third summit it became clear that there would be no change in this position. Non-alignment and continental solidarity remained fused. The 1969 Belgrade Consultative Meeting produced a very vague and general formula

. . . that those interested countries that proclaim their adherence to the policy of non-alignment and particularly those who had won their independence after the Cairo Conference and all members of the O.A.U. should be invited to the future gatherings of the non-aligned countries in accordance with the principles and criteria observed at the Belgrade and Cairo Conferences.[53]

The reference to Belgrade and Cairo was a reaffirmation of the policy that members of Western military alliances could not join the Non-Aligned. It seems to have been inserted solely to confirm that India had been successful in blocking Pakistan, a member of CENTO and SEATO, in her attempt, at the Consultative Meeting, to be included amongst the Non-Aligned.[54] The Dar es Salaam Preparatory Meeting was even more general in saying that invitations to Lusaka 'would be issued by the host State [sic] to countries on the basis of the criteria of non-alignment laid down in 1961 and 1964'.[55] Since then most newly independent countries have joined the Non-Aligned Movement and more recruits have also been made in Latin America. The summit conferences have remained broadly based and have steadily increased in size from 25 members in 1961 to 47 in 1964, 53 in 1970, 75 in 1973 and 85 in 1976.

As an historical phenomenon, non-alignment arose from the situation in 1960, in which there had been a setback to hopes of a relaxation of the Cold War, violent conflicts were impeding the decolonisation process, and there was the prospect of heavy involvement of the Great Powers in Africa and Asia. Tito, Nasser and Nehru, who had already been co-operating during and since the Suez crisis, responded by calling a conference of like-minded states, that were disturbed by the international situation. Because of the divisions between Nasser and the conservative Arab states, between Nehru and the Western military allies in Asia and between the Casablanca and the Brazzaville Groups in Africa, the first Non-Aligned summit was only attended by a minority of the Afro-Asian states. Subsequent developments led the Non-Aligned to block the holding of a second Bandung Conference, but at the same time the Non-Aligned dropped their radical exclusiveness and expanded their membership to include the vast majority of the Afro-Asians.

Identifying the components of the ideology

Having considered the early diplomatic history of the movement it is now appropriate to begin to define the ideology of non-alignment. The argument for a general, behavioural approach given at the beginning suggests that we should not fall into the trap of offering our own personal definition of the ideology. It would not be much better to draw upon the writings of one or two prominent leaders. We should study all the speeches and other materials in which reference has been made to non-alignment. Only in this way can the full range of ideas be encompassed. Unfortunately, it is a mammoth task for one researcher to read all the documents that are available, let alone to undertake a full, systematic, content-analysis. A more fundamental problem is that there is no straight-forward answer to questions such as the relative weight to give to the ideas of different leaders or of the importance of the occasion when the ideas were expressed. There are no quantitative methods nor indeed any non-quantitative methods to handle each individual country's foreign policy statements, in order to answer the question 'What is the essence of non-alignment?' Fortunately, there is an easy way out. The Non-Aligned leaders have themselves produced a consensus opinion on what they consider non-alignment to be. The communiqués of the Non-Aligned summit conferences will be relied upon as the most authoritative statements of the principles of non-alignment. The negotiation between the diplomats on the wording of a communiqué is designed to give a balance between the ideas of the major leaders and those of the many smaller states. The balance is struck by the Non-Aligned themselves rather than by our own perceptions of non-alignment. On the whole, all the important ideas had been developed by 1970 and so the main reliance will be placed on the communiqués of the first three summits.

Neutrality and non-alignment

Despite the enormous amount of documentation, it is relatively rarely that the Non-Aligned have collectively and explicitly given a concise definition of non-alignment. One of the few occasions on which this had been done was at the very first Non-Aligned gathering, the Cairo Preparatory Meeting in June 1961. The Foreign Ministers drew up the criteria by which the Committee of Ambassadors was supposed to issue invitations to the first summit. These were:

(i) an independent policy based on the co-existence of states with different political and social systems and non-alignment or a trend in favour of such a policy;

(ii) consistent support to movements for national independence;

(iii) non-membership of a multilateral military alliance concluded in the context of Great Power conflicts;

(iv)   in case of bilateral military agreement with a Great Power, or membership of a regional defence pact, the agreement or pact should not be one deliberately concluded in the context of Great Power conflicts; and

(v)   in case of lease of military bases to a foreign power, the concession should not have been made in the context of Great Power conflicts.[56]

This definition is highly important as it shows that even at this *very* early stage the Non-Aligned were not identifying themselves solely on the basis of a lack of military alignment in the Cold War. The definition highlights, as its first two criteria, peaceful co-existence and anti-colonialism. While there was obviously a great deal of overlap between the concepts, the overlap was far from complete. At the end of the 1950s there were non-bloc countries such as Finland, Sweden, Austria and Ireland that generally voted with the colonial powers in the U.N. on colonial issues and on the other hand there were bloc countries notably of course all the communists but also Greece and to a lesser extent Pakistan and the Philippines that were consistently anti-colonial.[57]

Despite the fact that the Non-Aligned are not neutral states and are not comparable to the small states of the 19th century, many writers have persisted in maintaining that non-alignment is merely a synonym for neutralism. Peter Lyon admits of a minor difference in that the 'neutral' states, in the past adopted a policy of 'neutrality', and were bound by a generally recognised set of legal rights and obligations, whereas today's 'neutralist' states with their policy of 'neutralism' are not recognised in international law.[58] Lyon's analysis is inadequate in that he admits only one of the many distinctions between neutrality and non-alignment. Many of the essays in Martin's book *Neutralism and Non-Alignment* simply take it for granted that there is no difference between the two concepts.[59] Sayegh offers more promise in his attempt to give a classification of neutralism involving four types: (a) passive neutralism, (b) negative neutralism: non-alignment, (c) positive neutralism and (d) messianic neutralism, but then he confuses the issue by saying that these are not distinct categories and that any combination of the four approaches (except passive and messianic) may be typified by the same state at one point in time.[60] What is more relevant to the present point is that Sayegh only offers these distinctions as representing different reactions to the Cold War and as different variants of the old phenomenon of neutrality.

The quotation of the criterion of non-alignment adopted by the 1961 Cairo meeting shows how, with the emphasis on anti-colonialism, non-alignment has always involved more than a new form of neutralism. But, before leaving this issue, it is worth considering further how the neutralist *component* of non-alignment is different from traditional neutrality. It has already been noted that traditional neutrality was a recognised legal status. This had an important consequence, that neutrality was respected by the Great Powers (even if this was only because respect for neutrality was one of the 'rules of the system', which would invoke counter-moves against any power that violated it).[61] By contrast the Cold-War belligerents, with their 'those who are not for us are against us' approach, do not recognise or respect any decision to abstain from the Cold War. Dulles was the most famous opponent of neutrality. He claimed that it

. . . pretends that a nation can best gain safety for itself by being indifferent to the fate of others. . . . It is an immoral and shortsighted conception.[62]

Neutrality was a passive, isolationist policy of non-involvement and generally was practised by stable, established states, that had a clear sense of identity. Non-alignment is a policy of new states that are still involved in a search for their identity. It rejects the claim that the Cold War is everybody's business and rejects the attempt to impose alien ideas. It is mainly due to ideological pressure coming from the bloc leaders and the need to develop a coherent and distinct reply that non-alignment could not remain a policy but itself had to develop into an ideology. Thus India's approach based upon an appeal to morality made a useful contribution. It allowed the small states not only to refuse to join alliances but to counter-attack:

. . . war between peoples constitutes not only an anachronism but also a crime against humanity. This awareness of peoples is becoming a great moral force, . . . (the Non-Aligned) resolutely reject the view that war, including the Cold War, is inevitable, as this view reflects a sense both of helplessness and hopelessness. . . . The existing military blocs . . . by the logic and nature of their mutual relations, necessarily provoke periodical aggravations of international relations.[63]

Neutrality involved abstention from all conflicts, whereas non-alignment only involves abstention from the Cold War. Non-alignment has not implied neutrality in the anti-colonial struggle nor in conflicts between the developing and the developed nations. Indeed the claim has often been made that non-alignment may involve active participation in Cold-War disputes provided that each issue is decided 'on its merits', rather than by regular support of a bloc leader. The distinctions between non-alignment and neutralism may be summed up by the difference between an activist and an isolationist approach.

The participants in the (Belgrade) Conference are convinced that, under present conditions, the existence and the activities of non-aligned countries in the interests of peace are one of the more important factors for safe-guarding world peace.

The participants

. . . consider it essential that the non-aligned countries should participate in solving outstanding international issues concerning peace and security in the world as none of them can remain unaffected by or be indifferent to these issues.[64]

The main way in which this activism is to be expressed is in support for the United Nations. Each of the main Non-Aligned conferences have had on their agenda an item concerned with strengthening the United Nations and each conference has endorsed the U.N. in its resolutions.[65]

Non-alignment and the United Nations

There are three important ways in which the United Nations has been of crucial relevance to the Non-Aligned and thus helped to give non-alignment an internationalist component. In the first place, as soon as a new country has become independent it has sought to join the United Nations. This sets the final seal on its independence, with the achievement of international recognition and the granting of formal equality, 'one state one vote'. The importance of this point is emphasised when it is remembered that the refusal to admit Mauritania and Mongolia to the U.N. until 1961 was explicitly intended as a denial of their independence. Secondly, once a state has joined the U.N. it is called upon to vote on many issues the majority of which may be of no immediate concern to the state's own interests. Two of the smallest states, Gambia and the Maldives, do not face this problem because of persistent absenteeism, but the vast majority engage in at least the minimum participation of attendance at Plenary Sessions. As a matter of prestige the delegates do not like to vote 'Abstain' regularly and thus an isolationist neutralism is, to this extent, made impossible. Lastly, in the areas where the Non-Aligned wish to effect changes in the international system, colonial emancipation or economic development, one of the main ways they have of making an impact is through collective action at the United Nations. It is important to note that any attempt in the fields of decolonisation or development to extend the U.N.'s role, by the partial surrender of national sovereignty, is not at the expense of the small states but only at the expense of big power sovereignty. When it comes to the pacific settlement of disputes, which often threatens the sovereignty of small states rather more than it does large states, the Non-Aligned are no more willing to accept the legitimacy of a result of which they disapprove (as may be seen in radical Africans' hostility to some decisions of the U.N. forces in the Congo) than are any other states.

Support for the United Nations is not derived from any underlying internationalism in non-alignment. The reverse is the case. The U.N. offers recognition of independence, forces at least limited involvement in international issues and is a highly useful forum for promoting the interests of the Non-Aligned. It is the pragmatic value of the U.N. that has injected a strong dose of internationalism and support for the expansion of the U.N.'s role, that might otherwise be absent from non-alignment.

Given that non-alignment is an activist ideology, it will be the intention of Chapter 2 of this study to examine how active the Non-Aligned have been in the United Nations. They will be compared with other small, non-bloc, states that have not attended Non-Aligned conferences and with other states that can make no claim to being Non-Aligned. It is expected that after allowing for the small size of many of the Non-Aligned they will be found to be more active than average. Then, in Chapter 3, the overall voting patterns in the United Nations General Assembly will be examined to see whether or not the Non-Aligned do form a coherent bloc.

Non-alignment and the Cold War

The word 'non-alignment' was originally coined because it sounded less negative for the states concerned than 'neutralism', 'the uncommitted', 'positive neutralism' or any of the other phrases that were used in the late 1950s. But like the various alternatives, 'non-alignment' was adopted because it had the clear implication that these states were not going to be involved in the Cold War. One of the many things that the three founders of non-alignment had in common was their opposition to Great Power alliances. Egypt was opposed to the Baghdad Pact; India was opposed to the Baghdad Pact and to SEATO; while Yugoslavia was opposed to the Warsaw Pact. Yet, despite this background, it is one of the oddities of the Non-Aligned conferences that Cold-War alliances have received relatively little attention. This is shown clearly by examining the agendas for the summit conferences, which are given in Appendix 1. At Belgrade the 'problem of foreign military bases' was grouped together with disarmament and nuclear tests and did not form a main item but was merely the fourth of six sub-heads to the item on 'peace and security'. Similarly at Cairo 'military pacts, foreign troops and bases' was only the eighth of nine sub-heads and at Lusaka the fourth among four. The subject also received relatively low priority in each of the final communiqués. Most surprising of all are the qualifications that hedge around the anti-pact elements of the Cairo 1961 criteria of non-alignment quoted earlier. The opposition is not to all Great Power alliances but only to those with a Cold-War flavour, 'concluded in the context of Great Power conflicts'. The qualifications were made because nine of the Belgrade participants had strong military ties, outside the main Cold-War alliances, with America or Britain, and of these nine, three could not have been left out of the Belgrade meeting.[66] Morocco was a member of the Casablanca group; Ceylon was close to India and had attended the Casablanca meeting as an observer; while Cuba needed support after the Bay of Pigs invasion attempt. The case of Cuba, which had and still has an American naval base at Guantanamo, points to what would have been a more logical qualification: namely, that if a country had inherited Great Power military links it should be actively trying to eliminate them.

However, although it has not been given prominence, each of the main conferences has endorsed a brief general condemnation of bases. The Belgrade communiqué said they

. . . consider the establishment and maintenance of foreign military bases in the territories of other countries, particularly against their expressed wishes, to be a gross violation of the sovereignty of such states. . . . They call upon countries which maintain foreign bases seriously to consider their abolition as a contribution to world peace.[67]

The Cairo communiqué was almost identical but expanded the statement a little. The Lusaka Conference introduced two new elements. It explicitly called for '*the dissolution* of great power military alliances'[68] and introduced a discordant note by agreeing

to safeguard international peace and security through the development of social, economic, political and *military strength of each country.*[69]

Once again we can see that the real underpinning of non-alignment is not a 'moral approach' but the national interests of the states concerned.

The purpose of Chapter 4 will be to examine the pattern of military relations of the Non-Aligned and to see to what extent they are free from entanglement with the Great Powers. In addition as alignment is commonly taken to mean that a state can be regularly relied on for support, the chapter will examine whether the diplomatic relations and U.N. voting patterns show any tendencies to regular alignment to the East or West.

Non-alignment and disarmament
The general increase in international tension from April 1960, in

particular the building of the Berlin Wall and the explosion of the world's largest nuclear bomb, by the Soviet Union, on the day the conference opened, made questions of security and disarmament immediately relevant to the Belgrade Conference. Even so it required Nehru's leadership to draw the conference along with India onto the world stage. On his initiative,[70] the conference adopted a special 'Statement on the Danger of War and an Appeal for Peace'[71] and also sent Sukarno and Keito to Moscow and Nehru and Nkrumah to Washington as special emissaries with letters appealing for further talks between Kennedy and Khrushchev.[72] In addition the main communiqué devoted six of its 27 points to questions of disarmament, including a demand that 'the non-aligned Nations should be represented at all further world conferences on disarmament'[73] and the assertion that 'the moratorium on the testing of all nuclear weapons should be resumed'.[74] It was this last issue of nuclear testing that made disarmament salient to most countries. At the time the dangerous effects of radioactive fall-out were receiving wide publicity. The Asians were worried about tests in the Pacific and the Africans were furious about French atomic tests in the Sahara.

The Cairo communiqué gave even more attention to security problems with four separate sections on the codification of Peaceful Co-existence (which was a special concern of Tito), on Respect for Sovereignty, on Settlement of Disputes without force, and on Disarmament. The last section, *inter alia*, gave support to the Moscow test-ban treaty, called for its extension to underground tests and, in a blow to the pro-Chinese elements, gave a detailed programme of non-proliferation measures. But China did gain support in the call for a 'world disarmament conference under the auspices of the United Nations *to which all countries would be invited*'.[75]

At the third summit in Lusaka 'Peaceful co-existence' was not even explicitly on the agenda and disarmament and general security questions received relatively little attention. They are barely mentioned in the 'Declaration on Peace . . .', which contains the reference, already mentioned, to building 'the military strength of each country'. One of the 15 resolutions (which are clearly meant to be of less importance than the two Declarations), is on disarmament. Its strongest demand is for the finalisation of a convention on damage caused by space satellites; there is only a very weak call for a World Disarmament Conference; and there is no reference at all to the Non-Proliferation Treaty, even though it had only been in force for six months and still lacked ratification by many of the most important countries. The resolution on the United

Nations does also include a call to celebrate the 25th Anniversary of the U.N. by the adoption of two Declarations on peaceful co-existence.

The overall trend from 1961 to 1970 shows that, while belief in disarmament and promotion of peaceful inter-state relations is still honoured as part of the ideology of non-alignment, this component has clearly declined from a near pacifist crusade at the beginning of the decade to being only of secondary importance at the end of the decade. Indeed the improvement in international relations, which was so desired in 1961, has been found to have its disadvantages, as 'there is an unfortunate tendency on the part of some of the big powers to monopolise decision-making on world issues which are of vital concern to all countries'.[76]

Non-alignment and anti-colonialism

We have already seen how historically the formation of the Non-Aligned Movement (in distinction to the non-alignment ideology), was based on anti-colonialism. The Suez crisis brought the three founding countries, Egypt, Yugoslavia and India more closely together, and the disputes over Algeria, the Congo and Mauritania's independence split the more anti-colonialist from the conservative African states. Were it not for this split there might well have been Pan-African meetings, Afro-Asian conferences and tripartite co-operation but no Non-Aligned conferences. It has already been pointed out that from the beginning anti-colonialism was one of the criteria of non-alignment. Now we will consider the contribution of anti-colonialism to the ideology.

At Belgrade 'self-determination' and 'liquidation of colonialism' took the most prominent position on the agenda but, although these issues were given emphasis in many speeches, Nehru set out to downgrade the importance of anti-colonialism.

. . . in so far as any historical perspective is concerned, the era of classic colonialism is gone and is dead, though of course it survives and gives a lot of trouble yet, but essentially it is over.[77]

He emphasised the 'dangers of modern nuclear warfare',

. . . we should . . . not talk about other subjects . . . while the world goes to its doom.[78]

Under Nehru's influence the 'Statement on the Dangers of War . . .' and the letters to Kennedy and Khrushchev made the greatest impact but the main declaration did devote the first eight of the twenty-seven specific points, with which it ended, to anti-colonial issues, notably the wars in Algeria and Angola, the French base at Bizerta, civil strife in the Congo and *apartheid* in South Africa.[79]

As with the Belgrade agenda, the provisional agenda drawn up for Cairo by the Colombo Ambassadors Meeting put anti-colonialism as a sub-head (along with disarmament, bases, the U.N., etc.) under the main item '. . . strengthening world peace and security. . .'. But, unlike Belgrade, Colombo gave priority to 'Peaceful co-existence' and included self-determination under 'Settlement of disputes without . . . force. . .'. These decisions were reversed at Cairo, when the Foreign Ministers, before the Heads of State met, emphasised self-determination by making it a separate sub-head and putting it, along with two other anti-colonial sub-heads, at the top of the list, with priority over peaceful co-existence.[80] The final communiqué 'The Programme for Peace and International Co-operation', used the agenda sub-items as the headings for each of its sections and used the same order, with the result that *ipso facto* it gave priority to '. . . elimination of colonialism, neo-colonialism and imperialism'. Not only did this section appear first but it was also twice as long as any of the other sections.[81]

At Lusaka anti-colonialism was raised to being a main agenda item and was no longer a set of sub-items under 'peace and security'. Furthermore, the clear implication of the 'Declaration on Peace . . .' seemed to be that 'the forces of racism, apartheid, colonialism and imperialism'[82] were the main threat to peace. Of the 15 resolutions, four were on the problems of Southern Africa and one was a 'General Resolution on Decolonisation'. It can be seen from these resolutions that it was the African countries that took the lead and one must assume that the Asians were not particularly concerned with anti-colonialism. The 'General Resolution . . .' is in fact only general with reference to Africa. It

makes an urgent appeal to France and Spain to permit . . . their colonies . . . freely and under the control of the U.N. and the OAU [sic] their right to self-determination.[83]

There was no mention at all of British, French, American, Australian, New Zealand, Dutch or Portuguese colonies in Asia, Latin America or the Caribbean.

Nevertheless the trend over the decade showed an increasing concern by the Non-Aligned for the problems of colonialism. Chapter 5 will examine the record of the Non-Aligned on colonial issues at the United Nations. Special attention will be given to the campaign to isolate South Africa and Portugal, because the problems of *apartheid* and Portugese colonialism were highlighted at each of the first three Non-Aligned conferences.

Non-alignment and the problems of economic development
Although Belgrade had 'Problems of unequal economic development . . .' as a main agenda item, the matter received very little
attention in 1961. There is nothing on the subject in the main part of
the Declaration and the 27 points at the end simply include a call for
a U.N. Capital Development Fund, better prices for primary products and free determination of the uses of aid.[84] However, there
was a clear feeling that economic problems had received inadequate attention, as the conference invited 'all the countries
concerned to consider convening an international conference,
as soon as possible, to discuss their common problems'.[85]

Only two months after Belgrade Tito, Nasser and Nehru met in
Cairo and discussed the idea of an economic conference.[86] Nehru
again was not keen[87] but Tito and Nasser had another meeting in
early 1962, held consultations with other governments and went
ahead with calling the Economic Conference in Cairo for July
1962.[88] Despite a Yugoslav assertion that 'with the exception of
Pakistan, all the participating countries were non-aligned',[89] it did
not fit the pattern of other Non-Aligned conferences in the early
1960s, in that three Latin Americans were full members and Malaya
was also present.[90] The conference received low-level support, as
less than a third of the participants sent Ministers.[91] The conference was mainly significant in that it helped to build up support
for the calling of the United Nations Conference on Trade and
Development.

After the moderate success achieved by the Group of Seventy-
Seven developing countries at the Geneva UNCTAD, which was
tempered with the feeling that 'the results achieved were neither
adequate for, nor commensurate with, the essential requirements
of developing countries',[92] economic affairs received much more
attention at the second Non-Aligned summit in 1964. The section
on 'Economic Development and Co-operation' in the final document was second only to the section on colonialism, in length.
However, the proposals adopted were mainly a reiteration of
previous demands on the U.N. and the developed countries for an
increase in Development Decade targets, more and better aid,
better terms of trade, a new U.N. industrial agency and a
conference on the rights of landlocked countries.[93] Only the last
item was likely to be of immediate practical value. The potentially
more important idea of mutual economic co-operation was not
elaborated in any detail.

At Lusaka economic matters were given greater weight on the
agenda (but were still definitely in third place). For the first time
they were given *major* emphasis in the final documentation.

President Nyerere made an important contribution to this process by making economic relations the centre of his 'keynote' speech at the Dar es Salaam Preparatory Meeting

The real and urgent threat to the independence of almost all non-aligned states thus comes not from the military, but from the economic power of the big states. It is poverty which constitutes our greatest danger and to a greater or lesser extent we are all poor.

It is in these facts that lies the real threat to freedom and to non-alignment.[94]

While there were fifteen resolutions, the decisions on 'Non-Alignment and Economic Progress' were given a greater status by separating them out as a 'Lusaka Declaration'. This time there was much less concern with the policies of the developed countries. The appeal for aid was not based on the conscience of the rich but on the idea of a system out of balance

. . . the poverty of developing nations and their economic dependence on those in affluent circumstances constitutes a *structural weakness* in the present economic order.[95]

International co-operation for economic development is not a one-sided process of donor–donee relationships; the development of developing countries is a *benefit to the whole world*, including the more advanced nations.[96]

The Declaration went into details of co-operation by joint planning, mutual trade preferences, exchange of information and joint infrastructure projects. If it were implemented, the programme would greatly improve the economic position of the Non-Aligned but the weakness of the Lusaka Declaration (which was later remedied) is that no ongoing machinery was set up and there was only vague commitment 'to review and appraise periodically the progress of mutual co-operation in the field of development in pursuance of the programmed action'.[97]

Over the decade from 1961 to 1970, there was a change from giving very little attention to economic matters to treating them as being of prime importance. Later in this chapter we will see how practical economic co-operation developed in the 1970s. Chapter 6 will examine some of the data on international trade and the receipt of foreign aid, and consider to what extent a state's economic position is related to other aspects of its foreign relations.

Non-alignment as an ideology

An ideology may be defined as 'the programmatic assertion of political values, which are held to be of universal validity for their proclaimed domain'.[98] On this basis, non-alignment *is* an ideology. It is different from other ideologies in that an ideology is usually concerned with the role of individuals in society, whereas non-alignment is concerned with the role of states in the international system. The ideology arises from the need for identification for new states entering a complex and demanding system; as a counter-ideology to the pressures from the 'free world' and the 'socialist system'; and in many cases as a result of specific situations of stress, that some of the states were facing. Particularly in relation to economic needs the ideology serves the purpose of interest articulation. Just as with ideologies concerning man and society the origins of non-alignment lie in identification, stress and interest.

Non-alignment is the assertion of state sovereignty in Afro-Asia. The consequences of this assertion have been worked out and proclaimed mainly in the fields of peace and security, colonialism and economic relations. Between them these fields cover almost all aspects of international relations. (The major omission is how to react to civil wars, when the definition of a state or of a nation is brought into question.[99]) As the Non-Aligned put it themselves, their purpose is 'ensuring national independence and full sovereignty of all nations on a basis of equality'.[100]

There is one aspect of the ideology of non-alignment that has never been fully elaborated: how wide is the domain over which it lays claim? The practice on invitations shows that all African and Arab states are considered as candidates and must be regarded as deviants when they refuse to attend Non-Aligned conferences or to support the Non-Aligned on specific questions. Presumably it would be warmly welcomed if the Asian aligned states ended their alignment (though India might be none too happy were Pakistan to leave SEATO and CENTO). In the 1960s, there seemed to be little interest in expanding the movement beyond Afro-Asia. The attendance of the Latin Americans and the neutral Europeans as observers was haphazard. Yet, in terms of the policies enunciated, the demands are completely universal. Peaceful co-existence, equal state relations, co-operation for development and the ending of colonialism are demands upon all countries, and together constitute a comprehensive 'foreign policy programme'.

Over the decade different emphasis was given to different aspects of the 'programme'. It is a gross simplification to say that at the beginning of the 1960s the Non-Aligned were mainly concerned with peace and security, in the middle of the decade anti-colonialism had priority, while at the end of the decade economic development was the main concern, but the simplification has some truth in it. The 'programme' has the coherence that is expected of an ideology because, although they have been analysed separately, the elements are closely inter-related in the thinking of the Non-Aligned. Thus within the same paragraph, peace and colonialism are linked:

(Non-alignment) is the product of the world anti-colonial revolution. . . . At a time when the polarisation of the international community on a bloc basis was believed to be a permanent feature . . . the non-aligned opened up new prospects.[101]

or

. . . notwithstanding the conclusion and signature of the Treaty of Moscow, *sources of tension* still exist in many parts of the world.

This situation shows that the forces of *imperialism* [*sic*] are still powerful.[102]

or

Imperialism, colonialism and neo-colonialism . . . endanger world peace and security.[103]

The concept of neo-colonialism provides a link between self-determination and development:

. . . the persistence of an inequitable world economic system, inherited from the colonial past and continued through present neo-colonialism, poses insurmountable difficulties in breaking the bondage of poverty and shackles of economic dependence.[104]

Disarmament is also often linked with development. The Non-Aligned

Support proposals for the diversion of resources now employed on armaments to the development of underdeveloped parts of the world and to the promotion of the prosperity of mankind.[105]

or

The Conference is aware of the tremendous contribution which the technology of the peaceful uses of nuclear energy . . . can make to the economy of the developing world.[106]

Sometimes all three components of the ideology are linked together:

. . . interference by economically developed foreign states in the internal affairs of newly independent, developing countries and the existence of territories which are still dependent constitute a standing threat to peace and security.[107]

While it has been possible to analyse separately the reactions to the Cold War, anti-colonialism and concern with economic development the Non-Aligned have by the 1970s fully integrated these concepts into a coherent ideological framework.

Earlier in this chapter we examined the criteria of non-alignment which were adopted at the very first Non-Aligned meeting, the Cairo Preparatory Meeting of June 1961. The only other reasonably concise definition of non-alignment occurs in the 'Lusaka Declaration on Peace . . .' issued by the conference in September 1970. The Lusaka Conference declared that

. . . the following continue to be the basic aims of non-alignment:
the pursuit of world peace and peaceful co-existence by strengthening the role of non-aligned countries within the United Nations so that it will be a more effective obstacle against all forms of aggressive action and the threat or use of force against the freedom, independence, sovereignty and territorial integrity of any country;
the fight against colonialism and racialism which are a negation of human equality and dignity;
the settlement of disputes by peaceful means;
the ending of the arms race followed by universal disarmament;
opposition to great power military alliances and pacts;
opposition to the establishment of foreign military bases and foreign troops on the soil of other nations in the context of great powers conflicts and colonial and racist suppression;
the universality of and the strengthening of the efficacy of the United Nations;
and the struggle for economic independence and mutual co-operation on a basis of equality and mutual benefits. [108]

A comparison of the June 1961 and the September 1970 definitions gives a simple summary of how the ideology of non-alignment has grown in complexity over the decade.

Recovery from decline and disunity

Since the 1970 Lusaka summit there have been no fundamental changes in the approach to membership of the Movement nor in the principles of the ideology. Furthermore there is no longer any need to explain why each conference takes place in terms of the impact of preceding events and which countries take the diplomatic initiative. Summit conferences now occur at regular intervals of three years and in many other ways the Movement has become institutionalised. However, we must first consider how the 1970 summit came to be called before we can examine the process of institutionalisation.

While the Cairo summit met with a spirit of optimism during the first stages of *détente*, within a year the small states of the Third World were faced with the facts of their powerlessness and the realisation that *détente* in Europe might actually increase the dangers of Super-Power military action elsewhere. First the Congo went through a new round of crisis when Lumumbist forces seized the provincial centre of Stanleyville and set up a rival government. This regime, which has the support of many of the Non-Aligned leaders, fell in November 1964, when Tshombe (who was now Prime Minister in the central government) re-took the town with the support of a Belgian paratroop drop from American planes. Similarly in the Dominican Republic in April 1965, after a coup designed to bring back to power the populist former President Bosch, the Americans intervened with some 20,000 troops because President Johnson said they 'cannot, must not, and will not permit the establishment of another communist government in the Western Hemisphere'.[109] In Vietnam the major escalation of American involvement occurred in early 1965; with a sustained programme of bombing North Vietnam starting in February; the first combat troops, as opposed to 'advisers', committed in March; and the number of men brought up to 45,000 by May. Thus, as many of the Non-Aligned saw it, American military might could be used unchallenged in Africa, in Latin America and Ghana in Asia to suppress the authentic nationalists.

One might have expected that these problems would lead to some form of joint activity by the Non-Aligned, but this could not occur because they were divided. Despite the formation of the O.A.U., the Brazzaville Group re-emerged with the formation of the Organisation Commune Africaine at Malgache in February 1965.[110] Eight of its fourteen members were at the Cairo summit and endorsed the decision to exclude Tshombe from the Non-Aligned, but only a few months later Tshombe was accepted as a member of O.C.A.M. On the Vietnam issue, a Yugoslav initiative in March 1965 led to a joint declaration calling for an end to hostilities and unconditional negotiations, but only 17 states supported it. On the one hand Cuba and Mali rejected it because it was not strongly enough worded and on the other hand many of the Non-Aligned did not want to antagonise America on this issue. This group of seventeen did include a majority of the original Belgrade Non-Aligned but were only a minority of the larger number of Cairo states.[111]

Further set-backs for the Non-Aligned included the imposition by the Soviet Union and the United States of a ban on voting in the nineteenth session of the General Assembly,[112] the Rhodesian Unilateral Declaration of Independence[113] and a series of six coups within a year in Africa which included the removal of such important leaders as President Nkrumah of Ghana and President

Ben Bella of Algeria. In Asia a short while later another major leader, President Sukarno of Indonesia, was also ousted by the army. Matters became even worse with the rout of the Arab armies by Israel in the Six Day War of June 1967.

Once again it was the Yugoslavs who took the initiatives that rescued non-alignment from its period of decline. After extensive consultations, Tito formally proposed a new conference, in a letter sent out on 1st March 1968 to the other leaders.[114] The response was not very favourable, so the Yugoslavs decided to call together a low-level Consultative Meeting of the Cairo states.[115] Most of the delegations, that eventually met in Belgrade in July 1969, were of no more than three people and only a minority contained any politicians. A quarter were led by their Ambassador to Yugoslavia. Controversy was played down by the Yugoslavs proposing an agenda that did not specifically mention any of the current conflicts.[116] In these circumstances, the result was a meeting that, in effect, discussed whether or not the Non-Aligned could still usefully identify themselves as a group.

The Yugoslavs, at the beginning, affirmed it was only by a 'programme of action' and joint activity, particularly in having another summit, that the Non-Aligned could make an impact on the problems of Vietnam, the Middle East and Southern Africa. The Algerians were quick to attack, what they euphemistically called 'every premature initiative', because too many countries could 'remain indifferent or adopt an attitude of cautious optimism' in the face of 'the resurgent aggressiveness of the imperialist powers'.[117] In other words they feared that it would not be possible to get a majority for radical resolutions at any Non-Aligned conference. At the other end of the political spectrum the Senegalese delegate opposed any conference that would repeat 'the routine verbiage of timeworn platitudes'.[118] Burma, Kuwait, Yemen, Congo (Brazzaville), Guinea and Mauritania also opposed the calling of another summit. The strongest support for Yugoslavia came from Indonesia, Tanzania and Ceylon, with it being likely that each of these three countries hoped to act as hosts for a third summit. Only twenty, of the thirty-nine delegates that spoke, were in favour and many of them seemed lukewarm. More significantly neither Egypt nor India offered any support at all to Yugoslavia.

The depth of antagonism to the West, felt, at this time, by the more radical states, comes out indirectly in the fact that there was no significant mention of the Soviet Union's invasion of Czechoslovakia in August 1968. Even Yugoslavia, which had in other forums strongly denounced the invasion, simply made an oblique reference that in Europe there had been 'adverse happenings in the past year'. Ceylon was the only country to speak against the Brehznev Doctrine, but without mentioning Czechoslovakia or the Soviet Union by name. Ceylon 'unequivocally' opposed 'an oft repeated declaration seeking to qualify the sovereignty of States coming within a sphere of influence'.[119]

Syria explained why they could not agree to attack the Soviet Union, as 'the assurance and support from the Socialist countries' on the Middle East and Vietnam 'have prompted us to reject the idea . . . the Soviet Union should be placed on the same plane as the United States'.[120] In the final communiqué the radicals won a statement of 'support for the heroic struggle of the people of Vietnam' and avoided any acknowledgement of the invasion of Czechoslovakia. However, the extent to which they were forced to compromise with the more conservative states is shown by the call for 'immediate and unconditional withdrawal of all foreign troops from *South Vietnam*'[121] This was a formulation that could be interpreted as putting the United States and North Vietnam on an equal footing, rather than blaming the war on United States' intervention as the radicals would have wished.

In addition to the radical/conservative divide that went through the Meeting, there was a division over areas of concern between the Arabs and the Africans. The Arabs gave priority to the question of Palestine and Israeli occupation of Arab lands since the 1967 war. Several of the Arabs spoke of nothing else, while half of the non-Arab speakers made no mention of the Middle East. On the other hand, the Africans concentrated on Southern Africa. The difference in emphasis produced a procedural dispute, when the Arabs wanted the Palestine Liberation Organisation to take part in the meeting. The Africans resented this happening without the Southern African liberation movements also taking part. In the end the P.L.O. was allowed to speak but was not accorded any official status. Both sides were represented in the communiqué with strong statements on Southern Africa and on 'the full restoration of the rights of the Arab people of Palestine'.[122]

What came across most strongly at the meeting was a general regret that five years could have elapsed without any activity by the Non-Aligned and that divergencies in policy had developed. In a variety of ways, there was a desire for closer co-operation and more regular contact. Proposals ranged from 'small residual *ad hoc* committees' to meet between conferences,[123] to Jordan's idea of 'a non-aligned volunteer legion'.[124] The final communiqué did not endorse Yugoslavia's call for another summit, but did agree 'on the need for a more active approach . . . and concerted efforts within U.N. frameworks'.[125]

It soon became clear that despite a long period of inactivity and the seriousness of divisions which still appeared at the Consultative Meeting, the Yugoslavs had succeeded in convincing the majority of a need to reaffirm their identity as a group. At a ministerial meeting, just two months later in September 1969, at the U.N.'s headquarters, it was agreed to hold in Dar es Salaam a Preparatory Meeting for a summit. The final seal was set upon the consensus when Tito visited Algeria from 5th–9th November and the Algerians, who had been the main opponents of further joint activity agreed 'to support jointly the convening of a new summit'.[126]

Already, at the Dar es Salaam meeting, the continuance of the conflicts in Vietnam and the Middle East had begun to radicalise more of the Third World states and so noticeably stronger statements were made on these two subjects. The debate on Vietnam shifted to whether or not the Provisional Revolutionary Government of South Vietnam should join the Non-Aligned. No decision could be reached at Dar es Salaam, so the matter was referred to the Lusaka summit. By then the climate had changed further and the communist South Vietnamese P.R.G. was accepted as an Observer, which gave them an equal status to eight Latin American and three other governments. In addition, a resolution passed at Lusaka in September 1970, now went as far as directly blaming America, by name for 'the continuation and the escalation of the war'.[127] From 1972 onwards the South Vietnamese P.R.G. obtained the status of a full participant until in 1976 the reunified Vietnam became a member of the Non-Aligned.

The Palestine Liberation Organisation also achieved a similar success in receiving recognition from the Movement, but it took longer to do so. The turning point for the Arabs and the P.L.O. in getting African support on the Middle East was Israel's negative response to an O.A.U. mediation mission in November 1971. When it was clear that the attitudes of the sub-Saharan Africans were beginning to change, the Algerians switched from opposing Non-Aligned activity in 1969 to deciding in early 1972 that they should exercise leadership among the Non-Aligned. In September 1973, the fourth summit was held in Algeria. As the host country has a particularly strong influence on the wording of conference documents, the 1973 summit produced a noticeably more radical Political Declaration than any before or since.[128] The concerns of the Arabs, and the sub-Saharan Africans were brought together:

The case of Palestine, where zionist settler-colonialism . . . represents a very serious threat to their survival as a nation, is *exactly the same as the*

situation in Southern Africa, where racist segregationist minorities . . .
(pursue) the requirements of a single imperialist strategy.[129]

Despite such a strong statement, the Palestine Liberation
Organisation got no further than being accorded Observer status,
for the first time, at the 1973 Algiers summit. However, one of the
resolutions called for all the Non-Aligned to break off diplomatic
relations with Israel. Six African countries had already done so
in the previous twelve months; Cuba, Togo and Zaïre broke
immediately after the summit; and nineteen more African countries
broke with Israel in the month after the outbreak of the 1973 war.
Then at the 1975 Lima Foreign Ministers meeting and since, the
P.L.O. was promoted above the African liberation movements and
given the status of a full participant. The limits of Arab influence
were shown when the Non-Aligned refused to accept the attempts
to call for Israel's expulsion from the United Nations.[130]

Thus the issues of Vietnam and the Middle East which had been
so divisive in the late 1960s were increasingly adopted as major
areas of concern for the Non-Aligned in the early 1970s. The
radical/conservative split over how to respond to America's
involvement in Vietnam and the Arab/non-Arab split over relations
with Israel and the Palestinians were resolved by the majority
gradually changing their positions. Initially only a minority had
been hostile to America and Israel. The issues were integrated into
the ideology by emphasising opposition to power politics and the
struggle against colonialism.

The institutionalisation of the Non-Aligned Movement

With the re-establishment of a sense of solidarity at the Lusaka
summit there were four ways that the Non-Aligned began in 1970
to develop the features of a formal institution. First, they decided
to hold meetings on a regular basis at a variety of levels of
representation. In practice this now means that summit conferences
are held every three years. In 1972 both Algeria and Sri Lanka were
candidates for the summit in the following year.[131] Algeria won the
contest as she had the prior endorsement of the O.A.U. Council of
Ministers,[132] but the Algiers 1973 summit decided the next summit
would be in Sri Lanka in 1976. In its turn this conference decided the
following one would be in Havana in 1979. In a similar way it now
seems to be established practice that a Conference of Foreign
Ministers is held every three years, about twelve months before
each summit. Other Consultative Meetings are held less regularly as
required.

The second measure taken, at the end of the 1970 summit

conference, was to appoint as an official spokesman, the Chairman President Kaunda of Zambia. His first task was to contact the major Western powers to ask for an end to their support for the white regimes of Southern Africa. Kaunda was also given an ongoing role 'to maintain contacts among other member States, ensure continuity, and carry into effect the decisions, resolutions and directives of the Conference'.[133] This hybrid role of spokesperson/leader/administrator has been given to the country holding the Chair of each of the subsequent summits, for the three-year period until the following summit. In view of the development of many other forms of co-operation during the mid-1970s the role has not turned out to be very important, for the Head of State concerned. Its main significance is that each leader has gone to the United Nations General Assembly in person, in the year in which they are appointed, to present Non-Aligned decisions to the Assembly. However, the United Nations delegation of the country holding the Chair has increasingly had to assume heavy administrative responsibilities.[134]

Thirdly, the most important of the new institutional developments in 1970 was the beginnings of a permanent executive committee for the Movement. The Dar es Salaam Preparatory Meeting in April 1970 elected a small 'Standing Committee'. At the time it was not realised that this would develop into a permanent institution, the Co-ordinating Bureau. The job of the Standing Committee was 'to maintain liaison and co-ordination' with Zambia, to prepare for the summit conference.[135] This was no innovation as a similar committee had been elected to prepare for the previous summit. Sixteen members were elected at Dar es Salaam: they were:

Algeria, Egypt, Morocco, Sudan, Burundi, Ethiopia, Senegal, Tanzania, Zambia, India, Indonesia, Iraq, Malaysia, Sri Lanka, Guyana, Yugoslavia.[136]

Meetings were held in June 1970 in Delhi and in July and August in Lusaka, to discuss such matters as which countries to invite to the summit, the content of the Agenda and the apportionment of the expenses of running the conference.

It would have been anticipated that the Standing Committee would have no life beyond the September summit. However, in conformity with the decision that meetings should be more frequent, it was agreed that a Consultative Meeting should be held at U.N. headquarters, at the start of the 1971 Session of the General Assembly, and on the 19th August 1971 the Standing Committee was reappointed to its preparatory role.[137] In its turn the New

York Consultative Meeting on the 1st October decided on a Ministerial Meeting in late 1972 and designated the same group of sixteen countries as a 'Preparatory Committee'.[138] At Georgetown, it was decided for the third time that 'the mandate of the existing Preparatory Committee shall be extended' to prepare for the next summit.[139] Not surprisingly it was also recommended that the summit should consider making the institution a permanent one. This was duly done at the fourth summit and a new group of seventeen countries was elected, as follows:

> Algeria, Liberia, Mali, Senegal, Somalia, Tanzania, Zaïre, Kuwait, Syria, India, Malaysia, Nepal, Sri Lanka, Cuba, Guyana, Peru, Yugoslavia.

The group had been elected *en bloc*, because they had already served as the Bureau of the summit conference. Their origin was reflected in a change of title to the 'Co-ordinating Bureau'.[140]

TABLE 1.2   MEETINGS OF THE MINISTERIAL CO-ORDINATING BUREAU

1. Kabul, Afghanistan	13th–15th May 1973
2. Algiers, Algeria	19th–21st March 1974*
3. Havana, Cuba	17th–19th March 1975
4. Algiers, Algeria	30th May–2nd June 1976
5. New Delhi, India	7th–11th April 1977*
6. Havana, Cuba	15th–20th May 1978

*The membership of the Bureau changed at these points.

In addition to preparing for future conferences, the Co-ordinating Bureau was given a mandate to co-ordinate activity and policy in the United Nations and to supervise the growing range of work in the economic sphere. In practice the last meeting of the old Preparatory Committee in Kabul in May 1973 had operated in this broader way and retrospectively it was recognised as the first meeting of the Co-ordinating Bureau. The existence of the Bureau has made it possible for routine collaboration to take place among the Non-Aligned. This could not happen before, because only the major political issues received attention at summit conferences.

The fourth institution that developed from the renewal of activity at the Lusaka summit was the formation of a United Nations caucus group. It is extremely difficult to trace the history of this development. At the Cairo summit in 1964 it was recommended that the Non-Aligned should consult at each session of the United

Nations and frequent references of a similar nature occur in subsequent documents. However, it is clear that these decisions were not always put into effect, so the real sequence of events is uncertain. Another problem is that caucus groups are not officially recognised by the U.N. and so are not covered by the records. It seems that the Non-Aligned Group started to operate after 1971 on an *ad hoc* basis and became particularly active from early 1973. Statements were made condemning the American bombing of North Vietnam and later welcoming the cease-fire in South Vietnam. Statements followed 'on aggressive actions against Zambia, on the situation in Cambodia, the massacre in Mozambique and other issues'.[141] Some of this activity involved large groups, for example the statement on the Vietnam cease-fire was endorsed by 45 countries (note that this was less than the total of 58 Non-Aligned in the U.N. at the time).[142] But, in addition, just as the Preparatory Committee worked beyond its mandate at its Kabul meeting, the same group of sixteen countries began operating without explicit authority as a small caucus group within the U.N.[143] The process began to be regularised when the Algiers summit entrusted the Bureau with 'Co-ordinating the activities and positions of Governments, particularly in the United Nations', and at the next meeting the Bureau 'discussed the terms of reference to be assigned to the Co-ordinating Committee' [*sic*] in New York.[144]

The fifth summit conference at Colombo in 1976 sought to clarify the confused situation with a 'Decision regarding the Composition and Mandate of the Co-ordinating Bureau', the text of which is given in Appendix 3. Although the document treats the executive committee of the Movement and the U.N. caucus group as being one body, the Co-ordinating Bureau, it is reasonable to regard them as two separate bodies, distinguished by who the representatives are. The *Ministerial* Co-ordinating Bureau meets at the level of Ministers of Foreign Affairs, once a year, as a three- to five-day conference, in a Non-Aligned capital city. From the documentation it appears to take the main responsibility for reviewing economic co-operation, and for deciding on arrangements for conferences. The *United Nations* Co-ordinating Bureau meets at the level of Permanent Representatives to the U.N., at least once a month, as a more routine affair in New York. It has the main responsibility for deciding tactics on drafting resolutions, lobbying and negotiating with other groups in the General Assembly. It has to 'maintain constant working contact' with the full membership in the 'Group of Non-Aligned Countries in the United Nations', now consisting of 83 of the 85 participants at Colombo. The link between the two branches of the Co-ordinating Bureau is that they have the same

FIG. 1.1 ORGANISATIONAL CHART OF THE NON-ALIGNED MOVEMENT

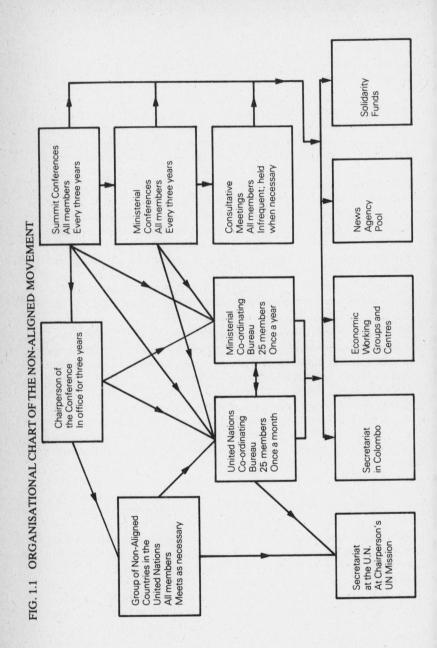

countries as members (because of the different levels of representation, completely different *people* meet in the two branches). At the Colombo summit the size was increased to 25 members and the following were elected for a three-year term:

12 Africans:	Algeria, Angola, Botswana, Chad, Guinea, Liberia, Niger, Nigeria, Sudan, Tanzania, Zaïre, Zambia.
8 Asians:	India, Indonesia, Iraq, P.L.O., Sri Lanka, Syria, Vietnam, with Bangladesh and Afghanistan sharing the term.
4 Latin Americans [*sic*]:	Cuba, Peru, Guyana, Jamaica.
1 European:	Yugoslavia.

A further overlap between the two branches of the Bureau is that both issue public, political statements on matters of current concern in the international situation. Finally, it is the United Nations Co-ordinating Bureau that will decide whether or not to agree to a request for an extraordinary meeting of the Ministerial Co-ordinating Bureau.[145] (There have not yet been any extraordinary meetings.) It has not been possible to establish how frequently the whole group of Non-Aligned countries actually meets nor what is its relationship with the U.N. Co-ordinating Bureau.

The combined impact of these changes has been recognised implicitly by the Non-Aligned themselves in the way there has been increasing reference from 1972 to the *Non-Aligned Movement*. In the early years very strong emphasis had been placed on the idea that the Non-Aligned would not form any third bloc. This tied in logically with opposition to the activities of the main blocs in the Cold War. However, it also reflected the desire to avoid financial commitments and possibly even caution by the smaller countries that the larger Non-Aligned countries might gain too much influence over them. Joint activity has grown without there being any compulsory financial obligations and with a clear emphasis on the equality of the participants.[146] The sense of identity and common membership in an institutionalised group finds expression in the use of the term Movement. No treaties or binding documents of any sort have been signed but regular meetings, an official spokesperson, an executive committee and a U.N. caucus group have been formed for the Movement.

These four main organs of the Non-Aligned have grown in importance because of their increasing involvement in supervising economic activity. We have already seen that the Lusaka summit placed special emphasis on the economic problems of development; this was followed up at the 1972 Georgetown Foreign Ministers meeting by the adoption of an 'Action Programme for Economic Co-operation'.[147] Despite its name the Programme contained little in the way of concrete proposals for action. It did begin to work out the implications of the Non-Aligned abandoning hope of development with help from the richer countries and turning instead to collective self-reliance. The most important decision was to appoint one or two members to act as 'Co-ordinating Countries' in four specialised fields. These countries were to use their own resources to come up with plans for detailed practical co-operation by the Movement as a whole. The first work was considered useful enough that Co-ordinators have now been appointed in eighteen fields, although they are not all equally active.[148] Results are slowly but surely beginning to appear. An International Centre for Public Enterprises has been established in Ljubljana, Yugoslavia, and statutes have been drawn up for a Centre for Science and Technology in Lima, Peru, and an International Centre on Transnational Corporations in Havana, Cuba. From 1977 a Research and Information System has got under way with annual meetings of economists to allocate priority research topics to institutes in the member countries. Co-ordinating Countries have arranged meetings of Groups of Experts on subjects as diverse as fishing and pharmaceuticals. All this activity is basically concerned with two aims. First to exchange information on the successes and the failures of development and secondly to increase the power of the Non-Aligned by joint activity, for example by combining in bulk purchasing of imports. On the whole the detailed work has been supervised by the Co-ordinating Countries reporting to the Ministerial Co-ordinating Bureau, while broad strategy and the formal authority for decisions has remained with the Foreign Ministers and the summit conferences.[149]

While in the long run the Non-Aligned wish to promote new industrial and agricultural development, the current concern of most of them is with Western dominance of their economies, particularly the marketing of raw materials. To have an impact on this power relationship, the Non-Aligned cannot act on their own and so at the Algiers summit two major initiatives were taken in their relations with other countries. President Boumedienne of Algeria, the new Non-Aligned Chairperson, went to the United Nations and called the Sixth Special Session of the General Assembly. This session in April and May 1974 substantially increased the pressure on the West by laying down principles for a New International Economic Order. In addition, all the Third World countries were brought together at a Conference of Developing Countries on Raw Materials at Dakar in February

1975. Although this was not a Non-Aligned conference, the Co-ordinating Bureau set up an Intergovernmental Group on Raw Materials to organise it. The conference in turn referred work back to the Bureau.

The two tactics of pressurising the West and working with other developing countries have been continued. Within UNCTAD and the Paris North-South dialogue the aim has been to obtain the agreement of producers and consumers to set up a Common Fund to stabilise commodity prices. At the same time the Non-Aligned, expecting that the West will not co-operate, have gone ahead with drafting an agreement for their own Special Fund for Financing Buffer Stocks. They have also attempted to strengthen their bargaining position by encouraging the formation of new associations of the producers of raw materials and the Bureau mandated a Group of Experts to draft statutes bringing together all the commodities in the Council of Producers Associations. Whether or not the Non-Aligned will have the power to restructure international economic relations remains to be seen. Work continues at a painfully slow rate, but before 1973 few people imagined oil prices could change so rapidly.

The conferences have also put some new political organs under the supervision of the Bureau. At Algiers in 1973 it was decided to set up a Solidarity Fund for the Liberation of Southern Africa to help the guerrilla movements and at Lima in 1975 a Solidarity Fund for Laos and Vietnam was recommended to help in the post-war reconstruction. Both were to be financed by voluntary contributions, however, it must be assumed that neither Fund has received much support, since they are not mentioned as being operational until the April 1977 Bureau meeting.[150] In another field, that of communications, the establishment of a Non-Aligned News Agency Pool is designed to break away from Western domination of the media. Work started in January 1975, when the Yugoslav agency, Tanjug, agreed to take stories from other countries, translate them and broadcast daily in English, French and Spanish.[151] The arrangements were extended and formalised in July 1976 at a Ministerial Conference in Delhi. Thus the practical co-operation within the Movement is gaining increasing momentum.

Conclusions

Critics of the Non-Aligned are prone to suggest that the concept of non-alignment has no meaning in an age of *détente* between the Super Powers. Alternatively, it is said that countries such as Cuba or Saudi Arabia are not *really* Non-Aligned. The problem with such arguments is that each of the critics have their own definition of what is 'essential' to non-alignment. The position adopted in this book is that it is not appropriate for observers from outside to set up their own definitions. Non-alignment is the ideology put forward by the states that call themselves Non-Aligned. Cuba and Saudi Arabia are Non-Aligned because they joined in forming the ideology, chose to attend conferences and were accepted as members of the Movement by the other members.

The ideology of non-alignment is relevant to the 1970s and the 1980s because it is concerned not only with preserving the independence of small states but also with finishing the process of decolonisation and promoting economic development. The literal meaning of the word non-alignment should not be allowed to confuse matters. There is as little reason to define the Non-Aligned in relation to the Cold War as there is to say that the members of the North Atlantic Treaty Organisation are the countries that catch fish around Iceland. The Non-Aligned had their origins in 1961 as a group of the more radical anti-colonial states, and continued in 1964 in order to avoid China making a successful claim to leadership of the Third World. They went into decline during a period when few states were willing or able to oppose the actions of the colonial powers or of Israel or America. And the Movement revived when a majority were willing to link the questions of the Middle East, Vietnam and Southern Africa in a single anti-colonial theme. The group of countries has enough sense of its own identity to refer to its 'members' and to call itself the Non-Aligned Movement. Institutional developments have given the Movement a high degree of organisation. Much of the activity is now directed towards practical co-operation to promote economic development, and it is possible that a powerful challenge will be mounted against the richer countries.

Non-alignment and foreign policy behaviour

Having considered the diplomatic history, the ideology and the institutionalisation of the Non-Aligned Movement, we can move on to consider the foreign policy decision making of the Non-Aligned states. Non-alignment is meaningful as a set of ideas. Is it also identifiable as a distinct pattern of behaviour? Activity within the Movement is just one of the many ways in which foreign policy may be expressed. Another approach is to examine participation in the United Nations, international trade, military links, and diplomatic exchanges to see what sort of behavioural identity existed when the Movement was being formed.

In order to obtain an understanding of how foreign policy is made and especially of how particular decisions are made, it is necessary to study in detail the history of each individual state. In so doing one would be liable to emphasise the unique aspects of each state's history. But statements about non-alignment must ignore these unique aspects and find what there is in common between a large number of states spread across four continents. The nature of this problem pushes us towards the use of quantitative methods to summarise the information. A common criticism of quantification in political science is that it offers a crude simplification of complex phenomena. However, to make general statements about what was by 1970 more than fifty Non-Aligned states, we must abstract what can only be relatively crude simplifications, from the mass of information about their foreign policy. To generalise is to simplify. In the following chapters, a variety of numeric indices will be constructed to examine the behaviour of the whole group of Non-Aligned states.

References

1. J. W. Burton, *International Relations: A General Theory* (London, Cambridge University Press, 1967), pp. 165–6.

2. J. W. Burton, A. J. R. Groom, C. R. Mitchell, A. V. De Reuck, *The Study of World Society: A London Perspective* (International Studies Association, Occasional Paper Number 1, University of Pittsburgh, 1974), pp. 53–4.

3. See the bibliography for a full list of publications on non-alignment. The only quantitative work has been:
   (a) N. Choucri, 'The Non-Alignment of Afro-Asian States: Policy, Perception and Behaviour', *Canadian Journal of Political Science*, Vol. 2, 1969, pp. 1–17. N. Choucri, 'The Perceptual Base of Non-Alignment', *Journal of Conflict Resolution*, Vol. 13, 1969, pp. 57–74. Both these articles are based solely on data for Egypt, India and Indonesia.
   (b) P. J. McGowan, 'Africa and Non-Alignment: A Comparative Study of Foreign Policy', *International Studies Quarterly*, Vol. 12, 1968, pp. 262–95. This article omits Asian states and anti-colonial issues from its consideration and does not explicitly consider African Non-Aligned states in comparison with the other African states.
   (c) H. Teune, S. Synnestvedt, 'Measuring International Alignment', *Orbis*, Vol. 9, 1965, pp. 171–89. This does not report many results and concentrates on the bloc states.

(d) B. Korany, *Social Change, Charisma and International Behaviour* (Leiden, A. W. Sijthoff, 1976). The book is predominantly concerned with theory, but in Chapter V contains quantitative work on diplomatic exchanges, developing ideas from an earlier conference paper by H. Hveem and P. Willetts.

4. G. H. Jansen, *Afro-Asia and Non-Alignment* (London, Faber and Faber, 1966). Chapter IX, reports on the debates at Bandung. The fifth of the Ten Principles asserted 'Respect for the right of each nation to defend itself singly or collectively, in conformity with the Charter of the United Nations'. This defence of military pacts was watered down by '6(a) Abstention from the use of arrangement of collective defence to serve the particular interests of any of the big powers'. But note this is not a prohibition of the membership of pacts. See Bibliography, Document (c).

5. In April 1955, Nasser paid a visit to Pakistan, during which he declared 'Pakistan is one of the countries nearest to my heart', *On Consolidation of the Cause of World Peace* (Cairo: U.A.R. State Information Service, 1966), p. 6. But since then Egyptian-Pakistan co-operation has not remotely matched the close bonds between Egypt and India.

6. India and Yugoslavia also supplied a substantial proportion of the troops for UNEF. No figures are available for when the force was first set up, but on 15th September 1957 India supplied 16% of the 5977 troops, while Yugoslavia supplied 11%. By 22nd August 1962 these proportions had increased: India supplied 24% and Yugoslavia 14% of the 5133 troops. Figures in G. Rosner, *The United Nations Emergency Force* (Columbia University Press, 1963), pp. 122–3.

7. *Op. cit.*, note 5. The quotations are from Nasser's speeches in Yugoslavia on 4/7/58 (p. 42) and in India on 30/3/60 (p. 48), respectively.

8. *Keesings Contemporary Archives 1953*, p. 12872.

9. *Ibid.*, p. 13660.

10. See for example Tito's address to the Federal Assembly, 7th March 1955, *Review of International Affairs*, No. 474, January 1970, documentation section, pp. 1–2.

11. See the Bibliography section on Documents for the references to the final communiqués of each of the main Non-Aligned conferences.

12. N. P. Nair, 'History, Ideology, Prospects' in K. P. Karunakaran (Ed.), *Outside the Contest* (New Delhi, People's Publishing House, 1963) or G. H. Jansen, *op. cit.*, p. 115.

13. Devdutt, 'India, National Interest', in Karunakaran, *op. cit.*, p. 65.

14. S. L. Poplai (Ed.), *Select Documents on Asian Affairs, India 1947– 50, Volume 2 External Affairs* (London, Oxford University Press for

the Indian Council of World Affairs, 1959), p. 15, emphasis added. This publication is hereafter referred to as *Indian Documents*.

15. *Ibid.*, p. 24

16. *Ibid.*, p. 24.

17. *Ibid.*, p. 24.

18. *Ibid.*, p. 29. For other references to India as a Great Power, see p. 18, p. 23, p. 26, p. 31, p. 79, p. 80 and p. 81. It is of interest to note that in the early 1950s the American State Department gave serious consideration to tackling the problem of Chinese representation in the U.N. by replacing China with India, as a permanent member of the Security Council, and seating the 'two Chinas' as ordinary members in the General Assembly. See Wilcox and Macy, *Proposals for Changes in the United Nations* (Brookings Institution, 1955), pp. 301–3. Trygve Lie also suggested that India could become the sixth permanent member of the Security Council, *In the Cause of Peace* (New York, Macmillan, 1954), p. 433.

19. *Indian Documents*, pp. 17–18.

20. Devdutt in Karunakaran, *op. cit.*, pp. 76–80.

21. 'India-China Agreement on Tibet', 29th April 1954, given in *Foreign Policy of India. Texts of Documents* (New Delhi, Lok Sabha Secretariat, various editions).

22. *Ibid.*, India-USSR Joint Declaration of 23rd June 1955.

23. '*Panchsheel: Its Meaning and History*' (New Delhi, Lok Sabha Secretariat, 5th edition), pp. 38–42.

24. *U.N. Official Records 12th Session*, Plenary, p. 624; First Committee, pp. 399–449; Annexes to Agenda Item 66, containing *inter alia* Soviet draft and India-Sweden-Yugoslavia draft resolution. The latter was adopted as Resolution 1236(XII). The Soviet draft contained the *Panchsheel* in exactly the form that India had been propagating. The West instead of treating it as being harmless, attacked the Soviet Union, e.g. the Philippines delegate said 'It was only too obvious that peaceful co-existence was not an end in itself but a means to world domination' (First Committee, p. 427, para. 39). The joint three-power draft resolution was adopted with only the first four Principles being mentioned.

25. The Goa invasion cannot be cited as a failure to live up to *non-alignment* because anti-colonialism has always been a component part of non-alignment and in more recent years the use of force against remnants of colonialism has been explicitly endorsed. On the other hand India had such a record of opposing force, that the survey, *India in World Affairs 1954–56*, M. S. Rajan (New Delhi, Asia Publishing House, 1964), claimed that India 'never considered' the use of force in Goa (p. 50).

26. In the General Assembly vote on the Treaty (95 in favour, 4 against, 21 abstentions) India was among the abstainers—Res. 2373(XXII) of 12th June 1968. India was also one of the 5 abstainers on the Security Council Resolution 255 of 19th June 1968, to provide a 'nuclear umbrella' for the non-nuclear states, and India has not ratified the Treaty.

27. G. A. Nasser, 'The Philosophy of the Revolution' in E. S. Farag (Trans.), *Nasser Speaks. Basic Documents* (London, Morssett Press, 1972), p. 45.

28. *Ibid.*, p. 55.

29. *Ibid.*, p. 57. Nasser even includes the Moslems of China and the Soviet Union as part of his 'homogenous whole'.

30. *Ibid.*, p. 56.

31. *Ibid.*, p. 45 and p. 57.

32. Nasser's attacks went as far as to claim that the conference was designed as an 'Islamic Pact' to replace the Baghdad Pact and 'place the Arab and Moslem countries under Anglo-Saxon influence', *Kesings Contemporary Archives 1965–66*, p. 21661.

33. A. A. Mazrui, *On Heroes and Uhuru-Worship* (London, Longman, 1967), the title of Professor Mazrui's chapter is 'Africa and Egypt's Four Circles'.

34. M. Heikal, *Nasser: The Cairo Documents* (London, New English Library, 1972 and Mentor Paperbacks, 1973). Chapter 8 is on Nasser's relations with Tito and Chapter 9 on his relations with Nehru. In both cases, private conversations and direct quotes from their correspondence are reported.

35. *U.N. Official Records 15th Session*, Plenary Meeting, 20th September 1960.

36. The U.A.R. and The Policy of Non-Alignment (Cairo, U.A.R. State Information Service, undated), p. 22 and *Documents, Activity of Non-Aligned Countries* (no publishing information but believed to have been circulated by the Yugoslavs at the Lusaka Conference), p. 1. The information that the meeting was at the Yugoslavs' permanent mission to the U.N. comes from page 228 of L. Mates, *Non-Alignment. Theory and Current Policy* (Oceana, Dobbs Ferry, New York, 1972).

37. U.N. Document A/4522, text in *Official Records 15th Session*, Plenary Meetings, p. 289.

38. The quote is from Nehru's speech to the Belgrade summit, *Conference of Heads of State or Government of Non-Aligned Countries* (Jugoslavija Publishing House, Belgrade, second edition, undated), p. 117. The main theme of this speech was a plea by Nehru that

colonial issues should take second place to issues of war and peace at the conference. Jansen, *op. cit.*, pp. 280–2, discusses in some detail Tito and Nasser's decision to ignore India's reluctance to convene a Non-Aligned meeting, 'uneasy, compulsory co-operation was the keynote of India's attitude'. See also *The Times* (London), 6th May and 5th June 1961.

39. There are very few references to the first official diplomatic initiative, to issue invitations for a Non-Aligned conference, having come from Tito and Nasser. The date of 26th April 1961 is in *Synopsis of the Second Conference of Non-Aligned Countries* (Information Department, Cairo, undated), p. viii. This is a highly inaccurate publication but the date does tie in with the reference to 'about a week later' than 22nd April in Jansen, *op. cit.*, p. 281. Both Jansen pp. 281–2 and the wording of the communiqué for the Cairo Preparatory Meeting refer to India joining as a sponsor after the initial invitations had gone out.

40. P. Willetts, *The Behaviour of the African Group in the General Assembly* (unpublished M.Sc., University of Strathclyde), see Chapter 4. For the full list of Belgrade states see Appendix 4.

41. Laos, the only other Asian state not having a military alliance with Britain or America, was excluded, presumably because Prince Boun Oum with United States' support was temporarily in control.

42. Jansen, *op. cit.*, p. 284. India wanted 'a minimum of fifteen more with a possible maximum of twenty-five extra'.

43. The U.A.R., *op. cit.* (note 36), gives Brazil, Bolivia, Ecuador, Mexico, Lebanon, Nigeria, Togo and Upper Volta, whereas Jansen, *op. cit.*, p. 288, omits Mexico and adds Cyprus. Usually one would assume that the official source is more reliable, but Jansen's inclusion of Cyprus is supported by P. Lyon, *Neutralism* (Leicester University Press, 1963), p. 183.

44. Jansen, *op. cit.*, Chapters XVII–XVIII.

45. The U.A.R., *op. cit.* (note 36), p. 33.

46. Jansen, *op. cit.*, p. 375.

47. *Ibid.*, p. 398.

48. In reading U.N. documents, there are currently many references to an African Group or an Asian Group, but not to an Afro-Asian Group. Although Security Council seats were allocated jointly to Africa and Asia in 1965, they have consistently been divided out, with three to Africa and two to Asia. In debates, when one might have expected a spokesperson for the Afro-Asians to take part, Algeria or now Sri Lanka has spoken on behalf of the Non-Aligned. If the Afro-Asian Group does still exist, it does not appear to be very active.

49. *Charter of the O.A.U.*, Article III, section 7.

50. The Asian states not invited were Iran, Israel, Japan, Malaysia, Pakistan, Philippines, Thailand, Turkey, Mongolia; and neither of the two Chinas, two Koreas or two Vietnams. Malaysia is rather the odd one out in this list and was excluded because of opposition by Indonesia, but attended the third summit in 1970.

51. U.A.R., *op. cit.* (note 36) and *Keesings Contemporary Archives 1964*, p. 20431.

52. Jansen, *op. cit.*, Chapter XVIII.

53. Last paragraph of communiqué given in *Consultative Meeting of Non-Aligned Countries* (Belgrade, Medunarodna Politika, 1970, no author given) or in *Review of International Affairs*, Nos. 464–5, 1969. It may be noted in passing that the criteria were not fully applied, as the Maldives did not receive an invitation to the Dar meeting in April 1970. Possibly, this was only an oversight on the part of the Tanzanian Ministry of Foreign Affairs. Alternatively, the Tanzanians were applying the criteria in a very strict manner and were excluding the Maldives, because from 1956 to March 1976 the U.K. Royal Air Force had a staging post on the island of Gan. The Maldives did attend the Colombo summit in August 1976.

54. Tunisia and Jordan strongly backed Pakistan's attempt to join the Non-Aligned and were supported explicitly by Ghana and Nepal and implicitly by Senegal and Ethiopia. *Op. cit. supra, Consultative Meeting* . . ., p. 82, p. 92, p. 73, p. 94, p. 83 and p. 143 respectively

55. *Op. cit.* (note 36), *Documents* . . ., p. 16.

56. *Indian and Foreign Review*, Vol. 7, No. 24, 1st October 1970. There are various other versions of these five criteria. Jansen, *op. cit.*, pp. 285–6; Lyon, *op. cit.*, p. 181; and Karunakaran, *op. cit.*, p. 50. All appear to be précising the version I have quoted, except that Lyon reports (v) as saying that bases must not be 'set up with their own consent', while Karunakaran gives (iv) and (v) in an unqualified form. A U.A.R. publication (note 36) seems nearer to Karunakaran but adds a reference to consent in (v).

57. L. H. Reiselbach, 'Quantitative Techniques for Studying Voting Behaviour in the U.N. General Assembly', *International Organisation*, 1960, pp. 300–1. A. Lijphart, 'The Analysis of Bloc Voting in the General Assembly: A Critique and a Proposal', *American Political Science Review*, 1963, p. 915.

58. P. Lyon, *op. cit.*, see note 43 above. On several occasions Lyon incorrectly describes the first Conference of Heads of State or Government of Non-Aligned Countries as the Belgrade Neutralist Summit (see p. 56, p. 70 and Appendix VI). He also in the text throughout fails to distinguish between the states that were and those that were not at Belgrade.

59. L. W. Martin (Ed.), *Neutralism and Non-Alignment* (New York, Praeger, 1962).

60. F. A. Sayegh, *The Dynamics of Neutralism in the Arab World* (San Francisco, Chandler Pub. Co., 1964).

61. The outstanding example was how the violation of Belgium's neutrality became the final trigger for the collapse of the nineteenth-century balance of power system.

62. J. F. Dulles, 'The Cost of Peace', *Dept. of State Bulletin*, XXXIV, 18th June 1956, pp. 999–1000.

63. Bibliography Document (e), p. 270 (page references for the second edition).

64. *Ibid.*, p. 271.

65. Belgrade final declaration points 1, 2, 4, 8, 10, 18(b), 20, 21, 24–6; Cairo Declaration Sect. I (13 references), II (1 ref.), III (2 refs.), IV (All aimed at U.N.), V (2 refs.), VI (All), VII (5 refs.), VIII (1 ref.), IX (All), X (7 refs.), XI (1 ref.); Lusaka Declaration on Peace paras. 1, 2, 12, 13(f), 13(g), 14, Declaration on Economic Progress, end of preamble, all of section C, and mention in 13 of the 15 resolutions.

66. The three observers and Cuba were members of the O.A.S.; Cuba in addition had the Guantanamo base on her soil; Ethiopia, Morocco and Saudi Arabia had American bases; Cyprus had British bases and Ceylon had a Defence Agreement with Britain.

67. Bibliography Document (e), p. 273.

68. *Review of International Affairs*, No. 491, September 1970, p. 25, para. 13(b), emphasis added.

69. *Ibid.*, emphasis added.

70. Bibliography Document (e), pp. 117–26, particularly p. 119.

71. *Ibid.*, pp. 267–8.

72. *Ibid.*, pp. 281–2.

73. *Ibid.*, p. 274, para. 18(a). The demand was met only 3 months later with the expansion of the Geneva Ten Nation Disarmament Committee, by the addition of eight 'neutral' members. Four of the eight, Burma, Ethiopia, India and the U.A.R. were at Belgrade as full participants and one, Brazil, had been an observer, at Belgrade.

74. *Ibid.*, para. 19.

75. *Review of International Affairs*, No. 350, November 1964, Section VII, para. 15, p. 85, emphasis added.

76. *Review of International Affairs*, No. 491, September 1970, p. 24, para. 7. See also p. 33, para. 2

77. Bibliography Document (e), p. 117.

78. *Ibid.*, p. 119.

79. *Ibid.*, pp. 272–5.

80. The U.A.R., *op. cit.* (note 36), gives the Colombo provisional agenda, but (as with other points) this publication is not very accurate in its comparison with the agenda adopted at Cairo, which is given in Appendix 1.

81. *Review of International Affairs*, No. 350, November 1964, pp. 80–2.

82. *Review of International Affairs*, No. 491, September 1970, p. 24, para. 8.

83. *Ibid.*, p. 30, op. para. 1.

84. Bibliography Document (e), pp. 274–5, paras. 21–3.

85. *Ibid.*, para. 22.

86. Supplement to *Review of International Affairs*, No. 461, June 1969, p. 3, Section (6).

87. Jansen, *op. cit.*, p. 313.

88. *Loc. cit.*, notes 86 and 87.

89. *Loc. cit.*, note 86.

90. Malaysia was accepted into the Non-Aligned at the meeting at the U.N. in September 1969 and subsequently attended both the Dar es Salaam and the Lusaka Conferences.

91. Jansen, *op. cit.*, p. 315.

92. *Review of International Affairs*, No. 350, November 1964, p. 87, para. 12.

93. *Ibid.*, paras. 19–24.

94. *The Nationalist*, daily newspaper, Dar es Salaam, 14/4/70, p. 5.

95. 'Lusaka Declaration on Non-Alignment and Economic Progress', *Review of International Affairs*, No. 491, September 1970, p. 26, preamble para. 8, emphasis added.

96. *Ibid.*, p. 28, Section C, 1(a), emphasis added.

97. *Ibid.*, p. 29, Section D(c).

98. See Appendix 2 for a discussion of this definition of ideology.

99. Even in this field one might make certain deductions from the logic of non-alignment, that it demands an attempt to mediate and diminish the level of conflict and certainly to oppose the extension of civil conflict by foreign involvement. On the other hand, state sovereignty implies the right to reject 'intervention in the internal affairs' of the state.

100. *Review of International Affairs*, No. 491, September 1970, p. 23, preamble para. 1.

101. *Ibid.*, p. 24, para. 3.

102. *Review of International Affairs*, No. 350, November 1964, p. 79, emphasis added.

103. *Ibid.*, p. 80, Section I, para. 2.

104. *Review of International Affairs*, No. 491, September 1970, p. 26, preamble para. 9.

105. *Review of International Affairs*, No. 350, November, 1964, p. 87, Section X, last para.

106. *Review of International Affairs*, No. 491, September 1970, p. 34, 'Resolution on Disarmament', para. 5.

107. *Review of International Affairs*, No. 350, November 1964, p. 79, para. 15.

108. *Review of International Affairs*, No. 491, September 1970, p. 25, para. 12. This has clearly been printed by the Review by copying the Republic of Zambia, Press Section, Information Services, 'Background No. 82/70'. In making the copy the Review omitted a sentence from the original and also copied what could only have been a typing error in the press release. The two corrections have been made in this quotation.

109. Television broadcast by President Johnson on 2nd May 1965, reported in *Keesings Contemporary Archives 1965–66*, p. 20814.

110. The twelve former Brazzaville Group members (Cameroon, Central African Republic, Chad, Congo-Brazzaville, Dahomey, Gabon, Ivory Coast, Madagascar, Mauritania, Niger, Senegal and Upper Volta) and Togo formed O.C.A.M. and Rwanda joined immediately afterwards.

111. A meeting took place on 14th and 15th March 1965 in Belgrade with representatives from Algeria, Ceylon, Cuba, Ethiopia, Ghana, Guinea, Mali, Tunisia, U.A.R. and Yugoslavia (note the absence of India). Cuba and Mali did not support the resulting declaration but nine others subsequently endorsed it. They were Afghanistan, Cyprus, India, Iraq, Kenya, Nepal, Syria, Uganda and Zambia. See *Keesings Contemporary Archives 1965–66*, pp. 20769–70.

112. The Soviet Union was in arrears on its assessments for the costs of the UNEF and ONUC peacekeeping operations. America tried to insist this brought Article 19 of the U.N. Charter into effect, so that the Soviet Union had lost its right to vote in the General Assembly. Rather than having a showdown it was agreed that all decisions would be by consensus, for that year.

113. The Smith regime's U.D.I. was a bad setback, but the O.A.U. response was more damaging. An emergency meeting of the O.A.U. Council of Ministers in December 1965 gave Britain an ultimatum that, if it did not 'crush the rebellion' within ten days, all members would break diplomatic relations. In the event only nine states did so. Z. Cervenka, *The Unfinished Quest for Unity* (London, Julian Friedmann, 1977), p. 123.

114. *Consultative Meeting of Special Government Representatives of Non-Aligned Countries* (Belgrade, Medunarodna Politika, 1970), p. 55.

115. There is no direct evidence that the response was not favourable. This statement is a deduction based on (a) the delay of sixteen months before any meeting took place, (b) the low level of representation and the non-specific agenda and (c) the strength of the opposition to a summit expressed at the Consultative Meeting.

116. The agenda was as follows:
'1. The role of the policy of non-alignment in the present day world, with special reference to the problems of peace, independence and development.
2. Consideration of possibilities for intensifying consultations, co-operation and joint activities by the non-aligned countries in various spheres.'
Consultative Meeting . . ., p. 171.

117. *Ibid.*, p. 55, p. 52, p. 54 respectively for the three quotes.

118. *Ibid.*, p. 84.

119. *Ibid.*, pp. 127–8.

120. *Ibid.*, p. 137. While the Syrians were not willing to criticise the U.S.S.R., the Algerians were on the grounds that they opposed *détente*. The U.S.S.R. was not explicitly mentioned but the Algerians attacked 'because the harmony has been achieved at the expense of all our peoples' (p. 52) and referred to 'regrettable passivity . . . of the progressive and revolutionary movement' (p. 54).

121. *Ibid.*, p. 172, emphasis added.

122. *Ibid.*, p. 172. On the objections to participation of the P.L.O. without the other liberation movements, see Nigeria p. 64, and Tanzania p. 112.

123. *Ibid.*, Sierra Leone p. 164.

124. *Ibid.*, Jordan p. 91. Other proposals included having meetings at regular intervals (Jamaica p. 76 and Nepal p. 94), continuity between summits (Guinea p. 70 and Morocco p. 105), one country to have co-ordinating responsibilities (Jamaica p. 76 and Tanzania p. 113) and several countries wanting more joint action in the U.N.

125. *Ibid.*, p. 174.

126. *Review of International Affairs*, No. 471, 20th November 1969, p. 29.

127. 'Resolution on South East Asia', in *Review of International Affairs*, No. 491, 20th September 1970, p. 30. Despite such a strong anti-American position, when the conference was faced with representatives of both Lon Nol and Sihanouk claiming Cambodia's seat, no decision could be taken. The continued change lead to Sihanouk's representative being seated at the 1972 Georgetown meeting.

128. 'Political Declaration of the Fourth Conference of Non-Aligned Countries' in *United Nations Document A/9330*. In a message to the summit Breshnev said 'The principal division in the world today is not between the "big" and the "small", the "rich" and the "poor", but between the forces of socialism, progress and peace, and those of imperialism, colonialism and reaction' (*Keesings Contemporary Archives 1973*, p. 26117). The Political Declaration came near to endorsing this Soviet position, by saying in paragraph 7, 'the policy of non-alignment, together with other peace loving, democratic and progressive forces, constitutes an important and irreplacable factor in the struggle for freedom and independence of peoples and countries'. Note also the implicit attack on state sovereignty in the reference, repeated elsewhere, to 'peoples'.

129. 'Declaration on the Struggle for National Liberation', *loc. cit. supra*, p. 27, emphasis added.

130. Resolutions VIII and IX of the 1975 Lima Foreign Ministers meeting, in *United Nations Document A/10217*, both call for measures against Israel 'including the possibility of eventually depriving it of its membership' of the U.N. The 1976 Colombo summit resolutions, in *United Nations Document A/31/197*, used a nearly identical wording.

131. *Review of International Affairs*, No. 536–7, 5th–20th August 1972, p. 14.

132. O.A.U. Council of Ministers Eighteenth Ordinary Session, 14th–19th February 1972, *Resolution CM/Res. 264 (XVIII)*.

133. 'Resolution on the Strengthening of the Role of the Non-Aligned Countries', in *Review of International Affairs*, No. 491, 20th September 1970, p. 34.

134. See the duties outlined in Sections 5, 6 and 8 of the first document in Appendix 3.

135. Bibliography Document (1).

136. *Guyana Journal*, Vol. 1, No. 5, December 1971 (Ministry of External Affairs, Georgetown), p. 41. *Indian and Foreign Review* reports 'the Committee decided that the expenses of the "summit"

will be shared according to the U.N. formula', Vol. 7, No. 24, 1st October 1970, p. 12.

137. *Guyana Journal, op. cit. supra*, p. 46.

138. *Ibid.*, pp. 46–7. *Review of International Affairs*, No. 516, 5th October 1971, pp. 15–18 contains the New York communiqué but omits the list of members of the Preparatory Committee. Meetings took place (1) 17th–19th February 1972 in Georgetown, (2) 17th March 1972 in New York, (3) 23rd–26th May 1972 in Kuala Lumpur and (4) 3rd–5th August 1972 in Georgetown. See *The Thrust of Non-Alignment* (Georgetown, Ministry of External Affairs, July 1972), pp. 27–28.

139. *The Georgetown Declaration, the Action Programme for Economic Cooperation and Related Documents* (Georgetown, Ministry of External Affairs, 1972), p. 45 'Resolution on Co-ordination'.

140. 'Decision regarding the mandate of the Bureau of the Conference', page 58 of *Fourth Conference of Heads of State or Government of Non-Aligned Countries. Fundamental Texts* (no publishing details given, but was produced by the Algerian government).

141. L. Mojsov, 'Non-Aligned Countries in the United Nations, *Review of International Affairs*, No. 562, 5th September 1973, p. 8.

142. J. Zivic, 'The Non-Aligned and Vietnam', *Review of International Affairs*, No. 554, 5th May 1973, p. 30.

143. L. Mojsov, then Head of the Yugoslav Permanent Mission to the U.N., writes of 'the fruitful activity of the Permanent Committee [*sic*] of Non-Aligned Countries in New York, which was established in this form and with its present competence at the ministerial meeting of 1971 . . . numerous meetings (were) devoted to coordinating activity and positions in the United Nations', *op. cit.*, p. 8. However, the 1971 meeting did *not* authorise any activity as a U.N. caucus group.

144. First quotation, *loc. cit.*, note 140. Second quotation, Final Document of the Co-ordinating Bureau March 1974, page 19 of *Review of International Affairs*, No. 576, 5th April 1974.

145. The position on this point is not completely explicit in the document. I have made my own interpretation of how Section 5(iii) is likely to operate in practice.

146. The statutes of the 'Solidarity Fund for Economic and Social Development', given in *United Nations Document A/10217*, make a major departure from other international financial institutions by giving each member one vote in the Board of Governors, instead of using weighted voting.

147. *Loc. cit.* in note 139 above.

148. See the second document in Appendix 3.

149. Information on the economic activity of the Non-Aligned is unless otherwise stated taken from the documents on the conferences and the Bureau meetings since 1970 listed in the bibliography.

150. Both these Funds underwent significant changes in title. At Algiers the first was actually a general 'support and solidarity fund' for liberation (*United Nations Document A/9330*, p. 30). The addition of Southern Africa to the title meant the exclusion of the P.L.O. The second Fund initially included Cambodia in its title, but the new regime made it plain that it did not want such help.

151. *Review of International Affairs*, No. 596, 5th February 1975, pp. 21–2.

CHAPTER TWO

Participation in the United Nations

If states are to achieve any success in influencing the outcome of processes in the international system, they must become active participants in the system. One problem for the small states is that they do not have the resources to participate with as many embassies or with attendance at as many conferences as they might wish. Therefore the United Nations is particularly important to them and we have already seen how the Non-Aligned have stressed this in their resolutions. As the United Nations has near universality in its membership, it compensates for the inability of many small states to staff more than a dozen or so embassies. As there are ample opportunities for any state to raise any issue for discussion in the General Assembly, the U.N. helps to compensate for the tendency of the Great Powers to discuss issues without regard to the interests of small states. Participation is worth while enough that up to 1970 only one state, the Maldive Islands, ever failed to take any part at all in the work of the General Assembly, and that was for only one session. The other small states do have varying levels of participation. As we have already seen in Chapter 1 that non-alignment is an activist ideology, let us now see whether the Non-Aligned are among the more active participants in the U.N.

The definition of analytical groups of states

Before proceeding further it is necessary for us to consider explicit definitions for two dimensions for classifying states that have already been referred to implicitly. First, the distinction has been made between Great Powers and small powers. Many inter-related factors, such as economic resources, industrial production, population size, land area or military forces, may be used as a measure of power. In practice there is no need for this study to tackle the problem of the multi-dimensionality of power. The words 'Great Powers' are used to refer to the five nuclear-weapon states, that are permanent members of the Security Council and would score high on almost any specific indicator of power. 'Small powers' encompasses all the other states and is not appropriate for rigorous use because it covers such a range from the very smallest to substantial intermediate level powers: but the term is sufficient for some descriptive purposes. The only need in this book for a precise operational definition of power arises later in this chapter and then a measure of economic size is clearly required. By *any* criteria of size, the vast majority of the Non-Aligned are small powers. But a few of the Non-Aligned are intermediate powers and many small powers are not among the Non-Aligned. Being a small state and being Non-Aligned are not always associated with each other.

The second dimension concerns the distinction between the Non-Aligned, bloc members and other states. As much of this study concentrates on behaviour in the United Nations, the caucus groups that operate in the General Assembly might seem to be a useful basis for classifying states. However, the groups that sponsor and negotiate on resolutions are not suitable, because they have changed across the years, have overlapping membership and do not have a formal status. The U.N. electoral groups have been more stable and more clearly identifiable. Initially a 'gentleman's agreement' governed elections to the Security Council and similar arangements followed for other organs. Then, at the 12th Session in 1957, Resolution 1192 formalised the groups for the first time, by specifying that the Assembly's Vice-Presidents

shall be elected according to the following pattern:
(a) Four representatives from Asian and African States;
(b) One representative from an Eastern European State;
(c) Two representatives from Latin American States;
(d) Two representatives from Western European and other States;
(e) Five representatives from the permanent members of the Security Council. [1]

Although the groups were named in geographical terms, their real identification was political. For example the 'Others' (including such states as Australia, New Zealand and South Africa) did not go in their *geographical* region with the Asian and African states but were put in the appropriate *political* positions with the West Europeans.[2] However, the composition of each of the groups was not specified and ambiguities remained in the situation. This is shown, at its extreme, by the case of Turkey, which was elected as an Asian Vice-President in 1959, held an East European seat on the

Security Council in 1961 and was a West European Vice-President in 1963.

A more substantial problem in using the U.N. electoral groups as a classification scheme for this study is that the 'Asian and African states' cannot be equated with the Non-Aligned. We have seen in the diplomatic history of the movement that there are some Afro-Asian states which have been considered to be aligned and others which while not being aligned are not members of the Non-Aligned group. As a result we will construct our own classification and use the following five groups for analysis:

> Non-Aligned
> Western Bloc
> Eastern Bloc
> Latin American
> Non-Bloc

A state is *defined* as being Non-Aligned in a particular year, if it attended the most recent of the Non-Aligned summit conferences. Thus the Non-Aligned group does not remain constant in its composition and varies according to whether the Belgrade states, the Cairo states or the Lusaka states are under examination. By contrast, the membership of the two blocs has remained constant. The Western Bloc consists primarily of the twenty states that have formed the Western multilateral military alliances of NATO, CENTO and SEATO. In addition five states (Nationalist China, Israel, Japan, South Africa and Spain), had such extensive bilateral military links that they were also included in the Western Bloc. This category has a high degree of overlap with the 'Western European and Other' group in the U.N. The difference is that the Western Bloc category includes seven Asian states, but omits the four European neutral states. For the Eastern Bloc category there is no difference, other than the name, from the Eastern Europe U.N. group. In both cases Mongolia is combined with the members of the Warsaw Pact.[3] When data concerning the U.N. is analysed, the group consists of ten members, but for other purposes the pseudo-states Byelorussia and Ukraine have to be excluded, reducing the Eastern Bloc to eight members.

There remain two groups, the Latin Americans and the Non-Bloc states, that neither attended the Non-Aligned summits nor were fully integrated into the bloc system. The Latin Americans have been taken separately from the Non-Aligned and the Non-Bloc states, because on the one hand their membership of the O.A.S. with the United States did give them a loose attachment to the Western Bloc and on the other hand the Afro-Asian Non-Aligned

FIG. 2.1 SUMMARY OF THE CLASSIFICATION SCHEME

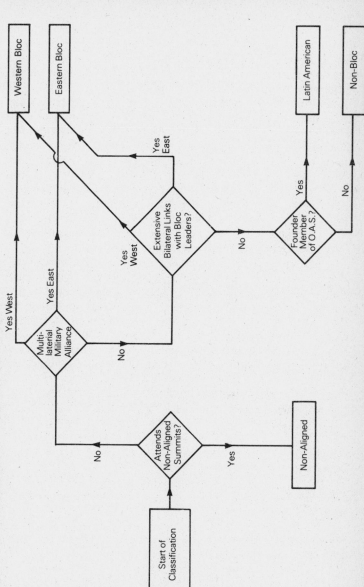

did not show much interest during the 1960s in recruiting from among the Latin Americans. As priority is given to identifying the Non-Aligned as a group, Cuba (a regular conference attender) has been included in the Non-Aligned category rather than with the other nineteen Latin Americans. When the new Caribbean states became independent, they were also omitted from the Latin American category.

The Non-Bloc are thus left as a residual category of states that are close to the Non-Aligned but are not actually found among them. The Non-Bloc comprise those African, Asian, Caribbean and European neutral states, without multilateral military ties, that have not attended the most recent Non-Aligned summit as full participants. At times some of the Caribbeans and European neutrals have demonstrated the reality of the idea that they are close to the Non-Aligned by attending summits as 'Observers' or 'Guests'. Like the Non-Aligned, the Non-Bloc category does not remain constant but varies in line with the attendance at the Belgrade, Cairo and Lusaka summits.

There are two main reasons why a state may be in the Non-Bloc category. First, it cannot attend a conference unless it receives an invitation to do so from the host state. We have seen that for the first summit in 1961 a deliberate policy of restricting invitations forced the Brazzaville states and others into the Non-Bloc category. Secondly, a state may receive an invitation but decline to accept it. This refusal to identify with the Non-Aligned has been the main reason for the existence of Non-Bloc states from 1964 onwards.

TABLE 2.1   THE DISTRIBUTION OF THE STATES INTO THE ANALYTICAL GROUPS

	1961	1964	1970
Western Bloc	25	25	25
Latin Americans	19	19	19
Non-Bloc	25	15	20
Non-Aligned	25	46	53
Eastern Bloc	10	10	10
	104	115	127
Not Independent	23	12	0
Total	127	127	127

The classification of each of the states, which were independent by 1970, members of the U.N. by its 25th Session and are used in this study, is shown individually in Appendix 4 and as totals in Table 2.1 above.

Delegation size as a variable

Participation in an international meeting may take many forms from speech making, to drafting resolutions, to lobbying and voting. Obviously all of these are of importance but it is generally recognised that the lobbying and bargaining that occurs in the corridors, at cocktail parties and in caucus is the most important route to success. Usually the more formal, official proceedings are merely recording the results of these informal processes. In order to achieve an impact in the lobbying, it is necessary to have enough personnel available to make contacts. For example, in the annual struggles during the 1960s led by Albania for the admission of communist China to the United Nations, there was not only a difference in the 'real world' physical power of Albania and America outside the U.N., but also a corresponding difference in the size of the delegations sent to the U.N. The small Albanian delegations of six to eight men had to cope with the vast number of documents and formal work of six main committees and the General Assembly plenary sessions. They either could not do this work effectively or had little time left to lead the campaign against America, which with sixty to ninety delegates was able to lobby every other country individually.

While it is only a partial reflection of the overall process, delegation size will be used as an index of participation in the United Nations. The decision by a state on how many delegates should be sent to a meeting does involve a real commitment of resources from the government's budget and, for all but the host state, involves the loss of foreign exchange. The expenses incurred by the delegates may well be the only concrete, non-verbal commitment that is made.[4] It has already been argued that the number of delegates a state sends will significantly affect its ability to influence the outcome of a meeting. Of course the number of delegates will by no means be the determinant of success, but it may be the only aspect of *participation* that affects success. Certainly the delegation lists are regarded as important documents by the participants themselves. The secretariat is usually expected to produce the lists early in the proceedings of any international meeting and the lists are almost always published in the official reports of the meeting.

The delegation lists for the Sessions of the United Nations General Assembly are published, in their final form, as *Prefatory Fascicle No. 2 of the Official Records*. Under Rule 25 of the Rules of Procedure each country is entitled to five Representatives and five Alternate Representatives. These are the only delegates that have the right to speak and to vote, though in practice more than ten

D*

people may be involved if a country changes its representatives for different parts of the session. For many of the smaller countries these are the only delegates sent and even the quota of ten may not be filled, but the vast majority of countries also send 'Advisers' and 'Special Advisers'. In addition, in the 23rd Session for example, four countries had 'Parliamentary Advisers' or 'Parliamentary Observers', six of the communist countries preferred to use the title 'Expert' and twenty-two countries had at least one from various categories of service personnel, including 'Secretaries', 'Interpreter', 'Administrative Officer', 'Research Officer' and 'Attaché'.

D*   In counting the total delegation size for each country, the decision was made to include all the names that were listed in the Official Records, irrespective of the titles they were given. This does mean that the figures for each delegation are not completely comparable, but the flaw cannot be remedied. Any other way of dealing with the problem would be equally likely to produce anomalies. For example, one might decide to exclude the service personnel, but it cannot be assumed that the minor members of a delegation never perform any political functions. Even the term Secretary can cover a wide range of status and duties. Finally, the very fact that a person is listed implies that the delegation leader thought that it would be useful for other delegations to be able to make contact through that person. Thus counting every person does have reasonable validity, based more on the practice of the diplomats involved than just the external judgement of the researcher.[5]

The U.N. Diplomatic Corps

Before we examine the pattern of delegation sending for various sub-groups within the Assembly, we will consider how large a diplomatic centre is New York; how it compares with some of the major capitals; and how stable across a long time period is representation in the U.N.?

It can be seen from Table 2.2 that in the late 1950s, after a group of sixteen states had joined in the 10th Session, the diplomatic corps at the United Nations consisted of some one thousand five hundred people. Then in 1960, at the 15th Session, when Cyprus and sixteen African states joined, the number of delegates increased to one thousand eight hundred. Apart from a slight drop in 1961, the corps continued to increase in size until in 1965 there was a total of over two thousand people attending the 20th Session of the Assembly and by 1970 the figure was 2316. The significance of the size of this diplomatic corps is emphasised when comparison is made with the

TABLE 2.2   U.N. GENERAL ASSEMBLY DELEGATION SIZES

Year	Session	No. of States	No. of Delegates	Mean Average
1956	11th	80	1535	19·2
1957	12th	82	1474	18·0
1958	13th	81	1512	18·7
1959	14th	82	1488	18·1
1960	15th	99	1820	18·4
1961	16th	103	1742	16·9
1962	17th	110	1856	16·9
1963	18th	111	1882	17·0
1964	19th	115	1964	17·1
1965	20th	117	2049	17·5
1966	21st	121	2053	17·0
1967	22nd	122	2086	17·1
1968	23rd	126	2181	17·3
1969	24th	126	2171	17·2
1970	25th	127	2316	18·2

Alger and Brams figures for the leading diplomatic capitals.[6] Their data is for 1963–64, so the comparison is best made with the U.N. 18th Session, from the same time period.

TABLE 2.3   DIPLOMATS RECEIVED AT TEN LEADING WORLD CENTRES 1963–1964

	Number of Diplomats	Number of States	Average Number of Diplomats
U.N. General Assembly	1882	111	17·0
Washington	1418	107	13·3
London	1305	96	13·6
Bonn	778	94	8·3
Moscow	732	69	10·6
Paris	716	98	7·3
Rome	707	85	8·3
Cairo	559	73	7·7
New Delhi	530	66	8·0
Tokyo	494	70	7·1

It will be seen that the U.N. outstrips even Washington and London, which are themselves in a class of their own compared to the other capitals.[7] Not only does the U.N. receive from more states, but also it receives a higher average number of diplomats and thus it has become the world's most important diplomatic centre. Apart from the U.N. in New York, there were only five countries that sent to or received from as many as 80 other countries and these were the five leading Western NATO powers. Thus New York is likely to be the only place where it is both physically convenient and politically acceptable to hold *ad hoc* diplomatic consultations amongst all the Non-Aligned. Cairo and New Delhi are also important centres outside the Western world, but even they would not receive diplomats from all the Non-Aligned states, particularly since the movement so broadened its ranks from 1964 onwards.[8]

The continuity of representation

While foreign embassies around the world are staffed on a permanent basis, the General Assembly meetings only last from the end of September to the end of December each year, with there sometimes being an extension into January and February. In the meantime, when the General Assembly is not sitting, much smaller Permanent Missions to the United Nations are maintained by most countries. Thus it would appear quite possible for the sizes of individual delegations to fluctuate substantially from year to year, as larger or smaller numbers of diplomats are brought in to supplement the Permanent Mission during the Assembly Sessions. The system allows the member states to decide the size of their delegations on an *ad hoc* basis each year. More diplomats may be sent when a particularly important issue is going to be discussed and less in a year when the state's interests are not so deeply involved.

However, the data shows that such *ad hoc* variations in the number of delegates are the exception rather than the rule. The pattern of representation at the U.N. has been remarkably stable over time. This is clearly shown by the extremely high values of the correlations given in Table 2.4. Each line of the table shows the correlations between the number of delegates sent by the various countries in one session and the numbers sent in subsequent sessions. The size of the correlation is a measure of how successfully we can predict most countries' delegation size in one year from its size in an earlier year. As one moves to the right along each line, or in other words as the time span increases, the correlations tend to drop, but they still remain very high. In the social sciences correlations of the order of 0·3 to 0·5 are generally considered worthy of comment; 0·5 to 0·7 would be considered moderately high; while 0·7 to 0·8 are very high. Thus the fact that all the correlations in the table are greater than 0·8 and one half the

TABLE 2.4 CORRELATIONS BETWEEN U.N. DELEGATION SIZES IN DIFFERENT SESSIONS OF THE GENERAL ASSEMBLY

	11th	12th	13th	14th	15th	16th	17th	18th	19th	20th	21st	22nd	23rd	24th	25th	Number of States
11th	—	0·97	0·94	0·92	0·87	0·89	0·89	0·87	0·87	0·82	0·81	0·84	0·86	0·87	0·89	80
12th		—	0·96	0·94	0·87	0·89	0·89	0·86	0·85	0·81	0·81	0·85	0·88	0·88	0·90	82
13th			—	0·96	0·90	0·89	0·91	0·88	0·88	0·86	0·85	0·88	0·91	0·90	0·90	81
14th				—	0·91	0·90	0·91	0·88	0·87	0·84	0·85	0·88	0·90	0·91	0·91	82
15th					—	0·91	0·92	0·88	0·88	0·85	0·87	0·88	0·88	0·90	0·89	99
16th						—	0·97	0·96	0·96	0·90	0·90	0·88	0·89	0·91	0·91	103
17th							—	0·97	0·95	0·92	0·91	0·92	0·92	0·93	0·92	110
18th								—	0·96	0·92	0·91	0·89	0·91	0·91	0·91	111
19th									—	0·94	0·94	0·89	0·89	0·89	0·90	115
20th										—	0·96	0·89	0·90	0·89	0·88	117
21st											—	0·88	0·89	0·90	0·90	121
22nd												—	0·95	0·95	0·92	122
23rd													—	0·96	0·95	126
24th														—	0·97	126
25th															—	127

N.B. The figures in each line have been calculated for the states that were U.N. members in that session. Thus as one moves down the columns the correlations are based on an increasing number of states.

FIG. 2.2 DIFFERENCES IN THE U.N. DELEGATION SIZES BETWEEN 1966 AND 1967

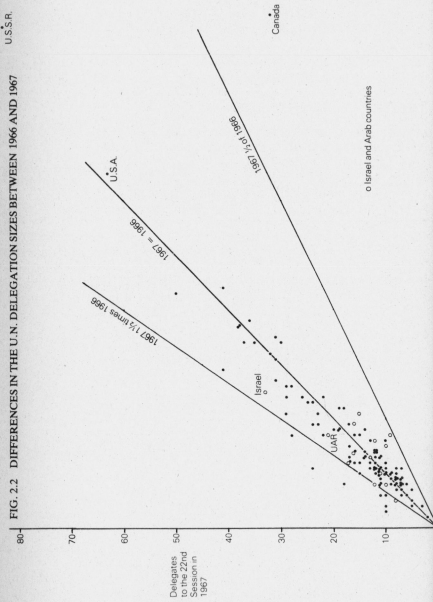

correlations are of 0·9 or more suggests an extremely stable pattern of behaviour. Even after fourteen years the countries that were in the U.N. in 1956 showed a correlation of 0·89 between the delegates they sent to the 11th Session and those to the 25th Session of the Assembly.[9]

It may not seem a very surprising discovery that countries tend to maintain continuity in their participation in the U.N. from year to year, but on the other hand there were plausible reasons to expect changing political factors to have made an impact. As a final investigation of this point, let us consider the lowest correlation in Table 2.4 between two consecutive sessions, which is the value of 0·88 between the 21st and 22nd Sessions. A reasonable explanation of this lower value is that the Arab states and Israel specially increased their participation in the 22nd Session, in the autumn of 1967, in order to wage a diplomatic battle in the aftermath of the Six Day War. But Figure 2.2, which graphs the delegates sent in 1967 against those sent in 1966, shows that such an explanation is not substantiated. One of the Arab states, the Yemen, is among the eight countries which increased their representation to more than one and a half times that of the previous year. However, this is a reflection of 1966 being the lowest figure for the Yemen for fourteen years, rather than 1967 being particularly high. Similarly, Lebanon and Tunisia both had relatively low representation in 1966, rather than high representation in 1967. When the number of

TABLE 2.5
CHANGES IN DELEGATION SIZES OF MIDDLE EASTERN STATES

	1961	1962	1963	1964	1965	1966	1967	1968	1969	1970
Algeria	—	19	21	20	18	21	15	30	18	28
Iraq	14	11	13	12	13	16	12	18	20	19
Jordan	7	7	9	8	10	13	13	12	9	9
Kuwait	—	—	10	11	8	10	11	11	14	17
Lebanon	10	11	13	8	13	8	12	14	11	9
Libya	6	7	9	9	8	8	10	11	9	16
Morocco	11	10	10	11	10	15	10	12	13	13
Saudi Arabia	11	12	14	19	16	19	16	18	17	17
Sudan	10	10	8	12	16	17	9	17	14	10
Syria	5	15	9	10	11	14	16	11	13	13
Tunisia	15	14	15	6	14	12	17	18	16	17
U.A.R	26	29	24	22	18	17	21	19	21	30
Yemen	10	10	6	6	8	5	8	7	6	9
Arab League Total	125	155	161	154	163	175	170	198	181	207
Israel	22	26	20	22	25	25	33	30	23	32

delegates sent by the Middle Eastern countries in 1967 is compared in Table 2.5 with the long-term trends for the 1961 to 1970 period, we find that only in Israel's case can one argue there has been an exceptional increase in 1967. In contrast five of the Arab states actually dropped their participation in 1967 and overall the 13 Arab League members as a group had five less delegates in 1967 than in 1966.

The states that did make particularly big changes mainly did so for more general reasons, rather than because of a specific political dispute. For the Congo (Kinshasa) 1967 marked a distinct turning point. After all the turmoil of the early 1960s the Congo received recognition from the other African states by being host to the fourth O.A.U. summit and her representation at the U.N. was significantly increased and has since remained at the higher level. Indonesia had a small delegation in 1966, after having temporarily left the U.N. the previous year, and 1967 simply marked the return to her normal level of representation. Barbados, Botswana and Lesotho were all new members in 1966 which only sent small delegations in their first year. There seems to be no obvious reasons for the changes in representation by Cuba, Malta and Canada. The drop of nearly two-thirds, from 94 to 32 delegates for Canada was particularly dramatic and on its own accounted for the relatively low correlation. When Canada is excluded the correlation is 0·96. Thus it appears that particular issues on the agenda at the U.N. have relatively little effect on the pattern of representation in the Assembly. Changes are due either to changes in a state's overall position in the international system or to a few unexplained fluctuations.

The differences between the groups

While there may be little evidence that short-term political factors are having any effect; the high correlations across the years could be consistent with longer term political factors being a determinant of delegation sizes. In Table 2.6 the total diplomatic corps is split up to see how many people were available to lobby for each of the five groups of states.

Throughout the 1960s the general pattern was that the Western Bloc had considerably more delegates than any other group and the Non-Aligned were the second largest group. The 'Non-Bloc' states usually had more delegates than the Latin Americans and the small group of ten East Europeans were the least well represented. The three smaller groups were of roughly the same size. The Latin Americans and the East Europeans kept their delegations relatively

TABLE 2.6   TOTAL NUMBER OF DELEGATES SENT BY EACH GROUP*

Year	Session	All States	Western Bloc	Latin American	Non-Bloc	Non-Aligned	Eastern Bloc
1960	15th	1820	668	241	239	379†	302
1961	16th	1742	658	236	257	360	231
1962	17th	1856	662	260	315	378	241
1963	18th	1882	661	280	352	364	225
1964	19th	1964	689	260	198	591	226
1965	20th	2049	760	267	204	571	247
1966	21st	2053	722	254	252	575	250
1967	22nd	2086	690	259	291	597	249
1968	23rd	2181	723	289	300	643	226
1969	24th	2171	696	274	325	631	245
1970	25th	2316	760	280	276	759	241

* For the membership of each group see Appendix 4.
† 24 states which were then independent and later attended the Belgrade Conference.

constant, except for 1960 when the communists made a big attempt to lead African anti-colonialism in the U.N. The 'Non-Bloc' group shows a steady increase in size, as new states become independent, only to drop down in 1964 and 1970 as more of its members are recruited into the Non-Aligned at the second and third summit conferences. The ending of the radical exclusiveness of the Belgrade Non-Aligned and their conversion to an Afro-Asian movement so broadened the ranks that by 1970 the Lusaka Non-Aligned had caught up with the biggest group of delegates, the Western Bloc.

TABLE 2.7   AVERAGE U.N. DELEGATION SIZE BY GROUP

Year	Session	All States	Western Bloc	Latin American	Non-Bloc	Non-Aligned	Eastern Bloc
1960	15th	18·4	26·7	12·7	10·9	15·4	30·2
1961	16th	16·9	26·3	12·4	10·7	14·4	23·1
1962	17th	16·9	26·5	13·7	10·5	14·5	24·1
1963	18th	17·0	26·4	14·7	10·7	14·0	22·5
1964	19th	17·1	27·6	13·7	13·2	12·8	22·6
1965	20th	17·5	30·4	14·1	11·3	12·7	24·7
1966	21st	17·0	28·9	13·4	12·0	12·5	25·0
1967	22nd	17·1	27·6	13·6	13·2	13·0	24·9
1968	23rd	17·3	28·9	15·2	11·5	14·0	22·6
1969	24th	17·2	27·8	14·4	12·5	13·7	24·5
1970	25th	18·2	30·4	14·7	13·8	14·3	24·1

While the Non-Aligned have throughout been the second largest group in terms of the absolute number of delegates sent, they do not appear so activist when we consider the average number of delegates for each country given in Table 2.7. Again the Western Bloc is in the lead with some 26 to 30 delegates each, but this time the Eastern Bloc is second with some 22 to 25 delegates each. Although, in total number of delegates, the Eastern Bloc is usually the smallest group, this is because there are few communist states in the U.N.: they are in fact relatively active. In the early part of the 1960s the Non-Aligned were the third most active group but in the later 1960s they fell behind the Latin Americans as well. However, there are only small margins between the last three groups. The Non-Aligned, the Latin Americans and the 'Non-Bloc' states all sent from 10 to 15 delegates on average throughout the 1960s, and were a long way behind the two Blocs.

TABLE 2.8

A. Proportional Distribution of Membership and Delegations

Each row totals 100%

	Western Bloc	Latin American	Non-Bloc	Non-Aligned	Eastern Bloc
16th Session					
Delegates	37·8%	13·5%	14·8%	20·7%	13·3%
Member States	24·0%	18·3%	24·0%	24·0%	9·6%
19th Session					
Delegates	35·1%	13·2%	10·1%	30·1%	11·5%
Member States	21·7%	16·5%	13·0%	40·0%	8·7%
25th Session					
Delegates	32·8%	12·1%	11·9%	32·8%	10·4%
Member States	19·7%	15·0%	15·7%	41·7%	7·9%

B. Net gain or loss in lobbying power

	Western Bloc	Latin American	Non-Bloc	Non-Aligned	Eastern Bloc
16th Session	+13·8%	−4·8%	−9·2%	−3·3%	+3·7%
19th Session	+13·4%	−3·3%	−2·9%	−9·9%	+2·8%
25th Session	+13·1%	−2·9%	−3·8%	−8·9%	+2·5%

Table 2.8 which gives data for the years when the Non-Aligned Conferences were held, shows how much the Non-Aligned have lost by consistently having a below average level of representation. The percentage distribution of the delegates between the groups is compared with the distribution of the number of states which are

members of the U.N. The Western and Eastern Blocs both sent large delegations and therefore they are better represented among the delegates than they are in voting power, while the opposite is true for the other groups. The Non-Aligned were 3·3% under-represented in the delegations sent in 1961 to the 16th Session; they were 9·9% under-represented in 1964 and 8·9% in 1970. Thus in 1961 while the Non-Aligned had an equal number of U.N. member states they only had just over half as many delegates as the Western Bloc; in 1964 with nearly twice the membership they still had less delegates than the Western Bloc; and in 1970 with over twice the membership they had practically the same number of delegates. A lead of 22% in members in 1970 still involved having one less delegate. In as much as it is important to have delegates available for lobbying and to attend the various plenary and committee meetings, the Non-Aligned are not able to exercise the influence to which they are officially entitled on the one state, one vote, system.

The disparity in delegation sizes at the U.N. must be seen as an even greater handicap when it is remembered that there is a more damaging disparity in the back-up facilities provided by the foreign offices in the home capitals. The American State Department in 1970 had some three hundred *senior* personnel with nine in the office for International Organisation Affairs, while many developing countries would have a *total staff* of less than twenty in their foreign affairs ministry and perhaps one or two would handle relations with all international organisations.[10]

Economic constraints on the level of representation

So far the delegation size has just been considered as a single variable on its own. But in practice it is not telling us much if we learn that Yugoslavia's delegation in 1961 was less than half the size of Britain's. It would be surprising if Yugoslavia's non-alignment led to such activism that it participated in the U.N. at the same level as Britain. Britain as a big power has an economy that is more than eight times bigger than Yugoslavia's and therefore we expect more participation from Britain. The delegations must be considered in relation to the size of each country, before we can claim to have made a complete comparison between the groups.

Gross National Product is commonly used as a measure of the size D* or power of states. It is an important measure for us to use, as sending delegations to the U.N. is almost solely a call upon economic resources.[11] In addition the U.N. itself does attempt to measure each state's ability to devote resources to international affairs. This is in the form of its sliding scale of assessments for contributions to the Regular Budget. Every three years the

Committee on Contributions fixes the percentage of the budget that each state will pay for the following three years. During the 1960s, the scale ranged from 0·04% for a group of the smallest states to just over 30% for America. The table below gives the correlation between delegation size and these two measures of a state's ability to afford the expenditure involved.[12]

TABLE 2.9
CORRELATION OF DELEGATION SIZE AND ECONOMIC SIZE

| | | | | *U.N. Regular Budget* | |
Year	Session	G.N.P.	Log G.N.P.	Assess %	Log of %
1960	15th	0·56	0·79	0·65	0·82
1961	16th	0·75	0·78	0·81	0·83
1962	17th	0·71	0·80	0·78	0·87
1963	18th	0·73	0·80	0·78	0·85
1964	19th	0·73	0·77	0·78	0·83
1965	20th	0·62	0·78	0·69	0·83
1966	21st	0·56	0·74	0·65	0·81
1967	22nd	0·60	0·79	0·67	0·86
1968	23rd	0·58	0·81	0·65	0·86
1969	24th	0·60	0·69	0·67	0·86
1970	25th	0·62	0·67	0·68	0·84

D* The correlations between delegation size and G.N.P. are all in the range 0·56 to 0·75, which is quite high, but the correlations between delegation size and U.N. budget assessments are all higher, being in the range 0·65 to 0·81. For both G.N.P. and the budget assessments the correlation is improved, sometimes markedly so, by taking the logarithm rather than using the raw data. This means that the data is showing a curved relationship rather than a straight line relationship. Instead of the delegation size continuing to increase steadily with the country's wealth, it begins to flatten out. Beyond a certain point a country has to be very much bigger before it begins to send noticeably more delegates. An economist would describe this situation as one of diminishing marginal utility. For example, this pattern may be shown with some of the countries from the Western Bloc in the 16th Session. If we were to use the data on Greece and Denmark to predict the delegation sizes for Italy and France on a linear basis, we would expect Italy to have about 71 delegates and France to have about 180. In actual fact Italy had 36 or a half what was expected and France had 49 or less than a third what was expected. Small differences in size are far more important among the small and medium states than they are among the large states.

One can test for such a curvilinear relationship by seeing whether   S*
the delegation sizes are directly proportional to the index of a
country's wealth or are proportional to the logarithm of the index of
wealth. This is the standard test, as the logarithm relationship is one
of a curve that gradually flattens out. Some of the data for the
Western Bloc in the 16th Session has been plotted in Figure 2.3 to
illustrate the point. The relationship when the raw data is used
shows a distinct curve but when the same data is converted to
logarithms the relationship is linear. The increase in the correlations is the statistical evidence of this pattern in the data.

The square of a correlation coefficient gives a measure of how   S*
much one variable is explaining the variation in the other variable:
that is if we can assume that the correlation is not spurious and is in
fact evidence of a causal link and such an assumption is a matter of
judgement rather than statistical proof. The term variation has a
precise statistical definition but it can be interpreted with its everyday meaning.

By squaring the correlation coefficients in the last column of   S*
Table 2.9 we find that, in the form of a log. relationship, the budget
assessments account for some two-thirds to three-quarters
(depending on which year is considered) of the variation in
delegation size between different countries. More specifically,
when the Non-Aligned conferences were held, in 1961 and 1964 the
budget assessment accounted for 68·9% of the variation in
delegation size and in 1970 it accounted for 70·6%. This is a high
proportion of the variation explained and it leaves relatively little
room for political factors other than size to have had any impact.

The results show a clear conclusion that the number of delegates a
country sends to the General Assembly is dependent upon the
economic size of the country. Contributions to the U.N. Regular
Budget, which are designed to assess how much each country can
afford, are a better predictor than the size of the G.N.P. As the
countries get more wealthy, the usefulness of larger delegations
does not increase so rapidly. This relationship, in which delegation
size relates to budget contributions on a curve that flattens out, as in
Figure 2.3, has high explanatory power.

The joint effect of economic constraints and group differences

However, we can still make a comparison between each of the five
groups and see if, after allowing for the size of the countries, there is
a tendency for the groups to show any differences in their
behaviour. This is done by plotting a series of regression equations.
While correlation measures the reliability (or explanatory power)

FIG. 2.3 ILLUSTRATION OF THE LOGARITHM RELATIONSHIP

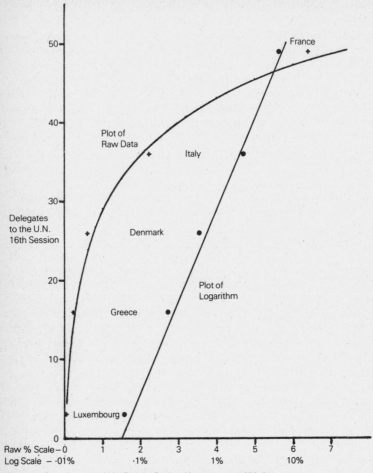

U.N. Regular Budget Assessments, 1959–61

The straight line, that has been drawn in, is actually the regression line for the states in the Western Bloc and not for all U.N. members. It has the formula:

Dels = 29·1 + 23·3 Log (Assess.)

with a correlation for the 25 states of 0·85.

of a relationship, regression is the technique for finding the equation of the one straight line that best represents the scatter of the points on the graph. A high correlation occurs when the countries are scattered close to the regression line. In the special case of a logarithmic curve, we can plot the graph as a straight regression line on logarithmic scaled axes. The following regression equations have been calculated separately from the data for each group on its own. The 16th Session was chosen because it was the session that opened immediately after the Belgrade Non-Aligned Conference in 1961. If non-alignment as a movement was going to have any effect on behaviour this would be the time it was most likely for the impact to be at its greatest.

TABLE 2.10   REGRESSION OF DELEGATION SIZE AGAINST BUDGET ASSESSMENTS, 16TH SESSION

Y = Number of Delegates, X = Log of Assessment for 1959–61

Western Bloc	$Y = 29 \cdot 1 + 23 \cdot 3 \, X$,	$r = 0 \cdot 85$,	$N = 25$
Latin Americans	$Y = 20 \cdot 8 + 8 \cdot 7 \, X$,	$r = 0 \cdot 75$,	$N = 19$
Non-Bloc	$Y = 22 \cdot 9 + 10 \cdot 6 \, X$,	$r = 0 \cdot 80$,	$N = 24^*$
Non-Aligned	$Y = 28 \cdot 9 + 13 \cdot 6 \, X$,	$r = 0 \cdot 78$,	$N = 25$
Eastern Bloc	$Y = 30 \cdot 3 + 22 \cdot 0 \, X$,	$r = 0 \cdot 81$,	$N = 10$

*Excluding Tanganyika, a new U.N. member.

The correlation of $0 \cdot 83$, for the Assembly as a whole in 1961, still   S*
remains high for each of the groups taken separately, which shows that economic size is still important in explaining variation within the groups. The equations are a little difficult to compare when we just look at the figures given in Table 2.10 (this is particularly so as the constant figure in a logarithm relationship does not represent the basic starting point of a zero assessment but an assessment of 1%, in the middle of the line). The picture is made clear when these regression lines are plotted in Figure 2.4. Each line is drawn solely to cover the economic range of states in that group. All the groups have at least one very small state so each line starts at the minimum assessment of $0 \cdot 04\%$. Amongst the Non-Aligned India is very much bigger than any of the others and so there is a continuous line only up to the value for Indonesia, the second largest, and then a broken line until the value for India.

The graph shows that, over the majority of the part that is relevant, the Non-Aligned for the same size economy were likely to send more delegates to the U.N. Indonesia only has an assessment of $0 \cdot 47\%$ of the budget, which may seem very low, but in fact 76% of the U.N.'s membership in 1961 had an assessment in the range of $0 \cdot 04$ to $0 \cdot 47\%$. Throughout the whole of this range, the line for the

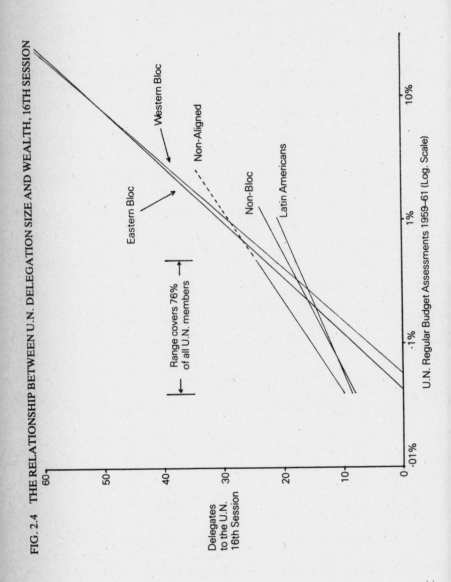

FIG. 2.4 THE RELATIONSHIP BETWEEN U.N. DELEGATION SIZE AND WEALTH, 16TH SESSION

Non-Aligned is above all the other regression lines. At the higher values the Western Bloc and the Eastern Bloc do overtake the Non-Aligned, but this is mainly due to the lines for the blocs being pulled up by large delegations from the Great Powers. With the exclusion just of the U.S.A. the line for the Western Bloc drops markedly and with the exclusion of the U.S.S.R. the position of the Eastern Bloc is almost identical to the Latin American's. The conclusion is that of all the smallest and medium size states, totalling three-quarters of the U.N.'s members, the Non-Aligned tended to be the most active.

This conclusion does not contradict the earlier discussion on how in the 16th Session the Non-Aligned sent on the average less delegates than the members of both the Western and the Eastern Blocs. The two main blocs are more active because their average economic size is greater than that of all the members of the Non-Aligned group, except India. Or looking at it from the other direction, despite having a higher desire to be active the Non-Aligned have a lower overall average performance, because the average Non-Aligned state is not wealthy.

TABLE 2.11   REGRESSION OF DELEGATION SIZE AGAINST BUDGET ASSESSMENTS, 19TH SESSION

Y = Number of Delegates, X = Log of Assessment for 1962–64

Western Bloc	$Y = 30 \cdot 9 + 23 \cdot 3\,X$,	$r = 0 \cdot 84$,	$N = 25$
Latin Americans	$Y = 24 \cdot 2 + 10 \cdot 8\,X$,	$r = 0 \cdot 76$,	$N = 19$
Non-Bloc	$Y = 27 \cdot 2 + 13 \cdot 1\,X$,	$r = 0 \cdot 92$,	$N = 15$
Non-Aligned	$Y = 26 \cdot 9 + 11 \cdot 7\,X$,	$r = 0 \cdot 70$,	$N = 46$
Eastern Bloc	$Y = 28 \cdot 4 + 19 \cdot 6\,X$,	$r = 0 \cdot 79$,	$N = 10$

TABLE 2.12   REGRESSION OF DELEGATION SIZE AGAINST BUDGET ASSESSMENT, 25TH SESSION

Y = Number of Delegates, X = Log of Assessment for 1968–70

Western Bloc	$Y = 33 \cdot 4 + 21 \cdot 8\,X$,	$r = 0 \cdot 83$,	$N = 25$
Latin Americans	$Y = 23 \cdot 5 + 8 \cdot 7\,X$,	$r = 0 \cdot 82$,	$N = 19$
Non-Bloc	$Y = 35 \cdot 1 + 18 \cdot 2\,X$,	$r = 0 \cdot 90$,	$N = 20$
Non-Aligned	$Y = 34 \cdot 7 + 16 \cdot 4\,X$,	$r = 0 \cdot 71$,	$N = 53$
Eastern Bloc	$Y = 30 \cdot 4 + 21 \cdot 0\,X$,	$r = 0 \cdot 83$,	$N = 10$

The second and third Non-Aligned summit conferences in Cairo in 1964 and in Lusaka in 1970 also met immediately before the corresponding 19th and 25th Sessions of the General Assembly. The data on the regression lines for these two points of time is given in Tables 2.11 and 2.12 and is presented pictorially in Figures 2.5

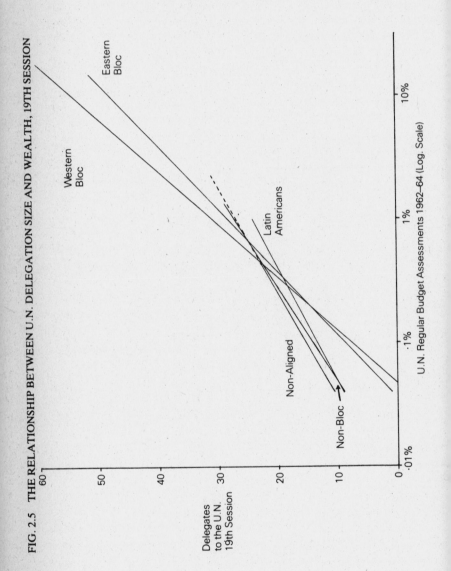

FIG. 2.5 THE RELATIONSHIP BETWEEN U.N. DELEGATION SIZE AND WEALTH, 19TH SESSION

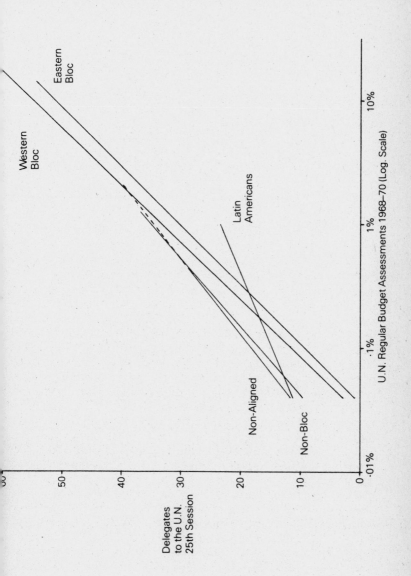

and 2.6, to see whether the pattern of behaviour that was observed in 1961 was repeated later when the Non-Aligned were recruited on a much wider basis. On the relevant parts of the graphs the Non-Aligned are still clearly more active than either of the main blocs, but they are only very marginally in the lead over the Non-Bloc states. In 1964, by comparison with 1961, the lines for the Non-Bloc and for the Latin American states have moved up, thus narrowing the gap with the Non-Aligned. Then in 1970 the Non-Aligned and the Non-Bloc states have moved up further together, leaving behind the Latin Americans. The relative positions of the Non-Aligned and three of the other groups have shown no more than minor fluctuations from year to year, but after originally being quite distinct the Non-Aligned and the Non-Bloc states have become virtually indistinguishable. The fact that this change has occurred since 1961 is not surprising. By broadening its ranks in 1964, the Non-Aligned movement became much more heterogeneous and lost its radical exclusiveness. At least from the point of view of the level of participation in the U.N., it has become less easy to separate the Non-Aligned from the Non-Bloc states.

Non-Aligned success in United Nations elections

A completely different measure of activism is to see to what extent the Non-Aligned obtained high prestige posts in the U.N. The most important posts, that are open to them, are the elected seats on the Security Council and the Presidency of the General Assembly. To count successes is a less precise form of measurement than delegation size, both because the amount of data is smaller and because its interpretation is more open to dispute. Election success is a measure of activism, in that the first requirement is for the country to promote its own candidacy. If the Non-Aligned were more inclined to support one of their own group, then success is a measure also of the group's cohesion in supporting the candidate. But, in order to be elected, votes are needed from members of other groups in the Assembly and so success is not solely determined by the Non-Aligned's own activity.

From 1946 until 1965, the seats on the Security Council were allocated by an unofficial arrangement, with two for the Latin Americans, one for the Commonwealth, one each for Western and Eastern Europe and one for the Middle East.[13] There was no direct provision for much of Africa and Asia. The arrangement began to come under strain when in the late 1950s Asian states, such as the Philippines and Japan, won the seat for Eastern Europe and in 1961 Liberia held the Western European seat. The Non-Aligned were relatively successful in this situation by using the old arrangement to their advantage. From among the Belgrade states, first Ceylon and then Ghana won the Commonwealth seat and the United Arab Republic followed by Morocco won the Middle Eastern seat. In 1965, Jordan (which had joined the Non-Aligned at Cairo) took over from Morocco. For comparison, the Non-Bloc states were represented by Liberia in 1961, Ireland in 1962, Ivory Coast (replacing Ghana) in 1964, and both Ivory Coast and Malaysia in 1965. Thus, from 1961 to 1963, the Non-Aligned did better, with two seats, than the Non-Bloc states, with first one and then no seat. In 1964, the two groups were equally represented and in 1965 the Non-Aligned were actually worse off, with only one seat while the Non-Bloc had two. This later situation was a particularly marked reversal of fortunes, because Non-Aligned Indonesia had bitterly opposed the election of Non-Bloc Malaysia. The point should not be exaggerated too much. By 1964, when Malaysia's election for the following year took place, Indonesia was out of line with a majority of the Cairo states. [14]

From 1966 there have been ten elected seats on the Security Council, allocated two to Latin America, two to "Western European and Others", one to Eastern Europe, and five to Afro-Asia, in practice two being to Asia and three to Africa. [15] From this point onwards the Non-Aligned have had a remarkable success. Each year up to 1978 they have held at least four seats; half the time they held five seats; and in 1973 they went up to seven seats. In the whole thirteen years not one African or Asian country was elected unless they had already joined the Non-Aligned. In more recent years the Non-Aligned have expanded so greatly that few Non-Bloc states remain. But throughout the first half of the period, before the Algiers summit, there were still sixteen to twenty-two Non-Bloc Afro-Asians and *none* were elected. The only success among the Non-Bloc states is that three of the European neutrals have each served one term for Western Europe.

In the elections to the Presidency of the General Assembly, the Non-Aligned have also been very successful. In the first fifteen years of the U.N., before the Non-Aligned were formed as a group, eight of the Presidents came from the Western Bloc, four were Latin Americans and only three were outside the bloc system. By contrast in the next fifteen years, the Western Bloc reduced to four Presidents; the Eastern Bloc obtained their first two; the Latin Americans dropped to three; and the Non-Aligned won six, while at no point since 1960 has a Non-Bloc country been elected President. The only break in this pattern of success for the Non-Aligned was that in 1962 a Western Bloc Asian state, Pakistan, was elected.

In the more recent years the achievement of the Non-Aligned

Movement has been particularly striking. In 1974, Algeria held the Presidency, the year after being the host country for the fourth summit. In 1976, Sri Lanka was President, after hosting the fifth summit in the same year. In 1977, Yugoslavia obtained the Presidency when it was the turn of Eastern Europe and Yugoslavia had in April 1977 already obtained the prior endorsement of the Ministerial Co-ordinating Bureau for its candidacy.[16] For the U.N.'s 33rd Session in 1978, it will be the turn of the Latin Americans to provide the President. If the Non-Aligned predominance continues, we may expect Panama or, with less likelihood, Argentina to be elected. The strongest possible evidence of Non-Aligned solidarity would be the election of Cuba, which is due in 1979 to host the sixth summit.[17]

Conclusions

We have established that the patterns of representation of the U.N. are very stable and that even a major crisis, such as the Third Arab-Israeli War, may have little effect on the number of diplomats sent by the countries involved. The U.N. has become the world's largest diplomatic centre and the main determinant of a state's level of participation is simply its economic size. Because the Non-Aligned are predominantly small states, their average delegation size is well below that of the main blocs. The Non-Aligned have significantly less people available for lobbying than they have voting power. But, when allowances are made for the effect of their small size, the Non-Aligned, as their ideology would suggest, do appear as the most active states in sending delegates to the General Assembly. In the competition for elected seats on the Security Council, the Non-Aligned did well initially from 1961 to 1963, but not so well in 1964 and 1965. Since then they have been very successful in winning the Afro-Asian seats and occasionally some others as well. In the elections for the President of the General Assembly, with one early exception, they have dominated at every possible opportunity.

References

1. Annex to Resolution 1192 (XII) adopted on 12th December 1957, *The Yearbook of the United Nations, 1957*, p. 119 (Office of Public Information, U.N., New York). The resolution concerned the composition of the General Committee and in operative paragraph 1 also referred to the electoral groups for the distribution of the chairmanships of the Main Committees. The last paragraph of the Annex complicated the matter by specifying that the Commonwealth,

which cross-cuts the regional electoral groups, must always have at least one member on the General Committee. The latter provision was dropped when Resolution 1990 (XVIII) superseded Resolution 1192 (XII), in 1964.

2. We can be certain that 'Western European and other states' includes the 'white, Dominium', Commonwealth states, because the Annex to Resolution 1192 (XII) (*op. cit. supra*) explicitly refers to Commonwealth states being in this electoral group.

3. In a document received by the author from the United Kingdom Foreign Office, with a letter dated 17/9/69, Mongolia was listed as being in the East European Group. Cuba was also listed in this group, but with a footnote, 'Electoral status in East European Group obscure'.

4. Under Resolution 1798 (XVII) of the General Assembly, the travel expenses for one round trip to New York of up to 5 representatives for each state are met by the United Nations Regular Budget. However, this subsidy does not include the cost of offices, accommodation and living expenses that must be met for *at least* the three to six months each year that the General Assembly is in session.

5. Because the number of delegates is being considered as an indicator of political behaviour, the administrative problems faced by new states in establishing their foreign service bureaucracy should not be allowed to affect the results. For this reason new states that joined towards the end of a session and which only had token representation are excluded from the analysis for that year. To be more precise, a state was excluded if it joined the session after 31st October and its representation was at a level of less than two-thirds of the number of delegates at the following session. On this basis Ghana was first included in the 12th Session, Guinea in the 14th, Tanganyika in the 17th, Kuwait in the 18th, Kenya in the 19th, Barbados in the 22nd, and South Yemen and Mauritius in the 23rd Session. Zanzibar, which was only in the U.N. for four months, was ignored altogether. The figures for the 24th and 25th Sessions do not come from the *Official Records*, because there is a delay before they are published. The results were derived from the series *Delegations to the United Nations* ST/SG/SER.B/23 and ST/SG/SER.B/24. This source was checked by comparing ST/SG/SER.B/22 with the *Official Records* for the 23rd Session and there was a correlation of 0·998 between figures derived from the two sources.

6. C. F. Alger and S. J. Brams, 'Patterns of Representation in National Capitals and Intergovernmental Organisations', *World Politics*, Vol. 19, pp. 646–63.

7. The figures given for the U.N. do not include the five non-member Observer states. When these are included the totals come to 1905 diplomats from 116 states, giving an average of 16·4 people per delegation.

8. In 1970 only twenty-four of the fifty-three full participants in the Lusaka Non-Aligned summit were among the sixty-nine states represented in New Delhi (*The Statesman's Yearbook 1970–71*, Macmillan, London, 1970, pp. 330–2), while only thirty-eight of the fifty-three at Lusaka were among the eighty-six represented in Cairo (*The Middle East and North Africa 1970–71*, Europa Publications, London, 1970, pp. 835–6).

9. Pearson's product moment correlation was used. The high correlations do *not* indicate that states were sending the same number of delegates each year but that they were changing in the same way, so that the majority increased or decreased their delegation sizes in the same years.

10. M. J. Kerbec, *Legally Available U.S. Government Information Vol. II*, (Output Systems Corporation, Virginia, 1970). Kerbec gives a list of 292 senior personnel that are at the level of Department head, 9 come within the office for International Organisation Affairs. The Report of the Committee on Foreign Affairs Personnel, *Personnel for the New Diplomacy* (Taplinger Publishing, New York, 1963), gives a figure for 1962 of 3687 total Foreign Service Officers plus 1235 Foreign Service Reserve Officers (p. 149). Of the F.S.O.s 46 were classified as working on International Organisation (p. 151). By contrast M. A. East gives a figure of 23 at the level of F.S.O. in the Ugandan Ministry of Foreign Affairs, of which one person worked on the United Nations, 'Foreign Policy-Making in Small States: Some Theoretic Observations Based on a Study of the Uganda Ministry of Foreign Affairs', *Policy Sciences*, December 1973, pp. 491–508.

11. Only the smallest and poorest of states might find that forming U.N. delegations is a strain on their personnel resources. Unemployment amongst school leavers is a well-known phenomenon in developing countries but in many countries university graduates also find that they are no longer in a 'seller's market'.

12. The first two columns of Table 2.9 exclude Byelorussia and the Ukraine as no meaningful G.N.P. data can be estimated for these two 'states'. The data on the G.N.P. was derived from the figures for G.N.P. *per capita* and population size in the third to sixth editions of the *World Bank Atlas* (International Bank for Reconstruction and Development, Washington D.C.), covering the years 1966 to 1969 respectively. (The third edition of the Atlas reports population figures that are labelled 1968, while the *per capita* income figures are labelled as being for the year 1966. However, on checking the population figures they are the same as those given by the *United Nations Demographic Yearbook 1966* for mid-1966. It has been assumed that the year is wrongly reported in the Atlas.) In Table 2.9 the delegates to the 15th–21st Sessions have been correlated with the 1966 G.N.P. figures, as no sources are available

which give comprehensive data for the earlier years. Similarly both the 24th and the 25th Sessions were correlated with the G.N.P. data for 1969. However, with a time span of only ten years it makes very little difference which year's G.N.P. data is used. The correlations between the figures for the different years are all within the range 0·989 to 1·000. There was no data for Mongolia in 1966 so the figure of $0·4377 thousand millions was calculated by assuming a growth rate of 9·6% for 1966. This was the average of the 8·5% rate for 1967 and 10·6% for 1968. The sixth edition of the *World Bank Atlas* no longer gives the G.N.P. *per capita* for twenty states with less than $100 p.a. For these states the 1969 G.N.P. was estimated by multiplying the 1969 population by the 1968 *per capita* income.

13. R. Hiscocks, *The Security Council. A Study in Adolescence* (Longman, London, 1973), p. 70. S. D. Bailey, *The General Assembly of the United Nations* (Stevens and Sons, London, 1960), pp. 165–7.

14. The Indonesians tried and failed at Colombo in March 1964 to get the second summit to discuss the calling of a conference of 'new, emerging forces', *Asian Recorder*, 15th–21st April 1964, p. 5772. At the summit, they tried and failed to obtain an endorsement of 'confrontation' with 'old forces of imperialism', *Keesings Contemporary Archives 1964*, p. 20433. There was so little sympathy with the Indonesians that President Nasser even urged the Malaysians to send observers to Cairo, *Ibid.*, p. 20432.

15. *United Nations General Assembly Resolution 1990 (XVIII)*.

16. *United Nations Document A/32/74*, p. 20.

17. The President will be a Latin American in 1978, by virtue of Resolution 1990 (XVIII), which from 1964 established a five-year pattern of rotation. The only Latin Americans, other than Cuba, Panama and Argentina, that have been full participants in Non-Aligned conferences are Allende's Chile and Peru. The Non-Aligned have not accepted Allende's successor, Pinochet, and Peru is highly unlikely to be elected, as Peru was President in 1959 and no country has yet held the Presidency twice. Cuba's standing has declined since it was chosen in 1976 to host the sixth summit in 1979. Opposition, even amongst the Non-Aligned, to Cuba's involvement in Afria means that it would be surprising if Cuba were to be elected President.

CHAPTER THREE

Voting in the General Assembly

Having found that the Non-Aligned do appear to be more active than other states in sending delegates to the meetings of the United Nations General Assembly, the question now arises of how coherent a group the Non-Aligned form in the political processes that lead to resolutions being passed by the Assembly. In as much as the declarations passed by the Non-Aligned conferences have relevance to the various items that come up on the U.N.'s agenda, we may expect the Non-Aligned to take a position that accords with their ideology. Even if issues arise, which are not relevant to non-alignment, the Non-Aligned may still develop a common stand in order to enhance their bargaining power on the more central issues.

Once again it will not be possible to form a complete picture of the political processes at the U.N. Three distinct categories of activity take place, they are lobbying, sponsoring resolutions and voting. Data on lobbying is not available and it is difficult to see how a research team could gather a reliable and complete data-set, given that it would require continuous monitoring of the activities of more than 2000 people for up to six months. Provided a complete set of Assembly documents is available, both sponsorship and roll-call voting can be coded in a reliable and valid way. As in a formal sense voting is the most important activity, it is the roll-calls that will be analysed, to see whether the Non-Aligned do engage in joint activity.[1]

Voting procedure in the General Assembly

Resolutions, amendments and procedural questions may be decided upon in several ways by the General Assembly. If the issue appears not to be controversial, the President may just indicate what he believes the consensus to be and unless any member objects

89

this is recorded as the decision of the Assembly. Even quite important resolutions, such as authorisation of the budget, may be approved unanimously, because during committee a generally acceptable formula has been worked out. Voting, on issues that are not too controversial, can take place by a 'show of hands'. In this case the *Offical Records* will give the total number of votes cast, but there is no way of knowing how each individual state voted. Roll-call voting provides the only completely public form of decision taking in the General Assembly. When any member requests a roll-call vote, the President selects one state at random, which is then asked to call out its vote. The remaining states are called in turn in the English alphabetical order until Z is reached and then those starting with A continue on in order until all have voted.[2]

Since the 23rd Session in 1968, machine voting has been used. Members have buttons to push on their desk and these operate coloured lights on two large boards at the front of the auditorium on either side of the President's podium. After adequate time has been allowed, the President throws a switch, the machine is locked and no more votes can be cast or changes made. The equivalent of the old 'show of hands' vote is made, when the machine only records the total voting each way. If a member so requests, a 'recorded vote' is taken and the machine prints out how each state voted.[3] However, not so much time has been saved as the Secretariat must have hoped for, because sometimes members still insist on the recorded vote being taken with the full roll-call procedure. In 1970, 21 of the 67 recorded votes were in fact roll-calls. What is important from our point of view is that for both recorded votes and roll-calls we can see how each state voted in the *Official Records*. (From now on the more common term, roll-call, will be used to describe both types of votes.)

Although only a minority of the decisions are taken by roll-call, the selection of these votes for analysis is not arbitrary. The decision is taken for us by the delegates when they decide whether or not to ask for a roll-call. It is their decision and not ours that an issue is important and/or controversial enough to require a roll-call. There is only one category of important decisions that is not covered. Except for those which are unopposed, all elections to bodies such as the Security Council, the Economic and Social Council, the International Court, the Assembly's General Committee and other subsidiary bodies are by secret ballot, so that it is impossible to record and analyse these votes.

D*   When roll-calls are held they need not be solely on the full text of a resolution. It is very common for the separate paragraphs of a resolution to be voted on separately and occasionally this is not followed by a vote on the whole resolution. For example in the 16th Session a draft resolution on technical assistance to developing countries came to the plenary from the Second Committee. A roll-call was held on the paragraph which requested the developed countries to increase their aid to 1% of their G.N.P., but, after this was passed, the whole resolution went through without any further voting.[4] Similarly, in the same session, the only controversial question, in a Sixth Committee draft resolution to call the Vienna Conference on Consular Relations, was whether or not China and other non-members of the United Nations should be invited to attend. Thus a roll-call was held on an amendment proposing that 'all states' be invited, but, after this failed no further voting took place.[5]

A variety of procedural questions may also lead to roll-call votes.   D* In the 16th Session there were three roll-calls on whether an item should be put on the agenda; three to request that there should be separate votes on individual paragraphs of three resolutions; two on motions that a resolution was 'important' and therefore must receive a two-thirds majority to be passed; two on motions to adjourn; and one on the order in which resolutions should be voted upon.[6] The decision was made to include all these procedural roll-calls in the analysis. In some cases, such as the request for a separate vote on the most controversial paragraph of a resolution, it is obvious that the procedural question is politically significant. In other cases, it only requires a brief reading of the *Official Records*, to find the context in which the procedural vote was called for, to realise its political significance. As was mentioned before, the fact that a roll-call was held indicates that at least one delegate thought the matter important.

Roll-calls as a source of data

At least one study of U.N. voting has used the roll-calls that are   D* reported in the United Nations Yearbooks.[7] The present author started by using this data source, but later on the Inter-University Consortium for Political Research data file of U.N. roll-calls became available and so a comparison was made between the two. The Yearbook has only a selection of the roll-calls. The choice is made by the members of the United Nations Secretariat who are responsible for editing the Yearbook. No reference is given to their criteria for choosing whether or not to report a roll-call. It would appear that they have a rather formal orientation towards giving priority to roll-calls that take the final decision on a resolution, while they often omit roll-calls on individual paragraphs or amendments. In contrast the I.C.P. R. file contains every single roll-call that has been held. Because the roll-calls that are omitted from the Yearbooks are sometimes the more divisive, use of the Yearbooks tends to over-estimate the amount of consensus in the Assembly, as compared to the results that are found from using all the roll-calls.[8] In view of this finding the I.C.P.R.data will be used in this study.

D*   The next decision that had to be taken was whether to use the roll-calls that are held in plenary session or those in the seven Main Committees of the Assembly or both sets of roll-calls. If both sets are used, the problem arises that some roll-calls are duplicated, by being held in committee and then repeated again when the same resolution goes through the plenary session. In addition we are particularly interested in the voting patterns of the small states, but often they are not able with their small delegations to attend all the meetings of the Main Committees and cope with all the other diplomatic work. The following table illustrates the situation.[9]

TABLE 3.1
U.N. 20TH SESSION, ROLL-CALL ATTENDANCE OF THE GROUPS

	Plen. Sess. %	1st Comm. %	2nd Comm. %	3rd Comm. %	4th Comm. %	5th Comm. %	6th Comm. %	Spec. P. Comm. %
Western Bloc	98·3	96·4	80·0	92·2	90·1	88·0	96·0	91·7
Latin Americans	90·2	73·9	57·9	78·4	76·7	57·9	75·4	59·6
Non-Bloc	84·8	67·9	61·1	66·9	71·4	72·2	50·0	66·2
Non-Aligned	90·0	84·5	62·2	75·6	88·0	73·3	68·9	85·0
Eastern Bloc	95·9	93·6	50·0	88·5	94·0	100·0	90·0	97·5

It seemed appropriate for this study solely to analyse those roll-calls which were held in plenary.

D*   In the United Nations there are three recognised ways of casting a vote. In addition to voting in favour or against a proposal, abstention is accepted as being the result of a definite decision, usually implying that the member is not completely opposed to a proposal but does have some doubts about it. During the 1960s a few states very occasionally announced that they were 'Not Participating'.[10] This implies strong opposition to a proposal and a denial that the United Nations had any right to be discussing and voting on the issue concerned, usually because the issue was alleged to be concerned with a state's internal affairs. Any such cases will be treated as a vote against the proposal. Finally, a state may be absent from a particular roll-call because the delegates were all engaged in other business. In this case no assumptions can be made on how the state would have voted and so absence is treated as 'missing data'. Another form of 'missing data' is when a state was not a member of the U.N. at the time the vote was taken and it became a member later in the session.

The choice of a methodology

Several methods of legislative roll-call analysis have now been developed. The best known involves using one or another form of factor analysis.[11] There are two important reasons why this could not be used. The first is a practical one, that none of the computer programmes that were available to the author would handle more than 80 variables, yet in all the sessions of interest there are 104 to 127 states that were members. Secondly, the method of factor analysis does not offer a convenient way of presenting each state's position in relation to the whole Assembly. An alternative method called cluster-bloc analysis has been developed so that with various new indices it is possible both to examine pre-specified groups, such as the Latin Americans, the Non-Aligned, etc., and as an alternative approach to see without pre-specification what were the empirical groups to be found in the voting data. These methodological questions are discussed in detail in Appendix 5.

The first step in cluster-bloc analysis is to measure for every pair of states how much they were in agreement. The simplest method would be to count what percentage of times the two states voted in the same way. Lijphart has proposed an index of agreement that is suitable for analysing United Nations voting, as it takes into account the fact that 'Abstain' is a frequent decision.[12] The assumption is made that abstention can usually be regarded as representing a position that is half way between 'Yes' and 'No' on an imaginary metric of the issue dimension. The second implicit assumption is that all roll-calls are of equal weight and that all forms of agreement are of equal weight. This assumption is not very strongly based, as one might argue that the decision of one state to join another in a small minority group is of more weight than a decision to join a third state which is with the majority. However, it is in the nature of research in the social sciences that there is going to be some gap between a concept and the method by which it is measured. In this case the Lijphart Index of Agreement seems a reasonable measure of how close a pair of states are in their voting patterns.

The Index is defined in the following way –

$$I_A = \frac{(f + \frac{1}{2}g)}{t} \times 100$$

where t is the total number of roll-calls that both states participated in, *f* is the number in which they cast identical votes and *g* is the number in which they showed 'partial agreement'. This later situation is said to occur when one state votes either in favour or against a proposal and the other state abstains. The two have not directly opposed each other, so they are in partial agreement. As an example of the use of the index, we may calculate the agreement between the Cameroons and the United States in the 16th Session. There were 76 roll-calls held in plenary and the Cameroons was absent from 3 of them. The two countries voted in exactly the same way 38 times, they showed partial agreement 19 times and they were opposed to each other the remaining 16 times. Thus the index is calculated as –

$$I_A \text{ (Cameroon-America)} = \frac{(38 + \frac{1}{2} \cdot 19)}{73} \times 100 = 65 \cdot 1\%$$

Similar calculations may be made for every possible pair of states. There were 104 members in 1961, so this means that there were 104 × 103/2 = 5356 values of the index to be calculated, for the 16th Session.

As we wish to know whether the states are co-operating together to form voting blocs, we must have some criteria for deciding whether an agreement score is to be regarded as high, medium or low. The standard that has been adopted is to compare the scores, that resulted from the political decisions of the members, with the scores that we would expect to occur, if they had been voting at random, for example by picking 'Yes', 'No'. 'Abstain' labels out of a hat. This reasoning is explained in detail in Appendix 5 and the cut-off points for high agreement and high disagreement (that is low agreement) are given in Table 6 of the Appendix. In practice for the numbers of roll-calls being analysed later in this chapter the cut-off points are generally from 50–75%, to mark high agreement or below 35–40% to mark high disagreement.

D* In addition to this statistical decision on cut-off points, there is also a more substantive problem when some states have a low attendance record. In the 16th Session there were 76 roll-calls and so from the probability distribution for random voting we find that (with $p \leqslant 0 \cdot 001$) any scores of $69 \cdot 1\%$ or more should be considered as high agreement. In the case of the Guatemala-Mexico agreement score this cut-off cannot be used. Guatemala missed 2 of the roll-calls, while Mexico was absent from 3. Their resulting joint participation was 71 roll-calls. The probability distribution for random voting on 71 roll-calls gives us a slightly higher cut-off point of $69 \cdot 7\%$ or more for high agreement. Similarly we find that Mauritania and Tanzania only attended 22 roll-calls together and that the distribution for 22 roll-calls gives a noticeably higher cut-off of 81·2%. By this criterion their actual agreement score of 81·8% must be considered to be showing high agreement. This statistical argument is still valid, but we may ask whether we are comparing like with like, when we say that Guatemala and Mexico achieved high agreement on the 71 roll-calls they attended and Mauritania and Tanzania achieved high agreement on the 22 roll-calls they attended. We cannot be certain and can only make an intelligent guess, if it is asserted that Mauritania and Tanzania would still have achieved high agreement had they attended all the roll-calls. For this pair of African states, so much of the data is missing that the question of 'common sense validity' arises before that of statistical validity. The decision was taken that most of the time a state would be excluded from the analysis if it attended less than three-quarters of the roll-calls. In consequence this means that each *pair* of states must have jointly attended at least half of the roll-calls.[13]

As was the case with data in Chapter 2, it would be preferable to analyse the voting in the 16th, 19th and 25th Sessions, which each opened a month after the three Non-Aligned summit conferences. It is in these years that the Non-Aligned were most likely to be acting as a voting bloc and to have common policies. However, in 1964 the United Nations was deadlocked over the United States' attempt to deprive the Soviet Union of her right to vote in the General Assembly, because of her arrears in payments towards U.N. peace-keeping operations. As a result a temporary consensus was obtained that there should be no roll-call voting in the 19th Session. By the following year voting was resumed and so the 16th, 20th and 25th Sessions will be analysed.

Cohesion within the groups

The first question that we are now able to tackle is how coherent have the various groups been: have they voted together enough for the members of each group to be in high agreement with each other? Table 3.2 gives the values of two indices for each group for each session.[14] The first, I_α, is an index of agreement for the group as a whole and measures the percentage of all the pairs of states in the group that were in high agreement with each other. Thus in the 16th Session the Non-Aligned had 25 members, which gives 25 × 24/2 = 300 pairs of states. A total of 299 of the pairs were in high agreement, only Cuba and Cyprus at 64·7% did not have a high enough score, so 299/300 gives a value of 99·7% for I_α. The second index, I_β, is comparable. It measures the percentage of all the pairs in the group, that were in high disagreement, i.e. low agreement.

The table shows that there was a clear bloc structure in each of the

TABLE 3.2   GROUP COHESION ON ALL ROLL-CALLS IN PLENARY
SESSION ($p \ll 0.001$)

	16th Session		20th Session		25th Session	
	% with High Scores I_α	% with Low Scores I_β	% with High Scores I_α	% with Low Scores I_β	% with High Scores I_α	% with Low Scores I_β
Western Bloc	90·6	0·0	69·0	0·7	74·4	0·0
Latin Americans	100·0	0·0	100·0	0·0	97·5	0·0
Non-Bloc	71·9	0·0	63·8	0·0	76·9	0·0
Non-Aligned	99·7	0·0	99·5	0·0	93·4	0·0
Eastern Bloc	100·0	0·0	100·0	0·0	100·0	0·0
Whole Assembly	49·8	13·6	55·8	1·0	62·0	3·1

three sessions. Earlier studies have found the Soviet bloc to be
highly cohesive and this situation has continued in more recent
years.[15] Not only do all the ten states achieve high agreement with
each other, but they so rarely fail to vote together that most of the
scores are 100% agreement. In the 16th Session, of the 752 votes
cast by the bloc on 76 roll-calls only 3 votes were out of line with the
Soviet Union and 2 of these appear to have been mistakes. In the
20th Session only 5 out of 393 votes cast were out of line, but on
these occasions Romania and Albania were clearly expressing their
own attitudes to disarmament questions. Albania achieved the
distinction of being the only state to vote against a resolution calling
for the suspension of all nuclear testing. (In so doing she was acting
as a surrogate for China in the United Nations.) By the 25th
Session, in comparison to the former tight discipline of the Soviet
bloc, a definite change has occurred. Romania cast eleven votes,
that is one-sixth of her votes, differently from the Soviet Union.
Poland, Mongolia and Ukraine cast another eight out of line, from a
total of 615 votes cast by the whole bloc. For any other group of
states, this record would still represent an impressive degree of
co-operation, but nevertheless it does show at least an important
change in Romania's position. She was able to take an independent
stand on a wide range of issues covering the Middle East, the Law of
the Sea, Namibia and UNCTAD.

The second most cohesive group was the Latin Americans.
Among the 19 states there were frequently pairs of states that
achieved 90–95% agreement, but unlike the Soviet bloc 100%
agreement was a rarity which did not occur in the 16th Session, only
twice in the 20th and once in the 25th Session. However, the scores
were high enough that in both the 16th Session and the 20th Session

they were all statistically significant and by this less stringent criterion the Latin Americans formed a completely cohesive group. In the 25th Session, there was a slight drop in the cohesion of the group. This was due to the new position adopted by the Chilean government after Dr. Allende was sworn in as President on 3rd November 1970. Chile still achieved high agreement with twelve of the Latin Americans, but failed to do so with Brazil, Dominican Republic and Nicaragua. (The three other Latin Americans were deleted because of low attendance.) Chile was the only member of the group that in this session achieved high agreement with the members of the Soviet bloc. The other members of the group maintained the same level of high agreement among themselves as in the previous sessions.

The third most cohesive group was the Non-Aligned. As has already been mentioned, in the 16th Session only Cuba and Cyprus failed to achieve significantly high agreement. However, the scores were generally not as high as those for the Latin Americans, being in the range 80–90%. No two countries reached 100% agreement. Within the whole Non-Aligned group, in the 16th Session, there were two sub-groups, that appeared to show above average cohesion. One was a radical group of the five 'Casablanca' states, Ghana, Guinea, Mali, Morocco and the U.A.R., with Iraq, Ethiopia, Yugoslavia and Indonesia. The second sub-group was formed from the four Asian states, India, Nepal, Burma and Ceylon. These two sub-groups and a few other isolated links all had scores showing over 90% agreement.

The value of I_α was almost the same in the 20th Session as in the 16th, but in the meantime the Non-Aligned group had increased in size from 25 to 41 members.[16] Four links were not high enough to be considered as significant agreement, they were between Togo and three of the more radical states and between Ceylon and Somalia. The average agreement score was in fact rather higher in the 20th Session and 15 pairs of Non-Aligned states did reach 100% agreement.

By the 25th Session there is a more substantial drop in the cohesion of the Non-Aligned group, although it still remains clearly more united than the remaining two groups. This time there were as many as 68 links that did not show high agreement. Again there were two sub-groups, one of the Arabs and the more radical African states, the other of seventeen relatively conservative Afro-Asian and Caribbean states. The 68 medium level agreement scores were all between pairs of states consisting of one member from each sub-group. Within each sub-group the scores were usually over 90%, while the general level between the sub-groups was 80–90%

agreement. Two of the conservative states were distinctly out of line with the rest of the Non-Aligned. Liberia and Swaziland between them were responsible for over half of the 68 medium level scores. They both failed to reached high agreement with 19 of the other 45 Non-Aligned.[17] Although the group became less cohesive in the 25th Session, the fact that 967 of the 1035 pairs of Non-Aligned states did achieve high agreement still represents a substantial degree of political unity.

The Western Bloc has a relatively low level of cohesion compared to the indices of over 90% in Table 3.2 for the Eastern Bloc, the Latin Americans and the Non-Aligned. However, before we make too much of this, it must be remembered that the group that has been called the Western Bloc is rather mixed in its composition. The only common link is that they are all tied militarily to the United States, mainly by the multilateral NATO, SEATO and CENTO treaties. This definition of the Western Bloc was an attempt to form a group from those countries that the Non-Aligned would perceive of as being Western.

One country immediately stands out as not belonging with the other Western states. Pakistan in the 16th Session only reached high agreement with 30·4% of the Western Bloc but did reach high agreement with all except Cuba amongst the Non-Aligned. In the 20th Session, Pakistan was down to agreement with only an eighth of the Western Bloc and now agreed with all the Non-Aligned and all the communist states. In the 25th Session it was back to a figure of 31·8% with the Western Bloc and still agreed with all except Laos among the Non-Aligned and all the communists. On the other hand it was Pakistan's high disagreement with Portugal and South Africa in the 20th Session, that produced the only non-zero values of I_β in Table 3.2. Of the others both Iran and the Philippines show a movement from the Western group towards the Non-Aligned. The same is true of Greece and Turkey. These two European NATO states appeared to be less central to the Western Bloc than Asian states such as Israel, Japan and nationalist China.

The Non-Bloc states also form a somewhat arbitrary grouping that was designed to cover those states that were eligible to join the Non-Aligned but chose not to do so. The group covers two distinct categories, the one being conservative Third World countries and the other being the four European neutral states. As a whole the Non-Bloc states only show slightly higher cohesion than the average for the whole Assembly. But the European neutrals had 100% cohesion amongst themselves in each session, while the Third World, Non-Bloc countries had figures of 100%, 98·2% and 77·8% in the three sessions.

Relations between the groups

Tables 3.3 to 3.5 show for each session how much there was agreement across the boundaries between the specified groups. Each figure gives:

$$IG_\gamma = IG_\alpha - IG_\beta$$

or in words, considering all the possible Lijphart agreement scores, the Inter-Group adhesion is

the percentage which show high agreement less
the percentage which show high disagreement.

Thus in the 16th Session there was almost complete overlap between the communists and the Non-Aligned on the one hand and also between the Latin Americans and the Western Bloc on the other, while there were many low scores between the communists and the Latin Americans and Western states. In the next two sessions the structure is not so strikingly clear. However, all the tables show a situation in which each group has considerably more than half its links with the next group at a high level of agreement. The amount of adhesion drops markedly as one moves away from the diagonal, until in the corner the relationship between the two extremes is one showing more disagreement than agreement.

TABLE 3.3
INTER-GROUP ADHESION ($IG\,\gamma$) IN THE 16TH SESSION ($p \leqslant 0.001$)

	East	Non-Aligned	Non-Bloc	Latin	West
Eastern Bloc	—	92·0	0	–83·3	–82·1
Non-Aligned	92·0	—	60·7	–7·8	–26·7
Non-Bloc	0	60·7	—	59·0	36·5
Latin Americans	–83·3	–7·8	59·0	—	94·2
Western Bloc	–82·1	–26·7	36·5	94·2	—

TABLE 3.4
INTER-GROUP ADHESION ($IG\,\gamma$) IN THE 20TH SESSION ($p \leqslant 0.001$)

	East	Non-Aligned	Non-Bloc	Latin	West
Eastern Bloc	—	97·6	59·3	0	–4·0
Non-Aligned	97·6	—	70·4	17·6	15·4
Non-Bloc	59·3	70·4	—	72·9	49·0
Latin Americans	0	17·6	72·9	—	78·1
Western Bloc	–4·0	15·4	49·0	78·1	—

TABLE 3.5
INTER-GROUP ADHESION (*IG* γ) IN THE 25th SESSION ($p \leqslant 0.001$)

	East	Non-Aligned	Non-Bloc	Latin	West
Eastern Bloc	—	66·9	2·9	2·1	–39·6
Non-Aligned	66·9	—	57·3	61·5	29·8
Non-Bloc	2·6	57·3	—	88·0	67·9
Latin Americans	2·1	61·5	88·0	—	75·3
Western Bloc	–39·6	29·8	67·9	75·3	—

The results all show that the General Assembly has a strong bloc structure in its patterns of roll-call voting. Furthermore the groups that were specified, on the *a priori* grounds that they were of interest in a study of non-alignment, do show themselves to have high explanatory power in summing up the patterns among some 5000 dyadic links. If these pre-specified groups were not relevant then there would not be any definite pattern in Tables 3.3 to 3.5. But in commenting on the results it has been necessary several times to point out how the figures for a group have been affected by changes in the behaviour of one or two individual states. An alternative way of examining the bloc structure is to drop the idea of looking at pre-specified groups and to see what are the empirical blocs that emerge from the data. Hitherto, it has not been possible to do this systematically with the results from cluster-bloc analysis, but the algorithm outlined in Appendix 6 does now offer one method.

The empirical identification of voting blocs

The Lijphart agreement scores for each state with every other state in the 16th Session gave a matrix of 104 × 104 scores. Six states were deleted because they did not attend at least three-quarters of the roll-calls, leaving a matrix of 98 × 98 scores. Then after testing each score to see whether it showed high agreement (by comparison to voting at random), medium agreement or high disagreement, a new matrix was constructed with a +1 to indicate agreement, –1 disagreement and 0 for medium scores. This matrix when printed out gave Figure 3.1. It can be seen that with the states still in alphabetical order, there is little coherence to the matrix. After using matrix algebra to move the +1's all as close to the diagonal as possible and the –1's all as far away from the diagonal as possible, the computer programme produced Figure 3.2.

As the depth of one line of computer print-out is a little greater than the distance between the individual characters on a line, Figure

FIG. 3.1   U.N. SESSION, THE START OF THE ATTEMPT TO FIND
CLUSTER-BLOCS

THE FOLLOWING MEMBERS WERE DELETED BECAUSE OF LOW ATTENDANCE –
HONDURAS PORTUGAL MAURITAN GABON   CONGO B, TANZANIA

3.2 is oblong in shape instead of being a perfect square. However, it is a symmetric matrix and it is only this feature of the printing that prevents it from being square. The columns across the top of the page are not headed, but they represent each of the countries in the same order as the list down the side of the page. Each of the points on the diagonal is a +, as each country was given a Lijphart agreement score of 100% with itself and is therefore in high agreement with itself. Reading down the first column we see that Albania reached high agreement with a bloc of countries that included nine other communist states, 23 of the 25 Non-Aligned and Libya, Sierra Leone and Jordan. Then comes a group of 24 countries from Lebanon to Finland with which Albania has medium scores and finally there are 38 Latin American and Western states with which Albania was in significant disagreement. If the columns had been headed, we would have gained exactly the same information by considering the points in the first row. Similarly the second to eighth rows representing the countries Bulgaria to Romania are the same as the second to eighth columns and also are the same as the first row/column for Albania. By any standard these eight countries form a voting bloc.

In the literature a cluster-bloc has not been defined in the above way, with all the countries having the same pattern of high agreements. A less demanding definition is for a cluster-bloc to be any group of states in which every member is in high agreement with every other member. By this standard the first 35 countries, from Albania to the Congo Democratic Republic, are a perfect cluster-bloc. Jordan can also be added to the bloc, on the grounds that only the one link with Mongolia failed to reach high agreement.

S*   Once one allows a cluster-bloc to have one or two links missing in this way, it is no longer always unambiguous as to where the boundaries should be drawn. This is not to say that the method turns out to be arbitrary. As the solution to the problem of how to order the matrix is a unique one, the whole process of converting the voting records into the final matrix of significant agreements is replicable by any other researcher. The question of where to draw the lines delimiting the cluster-blocs is of the same nature as deciding what words to use to describe the matrix. Sometimes, when the underlying pattern of political relationships is rather complex, description is not so easy.

In the 16th Session we find that there were five overlapping cluster-blocs. While these five blocs are related to the five groups that were specified earlier, they are by no means identical to them. The communists formed a bloc with 23 Non-Aligned and three other Afro-Asians. Then the communists are excluded, as all the

FIG. 3.2   CLUSTER-BLOCS IN THE U.N. 16TH SESSION

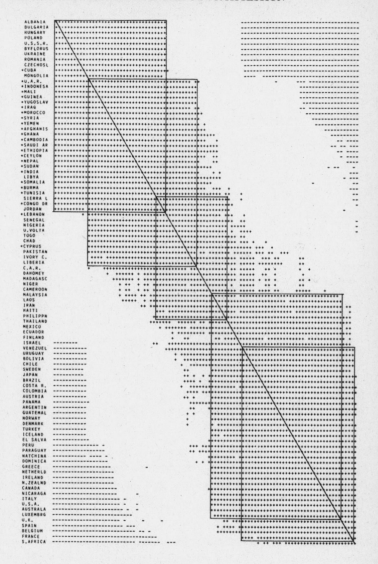

THE FOLLOWING MEMBERS WERE DELETED BECAUSE OF LOW ATTENDANCE -
HONDURAS PORTUGAL MAURITAN GABON   CONGO B.   TANZANIA

* ATTENDED THE BELGRADE NON-ALIGNED SUMMIT, 1961.

Non-Aligned except Cuba form a bloc with eleven other Afro-Asians. The third bloc includes only three of the Non-Aligned with all the Afro-Asian Non-Bloc states, three of the Asian allies of the West and Haiti the only black Latin American state. The final two blocs have a very high degree of overlap and consist of Malaysia and Laos, the four European neutrals, the Latin Americans and the Western Bloc states. Only South Africa is outside the bloc structure and she achieved the distinction of disagreeing with 38% of the other states, which is more than the 29% she managed to agree with.

In the 20th Session the problem of how to separate a series of overlapping, imperfect cluster-blocs becomes more acute. Ten cluster-blocs have been drawn on Figure 3.3 but only one of these has no links missing. The failure of the Congo Democratic Republic to reach high agreement with Malawi and the Maldives occurs so near to the centre of the matrix that it presents a flaw for five of the cluster-blocs. But it is the areas further away from the diagonal that are more indeterminate and might have led other researchers to define the boundaries of the cluster-blocs slightly differently.

There are only two clear breaks in the structure of Figure 3.3. The first 54 countries from the Congo (Brazzaville) to Gabon do form a perfect cluster-bloc, but it seems reasonable to group the next five countries down to Ceylon along with them. This gives a bloc of 59 members or over half of the Assembly. The bloc includes the nine communist states, 40 of the 41 Non-Aligned, Pakistan and 9 of the 11 Third World Non-Bloc states, but none of the European neutrals. At the bottom of the matrix there is a small bloc of six of the Western colonial powers. Another colonial power, the Netherlands, belongs to this bloc, but has been separated from it by the rather muddled pattern of high agreements shown by Spain and Finland.

Between these two blocs at either end of the matrix there is a continually changing pattern amongst the western Asians, the Latin Americans and the west European states. Some such as Greece and Iran have more links with the Non-Aligned than they do with the Western Bloc. Those further down, such as Uruguay and Venezuela, have links with all groups, including a fifth of the Non-Aligned and even some of the colonial powers. Finally those such as Belgium and New Zealand are only linked to Malaysia and none of the other Non-Aligned or Third World Non-Bloc states. The group of 36 states from Malaysia to the Netherlands form a mixed bloc, with only the Argentine, Haiti and Colombia preventing it from being a perfect cluster-bloc.

The situation in the 25th Session superficially appears to

FIG. 3.3   CLUSTER-BLOCS IN THE U.N. 20TH SESSION

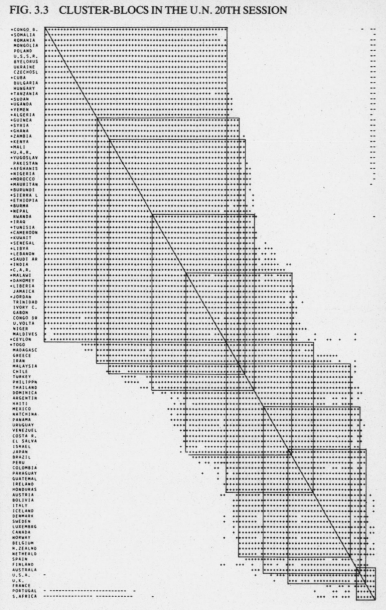

THE FOLLOWING MEMBERS WERE DELETED BECAUSE OF LOW ATTENDANCE -
NICARAGA   ECUADOR   MALTA   ALBANIA   CYPRUS   GAMBIA
CHAD   CAMBODIA   LAOS   SINGAPOR

* ATTENDED THE CAIRO NON-ALIGNED SUMMIT, 1964.

resemble that of the 20th Session. There is again a series of ten overlapping cluster-blocs. But unlike the previous two sessions, Figure 3.4 does not show the communist states and nearly all the Non-Aligned forming a single cluster-bloc. This time only 30 of the 46 Non-Aligned are in the bloc with the communists and they are joined by Saudi Arabia (which did attend the first two but not the third Non-Aligned summit), Pakistan and Chile. In addition, when we exclude the communists from consideration, the second cluster-bloc does not include all the Non-Aligned: six are still missing from the voting bloc.

In the previous years the Third World Non-Bloc countries were close together and followed by first the western Asians, then the Latin Americans and finally the main part of the Western Bloc. By the 25th Session not only the Non-Aligned but also all the other groups are much more spread across the matrix. Among the Non-Bloc states the Franco-phone states, Upper Volta, Ivory Coast, Madagascar and Gabon, have moved apart. Malawi has made a dramatic change from being in 1965 a Non-Aligned state that reached high agreement with the communists to being in 1970 a Non-Bloc state amongst the colonial powers and in high disagreement with the communists. Among the western Asians Iran has moved closer to the Non-Aligned, Philippines and Thailand are no longer adjacent and Japan has moved closer to the west Europeans. Among the Latin Americans Chile has clearly moved into the Non-Aligned voting bloc while Ecuador and Peru are also much closer to the Non-Aligned. Even two members of NATO, Turkey and Greece, can be found well towards the centre of the matrix and away from the other members of the alliance. Thus the middle, from Afghanistan to Gabon, shows much inter-mingling of the Non-Aligned, Non-Bloc, Latin American and Western Bloc states. In the 1950s the dominant majority in the General Assembly was a coalition of the Western Bloc and the Latin Americans. In the 1960s, if Figure 3.3 is typical, the dominant majority was a coalition of the Eastern Bloc and the Non-Aligned. Figure 3.4 tends to suggest that in the 1970s a new coalition of the less radical Non-Aligned, the Non-Bloc states (most of which joined the Non-Aligned in 1973) and the more radical Latin Americans would come to dominate the General Assembly.

The question posed by this chapter was to find to what extent the group of states that had defined themselves as Non-Aligned did form a distinct political grouping. The evidence for the 16th and the 20th Sessions, in 1961 and 1965, is quite definite. The Non-Aligned were a highly cohesive group that formed a voting alliance with the communist states.[18] By the 25th Session in 1970 the situation is

FIG. 3.4 CLUSTER-BLOCS IN THE U.N. 25TH SESSION

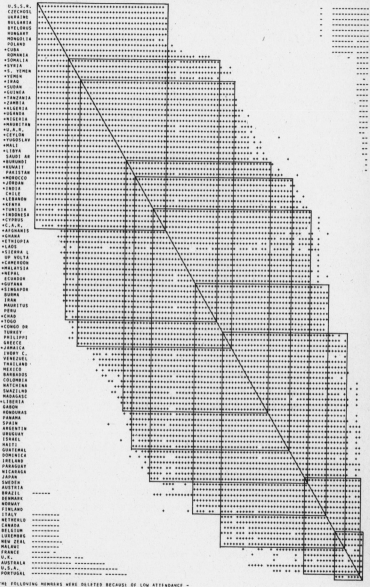

THE FOLLOWING MEMBERS WERE DELETED BECAUSE OF LOW ATTENDANCE -
ALBANIA   BOTSWANA   CONGO B.   EQ GUINF   LESOTHO   RWANDA
SENEGAL   TRINIDAD   CAMBUDIA   DAHOMEY   GAMBIA   FIJI
MALTA   NIGER   BOLIVIA   COSTA R.   EL SALVA   ICELAND
S AFRICA   MALDIVES

* ATTENDED THE LUSAKA NON-ALIGNED SUMMIT, 1970.

somewhat different, only two-thirds of the group still are in this alliance with the communists. In none of the sessions is there a perfect correlation between the pre-specified groups of interest and the empirical cluster-blocs. Cuba votes in a way that is more typical of the communists than the Non-Aligned and it is only the co-operation between these two groups that makes Cuba appear to be in the Non-Aligned voting bloc. In the 16th Session three states that did not attend the Belgrade summit, Libya, Sierra Leone and Jordan, voted closely with the Non-Aligned, while two states that did attend, Lebanon and Cyprus, were closer to the Afro-Asian Non-Bloc states. In the 20th Session two states from the Cairo summit, Ceylon and Togo, were relatively nearer the Non-Bloc states. In Ceylon's case this is rather surprising, as it will be recalled that Ceylon was one of the governments that took the initiative in calling the Cairo summit. Again, two states that were not then Non-Aligned, Pakistan and Rwanda, fit in with the Non-Aligned rather than the Non-Bloc states. In the 25th Session in 1970, the Non-Aligned group appears as a more cohesive voting bloc than it would have done if Malawi had been included. Yet Malawi did receive an invitation to the Lusaka summit and the Zambians appeared more pleased than embarassed when it seemed as though Dr. Banda might attend the summit.[19] Two other states that did attend, Liberia and Swaziland, were not close to the Non-Aligned in their voting. Thus the distinction between states that do or do not identify with non-alignment is usually but not always a guide to how the state will vote.

An interesting confirmation of the fact that non-alignment was a relevant behavioural dimension in the United Nations is the parallel history of the Afro-Asian Non-Bloc states. In both 1961 and 1965, with the exceptions noted above, they did form a group that were close to each other and midway between the Non-Aligned and the Western states. In 1970, like the Non-Aligned, they are much more dispersed. But in contrast the European neutrals have occupied a quite different position. In none of the sessions have they been close to the Non-Aligned or the Afro-Asian Non-Bloc states and, in as much as movement is discernible, it has been towards not away from the NATO states. Bearing this evidence in mind, it becomes less of a puzzle that the European neutrals have never been full participants in any of the Non-Aligned summits.

Among the Latin Americans until recently only Cuba has been an active member of the Non-Aligned group. The remaining Latin Americans have formed a cohesive bloc, but have not been clearly separated from some of the other pro-Western states. The one state, Chile, that did make a significant change in its voting, also followed this up by formally joining the Non-Aligned group at the U.N. in 1971 and attending the Georgetown Foreign Ministers meeting in 1972. Similarly among the more peripheral members of the Western Bloc only Pakistan has shown an interest in the Non-Alignment movement.[20] In 1970 she tried to obtain an invitation to the Lusaka summit, but was blocked by India. This anomaly in Pakistan's position was matched by a corresponding anomaly in the U.N. In the 1965 and 1970 voting Pakistan was closer to leaders of the Non-Aligned, such as the U.A.R. and Yugoslavia than India was.

Conclusions

The Non-Aligned did not operate with the highly disciplined bloc voting of the communist states, nor did they achieve as a high a degree of unity as the Latin Americans. But the Non-Aligned did reach an impressive degree of cohesion and were clearly identifiable as a distinct group. The states around America forming the Western Bloc would generally be considered to have a community of interests and outlook. The Non-Aligned showed a markedly higher cohesion than the Western Bloc. They were also more united than the residual category of Non-Bloc states.

The Indices of Inter-Group Adhesion and the computer identification of the empirical cluster-blocs both showed the Non-Aligned to be in an intermediate position between the communists and the Non-Bloc states. The sessions examined show a sharp decline in the gap between the Non-Aligned and both the Latin Americans and the Western Bloc, though it would need more comprehensive research to establish whether this was part of a longer term trend. Examination of the cluster-blocs shows that, although the five specified groups can be used to describe the main structure of the U.N. voting patterns, the details are much more complex. In each session there were two or three states that had *not* attended the Non-Aligned summits, which nevertheless voted with the Non-Aligned, while a few of the attenders were separate from the majority of the group. To say whether or not an Afro-Asian state was one of the Non-Aligned would usually, but not always, give a good prediction of its U.N. voting.

So far the analysis has looked at the overall bloc structure, when all the roll-calls in the various plenary sessions are considered. Now we must examine whether the cohesion of the Non-Aligned still holds in the issue areas that were found in Chapter 1 to be central to the ideology of non-alignment. While the United Nations is important and is particularly relevant, because of the strong support for it expressed by the Non-Aligned, it cannot be assumed that the General Assembly completely reflects the international scene. Measures of behaviour outside the United Nations must also be considered.

References

1. The activities of the various caucus groups at the U.N. are not recorded in the *Official Records*, so it is difficult to obtain information about them. As was outlined in Chapter 1, it would appear that the Non-Aligned did not meet with any regularity, until at the earliest October 1971. However, up to this point all except Cuba and Yugoslavia were members of the Afro-Asian Group, which did meet frequently. The question being asked in the analysis of the General Assembly's voting is 'Did the Non-Aligned behave as a coherent group, irrespective of there being any formal caucussing activity?'

2. *The Rules of Procedure of the General Assembly* (U.N. document A/8520. Rev. 12), Rule 87.

3. The procedure is described in detail in *Use of Mechanical Means of Voting* (U.N. Document A/INF/143, 20th September 1971).

4. *Official Records of the General Assembly* 16th Session, 1084th Plenary Meeting, 19th December 1961.

5. *Ibid.* 16th Session, 1081st Plenary Meeting, 18th December 1961.

6. The eleven procedural votes can be found in the *Official Records of the General Assembly* for the following Plenary Meetings of the 16th Session:

1014th PM 25th September 1961	Include Tibet on the Agenda,
1014th PM 25th September 1961	Include Hungary on the Agenda,
1033rd PM 11th October 1961	Nepal motion to adjourn,
1043rd PM 17th October 1961	Resolution on atomic radiation is 'important',
1080th PM 15th December 1961	Priority for motion that China is 'important',
1083rd PM 19th December 1961	Motion for separate votes on Angola resolution,
1086th PM 20th December 1961	Motion for separate vote on ONUC resolution,
1102nd PM 30th January 1962	Motion for separate vote on Angola resolution,
1104th PM 19th February 1962	Costa Rica motion to adjourn,
1109th PM 12th June 1962	Motion discussion of Rhodesia is 'important',
1109th PM 12th June 1962	Include Rhodesia on the Agenda.

7. A. Lijphart, 'The Analysis of Bloc Voting in the General Assembly: A Critique and a Proposal', *American Political Science Review*, Vol. 57, 1963, pp. 902–17.

8. Using data on roll-calls in the 16th Session, from the United Nations Yearbook the cohesion of the Assembly as a whole was found to be I_α = 62·3%, I_β = 3·9% and I_γ = 58·6%, whereas with the I.C.P.R. data the cohesion was I_α = 49·8%, I_β = 13·6% and I_γ = 36·2%. For the 20th Session the Yearbook gave I_α = 75·6%, I_β = 0·0% and I_γ = 75·6%, whereas the I.C.P.R. data gave I_α = 55·8%, I_β = 1·0% and I_γ = 54·8%. These indices are explained later in Chapter 3 and in Appendix 5.

9. The base for each of the percentages is the number of states in the group multiplied by the number of roll-calls held in the committee or in plenary. In the 20th Session there were 22 roll-calls in the First Committee, 1 in the Second, 20 in the Third, 35 in the Fourth, 1 in the Fifth, 3 in the Sixth, 12 in the Special Political Committee and 41 in Plenary.

10. The *Repertory of Practice of United Nations Organs*, Vol. 1, under Article 18 (1) gives a few cases of 'Not Participating' occurring very early on, with one roll-call in the 1st Session, two in the 4th Session and one in the 7th Session. However, enough ambiguity remained in the situation until 1963 that, when objections were raised to a delegation's having stated that it was 'Not Participating', the President of the General Assembly thought it was necessary to consult with the Secretariat and the Chairmen of the Main Committees to establish a standard procedure for dealing with this matter (*Official Records of the General Assembly*, 18th Session, 1255th Plenary Meeting, 6th November 1963).

11. The following works have all used factor analysis: H. Alker 'Dimensions of Conflict in the General Assembly'. *American Political Science Review*, Vol. 58, 1964, pp. 642–57; H. Alker and B. Russett, *World Politics in the General Assembly* (Yale University Press, New Haven, 1965); B. Russett, 'Discovering Voting Groups in the United Nations', *American Political Science Review*, Vol. 60, 1966, pp. 327–39.

12. Lijphart, *op. cit.*, p. 910.

13. The minimum level of attendance required by a pair of states was not written as a constant into the computer programme, but was left as a variable input parameter. In later chapters, when a much smaller number of roll-calls on particular issues is under consideration, the minimum attendance required is raised from 75% to 100%.

14. A precise definition of the indices is given in Appendix 5.

15. T. Hovet, *Bloc Politics in United Nations* (Harvard University Press, Cambridge, Mass., 1960), pp. 47–56.

16. Of the forty-six Cairo states, Indonesia had withdrawn from the U.N. and Cambodia, Chad, Cyprus and Laos attended less than three-quarters of the roll-calls in the 20th Session, leaving forty-one Non-Aligned in the analysis at this point.

17. Of the fifty-three Lusaka states, Botswana, Congo (Brazzaville), Equatorial Guinea, Lesotho, Rwanda, Senegal and Trinidad and Tobago attended less than three-quarters of the roll-calls in the 25th Session, leaving forty-six Non-Aligned in the analysis.

18. The statement that the Non-Aligned formed a voting alliance with the communist states says nothing about the political processes that were at work. It is necessary to go beyond the roll-call data to determine whether the Non-Aligned were supporting a communist viewpoint or the communists were accommodating to the Non-Aligned. The existence of a *de facto* voting alliance does not even imply that there was any form of joint caucussing.

19. *Zambian Daily Mail*, Lusaka, 8th September 1970.

20. At the 1975 Foreign Ministers Conference and at the 1976 Colombo summit, the Philippines was listed among the 'Guests'. This more recent development is not relevant to the position in 1970.

CHAPTER FOUR

Cold-War Alignments

It has been argued in the first chapter that non-alignment should not be equated with neutralism. Even if it is accepted that the Non-Aligned are activist rather than passive members of the international system, it is still a failure of comprehension to imagine that non-alignment simply has its literal meaning of a refusal to be aligned. Non-alignment is a complex and fluid ideology encompassing anti-colonialism, and North-South issues, as well as the East-West disputes. But this is not to say that abstention from alignment in the Cold War is not a *part* of non-alignment. In order to maintain their freedom of manoeuvre, the Non-Aligned claim the right to side with one of the Great Powers in any particular dispute, but not to do so on a regular basis. As Nyerere put it in 1970, 'It is thus a refusal to be party to any permanent diplomatic or military identification with the Great Powers'.[1] This chapter will examine data to see which of the small and the medium size states, by their behaviour, identified themselves with either side of the Cold War in the 1960s.

The practice of diplomatic exchanges

There are four states that became divided by the Cold War. After the Second World War both Germany and Korea were divided into temporary military occupation zones, for the victorious Allied powers to take over from the Axis powers. In both cases the zones, which were supposed to be temporary, solidified into competing political regimes. In 1949 the success of the Chinese communists, followed by Chiang Kai-shek's retreat to the island of Formosa, led to two more hostile regimes competing for diplomatic recognition. Finally the refusal of the Americans and the South Vietnamese to honour the 1954 Geneva Agreements led to another temporary dividing line lasting for a considerable time.

The most striking aspect of the diplomatic competition between the sectors of the four divided states of Germany, Korea, China and Vietnam is that, until the 1970s, each side claimed to be seeking the reunification of the two sectors. In addition, each regime has claimed that its authority extends to both parts of the territory of the divided states. East Germany is an exception in that it has all along accepted the legitimacy, in the international legal sense, of the Bundesrepublik. However, the D.D.R. maintained the political competition, as it never recognised West Germany's claim to speak for the whole of Germany and it often attacked West Germany's political legitimacy by alleging the continuation of Nazi and neo-Nazi influences. Thus during the 1960s, it was in practice possible to have diplomatic relations with one but not with both sides of the divided states.[2]

While an Index of Diplomatic Alignment based on exchanges with the divided states will be constructed for the years 1964 and 1970, such an Index would not produce comparable results for the period since 1970. Significant changes have occurred in each of the four cases. In West Germany Brandt became the first Social Democrat Chancellor in October 1969 and immediately initiated a new 'Ostpolitik' foreign policy. Treaties with the Soviet Union renouncing the use of force and with Poland accepting the post-war boundaries, were followed in 1972 by a Basic Treaty between East and West Germany and in September 1973 both states joined the United Nations. Communist China began to emerge during 1969 from the total isolation in which she had placed herself for the period of the Cultural Revolution. In July 1971 Nixon announced that he would visit Peking and on 25th October 1971 the communists replaced the Nationalist Chinese in the United Nations. The Vietnam peace talks opened in Paris in January 1969 and dragged on until a cease-fire agreement was produced in January 1973. A short while after the American withdrawal the South Vietnamese government collapsed under a new offensive and the Provisional Revolutionary Government took over in April 1975. North and South were reunified a year later and in September 1977 Vietnam joined the United Nations. Even in the case of Korea agreement on the principle of reunification by peaceful means was reached in July 1972. Thus in the 1970s the process of *détente* and the Vietnam War have changed the whole context in which diplomatic exchanges are made with the governments of Germany, China, Vietnam and Korea.

In the 1960s, if a state chose to extend recognition to all the communist or to all the Western regimes, then it was clearly taking sides in disputes that were central to the Cold-War conflict. It might be thought that the choice was rather remote and theoretical in nature for the states of the Third World, but because of the intensity of the diplomatic conflict the choice was actively put before them by the competing regimes. However, the decision to accord recognition did not necessarily mean that the Third World states had to staff new embassies. It is common diplomatic practice for Ambassadors to be received from another state without there being any need for the relations to be reciprocal. The receiving state need not itself send an Ambassador of its own to the sending state. This means that the decision to establish diplomatic relations, with one of the regimes, even at the Ambassadorial level, was a low cost one, that could have been contemplated by the smallest of states. All they had to do was agree to offer recognition and receive an Ambassador. Therefore the pattern of relations with the divided states gives an indicator of the extent of diplomatic alignment.

D*   The diplomatic world is highly hierarchical. There are not only distinctions between the various ranks, such as Ambassador, First Secretary and Second Secretary, but also different Ambassadorial postings are considered to be of different prestige. Britain has the practice of distinguishing the more important posts by appointing an Ambassador with a knighthood. However, information of this type is not readily available for more than a few countries. In order to collect data for all the independent countries, it is necessary to use one of the general reference annuals. The most satisfactory appeared to be *The Europa Yearbook*,[3] which despite its name does have world-wide coverage. Using this source, the only distinctions that could be made were between resident diplomatic missions, the accredition of non-resident Ambassadors and recognition without the exchange of diplomats. The situation of non-resident Ambassadors usually occurs when an Ambassador is accredited to two or more neighbouring states and is officially resident in only one of the states. Several countries have an Ambassador to the United States, who is resident with a mission in Washington and is also accredited as Ambassador or High Commissioner to Canada. A similar practice in the developing world is for many states to have their missions in Kenya accredited to Uganda. While the quality of airline and telecommunication links may be a factor in deciding where to site a mission, clearly the main factor is the relative importance attached to the different countries.

The construction of an Index of Diplomatic Alignment
D*   Bearing in mind these features of the diplomatic system, it is possible to assign a series of weights to the different types of

diplomatic links. In some earlier work[4] the following weights were assigned:

TABLE 4.1   WEIGHTS FOR AN INDEX OF
DIPLOMATIC ALIGNMENT

	Diplomats Sent	Diplomats Received
Resident Ambassador	5	4
Non-Resident Ambassador	3	2
Relations but No Mission	1	1
No Relations	0	0

It will be seen that greater weight has been given to the decisions   D*
by the sending country, which are directly under its control, than to
the decisions made by other countries as to which diplomats it will
be able to receive. In addition greater weight has been given
according to the level at which relations have been established. The
four divided countries each have two competing regimes and
diplomats can be both sent to and received from each regime, which
gives a total of sixteen possible diplomatic links to be coded. By
giving links with pro-Western regimes a negative value and links
with a communist regime a positive value, the sixteen weights can
be summed to give an index that may range from −36 representing
complete diplomatic alignment with the West to +36 representing
complete alignment with the East. An intermediate score of zero
may be attained either by having no relations at all with the divided
nations or by having a balancing pattern of relations with regimes
from each side of the Cold War.

As outlined above the Index gives a measure of the strength of the   D*
diplomatic links with either side in the Cold War. However, the
emphasis in studying non-alignment should be mainly on the extent
of deliberate commitment to either side. From this point of view a
weight of 4 is rather too high for the reception of a resident
Ambassador. For example, Uganda's decision on whether or not to
receive an Ambassador from South Korea is partly limited by South
Korea's decisions on whether it wishes to send any Ambassadors to
East Africa or to use multi-accreditation from Kenya or to send to
both Uganda and Kenya. To emphasise that residence or non-
residence is not determined by the host country, the two types of
links could be given the same weight of two. The argument could be
pushed even further, by considering only the decisions over which
each state has direct control and hence only coding diplomats sent
and not those received. The point turns out not to be of great
practical importance. As can be seen in Table 4.2, the correlations

between the three versions are extremely high.[5] As a compromise between running the risk of giving too great a weight to decisions not wholly under the control of each state and the alternative of not fully using the data that was available, the second version of the Index was chosen.

TABLE 4.2   CORRELATIONS BETWEEN
THREE VERSIONS OF THE INDEX OF
DIPLOMATIC ALIGNMENT

Year	(a)−(b)	(b)−(c)	(a)−(c)	No. of States
1963	0·997	0·993	0·982	108
1964	0·997	0·995	0·990	110
1965	0·997	0·993	0·987	113
1966	0·997	0·994	0·987	116
1967	0·998	0·995	0·991	120
1968	0·997	0·996	0·991	121
1969	0·997	0·996	0·992	124
1970	0·997	0·996	0·991	123

(a) Index coded as in Table 4.1.
(b) Index with Resident Ambassador Received coded 2.
(c) Index coding only Diplomats Sent.

There is one further aspect of the Cold-War diplomatic rivalry that may be taken into account. It might have been assumed that all states would have full relations with the two Super Powers, but the Alger and Brams data quoted in Table 2.3 shows that this is not so. In 1963–64 they found that the United States received diplomats from 107 countries, while the Soviet Union only received from 69 countries. To have relations with one or the other but not both of the Super Powers was another way of showing alignment. Changing the coding scheme in Table 4.1 to downgrade the receipt of a Resident Ambassador and including relations with the United States and the Soviet Union now gives an index ranging in value from −35 to +35, based on a total of 20 possible diplomatic links. These extreme values of the index would occur in the following way:

(1) reciprocal exchange of resident Ambassadors with one of the Cold-War regimes gives two links with the maximum score of seven (from the weights 5 plus 2);
(2) complete alignment with one side means full relations both ways with five regimes and no relations at all either way with the other five regimes;
(3) five scores of 7 gives an Index value of ±35, the sign depending on the side with which the alignment occurs.

For many states, including states that would often be regarded as highly aligned and including the two Super Powers themselves,[6] relations with the United States and the Soviet Union cancel each other out, giving Index values of ±28. Thus to have complete alignment of ±35 is to be 'plus royaliste que le roi'. In fact on the Eastern side, as the Soviet Union also had full relations with West Germany, to have a score greater than +21 was to be more aligned than the Soviet Union itself.

The Europa Yearbook was not a completely reliable data source. In particular the concept of diplomatic relations being established without missions being exchanged turns out in practice to be rather a nebulous one. Data of this type is only reported for a small number of countries. Most countries do not even report, in their diplomatic lists, the other countries to which they have sent but not received back Ambassadors. For example, in 1970 the page for Niger shows that it received an Ambassador from South Korea but under Korea there is no mention of relations with Niger.[7] Clearly, at least at the minimal level, relations must be regarded as being reciprocal. If country A accredits an Ambassador to B, then it is impossible for B to have no relations with A. But *The Europa Yearbook* also was found to have some simple errors of fact. For example, for 1964, under the Chinese People's Republic it is reported that there is an Ambassador from Denmark in Peking, while under Denmark there is supposed to be an Ambassador in Copenhagen from 'China, Republic of', which is the name commonly used by Nationalist China.[8] As a check against other less obvious errors the entries, for the divided countries, in *Keesings Contemporary Archives* were scanned for any mention of diplomatic activity. In most cases this yielded confirmation of the information in *The Europa Yearbook*. In earlier years even less detail was given in the Yearbook and so the diplomatic exchanges were only coded from 1963 onwards.[9]

The two graphs given below show that the Index of Diplomatic Alignment has a basic validity, in that it produces results that seem intuitively reasonable. Given that a concept such as diplomatic alignment is of an abstract nature and has no intrinsic units by which it can be measured, there must be some gap between the concept and its operationalisation. There is no inherent, magical validity in numbers and therefore the main criterion of validity for the Index must be whether those who work in the field feel that its results are reasonable.

Figure 4.1 shows the scores for five states that maintained a stable international position over the years 1963 to 1970. The Philippines, which is a member of SEATO and has close ties with the United

FIG. 4.1 ILLUSTRATION OF THE INDEX OF DIPLOMATIC ALIGNMENT

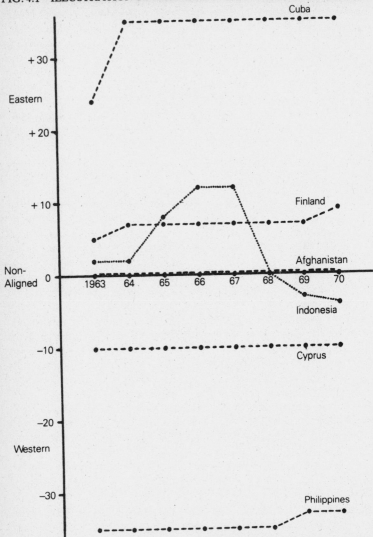

States, shows a high degree of Western alignment; Cyprus, which is not in any alliance but has close ties with Britain, is moderately Western aligned; Afghanistan is the only state to obtain the perfect non-aligned score of zero for every year; Finland, which maintains cordial relations with the Soviet Union, is slightly Eastern aligned; and Cuba, which is dependent upon support from the Soviet Union,

FIG. 4.2 DIPLOMATIC ALIGNMENT OF FOUR BRAZZAVILLE STATES

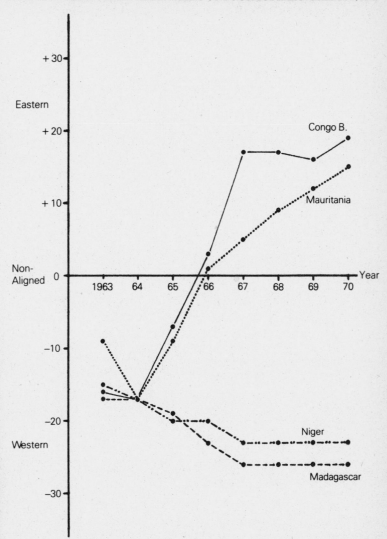

is highly Eastern aligned. By contrast, Indonesia from 1963 to 1965 moved into the period of 'confrontation' with Malaysia and then, with the removal of Sukarno in 1966–67, gradually disengaged again. The Index shows that there was a corresponding movement in Indonesia's diplomatic stance.

Figure 4.2 shows four of the twelve states that in the early 1960s

D*

formed the Brazzaville Group. In 1963–64 the four states are close in their behaviour and all are moving towards increasing Western alignment. Niger and Madagascar then continued to be among the most conservative of the African states, but Congo (Brazzaville) and Mauritania moved into the radical group. The Index rather dramatically plots this divergence in their positions.[10]

Differences between the groups in diplomatic behaviour

The overall distribution of the scores for all the 110 states that were independent at the beginning of 1964 is shown in Figure 4.3 as a frequency polygon. The results clearly show how much the Western states dominated the international system and in the divided states it was the Western regimes that had won the most diplomatic support. Eighty-three of the scores were in a Western direction, twenty-one in an Eastern direction and only six had a score of zero.[11] Furthermore the centre of gravity is not near the zero line.

FIG. 4.3 DISTRIBUTION OF THE INDEX OF DIPLOMATIC ALIGNMENT FOR 1964

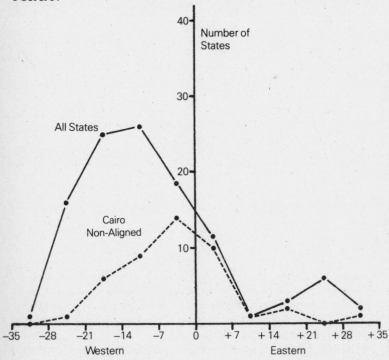

The median score is –13 on the Western side. The states that attended the second Non-Aligned summit in the same year of 1964 are also spread well across the spectrum, ranging from Jordan with –24 to Cuba with +35. However, the median for the Non-Aligned group at –4 is close to the middle.[12]

The pattern in Figure 4.4 for 1970, when the third Non-Aligned summit was held, is basically the same. But despite the general feeling that by 1970 the Cold War had begun to decline in importance there was in fact an increase in the diplomatic polarisation. The numbers at either extreme are larger. This is not just because more states became independent, as the numbers in the middle also dropped. The same trend has occurred within the Non-Aligned. They are both relatively more spread out and have suffered an absolute drop in numbers in the middle. By the criterion of the Index of Diplomatic Alignment, the Non-Aligned states were showing less non-alignment in their behaviour in 1970 than they were in 1964.

FIG. 4.4   DISTRIBUTION OF THE INDEX OF DIPLOMATIC ALIGNMENT FOR 1970

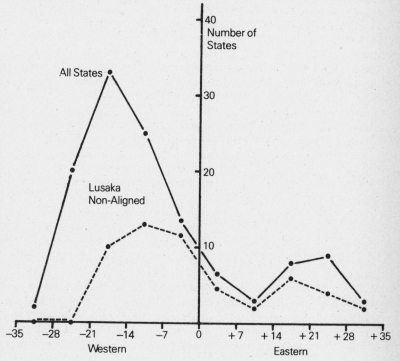

While a score of zero does represent the perfectly balanced position, it would be taking too rigid a view of non-alignment to say that only those with a score of zero were non-aligned. In the case of the competition between Peking and Taiwan, the Non-Aligned had collectively urged that Peking should hold China's seat at the United Nations.[13] Thus, if a member of the Non-Aligned group achieved a score of +7 through having full diplomatic relations with Peking, this can hardly be said to have detracted from its position of non-alignment. Equally, on the Western side, although there was from the point of view of non-alignment no ideological basis for choosing between the two Germanies, West Germany was so strong diplomatically[14] that to choose to recognise the Federal Republic rather than the D.D.R. was not *in practice* a significant act of alignment. Therefore a state can still be considered as having behaved in a non-aligned manner, if it had a score on the Index of Diplomatic Alignment anywhere in the range −7 to +7.

D*   It would not be reasonable to extend this range from −14 to +14 to take into account relations with either the United States or the Soviet Union. Although the exchange of diplomats with the Super Powers is not *per se* a sign of alignment, to have relations with one, rather than both, of the Super Powers does indicate some degree of alignment. The Index is designed so that relations at the same level with both the United States and the Soviet Union has no effect on its value. On the other hand relations with only one Super Power does contribute to an alignment score. Diplomatic non-alignment has been defined broadly by making allowance for relations with either West Germany or with communist China, but, if there are relations with both of these two, they will similarly cancel out in their effect on the score. The remaining scores, outside the range −7 to +7, which represent alignment with either side, may be split into scores of 8 to 21 representing moderate alignment and 22 to 35 representing high alignment. The ranges in the values of the Index are given in Tables 4.3 and 4.4, for each of the analytical groups that were derived in Chapter 2.

The results for 1964 show that broadly speaking there was a correspondence between the groups that were identified for analysing delegations and voting in the General Assembly, and the diplomatic behaviour outside the United Nations. As might be expected, the largest category for the Western Bloc had a high Western score on the Index of Diplomatic Alignment; for the Latin Americans and the Non-Bloc states the largest category had a moderately Western score; the majority of the Non-Aligned were in the middle range; and the Eastern Bloc had a high Eastern score. Using these expectations one would be correct in categorising (but

TABLE 4.3   DIPLOMATIC ALIGNMENT IN 1964

	Western Bloc	Latin American	Non-Bloc	Non-Aligned	Eastern Bloc	Total
High West	44%	16%	14%	2%	0%	15%
Mod. West	40%	84%	72%	34%	0%	46%
Non-Aligned	16%	0%	14%	55%	0%	27%
Mod. East	0%	0%	0%	7%	13%	4%
High East	0%	0%	0%	2%	88%	7%
	100%	100%	100%	100%	100%	100%
	=25	=19	=14	=44	=8	=110*

* The total of 115 U.N. members in 1964 is reduced by the exclusion of Byelorussia and Ukraine and by the fact that the diplomacy data is for January 1964, hence excluding Malta, Malawi and Zambia.

not in predicting the exact score) for 62% of the 110 states. But this is by no means a perfect correlation between the two variables. If one is willing to regard the Index as having the properties of an interval scale, then Analysis of Variance shows that the U.N. groups explained 63·0% of the variation in the diplomatic behaviour.

The results for 1970, the year of the Lusaka Non-Aligned summit, show a similar pattern, but except for the Western Bloc the scores for each group are now more widely dispersed. In particular, the Non-Aligned no longer have a majority in any category and the plurality has moderately Western rather than middle range scores. Putting states into the categories that might be expected to be correct, given their U.N. group, would only give a correct prediction for 48% of the 123 states. Similarly with the Analysis of Variance, the percentage of variation explained is found to have dropped from 63·0% in 1964 to 55·2% in 1970. This drop in the variation in the Index of Diplomatic Alignment explained by the U.N. groups indicates that the groups have become more diverse, but despite the drop, the result is still impressive. It is not common

TABLE 4.4   DIPLOMATIC ALIGNMENT IN 1970

	Western Bloc	Latin American	Non-Bloc	Non-Aligned	Eastern Bloc	Total
High West	52%	32%	17%	0%	0%	18%
Mod. West	44%	68%	61%	43%	0%	47%
Non-Aligned	4%	0%	17%	30%	0%	16%
Mod. East	0%	0%	6%	15%	25%	9%
High East	0%	0%	0%	11%	75%	10%
	100%	100%	100%	100%	100%	100%
	=25	=19	=18	=53	=8	=123

in social science research to discover a relationship in which more than half the variation in a variable can be explained. So even in 1970, the relationship between diplomatic behaviour and the U.N. groups must be considered to have been relatively strong.

The main reason for the decrease between 1964 and 1970 in the degree of association was the change in the Non-Aligned group. As can be seen in Table 4.5, this occurred in two ways. A comparison of

TABLE 4.5
THE CHANGING DIPLOMATIC ALIGNMENT OF THE NON- ALIGNED

| | Index Value 1964 | | Index Value 1970 | | |
	Belgrade Attenders	Cairo Attenders	Belgrade Attenders	Cairo Attenders	Lusaka Attenders
High West	0%	2%	0%	0%	0%
Mod. West	15%	34%	27%	39%	43%
Non-Aligned	69%	55%	31%	30%	30%
Mod. East	11%	7%	19%	17%	15%
High East	4%	2%	23%	13%	11%
	100%	100%	100%	100%	100%
	=26	=44*	=26	=46	=53

* 1964 data excludes Malawi and Zambia.

the first and the third columns shows that the original states, that got together at the first Non-Aligned summit in 1961 in Belgrade, changed in their diplomatic behaviour. Eleven of them, that is more than one-third, moved away from non-alignment. Four states, the Congo (Kinshasa), Ethiopia, Ghana and Morocco, moved towards a moderate Western alignment, which was partially compensated for by a movement of the Lebanon in the opposite direction. Algeria and the Yemen moved towards a moderate Eastern alignment while five states, Iraq, Sudan, Syria, the U.A.R., and the Cambodia of Prince Sihanouk, moved towards a high Eastern alignment, with scores in the range of +24 to +30. Thus the balance of the movement among the original Non-Aligned states was towards making the whole group on average more Eastern aligned.[15]

A comparison of the first two columns in Table 4.5 shows that the expansion of the Non-Aligned, by inviting many more states to the second summit in 1964 in Cairo, also changed the balance of the group as a whole. But the effect was quite different. At the time of their first summit, nearly two-thirds of the newcomers were Western aligned in their diplomacy. A comparison of the third and the fourth columns shows that this effect was maintained in 1970.

The Cairo states were still more Western than the original Belgrade states.[16] Furthermore, nearly two-thirds of the additional states that attended their first Non-Aligned summit in 1970 also were Western aligned,[17] and so the trend continues into the fifth column of Table 4.5.

Thus two very different types of changes were making the Non-Aligned less cohesive as a group. The older members were tending to move towards the East, while the new recruits to the movement, both in 1964 and in 1970, were shifting the balance more to the West. The overall result is a large drop in the proportion of Non-Aligned states that could be identified as being non-aligned in their diplomacy.

Alignment by military treaties

The second criterion of non-alignment given by Nyerere was a refusal to accept 'military identification with the Great Powers'. This appears to be simple to define but on close examination turns out to be more difficult to deal with than the concept of diplomatic alignment. At a minimal level military alignment means membership of formal multilateral alliances concluded by a treaty arrangement. However, the Non-Aligned Foreign Ministers in June 1961 declared that only alliances 'concluded in the context of Great Power conflicts'[18] were ruled out, but they did not specify exactly which alliances were or were not acceptable, by this criterion. Given that both Jamaica and Trinidad and Tobago attended the 1970 Lusaka summit as full participants, the O.A.S. must be acceptable under this definition. Equally, given the practice since 1964 of inviting all African states to all the Non-Aligned meetings, it seems that France's multilateral military arrangement with the Defence Council of Equatorial Africa is not considered to be a Cold-War alliance.[19] On the other hand, there is no question that membership of NATO, the Warsaw Pact, CENTO or SEATO rules out membership of the Non-Aligned group.[20]

In June 1961, the Foreign Ministers also said that 'bilateral military agreement with a Great Power' or 'the lease of military bases to a foreign power' was only acceptable if it was not done 'in the context of Great Power conflicts'. The concept of military alignment in the Cold War must be broad enough to include some bilateral military links, otherwise countries such as Spain and Japan would not be considered as being aligned. The question is how extensive do the military links have to be before a state is 'aligned'? Treaty relations cannot be the only criterion as practice in this area varies greatly. The United States tends to sign treaties even on such relatively unimportant matters as a small sale of arms or providing a general to head a military academy.[21] On the other hand the Soviet Union very rarely formalises military arrangements into treaties.

The United Kingdom has bilateral treaties with eleven countries.[22] All of these countries except South Africa have attended Non-Aligned meetings. In the case of Kenya, Uganda, the Maldives, Mauritius and Nepal, the agreements can perhaps be seen as falling outside 'the context of Great Power conflicts'. But the bases in Cyprus and Malta and in Libya, until Gaddafi closed them down, cannot be seen separately from Britain's role in NATO. Nor can arrangements with Malaysia and Singapore[23] be seen outside the context of the Vietnam War. It is true that Malaysia did not join the Non-Aligned until the third summit in Lusaka in 1970, but this was due to her earlier disputes with Indonesia, a leading member of the Non-Aligned Movement, rather than her military co-operation with Britain. Singapore also attended the 1970 summit, but had not been independent when the earlier conferences were held. Cyprus has attended Non-Aligned meetings since the first summit in 1961 and Libya since the second summit in 1964. In Malta's case, there was no desire to attend the 1970 summit, but she was accepted into the Non-Aligned group at the fourth summit in Algiers in 1973. The interesting point is that Malta was only accepted after an explicit assurance that the British bases would be run down when the current agreement expired.[24] Finally, although the reason for the Maldives not attending the Lusaka and Algiers Non-Aligned meetings is not definitely known, it is worth noting that the Tanzanian government did not extend an invitation to the Maldives to attend the Dar es Salaam Preparatory Meeting in April 1970.[25] This may have been due to the existence of the British base at Gan Island. After the base was closed, the Maldives did attend the fifth summit in 1976. On considering all these examples, the only conclusion that can be drawn is that, on this issue, the Non-Aligned have behaved in a relatively inconsistent manner, varying their decisions from country to country, rather than sticking to any clear general principles.

The strictest possible interpretation of non-alignment would be to say that all involvement by the small powers in military arrangements with a Great Power implies involvement in the Cold War. To make any distinctions as to the 'context of Great Power conflicts' is to make distinctions that are too fine to be recognised in the real world. With such an approach membership of the O.A.S., multilateral links with France or bilateral links with the U.S.A., the U.K. or France all imply military alignment with the West. Table 4.6 shows that when a strict definition of military alignment is used, we find that a large minority of the Non-Aligned are in fact aligned to

TABLE 4.6   MILITARY ALIGNMENT OF ATTENDERS AT
NON-ALIGNED SUMMITS

	Belgrade 1961	Cairo 1964	Lusaka 1970
Military links	4	15	17
No links	21	31	36
Summit attenders	25	46	53

the West. In 1961 one-sixth of the Belgrade summit group were aligned, while at the second summit in Cairo in 1964 and the third summit at Lusaka in 1970 one-third of the attenders were aligned.

A second approach, that is less idealistic and more influenced by considerations of *Realpolitik*, would be to argue that the Non-Aligned, like all other powers, are faced with security problems and that they must take steps to safeguard their own security. At times this may require membership of regional groupings, such as the O.A.S., even if a Great Power is also involved. At other times, bilateral pacts, such as the one between Kenya and Britain, may be thought necessary. It is the full membership of non-regional, multi-lateral pacts, created at the height of the Cold War that makes us perceive of countries such as Iran, Pakistan or the Philippines as being aligned. Using this line of argument the military links given in Table 4.6 would not be seen as detracting from non-alignment.

Arms supplies as data on military alignment

Another possible response to a security threat is to build up one's own military forces, by the purchase of modern weapons and equipment. By the end of the 1960s, only one-third of all the countries in Africa, Asia or Latin America produced any weapons at all and only six, Argentina, Brazil, Israel, the U.A.R., South Africa and India, produced either aircraft engines or armoured vehicles.[26] For the vast majority of states, if the decision was taken to build up a force of either aircraft or tanks, then purchases had to be made from Western or Eastern Europe, the United States or China. For many of the weapons there may have been a choice of only four or five countries from which to buy. If the decision to buy modern weapons is not taken to derogate from non-alignment, then, given the structure of the arms trade, making major purchases from countries such as Britain and France did not in practice violate non-alignment. The real choice for a small state to make was whether or not it would avoid making purchases from the United States, the Soviet Union or China.

The Stockholm International Peace Research Institute has done a detailed study of *The Arms Trade with the Third World*.[27] As it was concluded that 'the degree to which it is possible to identify the trade in military equipment in official trade statistics is inadequate for research work',[28] their methodology was to build up registers recording for each country what arms of what type had been supplied in each year. Direct U.S. Dollar valuations were put on each type of weapon, in order to avoid the problem of comparing the financial terms under which the weapons were supplied. The summation of these valuations gives a measure of the arms trade, that is comparable across different suppliers and different recipients. The researchers take the attitude that the resulting figures are more an indication of the relative order of magnitude of the flow of arms than a precise measure. They report for each country, for each year, whether its arms imports from each of the major suppliers falls under one of the following codes.

0 No purchases of major arms
1 Up to $10 million in value
2 In the range $10 to $50 million in value
3 In the range $50 to $100 million in value
4 Over $100 million in value.

The figures given cover only the flow of major weapons, that is aircraft, naval vessels, armoured vehicles and missiles. Small arms and artillery are not included.

If we take the approach, that was used earlier to construct the Index of Diplomatic Alignment, we may sum these codes in the SIPRI data to construct an Index of Military Alignment. Trade with the Soviet Union and China can be given a positive sign and trade with the United States a negative sign. (The problem of whether the split between the Soviet Union and China means that the Index ought to reflect a tri-polar rather than a bi-polar world can in practice be ignored, as only four countries were found to have any arms trade with China.) The resulting Index is clearly ordinal rather than interval in nature, that is it involves merely rankings rather than precise measurement. In the first place the original SIPRI codes are themselves only ordinal ranks, but secondly, where there was trade by one country with both Super Powers, the subtraction of the code for trade with the United States from that with the Soviet Union does not represent a genuine arithmetic operation. For example, when for 1961 Indonesia has a code of 2 with both the Super Powers, this does not mean that there was an equal level of trade. There could have been imports of $40 million from the Soviet Union and only $20 million from the United States. In constructing the Index we are saying that these two figures are of equal political significance. To have trade of the same order of magnitude with both sides, even if there may be a large absolute difference, represents the maintenance of a balanced position and should be regarded as military non-alignment. When in the following year Indonesia's arms trade with the Soviet Union increased to a level of 4 but the trade with the United States remained at a level of 2, there was no longer a balance between the two. However, the fact that there was still a medium level of trade with the United States reduces the political impact of the very high trade with the Soviet Union and the Index has a net value of +2 with the East.

An important problem with the SIPRI data is that the tables only include data for 78 of the 127 U.N. members in 1970. The section on Sub-Saharan Africa states that 'of the thirty-five independent states in 1969, only thirty have imported major weapons'.[29] The remaining five states can be identified elsewhere as being Botswana, Lesotho, Swaziland, Burundi and Sierra Leone,[30] and have been coded as having no arms trade, because they had no significant military forces. But in fact there were at this time 37 independent states of Sub-Saharan Africa,[31] and SIPRI have no explanation for the omisson of Equatorial Guinea and Mauritius. Similarly in other sections Barbados, Fiji, the Maldives and Nepal are omitted without explanation. These six tiny states will also be coded on the assumption that they had no trade in heavy weapons. One can find in the text that three Latin American countries, Costa Rica, Mexico and Panama, had no significant defence expenditure and that Cyprus and Malta had no important trade.[32] With the exclusion of Byelorussia and Ukraine from this analysis, there now remains Yugoslavia, the four European neutrals, eight Eastern Bloc states, 14 NATO states and the four members of the Western Bloc, Australia, New Zealand, Spain and Japan, to be accounted for. On the basis of data in *The Military Balance*, Austria was given a medium Western code of –2 for each year, Finland an Eastern code of +2 and Yugoslavia, Ireland and Sweden codes of zero.[33] The bloc states were all given the maximum alignment codes of +4 or –4 respectively in the appropriate direction. These allocations for states that were outside the scope of the SIPRI data-set are not above challenge. The scores certainly do not give an accurate assessment of their arms trade. Countries like Iceland and Luxembourg could not trade at the level of $100 million per annum, but the coding of the Index implies that membership of a major military alliance and a very high trade in arms represented an equivalent degree of military alignment.

As with the Index of Diplomatic Alignment, there is again no absolute criterion of validity to resolve whether or not the

D*

D*

manipulaton of the SIPRI data or the coding of the states not covered in the SIPRI tables is acceptable. The question must again be: does the process give results that seem reasonable? The values of the Index of Military Alignment have been plotted in Figure 4.5 for the same states as were used in Figure 4.1. The results this time are not so simple and clear, as there are many more fluctuations in the Index of Military Alignment. This might seem to suggest that the Index is unsatisfactory, but, while one does expect diplomatic exchanges to remain constant as long as there is no change in government policy, the same is not true of the trade in arms. A large order for tanks or aircraft may well be delivered over a period of one or two years and then be followed by a longer period during which there are only contracts for spare parts and maintenance. To some extent this is an explanation of the pattern for Cuba, which received a heavy supply of Soviet weapons during the period 1960–62 followed by a gradual decline in the level of supplies. But in addition the change would be partly due to a reduction in the Soviet military commitment in Cuba after the 1962 crisis and to the ideological disputes with Cuba that developed in the later 1960s. In Figure 4.5 Afghanistan, Cyprus and the Philippines maintained the same position relative to each other as they did in Figure 4.1, but there are now more fluctuations in the graphs and all three states were more to the East in their military alignment than in their diplomatic alignment. In Indonesia's case the period of confrontation with Malaysia was still evident, but less noticeably so. Overall these examples do illustrate that the Index can make sense substantively.

Differences between the groups in military alignment

The distribution of the Index of Military Alignment is given in Tables 4.7 to 4.9 and plotted as frequency polygons in Figures 4.6 to 4.8 for each of the years of the first three Non-Aligned summits.[34] (As the SIPRI data only covered up until 1969, that year had to be used instead of 1970 when the Lusaka summit was held.) It will be seen that the distributions are distinctly tri-modal. In each year the main peak is at the zero, non-aligned, position and there are two subsidiary peaks at each extreme. By 1969 the middle position has become dramatically dominant. This was due both to the arrival on the international scene of more small states that cannot afford large military forces and to a drop in purchases from either side.

Despite the fact that the Index was heavily biased towards the scores coming out on the Eastern side (by not taking into account the two major Western suppliers, Britain and France), the results still show in each year more than twice as many states with a Western score as with an Eastern score. This finding corroborates

FIG. 4.5 EXAMPLES OF THE INDEX OF MILITARY ALIGNMENT

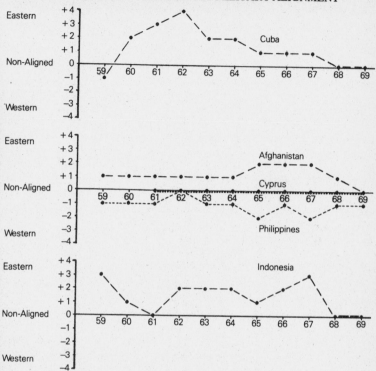

the previous finding that, in the field of diplomacy, the Western states had more weight in the international system. Clearly, if the Index took into account the arms trade with Britain and France, the distributions in Figures 4.6 to 4.8 would become highly skewed towards the West, as in Figures 4.3 and 4.4.

TABLE 4.7   INDEX OF MILITARY ALIGNMENT IN 1961

	Western Bloc	Latin American	Non-Bloc	Non-Aligned	Eastern Bloc	Total
High West	64%	5%	0%	0%	0%	17%
Mod. West	32%	58%	9%	29%	0%	28%
Non-Aligned	4%	37%	87%	42%	0%	38%
Mod. East	0%	0%	4%	21%	0%	7%
High East	0%	0%	0%	8%	100%	10%
	100%	100%	100%	100%	100%	100%
	=25	=19	=23	=24	=8	=99

Among the attenders at the Non-Aligned summits, the biggest category in each year was of those that had no significant arms trade. And, in direct contrast to the trends in diplomatic alignment, those that were militarily non-aligned have increased from under half of the Belgrade states, to just over half the Cairo states, to well over three-quarters of the Lusaka states. In this field there was neither a tendency for the original Non-Aligned to become more Eastern in their behaviour nor for the newcomers to be relatively Western. The increase in military non-alignment was due both to a

FIG. 4.6 DISTRIBUTION OF THE INDEX OF MILITARY ALIGNMENT FOR 1961

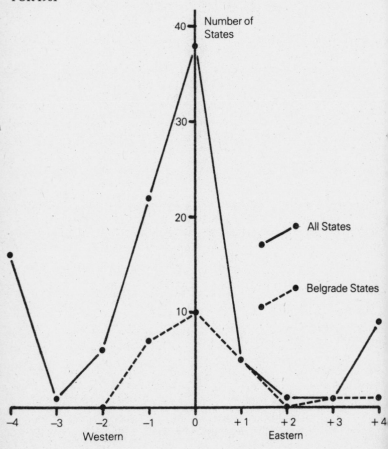

TABLE 4.8   INDEX OF MILITARY ALIGNMENT IN 1964

	Western Bloc	Latin American	Non-Bloc	Non-Aligned	Eastern Bloc	Total
High West	68%	0%	0%	0%	0%	15%
Mod. West	24%	74%	21%	18%	0%	28%
Non-Aligned	8%	26%	71%	57%	0%	38%
Mod. East	0%	0%	7%	23%	0%	10%
High East	0%	0%	0%	2%	100%	8%
	100%	100%	100%	100%	100%	100%
	=25	=19	=14	=44	=8	=110

FIG. 4.7   DISTRIBUTION OF THE INDEX OF MILITARY ALIGNMENT FOR 1964

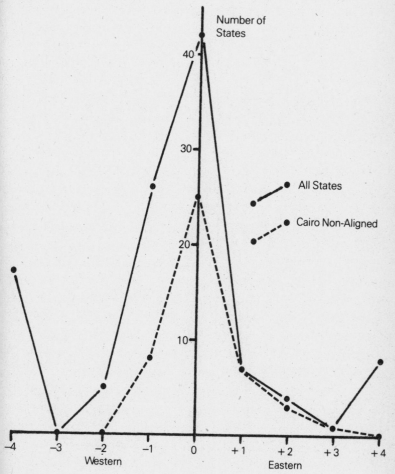

FIG. 4.8 DISTRIBUTION OF THE INDEX OF MILITARY ALIGNMENT
FOR 1969

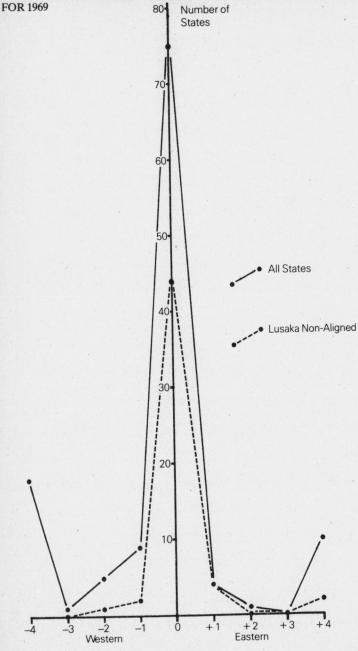

TABLE 4.9 INDEX OF MILITARY ALIGNMENT IN 1969

	Western Bloc	Latin American	Non-Bloc	Non-Aligned	Eastern Bloc	Total
High West	76%	0%	0%	0%	0%	15%
Mod. West	16%	21%	17%	6%	0%	11%
Non-Aligned	8%	79%	78%	83%	0%	61%
Mod. East	0%	0%	6%	8%	0%	4%
High East	0%	0%	0%	4%	100%	8%
	100%	100%	100%	100%	100%	100%
	=25	=19	=18	=53	=8	=123

drop in the number of Belgrade states receiving arms from the Super Powers and to the overwhelming majority of the newcomers being militarily non-aligned.

Since the Western Bloc and the Eastern Bloc groups were primarily defined in terms of their alliance with the Super Powers, it is not surprising that membership of these groups correlates with the Index.[35] The fact that the Latin Americans have at least a quarter of the group that were militarily non-aligned in each period is less expected, until it is remembered that among the Latin Americans are some very small states, that cannnot aspire to be of military significance. Nevertheless, there was by 1969 a very marked drop in the number of Latin Americans receiving arms from the United States and this change was in contrast to an increase rather than a decrease in the group's diplomatic alignment. The Non-Bloc group is of interest, as it is the only group that had a large majority in the non-aligned category in each year. This means that in the earlier years the Non-Bloc states could, if military links are the main criterion of non-alignment, have claimed that they were more 'truly' non-aligned than the Belgrade or the Cairo states.

The results from Analysis of Variance indicate a very strong S* relationship.[36] The U.N. groups explained 76·2% of the variation in the Index of Military Alignment in 1961; 77·8% in 1964; and 78·8% in 1969. There is no significance in the slight increases shown in the strength of the relationship, as analysis of the data for each of the years 1959 to 1969 shows that the increase was not part of any regular trend. This is in contrast to the drop in the explained variation in the Index of Diplomatic Alignment, which *was* part of a continuous trend over the years 1963 to 1970.

Differences between the groups in U.N. East-West voting

In addition to the exchange of diplomats and the flow of weapons, another way in which states can declare their alignment is in their voting on East-West issues in the United Nations General Assembly. This is another form of activity that might fall within Nyerere's definition of alignment as 'diplomatic identification with the Great Powers'. Voting in the U.N. is as much an act of diplomacy as is the exchange of diplomats, but it has two distinct features. Once the decision has been taken to support a minimal delegation in New York, the decision to cast a vote involves no costs.[37] It is also a decision that is highly visible: unlike almost all other international events and transactions, the record of a vote is automatically available to all other U.N. members, both at the time and later in the official documents.

D*   We have already considered the overall voting patterns in the previous chapter, but it cannot be assumed that the voting blocs on East-West issues would be the same as on all issues taken together. Rather than determine empirically which roll-calls may be identified as an East-West issue-set,[38] an *a priori* judgement was made as to which roll-calls would be generally recognised as being on aspects of the Cold War. In each of the 16th, 20th and 25th Sessions, roll-calls were held on the admission of China to the United Nations and on the maintenance of a U.N. Commission in South Korea. In the 16th and 20th Sessions there were roll-calls on the question of human rights in Tibet, and in the 16th Session there were also roll-calls on whether China should be invited to the Vienna conference on consular relations; on Cuba's complaint about the Bay of Pigs invasion; and on America's continued evocation of the Hungarian uprising in 1956.

The figures in Table 4.10, when compared with those in Table 3.2 show none of the groups had a higher cohesion in their voting on East-West issues than they did on all issues taken together. Indeed, except for the Eastern Bloc, the groups were considerably less

TABLE 4.10   GROUP COHESION ON EAST-WEST ROLL-CALLS ($p \leqslant 0.05$)

	16th Session		20th Session		25th Session	
	% with High Scores I_α	% with Low Scores I_β	% with High Scores I_α	% with Low Scores I_β	% with High Scores I_α	% with Low Scores I_β
Western Bloc	89.5	0.0	38.1	6.2	54.5	0.0
Latin Americans	100.0	0.0	77.2	0.0	72.5	0.0
Non-Bloc	54.3	0.0	18.2	0.0	39.6	0.0
Non-Aligned	71.0	0.0	17.5	8.9	18.7	18.7
Eastern Bloc	100.0	0.0	100.0	0.0	100.0	0.0
Whole Assembly	41.0	27.0	20.8	25.1	27.5	25.1

united to the extent of some 20 to 30% or more, in their voting on East-West questions. The Eastern Bloc remained solid and the Latin Americans maintained a substantial measure of cohesion. The Western Bloc was split in the 20th Session to the extent that several Western European states were not voting regularly with the bloc and Pakistan reached significant disagreement with 65% of the others. It remained split in the 25th Session, though not so severely.

It was the Non-Bloc and the Non-Aligned groups that can be seen really to have disintegrated, when East-West questions are isolated for separate analysis. By the 25th Session the Non-Aligned had reached the position that there were as many pairs of states within the group that were in high disagreement with each other as there were pairs in high agreement. Once voting cohesion had dropped to such a level, it is no longer meaningful to think the Non-Aligned were a separate distinct group. The empirically determined cluster-blocs, in Figures 4.9 to 4.11, show what had happened to the group. In the 16th Session, 21 of the Belgrade states were relatively close together and only four were out of line. In the 20th Session, the Assembly was split up into eleven, perfect, non-overlapping clusters and attenders at the Cairo summit are to be found in seven of these clusters. At one extreme Cuba, Algeria and Congo (Brazzaville) voted solidly with the communists, while at the other extreme Liberia and Togo were in complete disagreement with the communists voting solidly with the Western Bloc. In the 25th Session, there were nine clusters which form the basic structure of the voting blocs and Lusaka states were in every one of the clusters. As many as thirteen voted solidly with the communists; seventeen more were spread through the smaller clusters in between the two major antagonistic blocs; six voted predominantly with the Western Bloc; and five voted completely with the West. The various Non-Aligned states would no doubt offer widely different interpretations as to what was the 'true' non-aligned position on these roll-calls. Given that the Non-Aligned did urge collectively that China should be admitted to the U.N., it is difficult to accept that voting solidly with the West could have represented non-alignment. Whatever the balance of the argument may be, the Non-Aligned did themselves in their own voting decide it in a variety of different ways.

The voting agreement score is as near to being a genuine interval scale as we can ever hope to get in social science measurement. (It would only be above challenge, if we could somehow prove that each roll-call was of equal importance.) Therefore Analysis of Variance gives the most appropriate measure of association in this case. We find that in the 16th Session the groups explained 88·2% of the variation in the percentage agreement with the Soviet Union; in

S*

FIG. 4.9. CLUSTER-BLOCS ON U.N. 16TH SESSION EAST-WEST VOTES

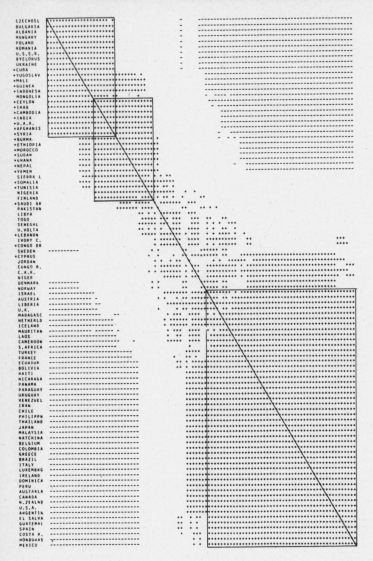

*Attended the 1961 Belgrade Summit.

FIG. 4.10 CLUSTER-BLOCS ON U.N. 20TH SESSION EAST-WEST VOTES

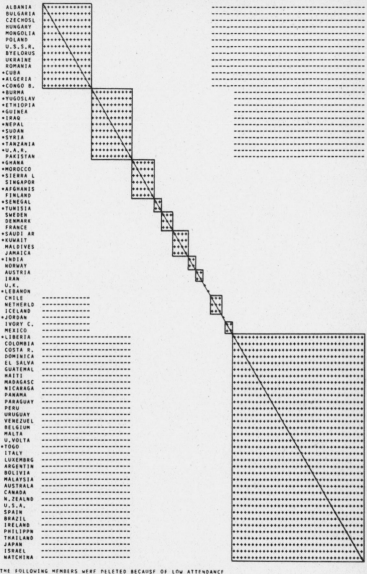

THE FOLLOWING MEMBERS WERE DELETED BECAUSE OF LOW ATTENDANCE

TRINIDAD	HONDURAS	ECUADOR	PORTUGAL	GREECE	CYPRUS
GAMBIA	MALI	DAHOMEY	MAURITAN	NIGER	CAMERUON
NIGERIA	GABON	C.A.R.	CHAD	CONGO DR	UGANDA
KENYA	BURUNDI	RWANDA	SUMALIA	ZAMBIA	MALAWI
S.AFRICA	LIBYA	TURKEY	YEMEN	CEYLON	CAMBODIA
LAOS					

*Attended the 1964 Cairo Non-Aligned Summit.

FIG. 4.11 CLUSTER-BLOCS ON U.N. 25TH SESSION EAST-WEST VOTES

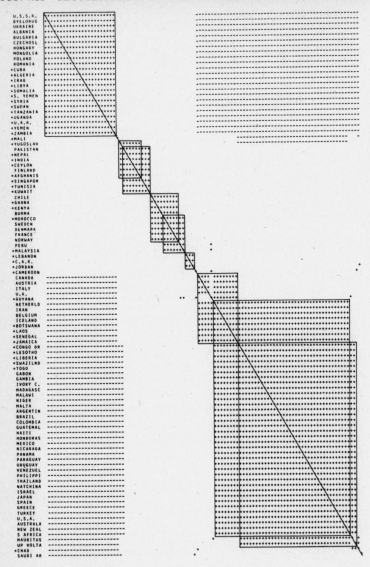

THE FOLLOWING MEMBERS WERE DELETED BECAUSE OF LOW ATTENDANCE —

BURUNDI	CONGO B.	CYPRUS	ETHIOPIA	EQ GUINE	GUINEA
INDONESA	MAURITAN	NIGERIA	RWANDA	SIERRA L	TRINIDAD
BARBADOS	CAMBODIA	DAHOMEY	FIJI	IRELAND	BOLIVIA
COSTA R.	DOMINICA	ECUADOR	EL SALVA	LUXEMBRG	PORTUGAL
MALDIVES					

*Attended the 1970 Lusaka Non-Aligned Summit.

the 20th this had dropped to 59·4%; and in the 25th Session it was down further to 51·4%.

The results of the Analysis of Variance reinforce the results from the other methods of presenting the data on East-West voting. In 1961 the pre-specified groups were a highly relevant way of categorising the various states in the U.N. and in accounting for almost 90% of the variation had exceptionally high explanatory power. The basic structure, of the communists on the one hand opposing the Western Bloc and the Latin Americans on the other hand, remained in the subsequent years and it was still possible to account for over half the variation. But, because the Non-Bloc and the Non-Aligned states ceased to behave as distinct groups, variation explained in 1964 and in 1970 dropped substantially compared to the very high level of 1961. Unfortunately there is not adequate data available on diplomatic exchanges in 1961, but the Index of Diplomatic Alignment for 1964 and 1970 gave results that were very close to those on East-West voting. With both sources of data, the variation explained in 1964 was approximately 60–63% and in 1970 was approximately 52–55%. It was also true by 1970 that, as with their East-West voting, the Non-Aligned and the Non-Bloc states had become highly diverse in their diplomatic behaviour. Thus, with two separate sources of data, very similar results have been found.

The comparability of the three sets of results

Three indices have been constructed to measure three forms of activity that are closely related to the concept of non-alignment in the Cold War. The three indices were derived from quite distinct data sources, involving information on the behaviour of different people, in the Foreign Ministries arranging diplomatic postings, in the Ministries of Defence arranging arms supplies and in the United Nations Delegations deciding how to cast their votes. With each index, the division of the states into five groups, the Western Bloc, the Latin Americans, the Non-Bloc states, the Non-Aligned and the Eastern Bloc, was able to account for more than half and in one case nearly 90% of the variation in the index.

The original group of 25 independent states, that met at the first Non-Aligned summit in Belgrade, did show a high degree of coherence in their behaviour in 1961, but less than one might have expected given that they came together explicitly as an ideological rather than a geographic or an economic grouping. In Table 4.6 we found 84% of the Belgrade states had no military alliances, but even as few as 16% having treaty alliances is different from an expectation of a perfectly non-aligned group with no treaty alliances at all. In Table 4.10, a cohesion score (I_γ) of 71·0% for the Non-Aligned group's voting on East-West issues was high, but it was lower than that of three of the other four groups and lower than the Non-Aligned themselves reached on all issues taken together. Using a broader concept of Military Alignment, based on arms supplies, over a quarter of the Belgrade states were categorised as being aligned to the West in 1961 and another quarter aligned to the East, with less than one-half being militarily non-aligned. Only if the two groups on either side are seen as somehow cancelling each other out can the group as a whole be considered to be non-aligned in this form of activity.

In 1964 the 46 states that attended the second Non-Aligned summit in Cairo were markedly less united than the Belgrade states in 1961. By now as many as one-third of the group were treaty allies of the West and the cohesion on East-West voting was down to I_γ = 8·6%. The Index of Military Alignment still gave just under one-fifth of the Cairo states trading in arms with the United States and one-quarter trading with the Soviet Union. On the Index of Diplomatic Alignment for 1964, six states did have a perfectly balanced set of diplomatic exchanges, giving a score of zero, but using a broad definition of non-aligned behaviour and taking scores from –7 to +7 included only 18 more of the Cairo states, leaving 20 (that is nearly half the total) aligned to one or the other side.

In 1970 the 53 Lusaka summit Non-Aligned states continued as a group to move slightly further away from non-aligned behaviour. Again one-third of the group had military treaty links with the West and the cohesion on East-West voting totally disappeared with I_γ = 0·0%. Only three states had perfect diplomatic non-alignment and only thirteen more had scores in the range –7 to +7, both figures being less than for the Cairo states, leaving 37 Lusaka states (that is over two-thirds of the group) aligned in their diplomacy. In 1970 the only movement against this general trend was in the Index of Military Alignment. There was an increase from just over half of the Cairo states to over three-quarters of the Lusaka states, which obtained no arms supplies from the Super Powers. But rather than being a positive increase in non-aligned activity this change represented simply an increased abstention from a high-cost alignment activity.

Conclusions

It is an important finding from this analysis that, although the dangers of overt military conflict between the Super Powers declined during the 1960s, the political conflict of the Cold War increased in intensity. When many of the medium sized and smaller states expanded their diplomatic activity, they strengthened their commitment to one or the other side in the diplomatic contest between East and West. In the United Nations voting, the Assembly as a whole became more deeply divided on East-West issues. Thus the decline in the variation in this behaviour explained by the five groups of states was not due to any decline in the Cold War. On the contrary the average variation (that is the dispersion in the scores) in both the Index of Diplomatic Alignment and the voting agreement with the Soviet Union in the U.N. increased substantially from the early 1960s to the end of the decade. The principal reason for both the increase in the overall dispersion and the decline in the amount explained was a spread in the diplomatic behaviour of the Non-Aligned group and a complete collapse in its coherence as a voting bloc. The overall conclusion is that by the end of the 1960s the Non-Aligned were no longer clearly identifiable as a group that behaved distinctly in East-West relations. As the Non-Aligned continue to operate as a diplomatic grouping, there must be some other concerns which held them together and gave them a sense of identity.

References

1. President Nyerere's speech opening the April 1970, Dar es Salaam, Non-Aligned preparatory meeting, printed in the *Nationalist*, 14th April 1970.

2. One important exception was that since 1955 the Soviet Union had full diplomatic relations with both East and West Germany.

3. *The Europa Yearbook 1963* (Europa Publications, London, 1963), and subsequent annual volumes until 1970 were used.

4. H. Hveem and P. Willetts, 'The Practice of Non-Alignment', paper at the Universities of East Africa Social Science Conference, Dar es Salaam, December 1970, pp. 8–11. P. Willetts, 'Towards a Theory of the Phenomenon of Non-Alignment', paper at the European Consortium for Political Research Workshop on 'Models of International Relations', Mannheim, April 1973, pp. 12–14.

5. The correlations are each calculated for the states that were independent and members of the U.N. by the January of the year concerned. The figures for the number of states in Table 4.2 are not the same as those for the U.N. Session of the previous year in Table 2.2, because of the exclusion of Byelorussia and Ukraine for each year and the addition of Kenya in 1964, Indonesia in 1966, Barbados in 1967 and South Yemen in 1968. The number of states in 1970 has

dropped from 124 to 123 due to the exclusion of Cambodia. The data on diplomatic exchanges in *The Europa Yearbook* for January 1970, when Prince Sihanouk was in power, cannot be used when Cambodia is regarded as a Non-Bloc country because of the Lon Nol regime's failure to gain a seat at the Lusaka Non-Aligned summit, later in the same year. Trade data is similarly affected by the change of regime. For this reason, Cambodia is excluded in the analysis of any data for 1970 in Chapters 4 to 6 of this study, except for Table 4.5. The Indices in Table 4.2 did include data on diplomatic exchanges with USA and USSR.

6. The United States and the Soviet Union were both coded as if they had full diplomatic relations with themselves.

7. *The Europa Yearbook 1970* (Europa Publications, London, 1970). This example also illustrates some of the minor inconsistencies to be found in the information in the Yearbook. Niger (Vol. II, p. 1075) and Dahomey (Vol. II, p. 438) are both reported as receiving a non-resident Ambassador from the Republic of Korea, based in the Ivory Coast, whereas the page for the Ivory Coast (Vol. II, p. 723) reports the Ambassador as being based in Paris. Finally the page for France (Vol. I, p. 659) does report the Ambassador in Paris as having multi-accreditation to Dahomey and the Ivory Coast but makes no mention of Niger.

8. *The Europa Yearbook 1964* (Europa Publications, London, 1964), Vol. I, p. 432 and Vol. II, p. 296.

9. With 20 links to be considered over 123 countries for 8 separate years there are nearly 20,000 items of data. In order to handle this amount of information, four computer programmes were written. One gave a printed copy of the data, a second gave a 'holecount' of the punches on each column and hence enabled any mis-codes to be identified, while a third programme made consistency checks. This made it possible to ensure that all exchanges were at least minimally reciprocal and to identify for checking all countries that were coded as having relations with both sides of a divided state. Finally another programme took the raw data on diplomatic links and constructed the scores on the three versions of the Index of Diplomatic Alignment.

10. The anti-quantitative scholar would ask 'What is the use of such quantitative work if it only produces results that an expert on African affairs already knew?' Even at this stage one may challenge with what verbal precision the 'expert' could have specified either the timing or the extent of the changes that have been illustrated. Secondly, no one scholar is likely to become an expert on all the differing regions of the world, whereas it is possible for one person to gather data on all countries. Thirdly, it is hoped that the results of the subsequent analysis using this data are not so immediately obvious.

11. In Figures 4.3 and 4.4, the zero scores are allocated equally with one half to each of the ranges, −7 to 0 and 0 to +7, on either side of the zero line.

12. With twenty-seven of the forty-four Cairo Non-Aligned having a pro-Western score, a median of −4 and a mean of −3·7, the balance of the Non-Aligned in 1964 was slightly but definitely towards the West.

13. In the Belgrade Declaration, the appeal for China's admission to the United Nations was worded in such a way that the Non-Aligned were not all fully committed to the policy. The wording was 'Those of the countries participating in the Conference which recognise the Government of the People's Republic of China recommend that the General Assembly, at its forthcoming Session, should recognise the representatives of the Government of the People's Republic of China as the only legitimate representatives . . .', *Conference of Heads of State or Government of Non-Aligned Countries* (second edition, Jugoslavija Publishing House, Belgrade, undated), p. 275. The Cairo final statement strengthened the support for China and at Lusaka it became an 'urgent need' to give China 'her rightful place'.

14. It can be seen in Table 2.3 that West Germany both received from more states and received a greater total of diplomats than even the Soviet Union.

15. In Table 4.5, the columns for 'Belgrade Attenders' include the twenty-five states at Belgrade plus Syria, which at the time of the conference was still part of the U.A.R.; Angola is omitted from both columns of 'Cairo Attenders'; Malawi and Zambia are omitted from the 1964 'Cairo Attenders' column, because they only became independent during 1964. The overwhelming majority of the Belgrade states were at the Cairo summit and the Cairo states at the Lusaka summit, so there is continuity across the columns. The exceptions may be identified from the attendance lists in Appendix 4.

16. Although it is not possible to detect it from Table 4.5, the newcomers at Cairo, like the original Belgrade states, did move slightly to the East. Tanzania moved from the middle to a moderate Eastern alignment, while Mauritania and Congo (Brazzaville) moved from a moderate Western to a moderate Eastern alignment between 1964 and 1970. Despite this movement, the Cairo newcomers were more Western than the Belgrade states in both years.

17. Against the general pattern, one of the newcomers at Lusaka, South Yemen, was in 1970 highly Eastern aligned in its diplomacy.

18. See Chapter 1, pp. 18–19.

19. *Keesings Contemporary Archives, 1961–62* (Keesings Publications, London), p. 18363, gives the members of the Defence Council of Equatorial Africa as being France, Central African Republic, Chad, Congo (Brazzaville) and Gabon.

20. As we saw in Chapter 1, it was Pakistan's membership of CENTO and SEATO that was used by India to block her admission to the Non-Aligned.

21. For example, see the *United Nations Treaty Series*, Vol. 54, p. 47 or Vol. 29, p. 349.

22. Keesings, *Treaties and Alliances of the World* (Keesings Publications Ltd., London, 1968), pp. 99–101.

23. Singapore did not sign a separate defence treaty with Britain, but 'since the secession of Singapore from the Federation of Malaysia on Aug. 9, 1965, Britain and Singapore have continued to co-operate in terms of the treaty', with Malaysia in 1957. Keesings, *loc. cit. supra.*

24. *The Times* (London, 5th September 1973).

25. A smaller inter-Ministerial committee in Dar es Salaam handled the detailed arrangements for the Non-Aligned meeting, on behalf of the group as a whole. A list of the invitees, seen by the author in Dar es Salaam, was given by the Foreign Ministry to this committee and the list did not include the Maldives.

26. Stockholm International Peace Research Institute, *The Arms Trade with the Third World* (Almqvist and Wiksell, Stockholm, 1971), pp. 724–30.

27. *Op. cit. supra.*

28. *Ibid.*, p. 804.

29. *Ibid.*, p. 597.

30. *Ibid.*, p. 601 footnote 6, '. . . Gambia, Botswana, Lesotho and Swaziland . . . rely on paramilitary elements in the police'; p. 633, Sierra Leone and Gambia '. . . have imported very few major weapons'; p. 662, the section on Burundi does not mention significant arms imports.

31. From 1968 to 1973 there were forty-one members of the O.A.U. SIPRI put the U.A.R. in the Middle East and treated Algeria, Libya, Morocco and Tunisia separately as North Africa. This leaves thirty-six Sub-Saharan members of the O.A.U., to which SIPRI have added South Africa, making thirty-seven.

32. *Ibid.*, p. 691 footnote 6, 'In Costa Rica and Panama there are no

armed forces as such, only a national guard'; p. 53, Mexico's defence expenditure is given as 0·7% of the G.N.P. and Costa Rica's as 0·5% of G.N.P.; p. 203, 'Cyprus became a Soviet recipient in 1964. . . . Total Soviet military aid to Cyprus has not been large'; p. 100, Malta is 'a country which has no stake in the arms trade either as supplier or recipient'.

33. *The Military Balance 1969–1970* (The Institute for Strategic Studies, London, 1969).

34. In Table 4.7 the 104 U.N. members in 1961 are reduced to 99 by the exclusion of Byelorussia, Ukraine, Syria, Sierra Leone and Tanganyika. In Table 4.8 the 115 U.N. members in 1964 are reduced to 110 by the exclusion of Byelorussia, Ukraine, Malta, Malawi and Zambia. In Table 4.9, Byelorussia, Ukraine, Fiji and Cambodia are excluded.

35. The fact that, in both 1964 and 1970, two states from the Western Bloc were militarily non-aligned is not of importance. In both these years, South Africa received no major supplies from the United States, but did so in 1962–63 and 1965–67. Israel received no supplies in 1964, but did so in 1959–61, 1963 and massively in 1968–69. Pakistan appeared militarily non-aligned in 1969 after a long period of American supplies followed by a brief period in which Chinese supplies were predominant.

36. The exceptionally high result obtained in the Analysis of Variance of the Index of Military Alignment is somewhat inflated by the inclusion of the extreme values of –4 for the 18 Western states and +4 for the 8 Eastern states, that were among the 31 states for which SIPRI had not collected data. When these 31 states are excluded from the analysis, the U.N. groups only explain 24·1% of the variation in Military Alignment in 1961; 27·3% in 1964; and 27·5% in 1969. While this is a long way from the 76–78% explained when all states were included, it is generally considered quite satisfactory to be able to explain a quarter of the variation in a social science variable. (For comparison, we may consider Analysis of Variance used in a completely different context. Parent's class is recognised as an important factor in the socialisation of British voters, yet father's class as a variable only explains less than 10% of the variation in the choice of the Conservative or the Labour Party. R. Rose, *Politics in England Today* Faber and Faber, London, 1974, p. 172.) However as one of the main sources of variation on any variable measuring political, diplomatic or military alignment in the Cold War must be the difference between the two main blocs, the picture is much more distorted by omitting the bloc states than by including them with a coding that cannot be strongly validated. If the same 31 states are excluded from the Analysis of Variance of the Index of Diplomatic Alignment, the variation explained for 1964 drops from 63·3% to

34·3%. This suggests that the major part of the relationship found with the Index of Military Alignment reflects the situation in the 'real world' rather than measurement error in the Index. The procedures used have not been beyond challenge, but the conclusion, that three-quarters of the variation in the Index of Military Alignment can be explained, seems a reasonable one and each of the steps taken can be justified.

37. Some might argue that U.N. votes are sold in return for economic aid and therefore the decision on how to vote does involve real costs. But, as it is not likely that an ongoing aid programme would be cut in response to a particular vote or set of votes, the most that is being lost is potential future aid. Given the diversity of sources of aid, the loss of aid from one donor or group of donors does not necessarily mean a net loss of aid.

38. It would not be useful for the present study to regard all roll-calls on which the United States and the Soviet Union were opposed to each other as East-West roll-calls. Nor would a more complex criteria, such as all roll-calls forming a single factor in a factor analysis, be any more appropriate. Such an empirically defined East-West dimension would be likely to include a variety of issues and be difficult to relate to the components of the non-alignment ideology discussed in Chapter 1. Alker and Russett, in *World Politics in the General Assembly* (Yale University Press, New Haven, 1965), do identify East-West factors in U.N. voting, but these include both Cold-War and anti-colonial issues. In this study it is particularly desired to make a detailed comparison of voting in these two issue areas. I share the view of T. Nardin: 'It is a property of factor analysis that it is unable to discriminate the covariation which arises because separate measurements represent partially overlapping indicators of a common underlying variable from that which arises between separate causally related variables. The fact of covariation, therefore, provides no justification for conceptual classification.' Quote from page 21 of 'Violence and the State: A Critique of Empirical Political Theory', *Sage Professional Papers in Comparative Politics*, Vol. 2, No. 01–020, 1971.

Anti-Colonialism and Relations with Southern Africa

From the very beginning of the movement, the Non-Aligned have been concerned with the problems of colonialism. This involved them primarily in trying to influence the behaviour of other states outside the Non-Aligned group and so they were likely to try to use the opportunities for international diplomacy provided by the General Assembly. The Charter of the United Nations states in Article 1 (2) that one of its purposes is 'To develop friendly relations among nations based on respect for the principle of equal rights and *self-determination of peoples* . . .' (emphasis added). Chapter XII of the Charter set up an International Trusteeship System for colonial territories that were placed under U.N. 'administration and supervision'. But Chapter XI also contained the commitment that all U.N. members responsible for other 'Non-Self-Governing Territories' accept in Article 73 'the obligation . . . (b) to develop self-government . . .' and '(e) to transmit regularly to the Secretary-General . . . statistical and other information . . . relating to economic, social and educational conditions in the territories . . .'. Although there was no time limit nor any sense of urgency, the Charter was written with the abolition of colonialism an explicit long-term goal of the Organisation. Both the Trusteeship Council set up under Chapters XII and XIII and the Secretary-General, in exercising his responsibilities under Chapter XI for the other colonial territories, came directly under the authority of the General Assembly. Thus the General Assembly was a particularly appropriate forum from which to mount an attack upon colonialism.

The United Nations and decolonisation in the 1960s
In 1960, when sixteen new African states joined the United Nations, the Soviet Union decided that the opportunity was offered

for a major propaganda offensive. Khrushchev personally came to address the Assembly and proposed a new item for the Agenda entitled 'Declaration on the Granting of Independence to Colonial Countries and Peoples'.[1] The General Committee allocated the item to the First Committee, but on the initiative of the Soviet Union the unusual step was taken of handling the question in Plenary Session without prior reference to a Committee. The Soviet draft resolution proclaimed that all colonies 'must be granted forthwith complete independence and freedom'.[2] The response of the Afro-Asians was interesting. While seeking strenuously to deny that they were in conflict with the Soviet Union, 43 Afro-Asian states tabled a lengthy, more carefully worded, alternative draft. At the end of the debate, the Soviet draft was voted down and a Soviet attempt to add to the Afro-Asian draft a call for all colonies to attain independence by the end of 1961 was also rejected. The Afro-Asian draft, in its unamended form, finally received a vote of 89 in favour, none against and nine abstentions, to become Resolution 1514 (XV).

In the following year, during the Assembly's 16th Session, a similar political process took place. The Soviet Union again took the initiative, demanding a programme for the final and unconditional liquidation of colonialism by the end of 1962.[3] The Afro-Asians again refused to engage in a full, uncompromising, attack upon the colonial powers and sought instead to move the general consensus as far as possible in an anti-colonial direction. Their resolution was passed, setting up a 'Special Committee on the Situation with Regard to the Implementation of the Declaration on the Granting of Independence to Colonial Countries and Peoples', with wide ranging powers to investigate and make recommendations on individual colonies.[4] The effect of this resolution was as if a major amendment had been made to the Charter creating a new organ to fulfil and expand the role that originally had been envisaged for the Trusteeship Council. The role of the Special Committee was further consolidated in the 17th Session by a re-affirmation of its mandate, expansion of its membership from seventeen to twenty-four states and its assumption of the tasks formerly assigned to the Special Committee for South West Africa.[5] In the 18th Session it also took on the responsibility for Article 73 (e) of the Charter, when the Committee on Information from Non-Self-Governing Territories was dissolved.[6]

During the 1960s, there were three specific areas on which the anti-colonial forces concentrated. They were the white minority regime in Rhodesia, the Portuguese colonies in Africa and the system of *apartheid*. But this attack on colonialism was not solely an activity of the Non-Aligned group of states. In the early 1960s the Non-Aligned did not formally meet at the U.N. The Non-Aligned operated through the Afro-Asian Group, which did meet regularly throughout the Assembly Sessions and led the lobbying to pass anti-colonial resolutions. The following summary of U.N. action does not seek to distinguish the role played by the Non-Aligned within the Afro-Asian Group, but an idea of their leading position can be gained from examining the composition of the Special Committee on Colonialism. Seven of the original seventeen members of the Special Committee appointed in January 1962 had been at the Belgrade summit four months earlier. These seven consisted of Yugoslavia and six from among the 22 Non-Aligned members of the Afro-Asian Group. In contrast, only one of the 27 Afro-Asians that had been excluded from Belgrade was appointed to the Special Committee.[7]

The 'Question of Rhodesia'

The first concern of the Special Committee on Colonialism, when it started work in February 1962, was with the situation in Southern Rhodesia. The failure of the African nationalists to make significant gains in the 1961 Rhodesian constitution and Britain's position that it could not interfere, because the colony had been self-governing since 1923, led to fears that white domination would become securely entrenched. The Afro-Asians succeeded in using the Special Committee and the General Assembly, to put pressure on Britain to call a constitutional conference for Rhodesia,[8] and forced Britain to use her veto in September 1963, to prevent a Security Council resolution, which would 'invite the United Kingdom Government not to transfer to its colony of Southern Rhodesia as at present governed any powers or attributes of sovereignty'.[9] A short while later, in May 1965, Britain had to let through a resolution which used almost an identical wording and which also called for a constitutional conference.[10] It is not possible to prove that the constant pressure on Britain, mounted under the leadership of the Special Committee on Colonialism, produced any direct effect. But it is reasonable to assume that the pressure was a major factor in preventing Britain granting independence to Rhodesia under the 1961 constitution.

When the Rhodesian unilateral declaration of independence took place, Britain, that had three years before been emphatically denying the right of any U.N. organ even to discuss Rhodesia,[11] herself took the initiative in calling a Security Council meeting.[12] Within 24 hours the Council had decided 'to call upon all States not to recognise this illegal racist minority regime'.[13] At the end of the three-week debate, the Council imposed an arms embargo and called upon all states 'to do their utmost in order to break all economic relations with Southern Rhodesia, including an embargo on oil and petroleum products'.[14] These measures went further than Britain's initial intention only to prevent arms supplies and to boycott Rhodesian tobacco and sugar[15] and so the resolution also included a specific call to 'the United Kingdom to enforce urgently and with vigour' the full measures. Normally, states will not tolerate having to receive direct instructions, to change their policy, from an international agency, yet Britain voted in favour of this resolution and went ahead and applied it.[16]

In April 1966, two oil tankers destined for Beira seemed likely to cause a serious breach in the oil embargo. On Britain's initiative, the Security Council passed a resolution authorising the first major military enforcement measures since the Korean War and the Royal Navy, acting on behalf of the Security Council, mounted a full-time blockade on Rhodesian oil supplies through Beira in Mozambique.[17]

At the time of writing the basic situation had not changed. The Rhodesia Front regime was not recognised by any other state and had to contend with international economic sanctions. The Afro-Asians had achieved a formidable success in the international isolation of Rhodesia, but had not made much progress towards their basic goal of undermining the domestic position of the regime. (It is assumed that the 'Internal Settlement' of March 1978 either will not make significant changes or will collapse in trying to do so.) The indices developed in this chapter will include data from the U.N. voting on Rhodesia, amongst the other colonial issues, and on trade with Rhodesia in defiance of the embargo.

The 'Question of Territories under Portuguese administration'

The Portuguese colonies presented a special obstacle to the move towards complete decolonisation, because Portugal refused to accept that they were colonies. Since 1951 Portugal had maintained that the colonies were part of a single state that extended across four continents. When Portugal joined the U.N. in late 1955, the Secretary-General sent a letter formally saying that he 'would be obliged if the Government of Portugal could inform him whether there are any Territories referred to in Article 73 of the Charter for the administration of which it has responsibility'.[18] Portugal replied that it 'does not administer Territories which fall under the category indicated"[19] and there followed four years of debate on what were the characteristics of a Non-Self-Governing Territory. This ended in December 1960 with the definition of a set of 'Principles . . . (for) Determining whether or not an Obligation exists to Transmit the Information called for in Article 73e . . .'[20] and a resolution listing nine territories that the Assembly considered to be colonies of Portugal.[21]

While much time and effort had to be expended to produce agreement on the simple proposition that the Portuguese Overseas Territories were colonies, the very care taken gave a sound base for arguing that action must be initiated against Portugal for disregarding the authority of the United Nations. The sudden increase in the level of fighting in Angola led to an immediate appeal to the Security Council in March 1961. However, at this stage, the Afro-Asians could not get sufficient support for a draft resolution affirming the right to self-determination in Angola.[22] In a subtle diplomatic manoeuvre, the Afro-Asians had a resolution of almost identical wording passed by an overwhelming majority in the General Assembly and then brought the issue back to the Security Council.[23] Only three months after the first attempt failed, the Security Council endorsed the Assembly's resolution.[24]

By the end of 1961, there were three committees, the Special Committee on Colonialism, a Committee on the Situation in Angola and a Special Committee on Territories under Portuguese Administration, all building up the pressures on the Portuguese government. The latter committee took what were then regarded as the exceptional steps of hearing petitioners from the African liberation movements and holding sessions in the African countries adjacent to the Portuguese colonies, in order to gather information from refugees.[25] Later, when the Special Committee on Colonialism took on the work of the other two committees, these new procedures became regular practice.

In the Assembly's 17th Session at the end of 1962, two resolutions were passed setting up a special education and training programme for Africans from Portuguese territories, calling on all states to refrain from supplying Portugal with arms and requesting the Security Council to take action.[26] During the debates Portugal had to face the fact that neither Britain nor America offered her any support and they both strenuously sought to deny that they were involved in supplying arms for the wars in Africa.[27] The follow-up by the Security Council endorsed the limited arms embargo and proposed a decolonisation programme, but avoided any commitment to further action.[28] Attempts by the Afro-Asians to extend mandatory sanctions against Portugal failed. In 1965 the Assembly did vote to urge all states to break diplomatic relations, to break sea and air links and to boycott trade with Portugal,[29] but the decisions of the General Assembly are only recommendations to the states and an attempt at the same time to have the Security Council order a trade boycott was voted down.[30] Even the Assembly's appeal to the International Bank to deny economic aid to Portugal was ignored by the Bank.[31]

The situation continued for several years with the Afro-Asians repeating the strong verbal assaults, while tensions began building up in Africa with an increasing number of border violations of Guinea, Senegal, Gambia, Zaïre and Zambia by the Portuguese forces. In 1969 Portugal was subject to condemnation by three Security Council resolutions over three separate border incidents.[32] When the situation worsened with a Portuguese invasion of Guinea in November 1970, the security Council responded with one of those relatively rare occasions when Article 25 of the Charter was specifically invoked to demand that Portugal pay compensation to Guinea for damage caused by the invasion and that it should end the colonial wars.[33] In the end it was not necessary for the Afro-Asians to substantiate the U.N.'s authority by forcing the Western powers to agree to sanctions or enforcement measures. The Portuguese government was not able to stand the combined effect of the international pressures and the prolonged guerilla wars. In April 1974 the Portuguese government was overthrown and replaced by a regime that engaged, as a first priority, in a process of rapid decolonisation.

The eighteen years of dispute over the Portuguese colonies shows both the strengths and the weaknesses of the U.N. It is possible to achieve a major change in the predominant diplomatic norms, such as the change from the acceptance of colonialism to its condemnation, and to bring intense diplomatic pressure to bear on those that reject the prevailing norms. Limited action, such as a poorly enforced arms embargo, may follow, but the U.N. is not an embrionic world government and cannot impose its will on a determined state or group of states in the minority. However, from the point of view of this study of non-alignment, the more important question that will be examined later is to what extent the majority respect the resolutions that they themselves have pushed through.

The United Nations and South Africa

In every single session of the General Assembly, from 1946 until the present day, South Africa's racial policy has been on the agenda and subjected to critical discussion. Initially the issue was India's complaint against South African legislation discriminating against citizens of Indian origin. From 1952 the wider question of racial conflict arising from *apartheid* formed a separate agenda item and a Commission was set up to try to persuade the South Africans to change their policy.[34] With the failure to obtain any response the Assembly's resolutions became increasingly critical. In 1960, under the impact of the Sharpeville shootings, the Security Council was involved for the first time in calling for the abandonment of *apartheid* and cautiously recognising that the 'situation is one that has led to international friction and if continued might endanger international peace and security'.[35] The move from the General Assembly to the Security Council represented a significant increase in the pressure on South Africa and the reference to 'international peace and security' represented an attempt to undermine South Africa's claim that the U.N. could not consider its domestic matters.[36]

Following the failure of Dag Hammarskold to make any progress in a visit to South Africa on behalf of the Security Council, the General Assembly in 1962 called upon all states to break off diplomatic relations with South Africa, to block air and sea communications to and from South Africa, to boycott South African goods and to refrain from exporting to South Africa.[37] The General Assembly also established a Special Committee on Apartheid,[38] which has built up an expertise on the situation and has been important for the U.N.'s role of disseminating information on *apartheid*. The Afro-Asian states were not able to obtain an endorsement by the Security Council of the general trade boycott, but in 1963 they did gain a call for an embargo first on the sale of arms to South Africa and then later on the sale of all equipment 'for the manufacture and maintenance of arms and ammunition'.[39] Much later on, the death of Steve Biko followed by the crackdown on the news media and Black Consciousness organisations provided the political climate for the adoption by the Security Council in November 1977 of a tightly defined, fully mandatory arms embargo. This was the first time that action under Chapter VII of the Charter had been taken against any U.N. member.[40]

Since the mid-1960s all the main organs of the U.N. have been involved in the attack upon *apartheid*. The Commission on Human Rights appointed a Special Rapporteur whose study detailed a long list of South African legislation that should be repealed; the Assembly established a United Nations Trust Fund for the legal defence of political prisoners, relief for their families and assistance to refugees;[41] the specialised agencies such as the International Labour Organisation adopted anti-*apartheid* programmes within their fields of interest, such as labour legislation, and South Africa was forced to withdraw from its membership of some of the main agencies;[42] the Assembly drew up as a treaty an 'International Convention on the Elimination of All Forms of Racial Discrimination';[43] and the Secretariat established a Unit on Apartheid which has run an intensive information campaign against *apartheid*.

South Africa has also been in continuous conflict with the United Nations, since its foundation, over the separate issue of the status of the territory of South West Africa. South Africa originally obtained control of this ex-German colony under a Mandate of the League of Nations and it was generally expected in 1945 that South West Africa would be transferred to the U.N. Trusteeship System. In response to a request for a judgement from the General Assembly, the International Court of Justice in 1950 delivered an Advisory Opinion that, unless a Trusteeship Agreement was made, the original Mandate was still in effect and that the General Assembly had inherited the League of Nations' supervisory powers.[44] South Africa refused to accept the Court's opinion and the issue continued as a dispute with the General Assembly, until in 1960 Ethiopia and Liberia, both former members of the League, instituted proceedings in the International Court against South Africa for breach of the Mandate. When judgement finally came in July 1966, the Court decided not to rule on the merits of the case on the grounds that Ethiopia and Liberia did not have any 'legal right or interest' in the case.[45]

During the 21st Session in the autumn of 1966, following the negative result of the case in the International Court and South African proposals to extend the system of *apartheid* to South West Africa,[46] the General Assembly decided to terminate South Africa's Mandate.[47] In May 1967, at a Special Session called solely to discuss the question of South West Africa, the Assembly set up a United Nations Council for South West Africa to administer the territory until it could become independent.[48] In the following year, as a symbolic change, South West Africa was renamed Namibia.[49] The Council has not exercised effective powers of government but it has been able to establish a programme of higher education overseas to train Namibian civil servants, technical and professional personnel and it issues documents for international travel as passports for Namibians in exile.[50] The authority of the General Assembly to take such action has been strengthened by a declaration from the Security Council that 'all acts taken by the Government of South Africa on behalf of or concerning Namibia after the termination of the Mandate are illegal and invalid'[51] and an Advisory Opinion of the International Court that all states are obliged to recognise the U.N.'s decisions and refrain from any dealings with South Africa implying recognition of its presence in Namibia.[52] In some respects it would appear that the Afro-Asians have not achieved any progress by pushing through decisions on Namibia that South Africa has been able to ignore with impunity. On the other hand, there has been a clear success in that South Africa has had to abandon the goal of incorporating Namibia as a fifth Province.[53] At the time of writing it still seems likely that South Africa will have to concede independence as promised on 31st December 1978 but intense conflict has now shifted to the question of what type of constitution should be drawn up for Namibia and in what way elections may be held.[54]

Data from a variety of sources will be examined to see to what extent each state has maintained normal relations or has joined the campaign to isolate South Africa. Voting in the General Assembly on the question of Namibia can be considered along with voting on Rhodesia, the Portuguese territories and other questions of de-colonisation. Although *apartheid* is not directly comparable to colonial domination by an external power, voting on this question will also be included in the analysis. Diplomatic exchanges, trading patterns and transport communications will provide three indi-cators on observance of the boycott resolutions passed against South Africa. Data on contraventions of the arms embargo will be disregarded because so few countries are arms exporters that the information is of little value for this study.

Differences between the groups in U.N. anti-colonial voting

As we have just seen, the United Nations has been deeply involved in the struggle against colonialism and has been a major factor in the confrontation over the future of Southern Africa. If non-alignment encompasses anti-colonialism, then one may expect the Non-Aligned to vote as a bloc on colonial issues in the United Nations. Anti-colonialism need not be considered the sole prerogative of the Non-Aligned. The voting may show that there has been an alliance with other groups, such as the other Afro-Asians or the com-munists, who are also anti-colonial in their ideology. Once again we may examine the patterns of voting that occurred on roll-calls in the General Assembly's plenary sessions, after each of the first three Non-Aligned summit conferences. This time all roll-calls concerned with Southern Africa or with the future of other territories which were under colonial rule have been selected for separate examina-tion. Roll-calls concerning Israel or the Palestinians are not included, because in 1970 the Non-Aligned still had not integrated these specific issues into their general anti-colonialism.

TABLE 5.1   GROUP COHESION IN VOTING ON COLONIAL QUESTIONS ($p \leqslant 0.001$)

	16th Session		20th Session		25th Session	
	% with High Scores I_α	% with Low Scores I_β	% with High Scores I_α	% with Low Scores I_β	% with High Scores I_α	% with Low Scores I_β
Western Bloc	59·8	0·0	45·0	0·7	31·2	7·6
Latin Americans	88·2	0·0	95·8	0·0	88·6	0·0
Non-Bloc	63·2	0·0	58·1	0·0	52·7	0·0
Non-Aligned	99·7	0·0	96·5	0·0	100·0	0·0
Eastern Bloc	100·0	0·0	100·0	0·0	100·0	0·0
Whole Assembly	41·5	10·1	44·3	2·7	65·2	4·8

The results in Table 5.1 show a contrast between on the one hand the high cohesion of the Eastern Bloc, the Non-Aligned and to a lesser extent the Latin Americans and on the other hand the lower cohesion of the Non-Bloc and the Western Bloc. On closer examination it is found that the lower cohesion of the Non-Bloc states is due to a division between the Third World and the European members of the group. In each session both the sub-groups showed a markedly higher cohesion than the group considered as a whole. However, the most important feature of the table is the steep decline in the cohesion of the Western Bloc and this runs in opposition to an equally steep *increase* in the cohesion of the Assembly as a whole. In the diagrams presented below, it will be seen that by the 25th Session the seven Asian members of the Western Bloc, along with Greece and Turkey, are all voting in significant disagreement with South Africa and some are also in significant disagreement with Portugal and the United Kingdom as well.

TABLE 5.2   INTER-GROUP ADHESION ($IG\,\gamma$) ON COLONIAL QUESTIONS ($p \leqslant 0.001$)

16th Session

	Eastern Bloc	Non-Aligned	Non-Bloc	Latin American	Western Bloc
Eastern Bloc	—	100·0	36·5	−19·4	−65·4
Non-Aligned	100·0	—	68·5	−1·7	−31·2
Non-Bloc	36·5	68·5	—	19·6	10·5
Latin Americans	−19·4	−1·7	19·6	—	62·7
Western Bloc	−65·4	−31·2	10·5	62·7	—

TABLE 5.3   INTER-GROUP ADHESION (*IG* γ) ON COLONIAL
QUESTIONS ($p \ll 0.001$)

20th Session

	Eastern Bloc	Non-Aligned	Non-Bloc	Latin American	Western Bloc
Eastern Bloc	—	95·0	53·3	0·0	−12·0
Non-Aligned	95·0	—	68·2	3·4	1·8
Non-Bloc	53·3	68·2	—	25·8	30·9
Latin Americans	0·0	3·4	25·8	—	38·8
Western Bloc	−12·0	1·8	30·9	38·8	—

TABLE 5.4   INTER-GROUP ADHESION (*IG*γ) ON COLONIAL
QUESTIONS ($p \ll 0.001$)

25th Session

	Eastern Bloc	Non-Aligned	Non-Bloc	Latin American	Western Bloc
Eastern Bloc	—	100·0	64·3	93·3	17·1
Non-Aligned	100·0	—	65·7	92·0	19·5
Non-Bloc	64·3	65·7	—	61·9	26·8
Latin Americans	93·3	92·0	61·9	—	26·2
Western Bloc	17·1	19·5	26·8	26·2	—

The relationships between the groups are given in Tables 5.2 to
5.4. In the 16th Session, with a 100·0% Inter-Group Adhesion score
between them, the Eastern Bloc and the Non-Aligned were not
distinguishable as separate voting blocs. Similarly the Western Bloc
and the Latin Americans were close to each other with 62·7% of all
the links between the two groups showing high voting agreement.
However, there were sharp divisions within the Assembly as can be
seen from the high negative Adhesion score between the Eastern
and Western Blocs. Two-thirds of the East-West pairs of states were
in significant disagreement.[55] The division even extended as far as
there having been slightly more disagreements than agreements
between the Non-Aligned and the Latin Americans. By the 20th
Session all the very low or negative scores have moved in a positive
direction, in some cases dramatically so. There were also some
further steep increases from the 20th to the 25th Session in the
Adhesion between the groups, the change of the Latin Americans
to scores of more than 90% Adhesion with the Eastern Bloc and the
Non-Aligned being particularly noticeable. Against the general
trend the mutual Adhesion of the Western Bloc and the Latin
Americans dropped to less than half of its original value. Thus over
the period, the Western Bloc, in addition to losing its internal

FIG. 5.1 CLUSTER-BLOCS ON U.N. 16TH SESSION COLONIAL VOTES

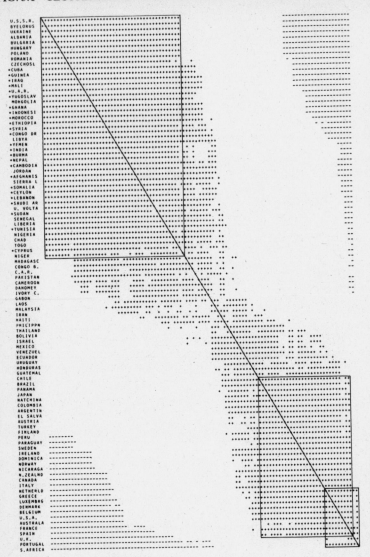

THE FOLLOWING MEMBERS WERE DELETED BECAUSE OF LOW ATTENDANCE –
MAURITAN TANZANIA CUSTA R. ICELAND

*Attended the 1961 Belgrade Non-Aligned Summit.

FIG. 5.2 CLUSTER-BLOCS ON U.N. 20TH SESSION COLONIAL VOTES

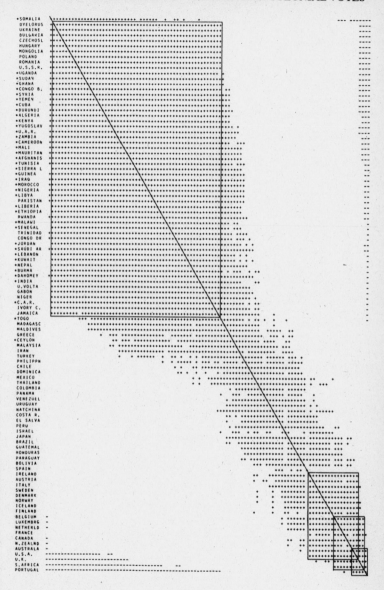

THE FOLLOWING MEMBERS WERE DELETED BECAUSE OF LOW ATTENDANCE –
ALBANIA   CAMBODIA CYPRUS   LAOS   CHAD   TANZANIA
MALTA   SINGAPOR GAMBIA   ARGENTIN ECUADOR   HAITI
NICARAGA

*Attended the 1964 Cairo Non-Aligned Summit.

FIG. 5.3 CLUSTER-BLOCS ON U.N. 25TH SESSION COLONIAL VOTES

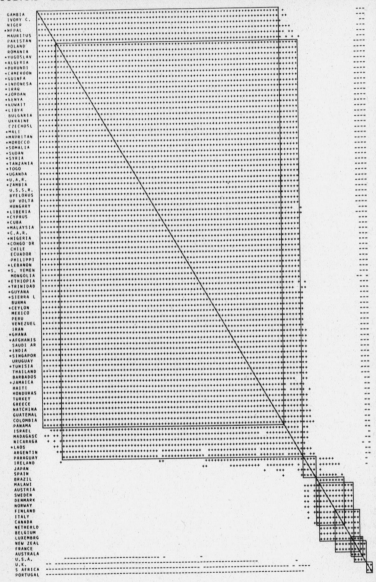

The following members were deleted because of low attendance –
ALBANIA   BOTSWANA   CHAD   CONGO B.   EQ GUINE   LESOTHO
*RWANDA   SENEGAL   SWAZILND YEMEN   CAMBODIA   DAHOMEY
GABON   FIJI   MALDIVES MALTA   BOLIVIA   COSTA R.
DOMINICA EL SALVA   ICELAND

*Attended the 1970 Lusaka Non-Aligned Summit.

cohesion, lost the regular support of the only other group that had been allied to it.

These patterns are illustrated in the diagrams of the empirically determined cluster-blocs in Figures 5.1 to 5.3. The main anti-colonial voting bloc increases from being a large minority in the 16th Session, to having a simple majority in the 20th Session, to having an overwhelming majority in the 25th Session. In the 16th and 20th Sessions, the anti-colonial bloc still had to bargain with other states to get a two-thirds majority required to pass resolutions on 'important' questions, though clearly the bloc was bargaining from a position of strength. By the 25th Session, when matters came to a roll-call vote, the anti-colonial majority could rely on almost always having its way.

In both the 16th and the 20th Sessions the diagrams have one dividing point that matches closely the divisions into the pre-specified analytical groups. The point is where Malaysia and Iran appear in each list. Below this point there are only the European neutrals, the Latin Americans and the Western Bloc states. Above this point are all the Afro-Asian Non-Bloc states, the Non-Aligned and the communists.[56] By the 25th Session, the anti-colonial majority is so all-embracing that no such division can be made.

Examination of the bottom right-hand corner of each diagram reveals the details of the collapse of the Western voting alliance on colonial questions. In the 16th Session, the United Kingdom and the United States are still within a cluster-bloc of 30 states, consisting of 17 that have been classified as Western Bloc, 9 Latin Americans and the 4 European neutrals. In the 20th Session, the United Kingdom is within a cluster-bloc of only ten states, while the United States is close to only 8 more states. Regular support has been reduced to the hard core of the Western Bloc and the European neutrals. Both the Latin Americans and the Asian members of the Western Bloc have distanced themselves from the colonial powers. In the 25th Session, the pro-colonial voting is no longer consolidated in one or two cluster-blocs, but is divided into a series of five smaller overlapping blocs. The United Kingdom and the United States are reduced to a grouping that solely includes Australia, New Zealand and France. The anti-colonial bloc is now so large because it has been joined by all the Latin Americans except Brazil and all the Asians except Japan. The only movement against the general trend is by Malawi, which in 1964 sent a low-level delegation to the Cairo Non-Aligned summit and voted with the anti-colonial majority, but in 1970 did not participate in the Lusaka summit and in the 25th Session is to be found in one of the pro-colonial clusters.

Within the general pattern, the two powers, Portugal and South Africa, that have been under the most sustained attack, have also become increasingly isolated. Even in the 16th Session, before the colonial voting strength had collapsed, Portugal and South Africa were not part of the main pro-colonial cluster-bloc. They were in a smaller grouping with nine other Western Bloc states. This position is maintained in the 20th Session, but in the 25th Session the two are completely isolated. They are not in significant agreement with any other states at all, while they are in significant *disagreement* with 80% of the rest of the Assembly.

S*   In each of the Sessions the Non-Aligned appear together in the empirically determined blocs. Only in the 20th Session do we find any of the Non-Aligned outside the main anti-colonial bloc and then only three states, Somalia, Togo and Ceylon, are marginally distant from it. The dispersion of the Non-Aligned in the 25th Session, scattered down a long list in the anti-colonial voting bloc, should not be taken as indicating a decreased cohesion.[57] There is so little difference in the patterns of pluses and minuses for the first 84 states, that there is little meaning to the ordering. For example, the 31 states from Poland to Hungary have an identical position in the cluster-bloc and their relative ordering is purely a construct of the computer programme. It is not the fact that the Non-Aligned apparently divide the Eastern Bloc into three groups, but that the nine Eastern Bloc states and twenty-two of the Non-Aligned states have an identical pattern that is meaningful.

While diplomatic action at the U.N. was formally in the name of the Afro-Asian Group, the diagrams give strong evidence that the Non-Aligned were setting the pace. Even though nearly all of the Western Bloc Asian states did caucus regularly with the Afro-Asian Group,[58] none of them are found in the anti-colonial cluster in the 16th Session. Only Pakistan has joined it in the 20th Session and Japan is still outside the anti-colonial cluster in the 25th Session. Similarly, only ten of the Afro-Asians designated as Non-Bloc are in the anti-colonial cluster in the 16th Session and nine are outside it. In the 20th Session six are in the less radical part of the anti-colonial cluster (with five of the six failing to reach significant disagreeent with Portugal), and three are outside it. When Afro-Asia is defined in a geographical rather than a political manner, including both the Western Bloc and the Non-Bloc Afro-Asians, then for these first two sessions as many as three-fifths of the Afro-Asians outside the Non-Aligned movement were not voting with the anti-colonial cluster. The mutual overlap between being an Afro-Asian state, being Non-Aligned and being anti-colonial was very high, but there was clearly a greater correlation between being

Non-Aligned and being anti-colonial than between being Afro-Asian and being anti-colonial.

The results of the analysis of U.N. voting on colonial issues are quite different from the results in the previous chapter. Although a broad anti-colonial consensus had developed, the same coalition did not always operate on all issues to produce an anti-Western majority. On East-West questions, over the same three sessions, the Assembly remained deeply divided and the United States was able to mobilise the largest voting cluster.

The most notable contrast is between the disappearance of the Non-Aligned as a coherent grouping on East-West questions and their emergence as the dominant grouping on colonial questions. This contrast helps to explain why the four European neutral states have never been full participants in the Non-Aligned movement. By their rejection of military alliances, Austria, Finland, Ireland and Sweden, might be expected to join the Non-Aligned. Yet, in Figures 5.1 to 5.3, we can see that these four states voted predominantly with the colonial powers. If anti-colonialism is a stronger identifying characteristic of the Non-Aligned than is abstention from East-West alignment, then it is not so surprising that the European neutrals have not joined the Non-Aligned.

Trade as an indicator of an anti-colonial foreign policy

As voting against colonialism in the General Assembly means taking a decision, which involves high visibility but low costs, the degree of commitment required need not be very high before a state is prepared to join the anti-colonial bloc. The question now arises whether the same states have backed up the policy by full implementation of the resolutions that they have voted for. Decisions on trade, diplomacy and other communication links are of lower visibility but may involve real economic costs.

In 1961 neither the General Assembly nor the Non-Aligned at the first summit had yet endorsed any call for *specific* action against the powers in Southern Africa, though the campaign against South Africa was already gathering momentum.[59] In the author's opinion, the issues were already clear enough that by 1961 one would expect the application of non-alignment to mean that a state would have no trade at all with South Africa. However, the contrast between the decolonisation policies of Britain and France and the obduracy of Portugal was not then sharp enough for non-alignment to imply a boycott of Portugal.

By the time of the second Non-Aligned summit in 1964, the U.N., in the resolutions discussed earlier in this chapter, had called for specific sanctions against South Africa, but the United Nations had not yet called for any action against Portugal. Nevertheless, the position of the Non-Aligned was clear. The Cairo summit produced a 'Programme for Peace and International Co-operation'.[60] In respect to South Africa the text

(a) calls upon all States to boycott all South African goods and to refrain exporting goods, especially arms, ammunition, oil and minerals to South Africa;

(b) calls upon all States which have not yet done so to break off diplomatic, consular and other relations with South Africa;

(c) requests the Governments represented at this conference to deny airport and overflying facilities to aircraft and port facilities to ships proceeding to and from South Africa,

and in respect to Portugal the text

calls upon all participating States to break off diplomatic and consular relations with the government of Portugal and to take effective measures to suspend all trade and economic relations with Portugal.

By 1970 one would expect that in addition no Non-Aligned states would have any trade with Rhodesia.

Using data in the various volumes of the United Nations' *Yearbook of International Trade Statistics*, we can construct an Index of Colonial Trade, that measures the percentage of each country's trade that was breaking the boycott of the Southern African powers. Thus for 1961 the Index is given by:

$$\frac{(\text{Value of imports from and exports to South Africa})}{(\text{Value of imports from and exports to all countries})} \times 100$$

The Index for 1964 adds in to the numerator the value of trade with Portugal and all the Portuguese colonies. The Index for 1970 also adds in trade with Rhodesia, the figures being taken from the report of the Security Council's sanctions committee.[61] In each year the Index was coded as a percentage to one decimal place.

Problems with the trade data

D* As, in succeeding editions of the International Trade Yearbooks, the figures may be slightly revised, the most recent volumes, which still contained the relevant data were used. For 1961 data this was the 1965 Yearbook, for 1964 data the 1968 Yearbook and for 1970 data the 1970–71 Yearbook, supplemented by the Security Council report. In the case of seven countries for all three years (Mongolia, Burundi, Equatorial Guinea, Maldives, Nepal, Yemen and Haiti), Guinea for 1964 and 1970 and Laos for 1961 and 1964, there is no data and a value of zero for colonial trade was assumed. With Albania and Nationalist China data for 1969 was used as an estimate for 1970. In the case of Kenya, Uganda and Tanzania, their mutual trade within the East African Community was added to their trade with the rest of the world to give the base for percentages.[62] Data for the Belgium-Luxembourg customs union could not be separated, so the two countries were given the same index values derived from their joint trade. In addition, Byelorussia and Ukraine were excluded from the analysis of trading patterns.

A special problem was presented by the existence of the Southern D* African Customs Union, which means that all published trade figures for South Africa include the trade of Botswana, Lesotho and Swaziland. In the case of Swaziland it was possible to obtain separate trade figures broken down by Swaziland's trading partners.[63] In the case of Botswana and Lesotho only figures for their total trade could be found.[64] In 1970 the trade of the three territories was 4·5% of that given in the U.N. Yearbook for the whole Customs Union. Half of this is attributable to Swaziland and can be accounted for by deducting each country's trade with Swaziland from its trade with the Customs Union. As at least half the trade of Botswana and Lesotho is with South Africa,[65] the remaining error in the trade figures for South Africa is no more than 1% overall. There seems to be no reason to suppose that this trade is distributed in such a way that it would produce a noticeable distortion in the Index of Colonial Trade for any individual countries. In the analysis Botswana and Lesotho will themselves be treated as trading partners of South Africa's, but excluded from any interval level statistics.

In addition to looking for entries for trade in the respective years D* with South Africa, Portugal and Rhodesia, under the separate pages for Afghanistan, Albania, Algeria, etc., a cross-check was made to see if the colonial powers had reported any trade that was not acknowledged by the other party. Due to time lags in the flows of trade, there are bound to be many discrepancies, so that for example South Africa's exports to the United Kingdom are not found to be the same as the United Kingdom's imports from South Africa. The decision was taken to use the figures reported by each country itself, except when it reported zero trade. Then the figures given by South Africa or Portugal were used. This cross-check also included going through the data in the U.N. Yearbooks for Angola and Mozambique. The value of any such trade to be added in was calculated in the appropriate currency using the exchange rates given in the U.N. Yearbooks.[66] For the 1970 data, although South Africa was not always reported as a 'Principal Country', trade with the South African union could always be identified under the heading 'Africa, Developed Economies'. A further check in the *World Trade Annual* revealed some separate data for trade with Guinea-Bissau, Timor and the smaller Portuguese colonies.[67] This trade was so marginal that it did not affect the Index values. After all the checks, any trade of less than 0·1% but greater than zero was coded as 0·1%, so that all traders at however low a level could be identified on the computer.

The impact of the trade boycotts

Of the three regimes involved in Southern Africa, South Africa has the largest economy, but an interesting finding from the statistics is that South Africa is not a major trading power. At no time during the 1960s did South Africa count for as much as 1½% of world trade and it was never among the top fifteen trading nations. It might perhaps be classified as one of the larger of the medium sized trading nations. Several of the Latin Americans, the Asians and the smaller countries of Europe have levels of trade that are the same order of magnitude as South Africa's. In particular, while South Africa trades far more than any one African country, it has never approached having as much as a third of the trade of the other African countries taken together. As South Africa's trade is not very large and is not highly concentrated with any particular countries, it is not even an important trading partner for any individual country other than those in the Southern African region with which it has historical ties. Not one of the independent states that were members of the U.N. at the beginning of 1961 had as much as 4% of their trade with South Africa in that year. It would seem that the states which were promoting a boycott of South Africa were operating from a position of strength against a weak enemy.

The only strong card held by South Africa was its dominant position in the gold markets, but in the 1960s even this did not have its former significance. South Africa's two main trading partners, the United Kingdom and the United States, both wished to eliminate the role of gold as the ultimate support for the international financial system; the Eurodollar market and SDRs were developing as alternative sources of international liquidity; and in 1968 the fixed price of gold at $35 per ounce was abandoned (except for the nominal valuation of official gold reserves), with the central banks agreeing not to buy or sell gold on the market nor to buy newly mined gold. For nearly two years South Africa was faced with the prospect that gold was going to have no more value than as a raw material for the production of jewellery and low resistance electrical components. In December 1969 the I.M.F. came to the rescue by providing a floor price for the free market in gold[68] and in the 1970s gold regained much of its former importance. Portugal and Rhodesia were both much smaller trading powers and had no special factors of this type working in their favour. If the political will were sufficient, there would seem to have been little reason to prevent the U.N. boycott resolutions having a major impact.

In any attempt to sever trade links, it will be easier to stop the exports rather than the imports of the outcast state. Other states can switch their purchases and generally will only suffer a marginal increase in costs. On the other hand, greater costs may seem to be involved in forgoing sales to the embargoed state, in the hope that compensating increases in sales can be made elsewhere.[69] Under this hypothesis, that any effects should be more noticeable on exports, data from the U.N. Yearbooks has been used in Figure 5.4 to plot total exports. The Yearbooks specifically define their area of interest to cover merchandise trade, excluding both refined and unrefined gold. It is not inappropriate for our purposes that the data does not cover the one area of economic strength for the Southern African powers.

The first impression given by the graph is that the boycotts have not been at all effective against South Africa and Portugal. The exports of both countries continued to rise throughout the 1960s, with the exports of the Portuguese Empire[70] fully keeping pace with the threefold expansion in world trade. However, although South Africa's exports also expanded substantially, they were significantly lagging behind those of the rest of the world. While total world trade trebled, South Africa's merchandise exports only doubled. It would require further research to see whether South Africa's performance was comparable to that of other nations with a similar economic structure; whether the South Africans deliberately relied on their exports of gold; or whether the South African government's pariah status was responsible for its poorer than average export growth rate. It is by no means impossible that the Afro-Asians' long campaign in the U.N. has had some effect on the South African economy.

In the case of Rhodesia, the evidence is unambiguous. In the year after U.D.I., Rhodesia's exports dropped by 39% on the previous year and it is not until 1972 that they have regained their 1965 level. If it is assumed that Rhodesia's trade would have expanded in line with world trade had U.D.I. not been declared, then the Security Council sanctions in 1972 were still costing Rhodesia at least two-fifths of her potential exports. In addition, of the exports actually

FIG. 5.4   THE EXPORT TRADE OF SOUTHERN AFRICA

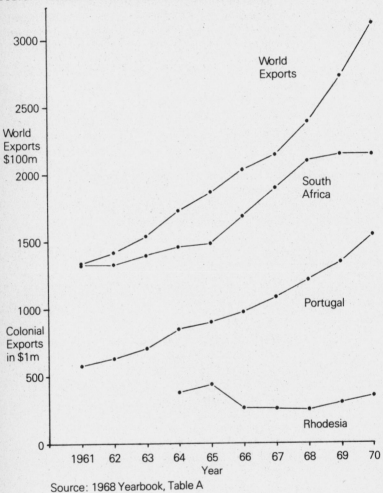

Source: 1968 Yearbook, Table A

taking place only one-third could be openly handled in the normal way, the remaining two-thirds having to travel on indirect routes under false documents.[71] Presumably, in order to allow a discount for those bearing the increased costs and taking the increased risks, the return to Rhodesia on such clandestine trade must be below the value of the goods sent out.

Differences between the groups in their colonial trade

When we break down the total trading patterns, it can be seen immediately from Table 5.5 that to attribute the failure of the attempts to isolate the Southern African powers to the support they gained from the Western Bloc would be a gross over-simplification.[72] In each of the years the Western Bloc states only formed a minority of the states engaging in what, for the sake of abbreviation, is described as colonial trade. With the expansion of the Non-Aligned group, there were actually more Non-Aligned traders than Western Bloc traders (though of course the contribution in terms of the total value of trade by the Non-Aligned would have been very much less than that of the Western Bloc). The Latin Americans made a switch from a majority, which did not trade with South Africa in 1961, to all but one coded as colonial traders in 1970.[73] Even the members of the Eastern Bloc gave no sign of completely eliminating their minute amounts of colonial trade.

TABLE 5.5   PARTICIPATION OF EACH GROUP IN COLONIAL TRADE

	1961		1964		1970	
	Trader	Non-Trader	Trader	Non-Trader	Trader	Non-Trader
Western Bloc	23	1	23	0	23	0
Latin America	5	14	11	8	18	1
Non-Bloc	12	11	9	5	15	3
Non-Aligned	15	10	27	17	32	21
Eastern Bloc	3	5	3	5	6	2
All states	58	41	73	35	94	27

Within these overall patterns, there have been changes that are not apparent in Table 5.5. For example, the three members of the East African Community all reduced their colonial trade, but by 1970 only Uganda had eliminated it. For Kenya the values of the Index of Colonial Trade were 4·5% in 1961, 0·4% in 1964 and 0·3% in 1970; for Uganda the values were 2·2%, 0·1% and 0%; for

Tanzania 1·7%, 0·1% and 0·1%. Thus in each case, in 1961 before they were independent, the East African countries were trading at a level above the world average with South Africa. By 1964, within one to three years after independence, their colonial trade had been drastically reduced. A more difficult problem was faced by Zambia. At independence in 1964, 12·2% of her trade was with South Africa and Portugal, while another 15·4% was with Rhodesia. By 1970 Zambia had found it possible to reduce this total from 27·6% to 9·2%.

On the other hand, changes in the opposite direction were also taking place. Iraq, which attended all the Non-Aligned summits, shows increased values of colonial trade, from 0·2% in 1961; to 3·7% in 1964; and 4·9% in 1970. This meant that, apart from the countries in geographical proximity to South Africa, Iraq had become of all the members of the U.N. the country that in 1970 devoted the largest proportion of its trade to colonial trade. Zaïre also showed an increasing proportion of its trade with the regimes that were supposed to be ostracised, so that, although Zaïre attended the Lusaka Non-Aligned summit, in 1970 it was the second largest colonial trader. Thus the United Kingdom, by this standard, appeared as not the largest but the third largest trading partner of the Southern African regimes. Two further striking anomalies are that each year the Non-Aligned states Sri Lanka and Congo (Brazzaville) had proportionally more colonial trade than did the United States.

It has already been mentioned that Botswana, Lesotho and Swaziland are members with South Africa of the Southern African Customs Union. The original customs agreement was signed in 1910 and it was revised in 1969, when the three High Commission Territories gained their independence. The revision for the first time changed the allocation of joint revenues from a fixed percentage for each territory to an allocation determined by the level of economic activity in each territory.[74] The South African Rand remains as a common currency for the area. If the U.N.'s 127 members in 1970 are listed by the size of their G.N.P., Botswana, Lesotho and Swaziland are each in the last six of the smallest states on the list. Their combined G.N.P. totalling together some $230 million compared with South Africa's G.N.P. of $16,850 million.[75] Swaziland, the only one for which detailed data was available in 1970, sent 21·2% of its exports to and received 92·0% of its imports from South Africa, giving a weighted average of 53·7% of its trade with South Africa. It can be estimated that the trade of Botswana and Lesotho is similarly dominated by South Africa. Clearly, these states that have their government revenue, their communications, their currency and their trade controlled by South Africa cannot be regarded as having freedom of action in their foreign policy decisions. It was an independent act of some significance for all three to participate in the Lusaka Non-Aligned summit, but for the near future it will not lie within their power to break their links with South Africa. Thus, to avoid distorting the picture for the Non-Aligned group as a whole, these three exceptional states are excluded from the following analysis.

TABLE 5.6   ANALYSIS OF THE VARIANCE IN
COLONIAL TRADE*

	1961	1964	1970
Number of states	99	108	115
Mean % trade for each group			
Western Bloc	0·92	1·53	1·17
Latin America	0·06	0·25	0·24
Non-Bloc	0·21	0·58	0·77
Non-Aligned	0·32	0·45	0·46
Eastern Bloc	0·05	0·07	0·09
Variation Explained	25·5%	23·4%	14·4%

* The group means given in the table are not weighted to account
   for each country's contribution to world trade.

The presentation of the Indices of Colonial Trade, which are   S*
sound interval scales,[76] in Table 5.5 as a dichotomous classification of traders and non-traders under-utilises the data. Furthermore, if many countries only had negligible amounts of trade while a minority engaged in more substantial trade, the results in Table 5.5 might exaggerate the failure of the sanctions. Analysis of Variance does fully use the interval properties of the data. We find in Table 5.6 a clear contrast is drawn between the behaviour of the two blocs. In each period the Western Bloc states averaged about 1% to 1½% of their trade with the colonial powers, while the Eastern Bloc states averaged less than one-tenth of a percent. However, in other respects the conclusions to be drawn from comparing the group averages are much the same as those drawn from the simple dichotomisation. None of the groups made a clear break in their trading patterns. The opposite occurred: all groups had a higher average level of colonial trade in 1970 than they had in 1961.

The picture could have been distorted by the emergence of new   S*
members of the international system, changing the base for the analysis, or by the changing definition of the indices. As the index for 1961 only covers South Africa's trade, while in 1964 Portugal's is included and in 1970 Rhodesia's is also included, it could be that

colonial trade has been declining, but not fast enough to eliminate the effect of broadening the definition of the indices. The results in Table 5.7 control for both these possible effects by examining the changes in South Africa's trade over the years among the states that were in the U.N. in 1961.[77]

TABLE 5.7   ANALYSIS OF THE VARIANCE IN SOUTH AFRICAN TRADE

	1961	1964	1970
Number of states	99	99	98
Mean % trade for each group			
Western Bloc	0·92	0·97	0·66
Latin America	0·06	0·09	0·13
Non-Bloc	0·21	0·46	0·33
Non-Aligned	0·32	0·26	0·25
Eastern Bloc	0·05	0·04	0·09
Variance Explained	25·8%	17·8%	13·5%

S*   Three of the groups increased their average level of trade with South Africa over the decade. The trade of the Non-Aligned dropped while that of the Non-Bloc states increased, so that their relative positions changed and came into line with the differences in their ideological commitments. However, the largest average drop was in the Western Bloc's trade with South Africa. On closer examination, it is found that the majority of the group had a steady level of trade and the drop in 1970 was attributable to three states, Iran, Pakistan and the Philippines, making big reductions in their trade. This is an interesting example of the processes of diplomatic pressure having some effect. As the three Asian, peripheral members of the Western Bloc moved from an intermediate position to strong anti-colonial voting in the U.N., they also made corresponding reductions in their trade with South Africa.

In whatever manner the data is presented, one is left with the conclusion that the Non-Aligned failed to back up their group solidarity in U.N. voting with a similar solidarity in their economic activity outside the U.N. All of the eight largest colonial traders in 1970 were Afro-Asian states, with six of these from among the Lusaka Non-Aligned. Even leaving aside the former 'High Commission Territories' and the former members of the Central African Federation, there were another four Non-Aligned and two Non-Bloc states, compared to only three Western Bloc states, with a score of over 2·0% on the Index of Colonial Trade for 1970. Allowing that the long campaign against South Africa is the core of the issue, we still find that of the four states, independent in 1961 and trading at least 2·0% with South Africa in 1970, three were at the Lusaka Non-Aligned summit. The importance of these breaches of sanctions by the Non-Aligned and other Afro-Asians was not so much the economic benefit to South Africa of the relatively low value of the trade as the political benefits South Africa gained from reducing the extent to which it appeared as a pariah in the international system. In as much as trade by the Afro-Asians eased the conscience of Western traders and blunted the opposition of anti-colonial groups within the Western Bloc states, this trade by the Afro-Asians may have been crucial in preventing sanctions having a wider impact.

Several times in the above discussion it has been necessary to comment on different patterns of behaviour within the groups and that the relatively large traders have been found across three of the five groups, so it is not surprising to find that the variation explained by the groups is quite low. In contrast to the ability of the groups to explain between a half to three-quarters of the variation in different indices on East-West relations, the figures in Table 5.6 show that only a quarter of the variation in the Index of Colonial Trade for 1961 and 1964 can be explained and for 1970 we are down to one-eighth of the variation explained. But, even the latter low figure was only obtained after making some adjustments to the analysis. When the results were first calculated with all the 119 states for which 1970 data was available,[78] the variation explained was as little as 1·9%, which implies that there was no relationship at all between the groups and the levels of colonial trade. Like all least-squares statistics, analysis of variance is greatly affected by individual extreme values in the data, and in this case two countries' trade is of a different order of magnitude from all the others. The

S*

TABLE 5.8   THE IMPACT OF EXTREME VALUES ON THE VARIATION EXPLAINED

	N	Variation Explained	Average Trade	
			Non-Bloc	Non-Aligned
All 1970 traders	119	1·9%	2·61	1·69
Omit Swaziland (trades 54·3%)	118	7·4%	2·61	0·63
Omit Malawi (trades 28·5%)	117	7·5%	1·09	0·63
Omit Zambia (trades 9·2%)	116	13·6%	1·09	0·46
Omit Mauritius (trades 6·2%)	115	14·4%	0·77	0·46

exclusion of Swaziland was enough to bring the variation explained up to 7·4% and the exclusion of the other states, that had more than 5% colonial trade, led to a further doubling of the variation explained. The details are given in Table 5.8.

S*   A second factor affecting the interpretation of the results is that analysis of variance does not take into account the ordinal arrangement of the groups, from being more to less identified with the West. Thus, in earlier results where the means of a variable did have a rank order corresponding to the ordinality of the groups, variation explained was a conservative measure to use. In Table 5.6 this is not the situation. The average levels of colonial trade for each group are not in the expected order and so variation explained is to an extent an over-estimate of the strength of the relationship. This point only strengthens the conclusion that the political differences offer a comparatively weak explaination of the differences in colonial trade.

Although it is a striking finding that the patterns of colonial trade were by no means as clear as the differences in behaviour on other indices and in particular there was a marked contrast between colonial trade and colonial voting in the U.N., the negative conclusions must not be overstated. In terms of the absolute value of their trade, both South Africa and Portugal throughout the 1960s relied heavily on the Western Bloc and especially on their major trading partners, the United Kingdom and the United States. Even when the perspective is changed from 'What was important for South Africa and Portugal?' to 'What was their relative importance to other states?', then the Western Bloc still had substantially more trade than the other groups. The low levels of trade of the Latin Americans may be explained by the fact that (with the exception of Brazil) there are few historical links between the Latin Americans and Portugal or South Africa. The minimal levels of colonial trade of the Eastern Bloc were as one would expect. What is quite contrary to expectations is that the behaviour of the Non-Bloc and the Non-Aligned groups was not clearly differentiated. Several states in both these groups had relatively high proportions of colonial trade.

The boycott of South Africa's air and sea communications

In addition to the campaign to break trade links, the boycott was extended to other forms of communication with South Africa. In 1961 this idea had not yet attracted much attention and South African Airways routes still remained as they were in the late 1950s. The main routes shown in Figure 5.5 were to the major West

European cities via Salisbury and Nairobi or via Brazzaville, while an infrequent service was also operated to Australia via Mauritius and the Cocos Islands. Thus South Africa had air links with six Western Bloc states and the one Non-Bloc state, Congo (Brazzaville), but none of the Latin Americans, Non-Aligned or Eastern Bloc.

By 1964 the O.A.U. had taken the initiative in organising a boycott of South African Airways and all independent African states withdrew their landing rights. This on its own was not so important, as South Africa's interest was in its communications with Western Europe. But in addition the African states withdrew S.A.A. rights to overfly their territory. As can be seen from comparing Figures 5.5 and 5.6, this considerably increased the airline's costs, by forcing them to route all their flights around the west coast of Africa. Luanda, Las Palmas and Lisbon became the crucial re-fuelling points and the Portuguese co-operated further by building a new international airport at Sal in the Cape Verde Islands. South African Airways only remained in business because it was given special dispensation by I.A.T.A. to charge passengers at the same rate as other airlines, rather than for the extra distances actually flown. The increase in costs of between 20 and 50%, between Johannesburg and the various European capitals had to be borne by the airline itself.

By 1970, instead of having been forced to contract further, S.A.A. on the contrary had managed to extend its network, by the addition of a route from Johannesburg to New York via Rio de Janeiro. This route across the South Atlantic was shorter, quicker and more convenient for passengers from Southern Africa than the trip via Europe and the North Atlantic to the United States. As is shown in Figures 5.7 and 5.8, S.A.A. had also built up a substantial regional network with Cape Town, Durban and Windhoek becoming international airports. With the exception of Madagascar, the regional co-operation with South Africa did not come from any of the O.A.U.'s original members, but from new states that became independent in the late 1960s. The net result of the various changes was an increase from six to seventeen in the number of states accepting S.A.A. flights. Of the five groups of states only the Eastern Bloc now had no such links. As well as nine of the Western Bloc states, Brazil among the Latin Americans; Austria, Madagascar, Malawi and Mauritius among the Non-Bloc and Botswana, Lesotho and Swaziland among the Non-Aligned were all breaking the boycott. As was the case for South Africa's trading relations the states that were most strongly out of line with political expectations were those within the Southern African region.

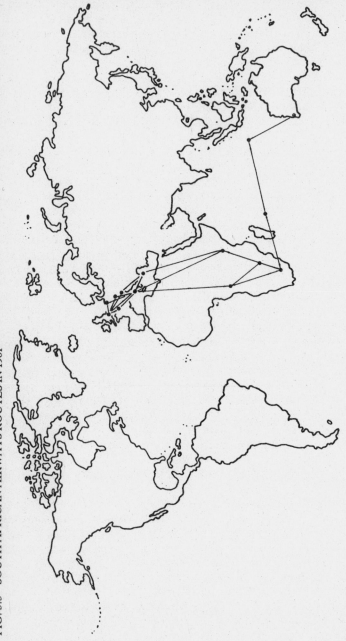

FIG. 5.5 SOUTH AFRICAN AIRWAYS ROUTES IN 1961

FIG. 5.6 SOUTH AFRICAN AIRWAYS ROUTES IN 1964

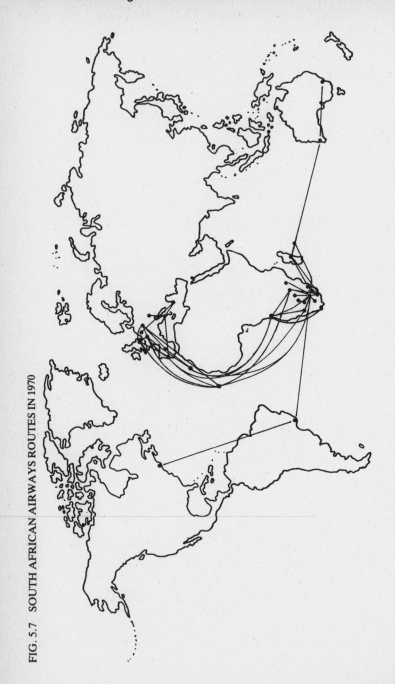

FIG. 5.7   SOUTH AFRICAN AIRWAYS ROUTES IN 1970

FIG. 5.8   SOUTH AFRICAN AIRWAYS REGIONAL ROUTES IN 1970

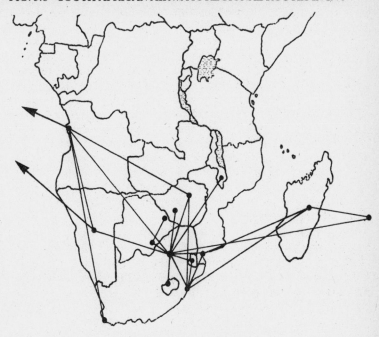

TABLE 5.9   COMPARATIVE PERFORMANCE OF SOUTH AFRICAN AIRWAYS

	South African Airways			World Total		
Year	Aircraft Departures	Passengers Carried	Passenger Miles	Aircraft Departures	Passengers Carried	Passenger Miles
1961	100·0	100·0	100·0	100·0	100·0	100·0
1962	108·8	114·2	114·2	102·9	113·1	115·3
1963	114·1	124·4	135·7	106·0	128·0	131·2
1964	114·2	128·0	167·2	110·6	143·4	154·5
1965	124·2	143·3	177·8	116·4	163·5	178·7
1966	154·7	190·9	239·5	126·9	187·2	207·8
1967	165·7	223·2	272·6	135·0	206·9	236·9
1968	170·2	227·7	298·5	146·8	226·8	261·1
1969	199·0	263·5	345·6	159·1	262·8	303·5
1970	238·5	332·7	491·1	167·0	298·7	361·2
1971	276·3	392·9	533·2	168·2	323·8	387·2

The statistics on international, scheduled, revenue, flights given as indices in Table 5.9 show how South African Airways has fared in comparison to the average for the other international airlines.[79] The most striking finding is that throughout most of the decade South African Airways' performance, in terms of the number of flights, the number of passengers carried and the number of passenger-miles, was considerably better than average. Only in 1963, 1964 and 1965 is there a noticeable impact on the number of passengers carried. The major re-routing round West Africa did not actually cause a reduction in the number of passengers, just a slow-down in their rate of growth and the ground lost was fully made up again by 1966. Presumably without this handicap S.A.A. would have been even more successful in capturing a larger share of the traffic and operating at a higher profit. The fact that the airline did not make a loss still does not alter the fact that it had to bear a high 'opportunity cost'.

In the case of shipping, the two companies, South African Lines Limited and South African Marine Corporation Limited, were not affected in any way, as their routes used to and still do run direct from South Africa to Western Europe and the United States, with no other ports of call.[80] Thus the shipping links are solely with a small number of the Western Bloc states.

The isolation of South Africa's sea and air flag-lines from all but a small minority of the other states might suggest that the majority were acting in accord with the wishes of the Non-Aligned. But a close reading of the 1964 Cairo summit resolution quoted on page 168 indicates that the aim was to boycott not only South Africa's own flag-lines, but also to prevent the ships and planes of any other country from going to and from South Africa. The results given below show that this policy has only been observed by the Eastern Bloc states. In all the other groups there has been at least a substantial minority that was willing to allow direct communications with South Africa. The results in Table 5.10 are similar to those for trade in Tables 5.5 to 5.7. There are relatively extensive links with the Western Bloc states, medium levels with the Non-Aligned and the Non-Bloc states and low levels with the Latin Americans. South Africa lies on one of the major shipping lanes of the world and ships from every major port in Africa and Asia call on their way round the Cape. A total of twenty-one air-lines flew to Johannesburg in 1970. Six of these were local lines such as Air Malawi and Swazi Air and the remaining fifteen had intercontinental routes. Alitalia went direct to Rome, Varig to Brazil and Qantas to Australia, leaving twelve lines flying to Europe with stop-overs at one or more of the main Sub-Saharan airports. As a result, six central and East African states and four West African states had direct air connections to South Africa.

If it was so easy to block South African Airways' own flights across most of Africa, the question arises why was the control of landing and over-flying rights not used to force other airlines to stop flying to South Africa? There would appear to be two answers to this question. In the first place, as most of the revenue from the flights must have come from the through trips between South Africa and Europe, it can be assumed that one result of a ban would have been to produce cancellations and to reduce the number of flights to the African states. Thus they would have lost both an important service and the foreign exchange derived from landing charges and airport taxes. Secondly, the South Africans would have gained from such a ban. If the European airlines had continued to operate by

TABLE 5.10   DIRECT SEA OR AIR LINKS WITH SOUTH AFRICA

	1961		1964		1970	
	Links	No Links	Links	No Links	Links	No Links
Western Bloc	19	5	20	4	18	6
Latin America	4	15	4	15	4	15
Non-Bloc	13	10	7	7	9	9
Non-Aligned	9	16	22	22	21	32
Eastern Bloc	0	8	0	8	0	8
All states	45	54	53	56	52	70

re-routing their flights round West Africa, then South African Airways would have been put on an equal footing with the European lines rather than facing a competitive handicap. On the other hand, if there had been a reduction in the total number of flights to and from South Africa, then S.A.A. would have gained a bigger share of the market. These arguments may not hold with the same strength in the late 1970s as they did in the 1960s. With the steep increase in fuel costs from 1973 and the independence of Angola and the Cape Verde Islands in 1975 leading to the possibility of further route diversions, the position of S.A.A. is becoming much weaker.[81]

Similar economic arguments against sanctions do not apply to the international shipping that passes round the Cape. As only a small proportion of the trade involves goods originating from or destined for South Africa, the trade would still continue, even if South African ports were closed down. While the Afro-Asian states would suffer no direct loss, the South Africans would lose the income from bunkering, which before the closure of the Suez Canal in 1967 was running at more than £2 million per annum and from 1968 jumped to £8 million per annum.[82] However, the political difficulties in the way of stopping the shipping are much more substantial. It has long been accepted that international air traffic can be controlled by individual states for a variety of political, economic and other reasons, but there is no such acceptance of interference with the 'freedom of the high seas'. Secondly, it would only seem reasonable to ask ships to forgo bunkering in South Africa if alternative bunkering were offered in the ports of West and East Africa and due to heavy congestion these facilities are not readily available. Thirdly, while action by only three or four states can drastically affect air flights to and from South Africa, it would require united action by nearly all the coastal states of Africa and Asia to have an impact on the shipping.

While the Non-Aligned have passed resolutions that called for a comprehensive boycott, in their behaviour they only attempted to use measures against South Africa's air and sea communications that they were able to put into effect themselves. South Africa was forced to pay a very limited but none the less a definite price in the re-routing of its flights to Europe. As with the trading patterns the behaviour of the Non-Aligned in this area was not markedly different from that of the Non-Bloc states. The break in the solidarity of both groups came from the links between South Africa and the other states of the Southern African region.

Diplomatic relations with South Africa and Portugal

A third aspect of the attempt to isolate the colonial powers has been the call by the Non-Aligned for all states to break diplomatic relations with South Africa and Portugal. Again we find that this idea had not gained prominence at the time of the Belgrade Conference and is explicitly called for by the Non-Aligned for the first time at the Cairo Conference. When East-West diplomatic exchanges were being considered in Chapter 4, it was essential to construct an Index of Diplomatic Alignment to summarise information on up to twenty exchanges for each state. With only two regimes under consideration it is possible to look at the data in more detail without having to construct an index. A further point in favour of a presentation by tables is that we are concerned not so much with the levels of the diplomatic exchanges as whether or not any exchanges existed at all. The sending and/or the receipt of either a resident or a non-resident ambassador all represented a breach of the diplomatic boycott. Relations with South Africa are given in Table 5.11 as a dichotomisation showing whether or not there was observance of the boycott.

TABLE 5.11   DIPLOMATIC RELATIONS WITH SOUTH AFRICA

	1961		*1964*		*1970*	
	Ambassador	*None*	*Ambassador*	*None*	*Ambassador*	*None*
Western Bloc	14	10	13	11	13	11
Latin America	2	17	3	16	5	14
Non-Bloc	3	20	3	11	4	14
Non-Aligned	2	23	0	44	0	53
Eastern Bloc	1	7	0	8	0	8
All states	22	77	19	90	22	100

In early 1961, it was still possible for two of the most important members of the Non-Aligned movement, Yugoslavia and the United Arab Republic, and even a member of the Eastern Bloc, Czechoslovakia, to send resident ambassadors to Pretoria.[83] All three countries broke their relations with South Africa later in 1961. For both 1964 and 1970 the boycott by the Non-Aligned and the Eastern Bloc was complete. Amongst the Non-Bloc states it was three of the European neutrals, Austria, Finland and Sweden, that were out of line with the others. The Afro-Asian, Non-Bloc states did also maintain a complete boycott, until in 1969 Malawi deviated by opening full diplomatic relations with South Africa and exchanging resident ambassadors. Among the Latin Americans South Africa was able to some extent to counteract her isolation elsewhere, by increasing the number of states with which she had exchanges. This increase though slight was in direct contrast to the movement by all but Brazil among the Latin Americans into the anti-colonial bloc in U.N. voting. As with all the other indicators, South Africa's main diplomatic support came from the Western Bloc, but there was an important division within the bloc. Of the eight Asian members seven had no relations while only Israel sent an ambassador. All, except four, of the West European and other members did have relations (exceptions being Iceland, Norway, New Zealand and Denmark after its break with South Africa in 1962).[84] In diplomacy even more than in its trade and its communications, South Africa was centred on Western Europe and America.

Portugal's diplomatic position was much stronger than South Africa's throughout the 1960s. It had ambassadorial relations with twice as many countries. Going through the groups in turn, we find that the Eastern Bloc had no relations at any point. In 1961 seven of the Non-Aligned had exchanges with Portugal and by 1964 they had been joined by three more. Then by 1970 the boycott campaign led to a break in relations by Indonesia, Ethiopia, Tunisia and the U.A.R. from the original seven, but Ceylon, Cuba and Morocco continued ambassadorial relations without there being any obvious, direct reason why they should do so.[85] The relations newly established by Congo (Brazzaville) did not last long, but Iraq and Lebanon went against the tide, in continuing their new links, again

TABLE 5.12   DIPLOMATIC RELATIONS WITH PORTUGAL

	1961		*1964*		*1970*	
	Ambassador	None	Ambassador	None	Ambassador	None
Western Bloc	21	3	21	3	22	2
Latin America	10	9	12	7	16	3
Non-Bloc	6	17	6	8	6	12
Non-Aligned	7	18	10	34	5	48
Eastern Bloc	0	8	0	8	0	8
All states	44	55	49	60	49	73

without obvious reason. Thus, in contrast to their boycott against South Africa, the Non-Aligned still in 1970 were a long way from applying a complete diplomatic boycott against Portugal.

Among the Non-Bloc states, the four European neutrals maintained uninterrupted relations from 1960 to 1970 and Malta did so from becoming independent in late 1964. The remaining Non-Bloc links with Portugal were all with states neighbouring on Portugal's African colonies. Senegal had reciprocal links for a brief while in 1961, Madagascar received a Portuguese Ambassador from 1961 to 1966, and Congo (Kinshasa) did so from 1963 to 1966. Malawi was the only Afro-Asian, Non-Bloc state to move clearly against the boycott, in receiving a Portuguese Ambassador in 1965, accrediting a non-resident Ambassador to Lisbon in 1968 and upgrading the link to a resident posting in Lisbon in 1970.

Among the Latin Americans the main determinant of their relations with Portugal was the size of the state concerned. The largest states had full reciprocal relations from 1960 onwards, while the smaller states established relations during the decade or upgraded lower level relations. Only Bolivia, El Salvador and Haiti remained without any Ambassadorial exchange by 1970, but Haiti was the sole one to have no exchange at all with either South Africa or Portugal at any point. Given that we have already found that

Haiti was the first Latin American state to dissociate itself from the colonial voting bloc in the United Nations, the absence of colonial diplomatic links in Haiti's case is probably based on principle rather than lack of activity by a small state.

Even more than South Africa, Portugal had a very strong diplomatic position within the Western Bloc. All but Israel and New Zealand had ambassadorial relations for most of the period and there is no reason to suppose that these two small states were refraining from links as a matter of principle.[86] The Philippines had no relations in the early 1960s, but sent a non-resident Ambassador from 1964 and a resident Ambassador from 1969. Thus the policy of the Western Bloc Asians in their colonial diplomacy shows a clear contrast. With the exception of Israel in each case, none of them had relations with South Africa, while by 1970 all of them had relations with Portugal.

The policy of boycott succeeded in isolating South Africa, so that her diplomatic contacts were reduced to the other white states, a quarter of the Latin Americans, Israel and Malawi. In Portugal's case the boycott was pursued with much less rigour and the only identifiable group to uphold it completely was the Eastern Bloc. Even in Africa Portugal's links were not confined just to the deviant state of Malawi. In Asia relations were maintained not just with the Western Bloc Asians but also with several of the Non-Aligned and Portugal ended the decade with exchanges with more than three-quarters of the Latin Americans. The Non-Aligned neither got full support for the boycott within their own group nor succeeded in isolating the majority of Portugal's links to the white states.

Comparisons between the four sets of results

Four separate types of data have been analysed to form a picture of the extent to which each state was adopting an anti-colonial foreign policy. As with the data on East-West relations, the indices were derived from completely independent sources and involved the behaviour of a variety of different people in areas of the international system as different as air and sea communications, the world of diplomacy, international trade and the politics of the General Assembly. In each of the four areas of the system, the Western Bloc countries remained the closest to South Africa and Portugal. However, the Asian members of the Western Bloc, that were generally loyal to the bloc in their East-West relations, did behave differently towards the question of colonialism. They had no transport communications nor diplomatic relations with South Africa and three of them made substantial reductions in their trade with South Africa. These Asian states also led the way in the splintering of the bloc in its U.N. voting. At the other end of the spectrum, the Eastern Bloc countries adopted a highly consistent anti-colonial policy.

The picture was not so clear for the other groups. The Latin Americans moved sharply in their U.N. voting from a pro-colonial to an anti-colonial position, but increased their trade, allowed South African Airways first trans-Atlantic route to open and expanded their diplomatic links with both South Africa and Portugal. Within the Non-Bloc group there is a contrast between the European neutrals and Malawi on the one hand and the remaining Afro-Asians on the other hand. The four neutral European states were as consistently pro-colonial as most of the European members of the Western Bloc. Between them they had all types of co-operation with South Africa and Portugal and even remained outside the U.N. anti-colonial voting bloc when it became an overwhelming majority. Malawi, that in 1964 appeared to be fitting into the anti-colonial majority, moved clearly into a pro-colonial position, so that in 1970 it was in the small group of just a dozen states which co-operated with South Africa in every one of the four areas of trade, diplomacy, communications and U.N. voting. The other Afro-Asian, Non-Bloc states moved from moderate to full anti-colonial voting, abstained from diplomatic links, but had some communication links and most of them traded, with several having relatively high levels of trade.

The Non-Aligned also showed a mixed pattern of behaviour. From the beginning they provided the core of the anti-colonial voting bloc and gave the leadership in the lobbying. The two states that sent Ambassadors to South Africa in 1961 broke off relations and from then on a complete boycott was maintained. In contrast the diplomatic boycott of Portugal was slow to get under way and was not even enforced within the Non-Aligned group with the result that it had no success overall. There was a similar contrast in the field of communications. The boycott of South African Airways international routes was fully carried out. While the tolerance of the new states in Southern Africa establishing local routes was understandable, it is surprising that resolutions calling on all countries to refuse to allow their own airlines and shipping companies to go to South Africa should be pushed so strongly at both the Non-Aligned Conferences and the U.N., when the Non-Aligned have made no attempt to carry them out. In the field of trade the majority of the Non-Aligned by 1970 had very little or no connections with the colonial regimes and some of them had done this by making significant reductions in their earlier levels of trade. But again the

Non-Aligned had by no means done all within their power to enforce the boycott. Even leaving aside the states bordering on South Africa, several of the Non-Aligned maintained or increased their relatively high levels of trade with South Africa and Portugal.

Although there is not always ideological consistency to the foreign policies of some states, there does appear to be behavioural consistency. The anti-colonial forces can be seen to have made a great deal of progress in all areas of the system, when the situation in 1961 is compared with that in 1970. Also, the attack against South Africa, in all areas, gathered more momentum than the attack against Portugal. South Africa has been in constant conflict with the international community on more than one issue since 1946. It was almost universally recognised to be a vicious and repressive regime, whereas Portugal's colonial policy was not in the limelight in the same way. Thus the pressures to act against Portugal were not so compelling as those against South Africa.

There was in addition a marked difference in behaviour in different areas of the system. The more visible, the more prestigious and the lower the cost of the activity, the more success there was for the anti-colonial forces. Voting in the United Nations involves high visibility, relatively high prestige and very low costs and the response was overwhelming. To break with South African Airways or to break diplomatic relations is not so visible, still is a prestige matter and does involve some low costs: the success was not so high, but what there was did represent more of an achievement. The other air and sea communications are of low visibility, would be damaging to South Africa's prestige if their rupture could be publicised, but involve both direct costs and the indirect cost of conflict with third parties. There was no success. To sustain a trade boycott is also of low visibility, but is potentially more damaging to South Africa and for most states the costs are more apparent than real. The response was rather mixed and unpredictable.

Conclusions

Even though the picture is not completely clear cut, anti-colonialism does provide a means of identifying the Non-Aligned.[87] During the 1960s the Latin Americans have very little to do with non-alignment and by 1970 they still had only a minimal commitment to anti-colonialism. The pro-colonial record of the European neutrals makes it completely explicable that these states remained so distant from non-alignment. Among Yugoslavia, the Caribbean states and the Afro-Asians which were invited to Non-Aligned Conferences, the odd one out was Malawi. Malawi was not only pro-colonial but also since 1964 had little to do with non-alignment.[88] Among both the Non-Aligned, that attended the summit conferences, and the Non-Bloc, that declined the invitations, the states that were least anti-colonial were all in the Southern African region. Botswana, Lesotho, Swaziland and Zambia were trying to distance themselves from a colonial heritage that bound them to South Africa and were accepted among the Non-Aligned. Madagascar and Mauritius had their links more by choice and remained outside the Non-Aligned group. All the others were committed to anti-colonialism, with several unexpected exceptions in colonial trade and diplomatic links with Portugal. Generally the Non-Bloc states had a little more colonial trade and adopted slightly less strong voting positions in the U.N. and the Non-Aligned provided the leadership. The data on East-West relations did not suggest a common identity for the Non-Aligned, but anti-colonialism did provide a bond between them. Furthermore it was a bond that is still as relevant to the Non-Aligned in the 1970s as it was in the 1960s.

References

1. United Nations Document A/4501.

2. Text read out by Khrushchev in the 869th Plenary Meeting of the General Assembly on 23rd September 1960 (*Official Records* for the 15th Session).

3. United Nations Documents A/4859, A/4889 amd A/L.355.

4. Resolution 1654 (XVI) passed on 27th November 1961 by a vote of 97 in favour to none against with 4 abstentions.

5. Resolution 1810 (XVII) on 17th December 1962 by a vote of 101 in favour to none against with 4 abstentions and Resolution 1805 (XVII) passed on 14th December 1962 by a vote of 98 in favour to none against with 1 abstention.

6. Resolution 1970 (XVIII) passed on 16th December 1963 by a vote of 84 in favour to none against with 26 abstentions.

7. *United Nations Yearbook 1961*, p. 51. The seventeen members of the Special Committee appointed by the President of the General Assembly in January 1962, categorised by the analytical groups used in this study were:
   Western Bloc — Australia, Italy, United Kingdom, United States;
   Latin America — Uruguay, Venezuela;
   Non-Bloc — Madagascar, Tanganyika;
   Non-Aligned — Cambodia, Ethiopia, India, Mali, Syria, Tunisia, Yugoslavia;

Eastern Bloc — Poland, U.S.S.R.
The Afro-Asian Group as it met at the U.N. included 6 of the 25 Western Bloc, 21 of the 25 Non-Bloc, 22 of the 25 Non-Aligned and 1 of the 10 Eastern Bloc states. The new state of Tanganyika, appointed to the Special Committee within days of attaining independence, is not in the text at this point referred to as having been 'excluded from Belgrade'.

8. Resolution 1747 (XVI) passed on 28th June 1962 by a vote of 73 in favour to 1 against with 27 abstentions (Portugal and U.K. 'Not Participating') and reaffirmed in Resolution 1760 (XVII) and Resolution 1883 (XVIII).

9. Draft resolution S/5425, proposed by Ghana, Morocco and the Philippines, voted on by the Security Council on 13th September 1963, receiving 8 votes in favour, 1 against (U.K.) and 2 abstentions (France and U.S.A.).

10. Resolution 202(1965), proposed as S/6329/Rev. 1 by Ivory Coast, Jordan and Malaysia, voted on by the Security Council on 6th May 1965, receiving 7 votes in favour to none against with 4 abstentions (France, U.S.S.R., U.K. and U.S.A.).

11. In the voting on resolutions in the General Assembly, instead of abstaining, voting 'No' or withdrawing in protest from the meeting, Britain had several times adopted a new tactic that implied a stronger protest. It was recorded as 'Not Participating' in the vote.

12. Letter of 11th November 1965, United Nations Document S/6896.

13. Resolution 216(1965), proposed as S/6921/Rev. 1 by Jordan, voted on by the Security Council on 12th November 1965, receiving 10 votes in favour to none against with 1 abstention (France).

14. Resolution 217(1965), proposed as S/6955 by Bolivia and Uruguay, voted on by the Security Council on 20th November 1965, receiving 10 votes in favour to none against with 1 abstention (France).

15. Statement by the Prime Minister, H. Wilson, in the House of Commons, 11th November 1965. Parliamentary Debates (*Hansard*) House of Commons, Fifth Series—Volume 720, columns 349–60.

16. In a statement by the Prime Minister, H. Wilson, in the House of Commons on 1st December 1965 it was announced that the British embargoes on Rhodesian exports were being extended to 'account for over 95 per cent of Rhodesia's exports' (*Hansard*, Volume 721, column 1431), and a separate Treasury announcement imposed stringent restrictions on the flow of current account funds to Rhodesia, *Keesings Contemporary Archives 1966* (Keesings Publica-

tions, London), p. 21176. A later statement by the Prime Minister on 20th December 1965 announced the imposition of an embargo on oil supplies to Rhodesia, *Hansard*, Volume 722, columns 1690–1.

17. Resolution 221(1966), proposed as S/7236/Rev. 1 by the United Kingdom, voted on by the Security Council on 9th April 1966, receiving 10 votes in favour to none against with 5 abstentions (Bulgaria, France, Mali, U.S.S.R. and Uruguay).

18. United Nations Document A/C4/331, in *Annexes to the Official Records* 11th Session, Agenda Item 34.

19. United Nations Document A/C4/347, *loc. cit. supra.*

20. Resolution 1541 (XV) of the General Assembly, passed on 15th December 1960 by a vote of 69 in favour to 2 against with 21 abstentions.

21. Resolution 1542 (XV) of the General Assembly, passed on 15th December 1960 by a vote of 68 in favour to 6 against with 17 abstentions.

22. Draft resolution S/4769, proposed by Ceylon, Liberia and U.A.R., voted on by the Security Council on 15th March 1961, receiving 5 votes in favour to none against with 6 abstentions, both U.S.S.R. and U.S.A. voting with Ceylon, Liberia and U.A.R. (*Official Records of the Security Council*, 16th Year, 946th Meeting, p. 33).

23. Resolution 1603 (XV) passed on 20th April 1961 by a vote of 73 in favour to 2 against with 9 abstentions.

24. Resolution S/4835, proposed by Ceylon, Liberia and U.A.R. as S/4828, amended by Chile S/4833/Rev. 1, voted on by the Security Council on 9th June 1961, receiving 9 votes in favour to none against with 2 abstentions.

25. *United Nations Yearbook 1962*, p. 410.

26. Resolution 1807 (XVII) passed on 14th December 1962, by a vote of 82 in favour to 7 against with 13 abstentions and Resolution 1808 (XVII) passed on 14th December 1962 by a vote of 96 in favour to 2 against.

27. *United Nations Yearbook 1962*, pp. 413–14.

28. Resolution S/5380, proposed as S/5372 by Ghana, Morocco and Philippines and amended by Venezuela by S/5379, voted on by the Security Council on 31st July 1963, receiving 8 votes in favour to none against with 3 abstentions (France, U.K. and U.S.A.).

29. Resolution 2107 (XX) passed on 21st December 1965 by a vote of 66 in favour to 26 against with 15 abstentions.

30. Resolution 218(1965), proposed as S/6953/Rev. 1 and amended on Uruguay's proposal by S/6965, was voted on and passed on 23rd November 1965, receiving 7 votes in favour to none against with 4 abstentions, but a separate vote on the operative paragraph calling for a boycott of trade with Portugal received 4 votes in favour (Malaysia, Jordan, Ivory Coast and U.S.S.R.) to none against with 7 abstentions resulting in the deletion of this paragraph.

31. The appeal to the International Bank was made as operative paragraph 9 of Resolution 2107 (XX), but the appeal had to be reiterated and the Secretary-General asked to consult with the Bank, a year later, in operative paragraphs 9 and 10 of Resolution 2184 (XXI), passed on 12th December 1966 by a vote of 70 in favour to 13 against with 22 abstentions.

32. Resolution 268(1969), on a complaint by Zambia, proposed as S/9360, voted on by the Security Council on 28th July 1969, receiving 11 votes in favour to none against with 4 abstentions (France, Spain, U.K. and U.S.A.); Resolution 273(1969) on a complaint by Senegal, proposed as S/9542/Rev. 1 and orally amended, voted on by the Security Council on 9th December 1969, receiving 13 votes in favour to none against with 2 abstentions (Spain and U.S.A.); and Resolution 275(1969), on a complaint by Guinea, proposed as S/9574, voted on by the Security Council on 22nd December 1969, receiving 9 votes in favour to none against with 6 abstentions (China, Colombo, France, Spain, U.K. and U.S.A.).

33. Resolution 290(1970), proposed as S/10030 by five Afro-Asian states, voted on by the Security Council on 8th December 1970, receiving 11 votes in favour to none against with 4 abstentions (France, Spain, U.K. and U.S.A.).

34. The Commission on the Racial Situation in the Union of South Africa was established by Resolution 616A (VII), passed on 5th December 1952 by a vote of 35 in favour to 1 against with 23 abstentions.

35. Resolution 134(1960), proposed as S/4299 by Ecuador, voted on by the Security Council on 1st April 1960, receiving 9 votes in favour to none against with 2 abstentions (France and U.K.).

36. South Africa's claim that *apartheid* cannot be discussed rests on Article 2(7) of the Charter: 'Nothing contained in the present Charter shall authorise the United Nations to intervene in matters which are essentially within the domestic jurisdiction of any state . . .' The reference to *apartheid* endangering 'international peace and security' is important, because, once the Security Council has determined 'the existence of any threat to the peace' (Article 39), Article 2(7) is no longer operative, as 'this principle shall not prejudice the application of enforcement measures under Chapter VII'.

37. Resolution 1761 (XVII), passed on 6th November 1962 by a vote of 67 in favour to 16 against with 23 abstentions.

38. *Ibid.*

39. Resolution 181(1963), proposed as S/5384, voted on by the Security Council on 7th August 1963, receiving 9 votes in favour to none against with 2 abstentions (France and U.K.) and Resolution 182(1963), proposed as S/5469, voted on by the Security Council on 4th December 1963, receiving unanimous support.

40. Security Council Resolution 418 (1977), adopted unanimously on 4th November 1977.

41. The appointment of a Special Rapporteur is detailed in the *United Nations Yearbook 1967*, pp. 84–5 and p. 499. A report was submitted to the Commission on Human Rights on 22nd November 1967 as U.N. document| E/CN.4/949 |with Corrigenda and Addenda. The United Nations Trust Fund was established by Resolution 2054B (XX), passed on 15th December 1965, by a vote of 95 in favour to 1 against with 1 abstention.

42. As early as 5th April 1956 Mr. Louw, the Minister of External Affairs, announced South Africa's withdrawal from UNESCO because of 'its interference in South Africa's racial problems by means of UNESCO publications' (*Keesings Contemporary Archives*, p. 14135). On 5th December 1963 the Conference of the F.A.O. adopted a resolution to exclude South Africa from all activities of its 'African region' and on 18th December 1963 South Africa gave notice of its withdrawal from membership of the F.A.O. (*United Nations Yearbook 1963*, p. 604). In June 1963 the Governing Body of the I.L.O. decided to exclude South Africa from all meetings 'the membership of which is determined by the Governing Body' (*United Nations Yearbook 1963*, p. 598). In 1964 the International Labour Conference adopted a 'Programme for the Elimination of *Apartheid* in Labour Matters' and two amendments to the I.L.O. constitution to permit the suspension or expulsion of members. In March 1964 the South African government decided to withdraw its membership (*United Nations Yearbook 1964*, pp. 492–3). On 30th July 1963, the Economic and Social Council by Resolution 974 D IV(XXXVI) excluded South Africa from membership of the Economic Commission for Africa (*United Nations Yearbook 1963*, pp. 274–5).

43. Resolution 2106 (XX), passed on 21st December 1965 unanimously, and came into force as a Convention on 4th January 1969, after 27 states had ratified it.

44. J. Dugard, *The South West Africa/Namibia Dispute* (University of California Press, Berkeley and London, 1973), pp. 128–43.

45. *Ibid.*, pp. 292–325.

46. The reference is to the Odendaal Commission Report of January 1964 which proposed the extension of the system of Bantustans to South West Africa. See Dugard, *op. cit.*, pp. 236–8 and pp. 431–5.

47. Resolution 2145 (XXI) passed on 27th October 1966 by a vote of 114 in favour to 2 against with 3 abstentions.

48. Resolution 2248 (SV) passed on 19th May 1967 by a vote of 85 in favour to 2 against with 30 abstentions.

49. Resolution 2372 (XXII) passed on 12th June 1968 by a vote of 96 in favour to 2 against with 18 abstentions.

50. Education and training for Namibians was first provided under Resolution 1705 (XVI), passed on 19th December 1961 by a vote of 94 in favour to none against with 1 abstention. Then the assistance to Namibians, South Africans, Southern Rhodesians and Africans from Portuguese territories was integrated under the U.N. Educational and Training Programme for Southern Africa by Resolution 2349 (XXII), passed on 19th December 1967 by a vote of 113 in favour to 2 against with 1 abstention. An attempt to expand the assistance through a U.N. Fund for Namibia made slow progress because of the failure to raise adequate voluntary contributions: see Resolution 3030 (XXVII), passed on 18th December 1972, by a vote of 124 in favour to 2 against with no abstentions. The first steps in gaining recognition for its travel documents, issued to Namibians, is reported by the U.N. Council for Namibia in its fifth report to the General Assembly (A/8024), and is endorsed in operative paragraph 12 of Resolution 2678 (XXV) passed on 9th December 1970 by a vote of 95 in favour to 5 against with 14 abstentions.

51. Resolution 276(1970), proposed as S/9620/Rev. 1 voted on by the Security Council on 30th January 1970, receiving 13 votes in favour to none against with 2 abstentions (France and U.K.).

52. Dugard, *op. cit.*, pp. 453–81.

53. In 1946 South Africa requested and the General Assembly refused to authorise the incorporation of South West Africa into the Union of South Africa. Nevertheless in 1949 the South African parliament passed the South West Africa Affairs Amendment Act which provided for the representation of South West Africa in the Union House of Assembly and Senate. Dugard, *op. cit.*, Chapter 5.

54. A constitutional conference based on representatives of the various ethnic groups in Namibia opened in Windhoek on 1st September 1975. Negotiations continued until March 1977 when a draft constitution was agreed. SWAPO refused to take part in the talks and they were condemned in the U.N. When the five Western members of the Security Council made it plain that they would not accept the proposals, they were abandoned by South Africa and on 6th July 1977 Justice Steyn was appointed as an Administrator-General. The Western 'contact group' have been acting as intermediaries between South Africa and SWAPO.

55. The definition of the index of Inter-Group Adhesion is given in Appendix 5.

56. The demarcation is not perfect, as in both Sessions Pakistan, from the Western Bloc, is on the anti-colonial side of this division and in the 20th Session this is also true of Greece.

57. In Table 5.1 the Non-Aligned group cohesion can be seen to have actually increased slightly in the 25th Session.

58. The exceptions are Israel and China, according to a mimeograph list of the U.N. groups received from the United Kingdom Foreign Office with a letter dated 17/9/69.

59. In April 1961 the Assembly had made a very general request to all states 'to consider taking such separate and collective action as is open to them' – Resolution 1663 (XVI) passed on 28th November 1961 by a vote of 97 in favour to 2 against with 1 abstention.

60. *Review of International Affairs* (Belgrade), Vol. XV, No. 350, 5th November 1964, pp. 79–88.

61. *Fifth Report of the Security Council Committee Established in Pursuance of Resolution 253 (1968), Concerning the Question of Southern Rhodesia*, United Nations document, S/10852/Add.2, Annex V. Appendix I, 2nd February 1973.

62. Data on Kenya's trade with Uganda and Tanzania came from *Statistical Abstract 1971* (Government Printer, Nairobi, 1971), p. 45, and data on Uganda's trade with Kenya and Tanzania came from *1970 Statistical Abstract* (Government Printer, Entebbe, 1970), p. 21 and p. 24.

63. *Annual Statistical Bulletin 1972* (Central Statistical Office, P.O. Box 456, Mbabane, Swaziland).

64. *Africa South of the Sahara 1975* (Europa Publications, London, 1975), p. 176 and p. 459.

65. 'Of Botswana's exports of animal products in 1966 18 per cent in value (31·6 per cent in 1965) went to South Africa. . . . Of the 1966 imports 65·4 per cent in value came from South Africa', *Europa Yearbook 1972*, Vol. II, p. 901.

66. For 1970 this was not necessary, as all the data in the *Yearbook of International Trade Statistics 1970–71* is expressed in dollars.

67. *World Trade Annual 1970, Volume I* (Walker and Co., New York, 1972). Although it is printed by a private firm, the United Nations is the source of the data for this publication. Thus it was rather surprising to find small discrepancies between this Annual and the U.N. Yearbook. None of the discrepancies were big enough to affect the Index of Colonial Trade, when calculated to one decimal place.

68. By an agreement on 30th December 1969 between South Africa and the I.M.F., South Africa could sell gold to the I.M.F. at $35 per

ounce to meet her foreign exchange requirements, whenever the London price of gold was at $35 or less per ounce: *Keesings Contemporary Archives 1970*, p. 23804.

69. This argument is basically a political one. If the state on which an embargo is being placed does have trade patterns that an economist could predict from the Theory of Comparative Advantage and in as much as the economic benefits are both substantial and specific to exports from that state, then it will be less likely that an embargo on exports can be successful.

70. The data in Figure 5.4 for Portugal includes the exports of its colonies, Angola, Mozambique, Cape Verde, Guinea, São Tomé and Principe. These gross figures for exports of the Portuguese Empire include trade within the Empire, for example from Angola to Mozambique. The net exports are $200–$400 million per annum less than the gross exports.

71. *Loc. cit. supra* in note 61, Annex VI.

72. In Table 5.5, the 104 U.N. members in 1961 were reduced by the exclusion of Byelorussia, Ukraine, South Africa and the new states Sierra Leone and Tanganyika. The 115 U.N. members in 1964 were reduced by the exclusion of Byelorussia, Ukraine, South Africa, Portugal and the new states Malawi, Malta and Zambia. The 127 U.N. members in 1970 were reduced by the exclusion of Byelorussia, Ukraine, South Africa, Portugal, the new state Fiji, and Cambodia, because of its change in regime.

73. No significance whatsoever should be attached to Haiti being coded as a non-trader. There was no data for 1970 for Haiti in the U.N. *Yearbook of International Trade Statistics 1970–71* and the coding was based on the author's assessment of the most likely figure.

74. 'Southern African Customs Union Agreement', *Standard Bank Review*, July 1970.

75. *World Bank Atlas* (seventh edition, International Bank for Reconstruction and Development, Washington D.C., 1972).

76. Even this Index is only interval level, if the assumption is made that trade with Rhodesia, South Africa, Portugal and its colonies was all of the same importance.

77. The number of cases drops to 98 in 1970 with the exclusion of Cambodia, because of the change in regime. When Cambodia is also excluded for 1961 and 1964, the variation explained is 25·8% and 17·7% respectively. The categories 'Non-Aligned' and 'Non-Bloc' refer respectively to the Belgrade, Cairo and Lusaka attenders/non-attenders. Use of the Belgrade Non-Aligned classification on the 1964 data gave a similar figure of 17·4% variation explained.

78. In addition to the six states excluded from Table 5.5 for 1970, Botswana and Lesotho were excluded at this point because the level of their trade with South Africa is not accurately known.

79. The indices were constructed from raw data in *Digest of Statistics No. 169, Series T No. 31, Traffic 1961–71* (International Civil Aviation Organisation, Montreal), pp. 116–37, for the World Total, which includes both IATA members and non-members, except the Soviet Union and China; and p. 372 for South African Airways.

80. *ABC Shipping Guide* (Skinner and Co. Ltd., London): No. 92, November/December 1961; No. 110, November/December 1964 and No. 179, December 1970.

81. From 8th April 1975 South African Airways decided of their own accord to discontinue their use of Luanda Airport, but it is believed that S.A.A. still overflies Angola: *Keesings Contemporary Archives 1975*, p. 27107.

82. The *Yearbook of International Trade Statistics 1968*, p. 747, under South Africa's 'Trade by Principal Countries . . .' gives the following figures in millions of Rands:

	1964	1965	1966	1967	1968
Ships stores and bunkers	16·27	18·66	18·95	46·12	65·67
of which bunker oil	11·54	14·10	13·68	—	—

    Substracting the second line from the first and converting from Rands to Pounds gives a net income from bunkering in 1964 of £2·4m; in 1965 of £2·3m and 1966 of £2·6m. Assuming a net income of about 25% of the gross income gives a figure of £8·2m for 1968.

83. The data is taken from *The Europa Yearbooks* for each of the respective years and applies to the situation in January of each year. In Chapter 4 an Index of Diplomatic Alignment was not constructed for 1961 because the data was not detailed enough in the early 1960s. This applied particularly to diplomatic exchanges with the two Vietnams and the two Koreas. The same limitation did not apply to exchanges with Portugal and South Africa.

84. Thus from 1962 the two Scandinavian states *outside* the Western Bloc did maintain ambassadorial relations with South Africa, but the three Scandinavian states *within* the Western Bloc did not do so. There is no apparent reason for this anomaly.

85. In Morocco's case the concern over the future of the Spanish Sahara may have been the indirect reason for maintaining relations with Portugal.

86. Israel could not have had anti-colonial motives for refraining from links with Portugal considering that she sent an Ambassador to South Africa during the whole period.

87. At this point the concern is with identifying differences between the Non-Aligned and the Latin American and Non-Bloc states. If the Non-Aligned are to be identified among all states then anti-colonialism is not a sufficient classifier. One variable from the East-West dimension of behaviour, that is membership of the multilateral military alliances, must also be used. This separates out on the one hand the strongly anti-colonial communist states and on the other hand the Western Bloc, Asian, states that have more recently become anti-colonialist.

88. Malawi has had an irregular pattern of attendance at some of the lower level Non-Aligned meetings. She was represented in 1969 at Belgrade, in 1970 at Dar es Salaam and in 1972 at Georgetown, but not at the 1970, 1973 or 1976 summits.

CHAPTER SIX

An Overall Portrait of the Non-Aligned

The object of this study was to identify what political ideas have been put forward under the name of non-alignment; to develop quantitative indicators of political behaviour that are relevant to these ideas; and to see whether or not the states that engage in the diplomacy of the Non-Aligned movement could be identified as having had distinct patterns of behaviour. Over the decade from 1961 to 1970, there were marked changes both in the political ideas expressed and in international behaviour. So far each of the indicators has been examined separately in turn. Now we will consider how the various forms of behaviour relate to each other and tentatively consider what theoretical explanations there may be of the results.[1]

East-West relations as a single dimension of foreign policy
The correlations between the three measures, from Chapter 4, of alignment in East-West disputes are given below.[2]

All the correlations are at least moderately high and remain so even for 1970. In Chapter 4 we saw that, contrary to any expectation that Cold-War conflicts had eased off by the end of the decade, the average variation in U.N. voting and in diplomatic exchanges with the divided states had increased. The high correlations between these two variables, both in 1964 at $r = 0.77$ and in 1970 at $r = 0.88$, show that the two forms of behaviour went closely together. Knowledge of how a state voted in the U.N. could give a good prediction of its diplomatic alignment and vice versa. This demonstrates that the two indicators refer to a single dimension of consistent foreign policy behaviour. The Index of Military Alignment also fitted into a common pattern with these two political variables, but the fact that some of the correlations with Military Alignment were lower indicates relatively less consistency

TABLE 6.1
CORRELATION OF INDICATORS OF EAST-WEST ALIGNMENT

		E-W votes in the U.N.	Diplomatic Alignment	Military Alignment
Data for 1961	E-W Votes in the U.N.	—		
	Diplomatic Alignment	. . .	—	
	Military Alignment	0·73	. . .	—
Data for 1964	E-W Votes in the U.N.	—		
	Diplomatic Alignment	0·77	—	
	Military Alignment	0·60	0·68	—
Data for 1970	E-W Votes in the U.N.	—		
	Diplomatic Alignment	0·88	—	
	Military Alignment	0·54	0·62	—

. . . Indicates data not available

for this variable. The absence of a drop across time in the correlations between voting and Diplomatic Alignment indicates that not only did the Cold-War divisions continue, but also behaviour remained generally in accordance with a consistent foreign policy on these issues throughout the decade. (It is one of the properties of the correlation statistic that, if there had been any tendency for states to move towards a middle position on one but not on both of a pair of variables, then the correlation would have dropped noticeably.[3]) However, the drop in the correlation between voting and Military Alignment from 0·73 to 0·60 to 0·54 suggests that competition in the supply of arms to the Third World countries did decline and became less directly related to the political alignments.

To say that the correlations show overall a consistent pattern of behaviour is not to deny for individual states there were many changes in U.N. voting, diplomatic exchanges and arms supplies. During the 1960s there was a substantial number of coups in the Third World countries, often resulting in a change of direction for the country's foreign policy. In other cases a government gradually stepped up its degree of commitment to the East or the West. The net effect of the changes was to increase the political and diplomatic alignment in the system. But such changes as occurred usually took place simultaneously in the U.N. voting and in the diplomatic exchanges, with the result that policy still remained consistent in the two areas. Although military alignment tended to follow suit, it was also subject to economic and strategic constraints rather than being solely a reflection of foreign policy.

Anti-colonialism as a single dimension of foreign policy

Four areas of activity involving relations with the colonial powers were examined in Chapter 5 and it can be seen from the correlations in Table 6.2, that these were not quite so closely associated with each other.[4] Once again it is U.N. voting and the exchange of diplomats that were most likely to go together, with $r = -0.61$ for 1961, $r = -0.68$ for 1964 and $r = -0.73$ for 1970. The negative correlation simply indicates an inverse relationship, because of the way the indicators were constructed. A higher percentage of anti-colonial voting in the General Assembly went with a lower level of diplomatic exchanges with South Africa and Portugal. The correlation for each year between the two was moderately high but it was less than the corresponding correlations between diplomacy and U.N. voting on East-West issues.

The remaining correlations between variables involving behaviour towards the colonial powers are markedly lower. The boycott of colonial trade and the denial of communications facilities for South Africa's ships and planes had only a medium link to the official foreign policy for most states. In the case of colonial trade the correlations of -0.28 and 0.27 respectively with U.N. voting and with diplomacy in 1970 indicates that, even after a decade, trade policy only had tenuous links with other aspects of foreign policy. On the other hand, policy on air and sea communications in each year went more closely with voting and diplomacy than did trade. Furthermore, these correlations show the communications boycott by the more anti-colonial countries coming into effect after 1961. The link between communications and voting increases from -0.36 to -0.46 to -0.55 and that between communications and diplomacy from 0.45 to 0.57 to 0.61. The increases show that there was a moderate success in making the issue of communications with South Africa a matter that had to be consistent with foreign policy, even if there was no progress along the same lines on colonial trade. U.N. anti-colonial voting, diplomatic exchanges with South Africa and Portugal and transport communications with South Africa had become for most states a single dimension of consistent foreign policy behaviour.

TABLE 6.2   CORRELATIONS OF INDICATORS
OF POLICY TOWARDS COLONIALISM

1961 Data

Anti-colonial U.N. votes	—			
Colonial Diplomacy	−0·61	—		
Colonial Trade	−0·20	0·29	—	
Sea or air Communication	−0·36	0·45	0·35	—

1964 Data

Anti-colonial U.N. votes	—			
Colonial Diplomacy	−0·68	—		
Colonial Trade	−0·30	0·39	—	
Sea or air Communication	−0·46	0·57	0·32	—

1970 Data

Anti-colonial U.N. votes	—			
Colonial Diplomacy	−0·73	—		
Colonial Trade	−0·28	0·27	—	
Sea or air Communication	−0·55	0·61	0·43	—

Delegation sending as a separate political dimension

In Chapter 2 we considered the size of delegations to the United   S*
Nations General Assembly as a measure of activism and found that,
after allowing for their small size, the Non-Aligned did tend to send
more delegates than other states. This was particularly evident in
1961 but not so markedly in 1964 and 1970. The activism turns out to
be a phenomenon that was completely independent of the two
foreign policy dimensions that we have just examined. The size of
the U.N. delegation for each year gave a correlation with the
East-West voting or the Diplomatic Alignment for the corresponding year of less than 0·1. Even when allowance is made for the size
of each country (by taking a partial correlation controlling for the
logarithm of their contribution to the U.N. Regular Budget), the
correlations are still less than 0·2, indicating that there was no
relationship between delegation size and East-West alignments.

The correlation of delegation sending with Military Alignment or   S*
Colonial trade in each year is below 0·3; with anti-colonial voting or
communications with South Africa is a little higher; and with the
Index of Colonial Diplomacy reaches 0·5. For each of these
variables the Western Bloc countries were all at one end of the
spectrum. The members of the Western Bloc were also a majority of
the larger countries sending the larger sized delegations. This is why
there are some medium level correlations. All of the partial cor-

relations have a magnitude of less than 0·2, when allowance is made for a country's economic size. (If partial correlations are taken of the results in Tables 6·1 and 6·2, they do not diminish in the same way). Delegation sending was not related in any direct way to alignment with the East or the West, nor was it related to the degree of anti-colonialism. It was a separate dimension of behaviour.

The relationship between the East-West dimension and the anti-colonial dimension

The figures in Table 6.3 show to what extent the two main issue areas were connected. The most striking finding is that in 1961 a public commitment to anti-colonialism, that is voting in the United Nations, went very closely with alignment on East-West issues at the U.N. The existence of this high correlation of 0·84 is illustrated by the similarity of the ordering of the states in the cluster-blocs shown in Figures 4·9 and 5·1. The Soviet Union's attempt to win support for its own interests, by identifying with the anti-colonial struggle, appeared at first to be meeting with some success, though even in 1961 the anti-colonial coalition was larger than the bloc that supported the Soviet Union on East-West issues. However, the situation did not last. A second striking feature of Table 6·3 is the drop in this high correlation between anti-colonial and East-West voting from 0·84 in 1961 to a moderately high level of 0·66 in 1964 to a medium level of 0·37 in 1970, indicating that only a weak relationship between the two still existed. This means that the breakdown of the Non-Aligned as a coherent voting bloc on East-West issues, described in Chapter 4, and the mobilisation of a massive anti-colonial majority described in Chapter 5, occurred as separate processes that brought about a differentiation between the two issues.[5]

A slightly different pattern occurred for the relationship between Military Alignment and anti-colonial voting. It was at a high level in 1961 with a correlation of 0·75 and dropped thereafter, but in this case the drop did not start in 1964 and a moderately high correlation of 0·60 was maintained in 1970. The drop was not so steep because there was little change at the extremes of the Military Alignment scale and hence there were no Afro-Asian countries in 1970 showing a combination (as they did on the previous pair of variables), of maximum Western alignment with maximum anti-colonialism. There was the drop caused by the broadening of the anti-colonial majority, but there was not in addition very much deviation from military non-alignment.

TABLE 6.3   CORRELATIONS BETWEEN VARIABLES ON THE EAST-WEST DIMENSION AND VARIABLES ON THE ANTI-COLONIAL DIMENSION

Data for 1961

	East-West U.N. Votes	Diplomatic Alignment	Military Alignment
Anti-colonial U.N. votes	0·84	. . .	0·75
Colonial Diplomacy	–0·36	. . .	–0·51
Colonial Trade	–0·18	. . .	–0·36
South African Sea or Air Communication	–0·22	. . .	–0·42

Data for 1964

	East-West U.N. votes	Diplomatic Alignment	Military Alignment
Anti-colonial U.N. votes	0·66	0·56	0·73
Colonial Diplomacy	–0·36	–0·35	–0·56
Colonial Trade	–0·08	–0·16	–0·38
South African Sea or Air Communication	–0·20	–0·25	–0·50

Data for 1970

	East-West U.N. votes	Diplomatic Alignment	Military Alignment
Anti-colonial U.N. votes	0·37	0·38	0·60
Colonial Diplomacy	–0·39	–0·40	–0·59
Colonial Trade	–0·13	–0·06	–0·27
South African Sea or Air Communication	–0·26	–0·27	–0·45

. . . Indicates data not available.

Unfortunately it was not possible to construct an Index of Diplomatic Alignment with data for 1961 that was comparable to that for 1964 and 1970. As we saw both in Chapter 4 and from the correlations in Table 6.1, behaviour on East-West voting and on Diplomatic Alignment was closely related. In the data that is available for 1964 and 1970, the two variables are also related to anti-colonial voting at the same levels. It is a reasonable assumption that in 1961 the exchange of diplomats with the states divided by the Cold War was highly correlated with anti-colonial voting and that this correlation dropped from 1961 through to 1970 in parallel with the drop in the correlation between the voting on the two issue areas. Thus all three indicators of behaviour in East-West relations show a decline in their association with U.N. voting on anti-colonial issues.

Colonial Diplomacy is in each year less closely associated with each of the indicators of East-West behaviour. However, in 1961 three states were out of line in their diplomacy. Czechoslovakia sent an Ambassador to South Africa, Cuba exchanged Ambassadors with Portugal and the U.A.R. had full relations with both South Africa and Portugal. This tended to depress the correlations for 1961 with the Index of Colonial Diplomacy. On the other hand in 1970 several Latin American states had increased their diplomatic activity, particularly with Portugal. This tended to increase the correlations for 1970 with the Index of Colonial Diplomacy. The net effect is that colonial diplomacy has correlated with East-West voting and diplomatic alignment at an intermediate level in each year and has not changed the strength of the relationship. The process over the decade was not the same, but the end result in 1970 was the same. Colonial Diplomacy like anti-colonial voting has intermediate correlations with both East-West voting and East-West diplomacy thus indicating a weak relationship in 1970 between the two dimensions.

The two indicators of foreign policy towards the colonial powers that involve economic factors have low correlations with the politics of East-West disputes, indicating that even in 1961 there was no relationship across these aspects of the main dimensions of policy. There are only correlations in the range -0.06 to -0.27, those between colonial trade and East-West voting and diplomatic alignment being lower in value than the corresponding correlations with South Africa's communications.

Colonial trade, colonial diplomacy and communications with South Africa all have higher correlations in each year with Military Alignment than they do with the two measures of political East-West alignment. This might suggest that Military Alignment is more closely related, except that there is a cross-cutting factor. These three measures of activity towards the colonial powers and Military Alignment itself are affected by a group of the smaller countries having a zero value on the four variables. For some of the small countries the situation arises because their lack of resources makes them inactive rather than because they have taken positive foreign policy decisions.[6] Countries such as El Salvador or Nicaragua in 1961 might fall into this category. But the same cannot be said for Afghanistan or Guinea, which although they are small states are more likely to be boycotting the colonial powers as a matter of principle. Thus it is not possible to say by how much the correlations between Military Alignment and the other three variables have been artifically inflated by the inactivity of some states on all the variables.

The overall picture drawn from Tables 6.1 to 6.3 together is that a dimension of Cold-War behaviour encompassing U.N. voting, diplomacy and Military Alignment continued in existence throughout the decade. There was also a dimension of anti-colonial behaviour, which was not as coherent, encompassing U.N. voting and diplomacy. South Africa's communications became increasingly related to this second dimension but trade remained only weakly associated. In 1961 the Cold War and the anti-colonial dimension were highly related within the United Nations, but less so outside. By 1970 the two dimensions were weakly related in the United Nations and in diplomacy and appeared not to be related at all on their more peripheral variables. The two areas of the international system that first concerned the Non-Aligned in 1961 had by the time of their third summit conference come to involve separate dimensions of behaviour.

Towards a theory of non-alignment

The question now arises whether there are any general explanations that bring together these results and suggest the processes by which a state may or may not join the Non-Aligned Movement or adopt non-aligned behaviour. There are two theoretical approaches that are relevant. Several neo-Marxist writers see most if not all of the Third World as being bound to the West by a complex network of links to maintain capitalist exploitation. It is argued that the extent of these links determines the extent to which each country is subject to Western political control. Alternatively, traditional international relations theory would postulate each state as having a degree of alignment with the West that depended on the government's perception of what best served that state's interests. The two approaches are not in automatic contradiction to each other on the predictions they make about particular states. But there is the implicit fundamental difference between Marxists and non-Marxists, in all areas of political science, on the extent to which there can be any autonomy from economic influences for political decision-making. To attempt to tackle these questions adequately would on its own be a major study, but it is possible to take a preliminary look at some of the evidence.

The Neo-Marxist approach

Four writers, Nkrumah, Woddis, Frank and Barratt-Brown will be considered as representative of the neo-Marxist approach.

Nkrumah's book, *Neo-Colonialism: The Last Stage of Imperialism*,[7] examines the problems of African development through an extension of Marxist ideas and the book's title deliberately echoes Lenin's *Imperialism: The Highest Stage of Capitalism*. Its argument is that the existence of colonialism explains the failure of Marx's prediction of revolution in the Western developed capitalist societies. The increasing immiserisation of the working class has not occurred, because increased profits were sought in the colonies. After the Second World War it was possible to buy off the workers by the provision of a Welfare State.

The developed countries succeeded in exporting their internal problem and transferring the conflict between rich and poor from the national to the international stage.[8]

Change within the colonies made it necessary to relinquish imperial control, but there was still the need for 'colonial earnings . . . to finance the Welfare State',[9] so a new system of neo-colonialism was necessary to keep up the economic exploitation.

The essence of neo-colonialism is that the state which is subject to it is, in theory, independent and has all the outward trappings of international sovereignty. In reality its economic system and thus its political policy is directed from outside.[10]

A complex network of finance capital and inter-locking directorships ensures the control of banks and companies operating in the Third World. Primary resources are extracted at low prices, but their processing has to be confined to the capitalist world. Foreign aid is dressed up in altruistic terms, but is the vehicle both for the control of decisions on economic policy and for the repatriation of profits. Organisations such as Moral Re-Armament, the Peace Corps and the United States Information Agency provide instruments of 'psychological warfare',[11] so that the economic exploitation can be made politically acceptable.

The dilemma for Nkrumah was that he could not accept that the whole of the Third World must be characterised as neo-colonial. The book was written while Nkrumah was still President of Ghana and there was a clear wish to make an exception for Ghana. He could see that on many objective indicators Ghana was not such an exception,

The issue is not what return the foreign investor receives on his investments. He may, in fact, do better for himself if he invests in a non-aligned country than if he invests in a neo-colonial one. The question is one of power. A state in the grip of neo-colonialism is not master of its own destiny.[12]

The analysis completely lacks an explanation of why some states do and some do not remain master of their own destiny. Later on Nkrumah appears to be denying that Third World states can gain enough power to have any real independence.

All the profits of neo-colonialism can be secured if, in any given area, a reasonable proportion of the States have a neo-colonialist system. It is not necessary that they *all* should have one.[13]

Economic exploitation will occur, 'whether they are under neo-colonialist control or not'.[14] Furthermore a developing country is subject to social pressures which can produce revolts

and therefore neo-colonialist nations have a ready-made weapon with which they can threaten their opponents if they appear successfully to be challenging the system.[15]

It would appear that for Nkrumah 'the policy of non-alignment as practised at present by many of the countries attempting to escape from neo-colonialism'[16] depends on political determination rather than a secure economic base and that in a totally un-Marxist manner he was asserting the primacy of political decision-making. The same un-Marxist approach is seen in Nkrumah's conclusion,

African unity . . . would destroy neo-colonialism in Africa. . . . Nevertheless, African unity is something which is within the grasp of the African people.[17]

Without further elaboration these ideas do not offer any direct hypotheses to discriminate the processes by which different states have shown varying degrees of non-aligned behaviour.

Woddis, in *An Introduction to Neo-Colonialism*,[18] offers a general analysis that is comparable to Nkrumah's, but differs in several important ways. Woddis sees colonialism at the end of the 19th century as the product of monopoly capitalism seeking wider markets and higher profits from cheap land and labour, but does not discuss either the concept of immiserisation or the rise of the Welfare State. While Nkrumah attributes the end of colonialism to political change within the colonies,[19] Woddis adds two other factors.

A coming together of three main political forces on the international scene – the socialist countries [with communist governments], the national liberation movements themselves, and the working class, democratic and peace movements in the metropolitan countries – . . . has spelt the doom of the system of direct colonial rule.[20]

The differences in emphasis between the two writers becomes important when Woddis defines the nature of neo-colonialism.

The old system of colonial rule was, in essence, an alliance between external imperialism and local pre-capitalist [feudal] forces . . . neo-colonialism generally represents a new alliance, one between external imperialism and sections of the local bourgeoisie and petty-bourgeoisie.[21]

This definition allows us to have a criterion, that Nkrumah does not provide, for distinguishing Third World states that are free to decide

either to take the capitalist path, or to strike out along the non-capitalist path in the direction of socialism.[22]

The extent to which there is a local basis for a capitalist class will determine the extent to which neo-colonial control is possible.

The existence of the communist states and of strong working-class movements in the Western capitalist states enables Woddis to accept the possibility that some Third World countries may start to develop socialism without passing through a capitalist stage.

Movements for national independence can no longer be confined within the limits of ordinary bourgeois democracy as in the nineteenth century, for these movements today are anti-imperialist movements taking place at a time of mounting socialist ascendancy in the world.[23]

Countries such as Burma, Cuba, Congo (Brazzaville) and the U.A.R. have 'seen the demise of neo-colonialist governments . . . overthrown by revolutionary forces',[24] while in other countries such as Guinea, Mali and Tanzania, 'where both feudalism and capitalism were exceptionally weak', 'the transition from neo-colonialism to liberation . . . will take place as a result of the slow maturing of events'.[25]

For Woddis, 'there are four main fields in which neo-colonialist activities are expressed — political, ideological, military and economic'[26] and it is clear that he means each field to encompass both domestic and international activities.[27] Thus Woddis, unlike Nkrumah, does lead us to suppose that from the domestic economic structure of a state we can predict whether or not it will adopt an anti-Western foreign policy.

Within the overall Marxist framework there is considerable room for disagreement on the nature of neo-colonialism. Frank, writing mainly about Latin America, maintains that there has been a process of 'dependent underdevelopment' with the Third World economies being satellites of the metropolitan-dominated, world-wide capitalist system.[28]

The world capitalist system . . . (has) incorporated and underdeveloped even the farthest outpost of 'traditional' society and no longer leave(s) any room for classical national or modern state-capitalist development independent of imperialism.[29]

Barratt-Brown in arguing against Frank is insistent that there has been some industrial development in the underdeveloped countries.[30] Like Woddis, Barratt-Brown sees the presence of an indigenous bourgeoisie as one of the crucial differences between colonialism and neo-colonialism. While Woddis does not discuss the issue of whether local capitalists are dependent upon or to some extent independent of the metropolitan countries, the logic of his argument is in opposition to Frank's.[31] Barratt-Brown's view of neo-colonialism is more complex than that of either Woddis or Frank.

What is emerging in the underdeveloped countries is a form of dualism . . . between a high profit/high wage international oligopolist capitalist sector and a low profit/low wage competitive local capitalist sector.[32]

Barratt-Brown borrows from Mao Tse-tung the concept of a comprador class, within the bourgeoisie, which is based on merchant rather than industrial capital and is engaged in buying or selling on behalf of a foreign industrial capitalist.[33] The political result is that

in the governments that have succeeded the colonial powers, three elements tend to appear in the successor ruling classes – native capitalists, feudal landlords and the comprador agents of capital. . . .[34]

Conflict with the Western powers may arise because 'even ruling elites in underdeveloped nation states may be forced to stand up to the transnational corporations'[35] or because of pressures when 'some development does take place; and in the process not only is there born an industrial working class . . . but also a frustrated rural peasantry'.[36] Barratt-Brown makes very few references to foreign policy issues, but it would not be inconsistent with his work to see foreign policy as reflecting the class interests of the ruling elites.[37]

The four writers examined in brief above are just among the more prominent in a large body of literature. Further consideration of other authors would revolve around the themes already discussed. While the neo-Marxists cannot be ignored, it is difficult to use their work to make predictions about the foreign policy of Third World states. In the first place this is not a subject to which they address themselves with any significant degree of concern. Secondly, as there are important differences among the writers, it is not obvious what predictions should be made. Therefore the author offers the following set of propositions, as being consistent with the basic approach shown by the different versions of the concept of neo-colonialism and extending its application to explain foreign policy behaviour: (a) neo-colonial control exists in order to further the economic interests of the Western, developed capitalist states; (b) these economic interests are served by a transfer of resources to the West, through the international banks, multi-national companies, interest on foreign aid and unequal trading relationships, based on high priced manufactured goods being exchanged for low priced primary products; (c) Western economic and political power, in alliance with whatever domestic interests there may be that benefit from the system, will be used to maintain governments that support the capitalist system, and (d) in order to maintain ideological consistency, governments under neo-colonial control will have a pro-Western foreign policy.

The hypotheses, that may be drawn from this set of propositions, need not depend upon us resolving the arguments about the class structure of the Third World countries. Whatever are the precise political processes at work, the combination of (b) and (d) imply that the greater the transfer of resources to the West the more a state will align itself with the West in its foreign policy. Unfortunately, data on banking and the operations of multi-national companies has not yet been brought together, so that comparisons aross many countries are not possible. However, data on aid and trade is available.

Aid and trade as predictors of foreign policy

Detailed information on the flows of foreign aid is given in the publications of the Development Assistance Committee of the Organisation for Economic Co-operation and Development.[38] Sixteen donor countries are members of the D.A.C. and data is given on their net bilateral official disbursements to all the other countries in the world outside the Eastern Bloc.[39] The disbursements of all the donors may be summed to give a figure for the volume of Western Aid to each recipient. In this context 'Western' does not have exactly the same meaning as elsewhere in this study, because the donors include the European neutrals and exclude Western Bloc states from Asia and southern Europe, which are recipients of Western Aid. In order to clarify the situation this data is presented with the groups labelled in a slightly different manner from usual in Table 6.4. In addition, to reduce some of the random effects of annual fluctuations in aid disbursements, the figures have been calculated as averages for two-year periods.

The results show that the Non-Aligned were not more free from aid ties than the other states. The exact opposite of what one would expect from neo-colonial theory was true. The Non-Aligned received the lion's share of Western Aid to independent states. In 1961–62 they received 41%, in 1963–64 59% and in 1969–70 55%.

TABLE 6.4   TOTAL VOLUME OF WESTERN AID p.a. IN $ MILLIONS

	1960–61	*1963–64*	*1969–70*
Spain, Greece, Turkey	326·5	230·1	263·8
Western Bloc Asians	623·5	749·1	745·2
Latin Americans	476·1	562·7	596·1
Non-Bloc Afro-Asians	538·5*	190·1	234·1
India	678·0	1008·2	773·5
Other Non-Aligned	711·4*	1475·3	1464·8
Eastern Bloc	0	0	0
All recipients	3354·0	4215·6	4077·6

* The figures for Guinea and Mali in 1960–61 are included with the Non-Bloc rather than the Non-Aligned as they could not be separated from the other Sub-Saharan, ex-French colonies.

Even if one excludes India, which received substantially more aid than any other country, the other Non-Aligned were far ahead of any of the groups which were more closely identified with the West. Various objections to the use of these gross totals will be considered below, but it must be remembered that from the point of view of the aid donors it is the gross totals that are important. It is a remarkable finding that in the middle and late 1960s more development aid went to the Non-Aligned than to southern Europe, military allies in Asia and the Latin Americans put together.[40]

TABLE 6.5   AVERAGE VOLUME OF WESTERN AID PER COUNTRY, p.a., in $ millions

	1960–61	*1963–64*	*1969–70*
Spain, Greece, Turkey	108·8	76·7	87·9
Western Bloc Asians	103·9	124·9	124·2
Latin Americans	25·1	29·6	31·4
Non-Bloc Afro-Asians	23·4*	19·0	14·6
India	678·0	1008·2	733·5
Other Non-Aligned	32·3*	32·8	29·5
All recipients	45·3	50·2	42·5

* See note to Table 6.4.

When allowance is made for the different number of countries in the groups by taking the average volume of aid for each country, the results appear more favourable to the neo-colonial theory. The southern Europeans and the Asian allies did on average receive much more aid than all the others except India. However, the

Non-Aligned still on average received more than would be expected when compared with the Latin Americans or the Non-Bloc states. But political significance cannot be readily attributed to these figures. If the volume of aid is to be taken as an indicator either of exploitation or of control, it must be further standardised by relating it to the G.N.P. of the receiving country.

TABLE 6.6
WESTERN AID PER COUNTRY, p.a., AS A PROPORTION OF G.N.P.
Averages not weighted by the size of the G.N.P.

	1960–61*	1963–64	1969–70
Spain, Greece, Turkey	(1·5%)	1·2%	0·9%
Western Bloc Asians	(2·6%)	2·5%	1·4%
Latin Americans	(1·5%)	1·9%	1·2%
Non-Bloc Afro-Asians	(7·2%)	4·5%	3·3%
Non-Aligned	(2·7%)	5·3%	3·4%
All recipients	(3·6%)	4·1%	2·8%

* The first column is not directly comparable to the next two.

D*   When the aid figures are calculated as a percentage of the G.N.P., India no longer stands out as a special case and has been included with the Non-Aligned again. The percentages for 1960–61 are slightly deflated, because it was not possible to obtain comprehensive G.N.P. data for 1961 and data for 1963 was used instead. For almost all countries the difference between the two years would not be large and the figures still give a guide for making comparisons.[41]

The averages in Table 6.6 only come near to supporting the theory of neo-colonialism with the data for 1960–61. Then the Non-Bloc Afro-Asians were receiving twice as high a proportion of aid as were the Non-Aligned. But this position was not maintained in subsequent years and the three groups that are closer to the West were all out of line. They received proportionally less not more aid than the Non-Aligned. Perhaps the most striking challenge to the neo-colonial theory was the difference between the Latin Americans and the Non-Aligned. It may be objected that the comparison is not a valid one because the figures are based on *net* official flows. As the Latin Americans had been independent for a longer time, they would have been paying back relatively more on previous loans than would the new states. The data for gross official aid is not available for earlier years. For 1969–70 the gross aid to the Latin Americans was 1·5% of their G.N.P. on average, which was still much less than half the net aid to the Non-Aligned, so the objection does not stand. Even when gross official aid, gross private export credits and net private long-term capital are added together the average proportion for the Latin Americans was only just above the net official aid to the Non-Aligned. The data does not support the idea that membership of the named groups was a determinant of the amount of Western Aid that a country receives. And vice versa, it cannot be Western influence exercised through aid that determined whether or not a country attended the Non-Aligned conferences.

The various problems over the different types of aid do not arise with data on trade. Definitions are reasonably standard and almost all countries provide details of the volume of trade with each of their main trading partners for the United Nations' Yearbooks of International Trade Statistics. In addition to there being some missing data, a few countries have to be excluded, because their data was not comparable. For example, the Kuwaiti trade figures have little use as they excluded petroleum products and the Rwandan data was incomplete with the failure to record the final destination of exports that used the transit port of Mombassa.[42]

Writers on neo-colonialism describe exploitation through trade as involving both low price exports of primary produce from the Third World to the West and the imports of high price manufactures from the West. Because our current interest is in the extent to which the West's dominance of trade leads to an impact on political decisions, it seemed more appropriate to use the export data on its own. A small state has some freedom of manoeuvre on where to purchase its imports, but usually will not want to lose any markets for its exports.

There is no obvious reference for deciding which countries should be regarded as the beneficiaries of the neo-colonial system. The original members of the European Economic Community, the United Kingdom and the United States would seem strong candidates and are mentioned frequently in the literature. As these eight countries take between them more than 40% of the world's exports, it seems sufficient to consider them for an indicator of trade with the West.

Taylor and Hudson advocate that, when trade concentration is being used as an index of external dependence, an index devised by Hirschman is preferable.[43] This means that instead of just taking the total exports to the West we should also take into account the extent that the exports were dispersed among the eight Western countries. Unless the capitalists are always able to work together in harmony in their relations with the Third World, it seems in accord with political reality to regard a country that sent 10% of its exports

D*

D*

to each of eight other countries as having been in a far less dependent position than another country that sent 80% of its exports to just one of the Western traders. For our purposes, to make an Index of Trade Concentration with the West, Hirschman's index becomes:

$$C = \text{Sum} \left\{ \frac{\text{Exports to each Western Trader}}{\text{Total of all Exports to World}} \right\}^2 = \sum_1^7 p_i^2$$

The summation occurs for seven rather than eight Western trading partners, because in all trading matters Belgium and Luxembourg are regarded as a single unit. The index figures are finally multiplied by one hundred. They are then comparable to the figures for the percentage of the exports that go to the West, with the percentage being weighted down by the amount of dispersion. As with the aid data, figures for two years have been taken, to iron out some of the annual fluctuations.

TABLE 6.7
AVERAGE INDEX OF TRADE CONCENTRATION WITH THE WEST
Averages not weighted by the volume of trade

	1960–61	1963–64	1969–70
Western Bloc	27·8%	27·6%	29·5%
Latin America	50·2%	47·0%	42·1%
Non-Bloc	52·2%	41·6%	37·0%
Non-Aligned	28·7%	35·9%	34·8%
Eastern Bloc	5·5%	5·9%	8·2%
All countries	36·1%	34·7%	33·8%

Amongst the Third World countries, the results given in Table 6.7 are fully compatible with neo-colonial theory. The Non-Aligned as a group were markedly less dependent upon the West than the Latin Americans or the Non-Bloc states. The biggest differences between the groups occurred in 1960–61, when the Non-Aligned were a smaller more exclusive radical grouping. The expansion of the Non-Aligned at the 1964 Cairo Conference brought with it an increase in the group's average trade concentration, but at the same time the trade concentration of the Latin Americans and the Non-Bloc states was dropping, so that by 1970 the three groups were closer together.

That the Western Bloc states should have had low trade with the West is not as odd as it appears at first sight. In order for them to have dominated trade with the Third World, they must have had

more trade with the Third World than do those countries themselves. Thus the U.K. and America were among the very lowest
traders with the West. However, when the Asian Western Bloc
states are considered on their own, their trade concentration was
not any higher than that of the other Western Bloc states. This
remains an anomaly that was out of line with the predictions of
neo-colonial theory.

While the evidence suggests that it was highly unlikely that
Western Aid had an impact on whether or not a small state adopted
non-alignment, the possibility of control through Western
domination of trade merits further investigation. So far the
economic indicators have only been considered in relation to the
analytical groups of states. This ignores both variation within the
groups and the fact that the groups might be of little importance.
The relationship between the economic indicators and the political
indicators developed earlier must now be examined.

An immediate challenge is raised by the earlier finding from
Table 6.3 that East-West alignment and the response to current
colonial problems after 1961 came to represent different
dimensions of behaviour. Under the neo-colonial hypothesis there
is no simple explanation of how this divergence could have come
about. No such phenomenon as a Western-aligned, anti-colonial
state should exist, yet by 1970 this was how several states behaved.
If economic control forced a state to support the West on Cold-War
issues, the same control would have produced support for the West
on colonial issues.[44]

The results in Table 6·8 show little evidence that there could have
been any general pattern of political processes whereby Western
economic domination was a determinant of the foreign policy of
small states. For each year, less than half of the correlations are in
the direction predicted by neo-colonial theory. For example, if the
volume of Western bilateral official aid was a determinant of U.N.
voting on East-West issues, then as the volume of aid went up,
voting agreement with the Soviet Union should have gone down,
producing a negative correlation in the table. In fact these variables
show a very low positive correlation each year, which was the
opposite to what was predicted.

Any confusing effects that might arise because both the main
Western Bloc states and the Eastern Bloc states have a zero score on
the aid indicators, are not present in these results. The correlations
were all calculated for just those states that were aid recipients. This
also means any effect due to the anomaly of some of the main
Western Bloc states having been low traders with the West has been
eliminated by their exclusion.

S*

TABLE 6.8   CORRELATIONS BETWEEN THE ECONOMIC AND THE
POLITICAL INDICATORS

Data for 1961

	Volume of Aid	Aid as % of G.N.P.	Trade Index	
East-West U.N. Votes	0·02	0·14	**−0·39**	Negative
Diplomatic Alignment	. . .	. . .	. . .	Relationship
Military Alignment	**−0·35**	0·03	−0·02	Expected
Anti-colonial U.N. Votes	−0·01	0·26	**−0·37**	
Colonial Diplomacy	**0·48**	−0·27	−0·23	Positive
Colonial Trade	**0·31**	−0·03	−0·27	Relationship
South African Sea or Air Communication	0·04	−0·06	−0·11	Expected

. . . Indicates data not available.

Data for 1964

	Volume of Aid	Aid as % of G.N.P.	Trade Index	
East-West U.N. Votes	0·16	0·13	−0·25	Negative
Diplomatic Alignment	0·18	0·06	**−0·34**	Relationship
Military Alignment	−0·09	0·13	−0·06	Expected
Anti-colonial U.N. Votes	0·06	0·32	−0·14	
Colonial Diplomacy	0·28	−0·33	−0·16	Positive
Colonial Trade	0·16	−0·07	−0·21	Relationship
South African Sea or Air Communication	−0·00	−0·10	−0·06	Expected

Data for 1970

	Volume of Aid	Aid as % of G.N.P.	Trade Index	
East-West U.N. Votes	0·07	0·03	**−0·39**	Negative
Diplomatic Alignment	0·03	−0·03	**−0·36**	Relationship
Military Alignment	−0·15	0·10	0·06	Expected
Anti-colonial U.N. Votes	0·02	−0·05	−0·09	
Colonial Diplomacy	0·22	−0·29	−0·08	Positive
Colonial Trade	−0·01	0·00	0·05	Relationship
South African Sea or Air Communication	0·09	−0·10	0·05	Expected

The correlations that were not only in the predicted direction, but
also were large enough to merit some attention, at a value of more
than 0·3, have been emphasised in Table 6.8. In each case these
correlations in heavy type were only at an intermediate level, none

were greater than 0·5, indicating that there was only a weak relationship between the variables concerned. In 1961, the volume of Western aid received by each state was weakly related to their military alignment, their colonial diplomacy and their trade with South Africa (colonial trade), while trade concentration with the West was weakly related to voting on colonialism in the U.N. It must be assumed that none of these four relationships was of much political significance, because they all disappeared in 1964 and 1970.

There were, however, two relationships that might be affirmed from the results. In each year concentration of trade with the West correlated at a level of 0·25 or more with East-West voting in the U.N. and with East-West diplomacy. If there is any evidence in this data for the impact of neo-colonialism on foreign policy, then it operated through the medium of trading relationships, not through foreign aid, and it had a limited effect on East-West disputes, not on the problems of decolonisation.[45] The correlations, of course, do not prove that even these relationships were caused by trade concentration being a determinant of policy on East-West issues. It may be that those states which moved politically some way towards the East adopted and put into effect a policy of trade diversification. The two weak links were consistent with neo-colonial theory, but could be explained in other ways.

Non-alignment and the formation of alliances

A completely different theoretical approach is to deny that international politics is predominantly the product of economic forces. Many writers on international relations focus on the concept of national interest and see states as continually striving to increase their power.[46] As Morgenthau puts it, 'Statesmen think and act in terms of interest defined as power'.[47] However, it was John Burton, a trenchant critic of the power theorists, who was until recently the only scholar to have had a prime concern with seeking a general explanation of the phenomenon of non-alignment. Burton saw the Cold-War alliances as being the product of a system in which power was considered to be both desirable and useful. With the advent of nuclear weapons on the one hand and a large number of small, relatively powerless nations on the other hand, power processes must and are being replaced by communications processes, and conflicts can be resolved by mutual adjustment. Non-alignment was perceived as the most prominent manifestation of this changing basis to the international system.

The options of adjustment and the use of power are dramatically featured;

non-aligned States cannot rely upon power and must adjust, while the major States have a technical capacity of power sufficient not to have to accept the course of adjustment.[48]

Despite Burton's claim to be describing non-alignment 'as a model in the academic or comparative sense' rather than 'a model in the exemplary sense',[49] his description was much more of an ideal world rather than of the real world. Egypt, India and Indonesia are significant powers. They have long had armies bigger than Britain's and since Burton was writing each has initiated one or more local war. The other Non-Aligned countries may be small by comparison, but there are large differences in size between them, so that the use of power politics within the Third World is not automatically ruled out.

Burton offered some more relevant ideas in his chapter on 'The Development of Alignments':

Non-alignment as an accomplished fact can be explained only by taking into account also the strength and causes of alignment pressures.[50]

In the Cold War many countries are aligned with one or other Great Power as though they were directly involved with it in a common ideological struggle. However, their alliances have in many cases very little to do with the central conflict.[51]

Burton suggested three reasons why Third World states may have wished to join alliances. First, if they were engaged in local conflicts, alignment was a means of trying to enlist support. A good example was Pakistan joining CENTO and SEATO in order to seek Western support against India.[52] Secondly, unpopular governments which faced demands for social and political change were able to label this communist subversion and to seek foreign military assistance. Thailand and the Philippines were early examples.[53] Thirdly, rejection by one of the Great Powers may have led to alignment with the other side. Burton's example was of the United States pushing Cuba into alignment with the Soviet Union.[54] The isolation of Israel and South Africa from the other states in their region, leading to their alignment with the West, was a similar process.

For Burton the Non-Aligned were merely states that wished to maintain their independence and did not have defence or other interests that required foreign support.

The nonaligned nations do not face, or do not believe they face, threats to their security with which they themselves cannot deal.[55]

In the belief that power politics is becoming an anachronism, the early moralistic attacks by the Non-Aligned on the big powers were taken at their face value.[56] Burton also accepted the protestations of Non-Aligned leaders that they did not wish to form another bloc.[57]

Unlike Burton, Liska is one of the power theorists and he writes about alliances with an emphasis on military factors and the balance of power.

All association depends on the existence of identical interests . . . provisionally disparate interests of members must be at least compatible with each other.[58]

. . . the question arises: interests and gains (or liabilities) in what? We answer in terms of internal and international security, stability, and status of states and regimes.[59]

Despite the differences between Burton and Liska, their conclusions about the reasons for forming alliances are markedly similar to each other. Liska says

. . . conflicts are the primary determinants of alignments. Alliances are against, and only derivatively for, someone or something.[60]

A dominant conflict affects the global system of a given time in its entirety; but lesser conflicts are often more immediately significant in filling out the complete pattern of alignments.[61]

Like Burton, Liska also suggests that domestic factors can be important.

A country's international alignment may, therefore, be determined by the ruling group's response to internal conflicts.[62]

In contemporary international politics, an opportunistic alignment occurs when parties to the internal economic and political conflict align themselves with one of the superpowers without adopting its view of the East-West conflict.[63]

As with Burton, the whole of Liska's chapter on 'Non-Alignment and Neutralism' is based on the assumption that non-alignment can simply be viewed as abstention from alignment and freedom from pressures to align.

The alliance of the Non-Aligned

In contrast to Burton and Liska, a more fruitful approach might be to regard non-alignment as no less than a new form of alignment. Such a theoretical conclusion to this study should not be seen as having been tested in the earlier empirical analyses. But, having found that the evidence to support the neo-colonial theory is relatively weak, it is a direction which could be pursued in further research and some of the questions it raises will now be examined. The main implication is that Burton and Liska are fundamentally wrong in thinking that the Non-Aligned are behaving differently from the bloc states. The denials by the Non-Aligned that they were forming a third bloc, though sincerely made, were not valid and functioned as a means of providing ideological distance from the two Cold-War blocs. This perspective suggests that, when the Non-Aligned met in Belgrade in September 1961, they were setting up an informal, non-military, alliance.

The idea of a non-military alliance does not seem so strange, if the functions of military alliances are examined critically. It can be argued that neither NATO nor the Warsaw Pact has in practice had much military significance. Under this interpretation, NATO did not contain Soviet expansion after the Second World War, as this had already come to a halt before NATO was formed. NATO did not react militarily to the Hungarian uprising of 1956 or the invasion of Czechoslovakia in 1968 nor did it affect military action between two of its members, Britain and Iceland. Most important of all NATO had no significant part to play in the Cuban missile crisis of 1962. Similarly, the formation of the Warsaw Pact in 1955 need not be interpreted as signifying closer military integration in Eastern Europe, but a loosening, after Stalin's death, of the hierarchical system and the first signs of respect for the sovereignty of the satellite states. There may be standardisation of military equipment within the Warsaw Pact, but it must be doubted that the alliance has any major role to play in crisis decision-making. The function of both NATO and the Warsaw Pact could be to provide a political alliance, for mutual ideological support and co-ordination of foreign policy interests. Military co-operation is then merely an expression of the political alliance

By an extension of the above argument, it does not seem unreasonable to imagine that some alliances could be solely political and not have any military component. In some situations the existence of military co-operation would not add to the political power of an alliance. For the Non-Aligned it would detract from the coherence of their ideology. In any case military co-operation would not be practical for such a disparate, geographically spread, group of states. The Non-Aligned have no formal legal commitment to each other, but we did see in Chapter 1 that, after their first ten years, they rapidly developed an informal, institutional structure. They now regard themselves as a Movement, with a defined membership. The Movement has regular meetings, a recognised spokesperson, an executive committee, a U.N. caucus group and many arrangements for economic co-operation. It is clear that the Movement is not in any sense an alliance in relation to the Cold War. But, with its concern for political emancipation and economic development, it may be characterised as a non-military, anti-colonial, alliance.

If the Non-Aligned are an alliance, then the reasons for a state joining the Non-Aligned will be the same as for joining any other alliance. One could start by considering whether the Non-Aligned have come together in accordance with the explanations of alliance formation given by Burton and Liska; that is, to seek support in a local conflict, to alleviate domestic political problems or because of pressure from a Great Power. In addition we may add a fourth reason. Small states may join an alliance, because it is necessary to join in order to maintain consistency in their foreign policy. This situation may arise either through the need to follow the example of an important regional power or because the ideological appeal of the alliance is close to the ideology of the regime.

As these pressures are offered as reasons both for joining with the Great Powers and for joining the Non-Aligned, it would seem that we have explained everything and thereby explained nothing. The remaining factor to be taken into account is that the choice of which alliance to join is largely determined by the state of the international system at the time. In the 1950s the Western alliance held a commanding position in the United Nations and backed this up with greater economic, diplomatic and military strength in the world outside. The West offered more potential support than the East, and the Non-Aligned did not exist then, so states under pressure joined the Western alliance. In the 1960s the Non-Aligned suddenly became the group most likely to be able to offer majority support in the General Assembly and also included all the major regional powers of the Third World. The Non-Aligned became the most satisfactory group to approach for support.

We may now see how well this analysis fits to the formation of the Non-Aligned group in 1961. The original core of the alliance was the bilateral alliance of Yugoslavia and the United Arab Republic. Ever since 1945 the central problem of Yugoslavia's foreign policy had been its relations with the Soviet Union. It also faced the pressures of building a common identity in a multi-national state. The U.A.R. had been invaded by Britain and France in 1956, was involved in the Algerian War and since 1948 had been in conflict with Israel. Following Tito and Nasser's initiative twenty-three other countries finally came to the Belgrade summit. Instead of going through the circumstances of each of the

FIG. 6.1 ALLIANCE FORMATION IN THE THIRD WORLD

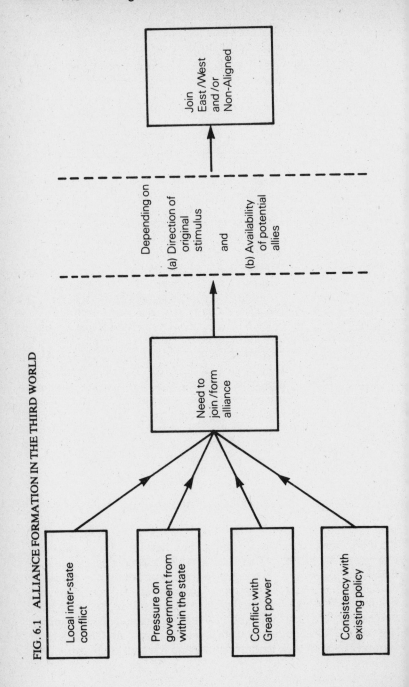

twenty-three in detail, possible reasons for joining the alliance are given in summary below.

India	Kashmir dispute with Pakistan, Western ally; follower of Yugoslavia and U.A.R.; and domestic pressures.
Afghanistan	Claims against Pakistan; and follower of India.
Algeria	War with France.
Burma	Domestic pressures; and follower of India.
Cambodia	Disputes with Thailand + S. Vietnam, Western allies; keeping distance from USA + China.
Ceylon	Domestic pressures; follower of India.
Congo (Zaïre)	Dispute with Belgium; secessionist problem.
Cuba	American-backed invasion attempt, etc.
Cyprus	Communal differences; possible pressures from Greece and Turkey.
Ethiopia	Dispute with Somalia; domestic Eritrean problem.
Ghana	Pan-African ambition source of local disputes.
Guinea	Independence in conflict with France.
Indonesia	Dispute with Malaya; domestic revolts.
Iraq	Break with Western alliance; anti-Israeli; claims on Kuwait; Kurdish revolt.
Lebanon	Domestic communal divisions; follower of U.A.R.
Mali	Independence in dispute with France + Senegal.
Morocco	Claims against Mauritania.
Nepal	Follower of India.
Saudi Arabia	(Follower of U.A.R.)
Somalia	Claims against Ethiopia and Kenya.
Sudan	Follower of U.A.R., domestic problem in south.
Tunisia	Bizerta conflict with France.
Yemen	Follower of U.A.R.

It will be seen that in no case is there any difficulty in suggesting that at least one of the four reasons for joining an alliance could be applicable. The list has not been drawn up in a thorough and systematic manner, so no doubt further reasons could easily be added. In particular all the states are to some extent facing domestic pressures, at least in the form of the social tensions arising from economic development. In addition an ideology that stresses national independence and anti-colonialism has some appeal to all of them. But development and nationalism are not peculiar to the Non-Aligned; they were a characteristic of many other states that did not come to Belgrade.

All alliances are likely to have some members that are more peripheral. The Non-Aligned are no exception and there are some cases in the list, where the suggested reasons do not seem quite so convincing. There are only seven countries that in 1961 had not recently been involved either in a local dispute or a dispute with a Great Power. That Ceylon and Nepal should follow India's lead and that Sudan should follow the U.A.R.'s lead does seem sufficient explanation, but the reasons for Burma, Lebanon, Saudi Arabia and Yemen seem relatively weak. It turns out that all these seven countries were among the nine that sent the smallest delegations, with less than a dozen people, to Belgrade. Furthermore, the four countries with the least reason for being present were peripheral in several other ways. Lebanon and Yemen were not invited to the preliminary meeting in June in Cairo and were only added because of India's pressures to expand the group. Saudi Arabia and Yemen were two among just four states, that failed to send their 'Head of State or Government' to Belgrade. And Burma and Saudi Arabia were the only Belgrade states to drop out of one of the subsequent summit conferences.

An intriguing feature of the list is that Ethiopia and Somalia, which were in dispute over the boundary between them, both turned to the Non-Aligned for support. Neither could afford to let the other win the group to its side, so both joined to block the other. This may also have been the spirit in which Lebanon and Saudi Arabia followed the U.A.R. into the Non-Aligned. They were wary of allowing the U.A.R. to have a forum for attacking the more conservative Arab regimes. That an alliance should have competing states both seeking to become members is not unique to the Non-Aligned. NATO similarly found itself taking in both Greece and Turkey and eventually in 1974 was nearly faced with an all-out war between them.

Just as it is necessary to explain why a state came to join the Non-Aligned, the argument to be convincing should explain why the Non-Bloc states did not join the Non-Aligned. A summary of the reasons is given below.

Cameroon, C.A.R., Chad, Congo (B), Dahomey, Gabon, Ivory C., Madagascar, Mauritania, Niger, Senegal, U. Volta	Brazzaville Group: friendly to France; support Mauritania; hostile to Ghana.

Jordan	Poor relations with U.A.R.; good with U.K. and U.S.A.
Laos	Regime under pressure seeking U.S.A. support.
Liberia	Good relations with U.S.A.; rivalry with Ghana; Monrovia Group.
Malaya	Good relations with U.K.; in conflict with Indonesia.
Nigeria	Good relations with U.K.; rivalry with Ghana; Monrovia Group.
Libya	Ideologically distant from U.A.R.; Monrovia Group.
Sierra Leone	Member of Monrovia Group.
Tanganyika	Not independent until after the Belgrade summit.
Togo	Conflict with Ghana; Monrovia Group.
Austria, Finland, Ireland, Sweden	Good relations with Great Powers; very stable government; local problems not at the time causing friction; ideologically distant from Non-Aligned.

In the case of the four European neutrals the essential position was the lack of any positive reason why they should join the Non-Aligned. In addition we have seen several times that, on an important behavioural dimension, anti-colonialism, these European states are not in sympathy with the Non-Aligned. For all the Afro-Asian, Non-Bloc states the reasons were much stronger. Each one, except Laos and Tanganyika, was in open conflict with one of the Non-Aligned. The African states were in the Monrovia Group, which encompassed the Brazzaville states along with others hostile to the leading African Non-Aligned states.

There were also rivalries and conflicts among the Latin Americans, so we must explain why at least a few more than just Cuba did not join the Non-Aligned. The Organisation of American States provided a forum for their local conflicts to be fought out. With the United States being the dominant power in the region, all the Latin Americans saw relations with Washington as the primary concern of foreign policy. Thus, the advantages to be gained by any Latin American state in joining the Non-Aligned were not likely to be sufficient to off-set the disadvantage of being regarded disloyal to the O.A.S. and the United States. The major exception was Cuba, which on coming into conflict with the majority of the O.A.S. had to turn elsewhere. Throughout the 1960s Cuba was the only Latin American state to join the Non-Aligned. In the 1970s a few more of the Latin Americans have joined the Movement, as a means of asserting their independence from the United States.

An interesting feature of all contemporary alliances is that, despite changing circumstances, membership remains very stable. Only CENTO has lost a member. After a dramatic upheaval in 1958, Iraq left what was then known as the Baghdad Pact; but Albania has not left the Warsaw Pact; France has not left NATO; Cuba has not left the O.A.S. and Pakistan has not left SEATO. In the same way, once a state has attended one Non-Aligned meeting, it receives an invitation to each subsequent meeting. Other alliances have to go through the cumbersome and difficult process of amending a treaty, in order to expel a member. The Non-Aligned would only have to withdraw invitations to conferences, for members they wished to expel. Coups have eliminated important Non-Aligned leaders, such as Nkrumah, Sukarno and Obote, without there being any response from the Non-Aligned group; Cuba has moved very close to the Soviet Union while remaining a member of the Non-Aligned. Only in the case of Chile, with the death of President Allende, has a member been expelled from the Movement. Like other alliances, some members have at times opted to be less active: three states missed the 1970 summit, only to attend again in 1973 and 1976. Again like other alliances, there comes a point when some members diverge from the alliance more than can be tolerated and their membership is temporarily suspended. In 1964 the Non-Aligned were unable to accept a delegation from Congo (Kinshasa) led by Tshombe, but had no objections in 1970 to a delegation sent by Mobutu. Similarly in 1970 representatives from the Lon Nol regime in Cambodia were not seated. Like the other alliances, the Non-Aligned have generally sought to maximise membership even at the expense of tolerating ideological diversity. Only in the most exceptional circumstances is a member suspended or expelled, in order to maintain the ideological justification for the alliance.

While several of the disputes that originally brought the Non-Aligned together proved to be temporary, the things that they had in common to build up a common ideology have remained. The great improvement in relations within both the African group and the Arab League made it possible to absorb most of the Non-Bloc states. The disputes over Southern Africa continue to make the alliance important for African states; the attempt to rally support against Israel makes the alliance important for Arab states; and development is important to all the Non-Aligned.

The approach to the Third World of the neo-colonial theorists was criticised because it did not offer any obvious hypotheses for discriminating between different dimensions of behaviour. The economic satellites of the West would be expected to follow the West both in the Cold War and on colonial issues. This problem does not arise in the same way if the Non-Aligned are seen as an alliance. It is only necessary to show that certain forms of behaviour were a useful strategy for the alliance to follow.

In 1961 nine of the twenty-five states that came together at Belgrade had been recently in direct dispute with one of the major Western powers. The Non-Aligned were an anti-Western alliance. At that stage it was not easy to separate out the politics of colonialism from the Cold War. For example, the Congo crisis seemed to many of the actors to be bringing the Cold War into the heart of Africa. Equally, the issue of nuclear weapon tests and the dangers of conflict between the two Super Powers made the Cold War relevant to all the small states. The Non-Aligned felt it necessary to distance themselves from the West on both East-West issues and on colonialism. Hence we have a possible interpretation of how these two issue dimensions came to be closely related.

After 1961 many colonial territories were granted formal independence and, with the notable exception of Indo-China, the threat of direct Western military action in Afro-Asia rapidly receded. With the ending of the Algerian War and the establishment of Mobutu's regime in the Congo, the main conflicts were with Israel and South Africa, both outside the Western alliance system, and with Portugal, a weak, peripheral member of NATO. The conflict with the big Western powers was indirect rather than direct and the goal was to weaken Western support for the main targets, South Africa, Portugal and Israel. It was no longer necessary to avoid all political links with the West. States that were committed to the West on East-West issues could join the Non-Aligned provided they were committed to anti-colonialism. Equally, states that wished to align themselves with the East could do so with less fear of Western intervention and would still contribute their anti-colonialism to the Non-Aligned. These processes allowed behaviour on the East-West dimension to become relatively independent of behaviour on the anti-colonial dimension.[64]

There was within the dynamics of alliance politics another process affecting the behaviour of the Non-Aligned. The weakness of the Non-Aligned both in relation to the Great Powers and at the local level in relation to Portugal and South Africa meant that the Non-Aligned were trying to build the maximum possible size to their anti-colonial coalition. This process was of benefit to most but not to all governments that had joined the Non-Aligned. Where the

Non-Aligned continued to offer support against a Great Power, then a maximal coalition was desired; where a regime faced domestic pressures, then acceptance in a larger alliance offered greater legitimacy; and, where it was logical to allow a geographical or ideological neighbour into the Non-Aligned, an increase in size made the logic more compelling. But the change was not necessarily to the advantage of those engaged in local disputes. In cases where one party remained outside the Non-Aligned, the other party still benefited. India gained by being in a larger grouping that was denied to Pakistan. In other cases the expansion of the Non-Aligned was a definite disadvantage. For example, Morocco lost by the inclusion of Mauritania and Somalia lost by the inclusion of Kenya. In such cases both sides still had to maintain their position in the Third World by remaining anti-colonial and staying in the Non-Aligned. Then they could seek support elsewhere by forming East-West alignments. The processes of alliance politics give a possible causal explanation for the decreasing correlation between behaviour in East-West relations and anti-colonialism.

This preliminary investigation of the evidence would suggest that explanations of foreign policy behaviour based on neo-colonial theory are not likely to be sustantiated and that it is more fruitful to regard the Non-Aligned as a non-military alliance. Further research would do more justice to the neo-colonial theory by gathering data on the foreign ownership of capital and control of finance in Third World countries, by making a more detailed breakdown of the effects of foreign aid and by investigating whether the medium link found between Western trade and East-West alignment is due to economic domination. The support for an alliance theory is only based on a nominal categorisation in which it was claimed that at least one of four general reasons did explain why each Afro-Asian state was or was not in the Non-Aligned. Further investigation is required to see whether changes in inter-state disputes and in domestic stability do lead to a changing commitment to the Non-Aligned and changing behaviour on the East-West and the anti-colonial dimensions. This requires the integration of some appropriate form of events-data into the analysis. Classification of the day-to-day events which are dominating the lives of politicians and other decision-makers can reveal whether there are certain general types of events that lead to the formation of inter-state alliances. If either neo-colonial theory or a theory of alliance formation is to prove useful, it must not only explain processes that are common to all the Third World states but also explain the large differences that have arisen between them in their foreign policy behaviour.

We have seen that the ideology of non-alignment developed by merging the ideas on foreign policy of the governments that first formed the alliance. In particular Tito's concern with peaceful coexistence, Nehru's moralist attack on the Great Powers with the *Panchsheel* and Nasser's Arab nationalism combined to produce an ideology that linked condemnation of the Cold War alliances to anti-colonialism. Later anti-colonialism received more emphasis and an analysis of economic development was added. The new alliance of the Non-Aligned was able to integrate a justification for rejecting the old alliances with an assertion of the new common interests.

In 1961 the Non-Aligned were a group of only 25 members that made themselves distinct from an equal number of Non-Bloc states. They had taken the initiative in forming the alliance and followed this up by being relatively more active in sending delegations to the United Nations. The ideological commitment was seen in the Non-Aligned voting as a bloc in the General Assembly, both on East-West issues and on colonial issues.

From 1964 the Non-Aligned expanded to include most of the Non-Bloc states and from 1970 became an established part of the international system. They were no longer clearly distinct from the Afro-Asian Non-Bloc states on any of the behavioural indicators, but were quite different from the European neutrals in being anti-colonial. The Non-Aligned remained marginally more active in delegation sending and acted as the core of an increasingly dominant anti-colonial majority. At the same time they lost their coherence on the East-West dimension. Despite the origin of the word, the Non-Aligned could not be described either as a group of states that had refused to join alliances or as a group that was distinguished by non-involvement in Cold War disputes. All that remained was a refusal to take membership of multilateral, Cold War, military alliances. In other respects some of the Non-Aligned were fully committed to the East and some to the West. A strong hypothesis was that the Non-Aligned became an alliance of states committed to anti-colonialism.

If these conclusions are correct, the continued operation of the Non-Aligned as a diplomatic and ideological group will not be significantly affected by the course of relations between the Super Powers or the conflict between capitalism and communism. The disappearance of the Cold War will not lead to the disappearance of non-alignment. On the other hand the course of events in Southern Africa and the Middle East will be of crucial importance. Differences of strategy on whether to attempt negotiations or to increase confrontation with South Africa or with Israel may cause severe temporary problems. The eventual achievement of majority rule for the Africans and a homeland for the Palestinians would not remove all *raisons d'être* for the Non-Aligned Movement. The very long-term problems of development will still keep the developing states working together against the rich, developed states. The greatest danger to the Non-Aligned is a dispute that cuts right across the Third World, such as a failure by the cartels of primary producers of oil and other raw materials to provide economic support for the poorest developing states. The future of the Non-Aligned will depend not on Cold War and *détente*, but on the politics of non-military alliances for the Third World.

References

1. We do not have any quantitative measures for the ideological structure of the conference documents examined in Chapter 1. However, there is a strong impression of a correlation between the changing ideological concerns and the changing political behaviour. As concern with East-West issues declined in importance, indicators of East-West behaviour ceased to give a means of identifying the Non-Aligned. Anti-colonialism became a major component of the ideology and also gave the Movement behavioural coherence.

2. In order to keep the number of cases constant for each year across Tables 6.1 to 6.3, states that were missing data on any variable for a particular year were excluded throughout for that year. Thus for 1961 the 104 U.N. members less Byelorussia, Ukraine, South Africa, Portugal, Sierra Leone, Tanganyika and Syria gives $N=97$; for 1964 the 115 U.N. members less the first four above, Malawi, Malta, Zambia and Indonesia gives $N=107$; and for 1970 the 127 U.N. members less the same four, Botswana, Lesotho, Swaziland, Malawi, Zambia, Maldives, Fiji and Cambodia gives $N=115$. In 1970 Malawi and Zambia were excluded because their extreme values on colonial trade would dominate correlations with this variable, rather than because of missing data. Cambodia was excluded because the coup in 1970 meant that data for that year was not comparable for the different variables.

3. The correlation would drop substantially if both East and West aligned states were equally likely to move to the centre on *either one* of the variables, and if few states moved on *both* variables. The point does not remain quite so valid if only one type of movement (e.g. only Western states moving on only one variable) occurred. Then the correlation need not necessarily drop.

4. The communications variable was created as a dichotomy, with value one indicating that the country accepted either South Africa's flag line's ships or South African Airways planes. A value of zero indicated that neither were accepted. The Index of Colonial Diplomacy used in

the correlation matrices in Tables 6.2, 6.3 and 6.8 is derived from
the data on diplomatic exchanges with South Africa and Portugal with
the same coding scheme as was used for the East-West Index of Diplomatic Alignment.

5. Perhaps the political link was that the willingness of the Non-Aligned
to tolerate divergences within the groups on East-West issues made
it possible for members of the Western Bloc and Latin Americans to
break away on colonial issues.

6. The Index of Military Alignment does not have a linear relationship
with the size of a state. Some of the larger countries are in NATO,
but some are at the other end of the scale, with Eastern alignment
in the Warsaw Pact. There is a curvilinear relationship. This means
that we cannot control for the effect of a country's size by taking a
partial correlation, as we did earlier when considering U.N. delegations.

7. Dr. K. Nkrumah, *Neo-Colonialism: The Last Stage of Imperialism*
(Thomas Nelson and Sons, 1965 and Heinemann, African Writers
Series, London, 1968). Page references are to the Heinemann edition.

8. *Ibid.*, p. 255.

9. *Ibid.*, p. xiii.

10. *Ibid.*, p. ix.

11. *Ibid.*, p. 248. Each of the organisations mentioned is explicitly
discussed in Chapter 18, by Nkrumah.

12. *Ibid.*, p. x.

13. *Ibid.*, p. xiii–xiv.

14. *Ibid.*, p. xiv.

15. *Ibid.*

16. *Ibid.*, p. 258.

17. *Ibid.*, p. 259.

18. J. Woddis, *An Introduction to Neo-Colonialism* (International
Publishers, New York, 1967).

19. Nkrumah, *op. cit.*, p. xiii and p. 258. Nkrumah does not mention
the existence of the communist states as a factor in the ending of
colonialism, but on p. xiv he does say that their existence 'makes it
impossible to enforce the full rigour of the neo-colonialist system'.
If anything, the contribution of Woddis's third factor is denied.
Nkrumah on p. xiii suggested the working class in the colonial
states after the war supported colonialism.

20. Woddis, *op. cit.* p. 32.

21. *Ibid.*, p. 56.

22. *Ibid.*, p. 57.

23. *Ibid.*, p. 51.

24. *Ibid.*, p. 123. The countries given as examples are from Woddis.

25. *Ibid.*, p. 124.

26. *Ibid.*, p. 70.

27. Woddis, *op. cit.*, Chapter 3 'Neo-Colonialism at Work', contains many references to foreign policy on pages 61 to 86.

28. A. G. Frank, *Capitalism and Underdevelopment in Latin America* (Monthly Review Press, New York and London, 1969).

29. *Ibid.*, p. xvi.

30. M. Barratt-Brown, *The Economics of Imperialism* (Penguin Modern Economics Texts, London, 1974), Chapter 11, particularly pages 265–8.

31. Woddis, *op. cit.*, pp. 58–9.

32. Barratt-Brown, *op. cit.*, p. 276.

33. *Ibid.*, pp. 261–2.

34. *Ibid.*, p. 274.

35. *Ibid.*, p. 277.

36. *Ibid.*, p. 281.

37. In an earlier work, Barratt-Brown does have a brief section on the Cold War, one aspect of which is 'the defence of capitalist positions against communist encroachment', *After Imperialism* (Merlin Press, London, revised edition, 1970), p. 204. Another section on 'Positive Neutralism', pp. 465–8, is prescriptive rather than descriptive or analytical.

38. *Geographical Distribution of Financial Flows to Less Developed Countries*, three separate volumes (a) Disbursements 1960–64, (b) Disbursements 1969, and (c) Disbursements 1970 (O.E.C.D., Paris).

39. The sixteen members of the Development Assistance Committee were Australian, Austria, Belgium, Canada, Denmark, France, W. Germany, Italy, Japan, Netherlands, Norway, Portugal, Sweden, Switzerland, U.K. and U.S.A. Portugal resigned in 1974 and Finland and New Zealand are now members.

40. The data does not include military aid. In as much as military aid is seen as an alternative rather than a supplement to development aid, neo-colonial theorists can accept the results in Tables 6.4 and 6.6 as being consistent with their approach. It could also be argued that the Non-Aligned received so much aid because the major capitalist powers were attempting to obtain influence and block the development of non-alignment. The correlations obtained in Table 6.8 suggest that there is not much substance to this argument.

41. The 1969–70 aid data was divided by the 1970 G.N.P. from the *World Bank Atlas 1970* (seventh edition, International Bank for Reconstruction and Development, Washington D.C., 1972) and both the 1960–61 and the 1963–64 aid data were divided by the 1963 National Income from the *United Nations Statistical Yearbook 1973* (Department of Economic and Social Affairs, Statistical Office, New York, 1972). This procedure was not very satisfactory for three reasons. First, National Income and Gross National Product are not the same. Secondly, some distortions in the relative positions of different countries will arise from using 1963 National Income data as a divisor for the 1960–61 aid data. The distortion will depend on the extent to which different countries have had different growth rates from 1961 to 1963. The *Statistical Yearbook* did not give data for China (Taiwan), Cuba or Yugoslavia, so estimates were made for these countries. It is a reasonable assumption that the sources of error are not sufficient to have a large effect on the correlations given in Table 6.8.

42. *Yearbook of International Trade Statistics* (Department of Economic and Social Affairs, Statistical Office of the United Nations, various editions). There was no data on Mongolia, Nepal and Yemen for any of the years; none on Laos for 1960–61 or 1963–64; inadequate data on Kuwait for 1963–64 and 1969–70; inadequate data on Rwanda for 1969–70; no data on Albania, Botswana, Equatorial Guinea, Guinea, Lesotho, Maldives and Swaziland for 1969–70; and data on China and Ecuador for 1969 but not for 1970. Belgium and Luxembourg were both given the results of calculating their trade concentration from their joint customs union data. Data on trade within the East African Community, taken from the sources given in note 62 to Chapter 5, was added to the totals for Kenya, Uganda and Tanzania. Data for Guinea 1963–64 was taken from *Directions of Trade 1962–66* (joint publiction of the International Monetary Fund and the International Bank for Reconstruction and Development, Washington D.C.) and data on Haiti for 1960–61 and 1963–64 was from the *Directions of Trade 1960–64* and *Directions of Trade 1962–66*, respectively.

43. C. L. Taylor and M. C. Hudson, *World Handbook of Political and Social Indicators, Second Edition* (Yale University Press, New Haven and London, 1972), p. 347.

44. Among the writers on neo-colonialism, Nkrumah, Woddis and Frank do not offer any basis for distinguishing between support for the West on the East-West dimension and on the anti-colonial dimension of foreign policy behaviour. Barratt-Brown's idea that there could be conflict between indigenous capitalists and the transnational corporations would allow for anti-Western nationalism occurring. This could be expressed in the form of anti-colonialism *without* necessarily also leading to any decline in anti-communism. Such a situation might be tolerated by the metropolitan colonial powers as not threatening their main interests. These arguments would explain divergences in behaviour on the two dimensions.

45. See note 44 for a discussion of how correlation with just one of the two dimensions may be explained. It might be argued in defence of neo-colonial theory that exploitation by means of aid and trade need not occur simultaneously in the same country and that the two were to some extent alternatives. This argument would suggest the calculation of a multiple correlation coefficient with the two used as independent variables in a multiple regression rather than two separate simple regressions. However, no increase in explanatory power is obtained when this is done for the results in Table 6.8. A further argument is that there has been an inadequate test of the theory because no data was obtained on the transfer of resources via the banks and the multi-national companies. As the operations of these institutions would be expected to relate closely to the trading patterns, it is hypothesised by the author that data on these variables would not yield substantially different results.

46. J. Frankel comments: ' "National interest" is a singularly vague concept.' 'On the other hand, the majority of political scientists attach considerable political significance to the concept', *National Interest* (Macmillan, Key Concepts in Political Science series, London, 1970), p. 15 and p. 18 respectively.

47. H. J. Morgenthau, *Politics Among Nations*, third edition (A. A. Knopf, New York, 1962), p. 5.

48. J. Burton, *International Relations, A General Theory* (Cambridge University Press, London, 1965), p. 235.

49. *Ibid.*, p. 163.

50. *Ibid.*, p. 169.

51. *Ibid.*, p. 173.

52. *Ibid.*, pp. 174–5.

53. *Ibid.*, pp. 176–8.

54. *Ibid.*, p. 184.

55. *Ibid.*, p. 185.

56. *Ibid.*, p. 200.

57. *Ibid.*, p. 209, p. 211 and p. 226.

58. G. Liska, *Nations in Alliance. The Limits of Interdependence* (John Hopkins Press, Baltimore, 1968 edition), pp. 27–8.

59. *Ibid.*, p. 30.

60. *Ibid.*, p. 12.

61. *Ibid.*, p. 18.

62. *Ibid.*, p. 21.

63. *Ibid.*, p. 22.

64. The Vietnam War threatened at first to confuse East-West relations and anti-colonialism again. In the late 1960s it did not become an East-West issue in the same way as the Korean War. The Sino-Soviet dispute produced complications in support for North Vietnam and the Americans got no significant military support from Britain while they faced condemnation from France. From 1969–70, the Non-Aligned were able to regard it solely as an anti-colonial issue.

The Agendas of the Conferences of Heads of State or Government of the Non-Aligned Countries

1. Belgrade 1st—6th September 1961

I. Exchange of views on the international situation.

II. Establishment and strengthening of international peace and security.
   (1) Respect for the rights of Peoples and Nations to self-determination, struggle against imperialism, liquidation of colonialism and neo-colonialism.
   (2) Respect for the sovereignty and territorial integrity of States; non-interference and non-intervention in internal affairs of States.
   (3) Racial discrimination and *apartheid*.
   (4) General and complete disarmament; banning of nuclear tests; problem of foreign military bases.
   (5) Peaceful coexistence among States with different political and social systems.
   (6) Role and structure of the United Nations and the implementation of its resolutions.

III. Problems of unequal economic development; promotion of international economic and technical co-operation.

IV. Other matters.

V. Communiqué of the Conference.

Source: *The Conference of Heads of State or Government of Non-Aligned Countries* (Publicisticko-Izdavacki Zavod, Belgrade).

2. Cairo 5th—10th October 1964

1. General discussion of the international situation.
2. The safeguarding and strengthening of world peace and security, promotion in the settlement of international problems of the positive role of new States and of national liberation movements:

(a) concerted action for the liberation of the countries still dependent; elimination of colonialism, neo-colonialism and imperialism;

(b) respect for the of right peoples to self-determination and condemnation of the use of force against the exercise of this right;

(c) racial discrimination and the policy of *apartheid;*

(d) peaceful coexistence and the codification of its principles by the United Nations;

(e) respect for the sovereignty of States and their territorial integrity; problems of divided nations;

(f) settlement of disputes without the threat or use of force, in accordance with the principles of United Nations Charter;

(g) general and complete disarmament; peaceful use of atomic energy; banning of all nuclear weapon tests; establishment of nuclear-free zones, prevention of dissemination of nuclear weapons and abolition of all nuclear weapons;

(h) military pacts, foreign troops and bases;

(i) the United Nations; its role in international affairs, implementation of its resolutions and amendment of its Charter.

3. Economic development and co-operation:
   (a) effects of disarmament on world economic development;
   (b) United Nations Conference on Trade and Development.

4. Cultural, scientific and educational co-operation; and consolidation of the international and regional organisations working for this purpose.

5. Any other subjects.

Source: *Review of International Affairs*, Volume XV, No. 350, p. 6.

3. Lusaka 8th—10th September 1970

I. CHARTER FOR PEACE, FREEDOM, DEVELOPMENT AND INTERNATIONAL CO-OPERATION AND GENERAL DISCUSSION ON THE INTERNATIONAL SITUATION.

II. PRESERVATION AND STRENGTHENING OF WORLD PEACE AND SECURITY IN THE CHANGED WORLD SITUATION:
   (a) the role of the non-aligned nations;
   (b) strengthening of the United Nations;
   (c) problems of disarmament;
   (d) military pacts, foreign troops and bases.

III. PRESERVATION AND STRENGTHENING OF NATIONAL INDEPENDENCE, SOVEREIGNTY, TERRITORIAL INTEGRITY AND EQUALITY AMONG

STATES AND NON-INTERVENTION IN THE INTER-
NAL AFFAIRS OF STATES:
- (a) action for the liberation of countries under colonial domination and support to liberation movements;
- (b) abolition of all forms of racial discrimination and
  apartheid;
- (c) neocolonialism;
- (d) preservation and strengthening of the independence of
  non-aligned countries.

IV. ECONOMIC DEVELOPMENT AND ECONOMIC INDE-
PENDENCE (DEPENDENCE ON ONE'S OWN RE-
SOURCES):
- (a) bilateral, regional and inter-regional co-operation
  between non-aligned countries and developing countries;
- (b) trade and assistance policy;
- (c) the second decade of the United Nations for development.

V. STRENGTHENING OF CO-OPERATION AMONG
NON-ALIGNED COUNTRIES.

VI. MISCELLANEOUS.

Source: *Review of International Affairs*, Volume XXI, No. 491
p. 14.

The Description of Non-Alignment as an Ideology

It is a surprising failing of political science that the discipline has not yet produced a generally acceptable, concise and value-free definition of 'ideology'. The word is often used as a term of abuse or criticism. As recently as 1970, Diggins was forced to end an article with the conclusion 'Too often, . . ., we American pragmatists [sic] tend to regard an ideologist as any one on the wrong side of the barricades',[1] while in a book on the subject Geertz has to devote a considerable proportion of his chapter to demonstrating that the concept of ideology is usually used in a highly perjorative way and makes the plea 'An ideologist is no more a poor social scientist than a social scientist is a poor ideologist. The two are – or at least they ought to be – in quite different lines of work'.[2]

In respect for this plea for a neutral concept we can immediately dismiss Johnson's definition that 'ideology consists of selected or distorted ideas about a social system or a class of social systems when these ideas purport to be factual and also carry a more or less explicit evaluation of the "facts" '.[3] Johnson lists the sources of ideology as social strain, advocacy of interests, bitterness and limited social perspectives. The later category shows the weakness of his definition. As an example of limited social perspectives he suggests many whites in the United States have 'been insulated to some extent against detailed knowledge of the relative deprivation that many Negroes suffer'. He continues 'consequently, many whites can innocently imagine that the value system is better realised than it actually is. This, of course, is ideology'.[4] Note that Johnson is not distinguishing 'innocent' ignorance from a deliberate refusal to accept established facts. Thus he is putting forward the absurd proposition that all the ignorant are ideologues.

Shils defines ideology as 'one variant form of (the) comprehensive patterns of cognitive and moral beliefs about man, society, and the universe in relation to man and society'.[5] An ideology is distinguished from an 'outlook' by being explicitly formulated, systematised, insistent on its distinctiveness, resistant to innovation, by having an authoritative promulgation and by maintaining collective discipline through complete individual subservience. 'All ideologies . . . entail an aggressive alienation from the existing society',[6] while beliefs which affirm the existing order are designated 'outlooks'. After such a restrictive definition one is not surprised by the assertion that 'ideologies are the creations of charismatic persons'.[7]

Shils's whole approach to the concept of ideology is in itself an ideological one. Implicitly he says ideologues are nasty, narrow-minded and dogmatic while we democrats have an open 'outlook'. His ideologues are simply an American stereotype of the communists who wish 'to acquire power, even by conspiracy and subversion'.[8] There can be no other explanation for Shils's extraordinary statement that 'even where the exponents of an ideology have . . . power . . . they continue to be alienated from the outlook and creeds of the society over which they exercise power'.[9]

Sartori offers a more challenging analysis of ideology as the product of a rationalist mind.[10] He sees rationalism as deductive reasoning that may only be modified by reason and not by evidence and hence is the opposite of empiricism. Ideology is characterised by the closed mind while its political opposite, pragmatism, is characterised by the open mind. He also adds another dimension by characterising ideology as having strong affect while pragmatism has weak affect but this dimension is clearly of secondary importance for Sartori.

Diggins effectively demolishes Sartori's framework by showing that *the* classical ideology, Marxism, is an empirical system of thought and its practitioners have been decidedly pragmatic in their approach to politics. Diggins points out that what Sartori is lacking is any reference to political values or the 'passion' of politics.[11] However, Diggins does not take the next step and give an alternative definition of the concept of ideology. Thus we have no choice but to be rash and offer our own definition:

An ideology is a programmatic assertion of political values, which are held to be of universal validity for their proclaimed domain.

An ideology has to be political to distinguish it from personal moral values, though it will be noted that almost any moral value may become political when it is no longer considered personal but universal. Thus even vegetarianism can be transferred into the political arena by the ideology of Jan Sang. The element of universalism in ideology is rarely given any weight yet it is a highly important element of ideology. The racist does not just consider the American Negro or the West Indian to be inferior to himself, but *all* coloured peoples inferior to *all* whites. The 'African socialist' does not just proclaim himself to be a socialist but asserts that all Africans are naturally socialist and have been under colonial influence if they are anti-socialist.[12] It is the fact that the political values have been translated into proposals for action that transforms the values into an ideology. It is proposals for the control of industry, provision of welfare and redistribution of income that translates the value of equality into the ideology of socialism. Finally, it is the strength of the assertion of the programme that makes us recognise it as an ideology. The more passionate the assertion the more quickly it is recognised as ideology.

The definition is a neutral one but one that does encompass the more restrictive definitions of other writers. The propagation of ideology may involve the distortion of facts and frequently will involve selection but this is not necessarily so, nor is it an *essential* feature of ideology. Equally some ideologies may, as for Shils, be the consolation and hope of alienated minorities but this is only one type of ideology.

We must also include Shils's 'outlooks' under the heading of ideology. Thus we are able to include conservation and liberalism within the term. As ideologies of the *status quo* they may only be implicitly rather than explicitly systematised into a programme but they are nevertheless ideologies, as is soon shown by any threat to the *status quo* from a competing ideology.

Contrary to Sartori's approach we cannot view pragmatism as the negation of ideology. Instead it is a matter for empirical investigation whether the supporters of a particular ideology are pragmatic or rigid and inflexible, in their attempts to win support for their programme, and whether they are willing to consider new ways to assert their values or are dogmatic in maintaining the original formulation. A pragmatic ideologist is simply one that is more likely to be successful.

In posing the question whether or not non-alignment is an ideology, we are not starting from the prejudicial viewpoint that non-alignment may give a rigid distorted picture of the international system, though much 'analysis' of non-alignment does start from such an ideological assumption. Instead, we are concerned with the neutral questions: What are the origins of non-alignment? What are its values? How wide is the domain over which those values lay claim? Are the values formulated systematically enough to constitute an ideology?

References

1. J. P. Diggins, 'Ideology and Pragmatism: Philosophy or Passion?' *American Political Science Review*, 1970, pp. 899–906.

2. C. Geertz, 'Ideology as a Cultural System' in *Ideology and Discontent*, Ed. D. E. Apter (Free Press of Glencoe, 1964).

3. H. M. Johnson, p. 77 of 'Ideology and the Social System' in the *International Encyclopedia of the Social Sciences* (Macmillan, 1968), Vol. 7, pp. 76–85.

4. *Ibid.*, pp. 80–1.

5. E. Shils, p. 68 of 'The Concept and Function of Ideology' in *International Encyclopedia of the Social Sciences* (Macmillan, 1968) Vol. 7, pp. 66–76.

6. *Ibid.*, p. 68.

7. *Ibid.*, p. 69. Note that not even Marx could be called charismatic.

8. *Ibid.*, p. 69.

9. *Ibid.*, p. 68.

10. G. Sartori, 'Politics, Ideology and Belief Systems', *American Political Science Review*, 1969, pp. 398–341.

11. J. P. Diggins, *op. cit. supra*, p. 901.

12. The universalism does not necessarily apply to mankind as a whole. It may be part of the ideology that it limits own horizons. Thus the Jan Sang leader deliberately limits himself to India and *all* Indians, while the African Socialist limits himself to Africa and *all* Africans.

Documents from Colombo on Institutional Arrangements

Decision regarding the Composition and Mandate of the Co-ordinating Bureau

I. The Conference, at its final session, adopted the recommendations on the Composition and Mandate of the Co-ordinating Bureau, made by the Conference of Foreign Ministers, which met in Colombo.

These recommendations are as follows:

1. In the intervening period between conferences of Heads of State or Government of Non-Aligned Countries, the Co-ordinating Bureau is the organ of Non-Aligned countries entrusted with the co-ordination of their joint activities aimed at implementing decisions and programmes adopted at Summit Conferences, Ministerial Conferences, meetings of the Group of Non-Aligned Countries at the United Nations and at other gatherings of Non-Aligned countries.

2. The Co-ordinating Bureau shall be composed of representatives of Non-Aligned countries (up to 25) chosen by the Conference of Heads of State or Government of Non-Aligned Countries, taking into consideration the principles of balanced geographical distribution, continuity and rotation.

3. The Co-ordinating Bureau shall meet:
   (i) at the level of Ministers of Foreign Affairs or special Government representatives once a year or as necessary;
   (ii) on a continuing basis, at the level of permanent representatives of Non-Aligned countries at the United Nations Headquarters in New York once a month as a rule.

4. In carrying out the functions entrusted to it by the Conference of Heads of State or Government of Non-Aligned Countries and Ministerial Conferences of Non-Aligned Countries, the Co-ordinating Bureau shall:

(i) follow the implementation of the decisions and programmes adopted by the conferences of Non-Aligned countries; ensure the co-ordination of activities of Non-Aligned countries aimed at carrying out the said decisions and programmes and propose measures for ensuring and promoting their implementation;

(ii) carry out work connected with the preparation of Conferences of Heads of State or Government, Ministerial Conferences and, if need be other meetings;

(iii) meet to consider international problems special crises situations or a matter of immediate common concern to the Non-Aligned countries. It may recommend appropriate action as necessary; it may also set up when necessary working or contact groups from among all the Non-Aligned countries;

(iv) review and assist in the implementation of the sectors of the Action Programme for Economic Co-operation among Non-Aligned in respect of which responsibilities have been assigned to various member States individually or jointly;

(v) co-ordinate the joint activities of Non-Aligned countries within the framework of the United Nations system on the basis of the decisions of conferences of Non-Aligned countries and carry out tasks assigned to it by the Group of Non-Aligned Countries in the United Nations, bearing in mind the necessity to co-ordinate activity with the Group of 77; keep the Group of Non-Aligned Countries in the United Nations continually informed of its activity and maintain constant working contact with it;

(vi) the Bureau may issue press releases or hold press conferences in order to inform the public about its activities and decisions.

5. The Chairman of the Co-ordinating Bureau shall be the representative of the host country of the preceding Conference of Heads of State or Government of Non-Aligned Countries.

The Chairman shall:

(i) convene meetings of the Co-ordinating Bureau as well as meetings of the whole Group of Non-Aligned Countries in the United Nations;

(ii) propose, in consultation with the members of the Co-ordinating Bureau, the agenda for meetings of the Co-ordinating Bureau; with other Non-Aligned countries, the agenda for meetings of the whole Group of Non-Aligned Countries;

(iii) consult other Bureau members to ascertain the existence of a general consensus for convening a meeting of the Bureau at ministerial or special government representatives' level if it is requested for by a Non-Aligned country or a group of Non-Aligned countries.

6. Any member of the Co-ordinating Bureau and any other Non-Aligned country has the right to request the convening of a meeting of the Co-ordinating Bureau.

The Chairman shall inform all the other members of the Co-ordinating Bureau at the United Nations of such a request and convene without delay an informal meeting of the members of the Co-ordinating Bureau. If the majority of the members present support the request the meeting shall be convened.

7. The decisions of the Co-ordinating Bureau shall be adopted by consensus in the spirit of, and in keeping with the practice of conferences of Non-aligned countries.

The decision taken by the Co-ordinating Bureau meeting at New York at the level of ambassadors or their deputies shall be incorporated in the records of the meeting and circulated among the members of the Co-ordinating Bureau and duly approved by them.

The meetings of Co-ordinating Bureau shall be open to all members of the Non-Aligned Movement. They shall have the right to participate in the proceedings, but shall not take part in decision-making.

8. In keeping with the need of efficient functioning and co-ordination, the Chairman of the Co-ordinating Bureau of the Non-Aligned countries shall arrange for the provision of supporting services and facilities at his permanent mission at the United Nations headquarters in New York supplemented, as necessary, by the mission of other member countries of the Co-ordinating Bureau.

II. The Conference decided that the Bureau will consist of 25 seats and that these seats will be allocated between the different regions in the following manner:

Africa	12
Asia	8
Latin America	4
Europe	1

III. The Conference also decided that each of the above regions will select on the basis of consensus, the countries which will occupy the seats allocated to it.

IV. The Conference further decided that a Co-ordinating Bureau elected during one Summit Conference will hold office till the election of a new Bureau at the following Summit Conference.

V. The following countries were elected to membership of the new Co-ordinating Bureau:

1. Algeria	10. Indonesia	18. Sri Lanka
2. Angola	11. Iraq	19. Sudan
3. Bangladesh/	12. Jamaica	20. Syria
Afghanistan*	13. Liberia	21. Tanzania
4. Botswana	14. Niger	22. Vietnam
5. Chad	15. Nigeria	23. Yugoslavia
6. Cuba	16. Peru	24. Zaïre
7. Guinea	17. PLO	25. Zambia
8. Guyana		
9. India		

*It was agreed that Bangladesh will occupy the seat for the first half and Afghanistan for the second half of the three-year term of office.

Fifth Conference of Heads of State or Government, Colombo 16th – 19th August 1976. Document NAC/CONF.5/S.5.

Action Programme for Economic Co-operation
III. CO-ORDINATION OF ACTION PROGRAMME

1. The co-ordinating countries will keep the Co-ordinating Bureau and all other non-aligned countries informed of the progress made in their respective fields of activities. The implementation of the Action Programme shall be reviewed annually at a meeting of the co-ordinating countries. The report of this meeting will be considered by the Conference of Foreign Ministers which would give appropriate direction taking into account the recommendations made on it by the Co-ordinating Bureau. In the field of economic co-operation covered by the Action Programme of the Non-Aligned Countries it is understood that other developing countries desirous of being associated with it may participate as appropriate and contribute to its successful implementation. Heads of State or Government of Non-Aligned Countries invite non-aligned and other developing countries to co-operate with the co-ordinating countries, and in consultation undertake action for the implementation of measures agreed upon.

2. They consider that measures and actions proposed by the

co-ordinating countries at their meetings held in Belgrade, Georgetown and Havana is of utmost importance for the carrying out of decisions contained in this Action Programme.

3. Bearing in mind the need to avoid duplication and the pursuit of [contradictory] initiatives in the promotion of economic co-operation among developing countries, the Heads of State or Government emphasize the need to ensure proper co-ordination in the implementation of the measures being undertaken under the Non-Aligned Action Programme and those envisaged in the resolution for Economic Co-operation among Developing Countries adopted by the Group of 77 at its Ministerial Meeting held in Manila. In this connexion the forthcoming conference on Economic Co-operation among Developing Countries to be held in Mexico should provide an opportunity to contribute to the above-mentioned purpose.

4. The Heads of State or Government of Non-Aligned Countries having reviewed the work carried out by the co-ordinators of the Action Programme, decide to extend the mandate of the existing co-ordinators until the next summit when the list will be reviewed. They also decide that additional co-ordinators should be appointed for the same period. The full list of co-ordinators is as follows:

Subjects	*Co-ordinating Country*
1. Raw materials	Panama, Algeria, Peru, Senegal, Indonesia, Iraq, Cameroon, Cuba, Afghanistan.
2. Trade, Transport and industry	Guyana*, Afghanistan.
3. Financial and monetary co-operation	India*, Indonesia*, Sri Lanka, Peru, Cuba.
4. Scientific and Technological development	India, Somalia, Algeria*, Yugoslavia*, Peru.
5. Technical co-operation and consultancy services	Panama, India.
6. Food and agriculture	Ethiopia, Korea, Sri Lanka, Morocco, Sudan, Tanzania, Somalia.
7. Fisheries	Cuba, Libya, Morocco, Somalia.
8. Telecommunications	Cameroon.
9. Insurance	
10. Health	Cuba.
11. Employment and human resources development	Panama, Tunisia, Sri Lanka.

12. Tourism	Cyprus, Cameroon, Tunisia, Morocco.
13. Transnational corporations	Algeria, Cuba.
14. Sports	Algeria, Cuba.
15. International co-operation for economic development	Panama, Egypt*, Nigeria*.

For the research and information system, the following countries have indicated their willingness to be the co-ordinating countries: India, Peru, Tanzania, Yugoslavia, Sri Lanka.

The Conference of Foreign Ministers of Non-Aligned Countries may review the above indicated list of co-ordinators at the request of interested member countries.

*Present Co-ordinating Countries.

Excerpt from *Fifth Conference of Heads of State or Government. Document NAC/CONF.5/S.4.*

The Membership of the Groups used for Analysis

(a) *Western Bloc*:

Belgium	Portugal	Israel
Denmark	Spain	Japan
France	U.K.	Pakistan
Greece	Australia	Philippines
Iceland	Canada	South Africa
Italy	New Zealand	Taiwan
Luxembourg	United States	Thailand
Netherlands	Iran	Turkey
Norway		

(b) *Eastern Bloc*:

Albania	Hungary	Romania
Bulgaria	Mongolia	Ukraine
Byelorussia	Poland	U.S.S.R.
Czechoslovakia		

(c) *Latin Americans*:

Argentina	Ecuador	Nicaragua
Bolivia	El Salvador	Panama
Brazil	Haiti	Paraguay
Chile	Honduras	Peru
Columbia	Guatemala	Uruguay
Costa Rica	Mexico	Venezuela
Dominica Republic		

(d) *Non-Aligned and Non-Bloc:*

The composition of these two groups has varied for two reasons. First, new states have emerged since 1961. Some have chosen to attend the Non-Aligned Conferences while others have not. Secondly, a few states have not been consistent in their behaviour and have attended some but not all of the conferences. The decision has not always been solely the preserve of each individual state. For example, Malaysia did not attend in 1964 because Indonesia was able to obtain a majority consensus to deny her an invitation. Thus the empirical definition of the Non-Aligned has two components. A state has chosen to identify itself with the Non-Aligned and in addition has received implicit acceptance from the others.

The following table lists all those states that had become independent by 1970 and for which data was gathered in this study. It indicates whether they took part in each of the five summits, as full participants. (The key to the table is at the end of Table A4.3.)

TABLE A4.1

FULL PARTICIPANTS AT THE NON-ALIGNED SUMMITS

Asian States	*1961* Belgrade	*1964* Cairo	*1970* Lusaka	*1973* Algiers	*1976* Colombo
Afghanistan	A	A	A	A	A
Burma	A	A	N	A	A
Cyprus	A	A	A	A	A
Fiji	—	—	N	N	N
India	A	A	A	A	A
Indonesia	A	A	A	A	A
Iraq	A	A	A	A	A
Jordan	N	A	A	A	A
Kampuchea	A	A	N	A	A
Kuwait	—	A	A	A	A
Laos	N	A	A	A	A
Lebanon	A	A	A	A	A
Malaysia	N	N	A	A	A
Maldives	—	—	N	N	A
Malta	—	N	N	A	A
Nepal	A	A	A	A	A
Saudi Arabia	A	A	N	A	A
Singapore	—	—	A	A	A
South Yemen	—	—	A	A	A
Sri Lanka	A	A	A	A	A
Syria	—	A	A	A	A
Yemen	A	A	A	A	A

TABLE A4.1

CONTINUED

African States	1961 Belgrade	1964 Cairo	1970 Lusaka	1973 Algiers	1976 Colombo
Algeria	A	A	A	A	A
Benin	N	A	N	A	A
Botswana	—	—	A	A	A
Burundi	—	A	A	A	A
Cameroon	N	A	A	A	A
C.A.E.	N	A	A	A	A
Chad	N	A	A	A	A
Congo (Brazza.)	N	A	A	A	A
Egypt	A	A	A	A	A
Equatorial Guinea	—	—	A	A	A
Ethiopia	A	A	A	A	A
Gabon	N	N	N	A	A
Gambia	—	—	N	A	A
Ghana	A	A	A	A	A
Guinea	A	A	A	A	A
Ivory Coast	N	N	N	A	A
Kenya	—	A	A	A	A
Lesotho	—	—	A	A	A
Liberia	N	A	A	A	A
Libya	N	A	A	A	A
Madagascar	N	N	N	A	A
Malawi	—	A	N	N	N
Mali	A	A	A	A	A
Mauritania	N	A	A	A	A
Mauritius	—	—	N	A	A
Morocco	A	A	A	A	A
Niger	N	N	N	A	A
Nigeria	N	A	A	A	A
Rwanda	—	N	A	A	A
Senegal	N	A	A	A	A
Sierra Leone	N	A	A	A	A
Somalia	A	A	A	A	A
Sudan	A	A	A	A	A
Swaziland	—	—	A	A	A
Tanzania	N	A	A	A	A
Togo	N	A	A	A	A
Tunisia	A	A	A	A	A
Uganda	—	A	A	A	A
Upper Volta	N	N	N	A	A
Zaïre	A	N	A	A	A
Zambia	—	A	A	A	A

TABLE A4.1 CONTINUED

Caribbean and Europe	1961 Belgrade	1964 Cairo	1970 Lusaka	1973 Algiers	1976 Colombo
Barbados	—	—	(N)	(N)	(N)
Guyana	—	—	A	A	A
Jamaica	—	(N)	A	A	A
Trinidad-Tobago	—	(N)	A	A	A
Cuba	A	A	A	A	A
Yugoslavia	A	A	A	A	A
Austria	N	N	(N)	G	G
Finland	N	(N)	(N)	G	G
Ireland	N	N	N	N	N
Sweden	N	N	N	G	G

TABLE A4.2 THE CHANGING SIZES OF THE TWO GROUPS*

	Non-Aligned	Non-Bloc	Not Independent
Belgrade Conference	25[a]	24	24
U.N. 16th Session	25[b]	25[f]	23
U.N. 17th Session	26[c]	30	17
U.N. 18th Session	26[c]	32	15
Cairo Conference	46[d]	15	12
U.N. 19th Session	46	15	12
U.N. 20th Session	45[e]	18	10[e]
U.N. 21st Session	46	22	5
U.N. 22nd Session	46	24	3
U.N. 23rd Session	46	26	1
U.N. 24th Session	46	26	1
Lusaka Conference	53	20	0
U.N. 25th Session	53	20	0

* The table covers the 73 states listed in Table A4.1 and, along with the 25 Western Bloc, 10 Eastern Bloc and 19 Latin Americans listed earlier, covers the 127 states for which data was gathered in this study.

[a] Includes Algeria (not then independent) but excludes Syria (then part of the United Arab Republic).

[b] Excludes Algeria, but includes Syria (now separate again).

[c] Includes both Algeria and Syria.

[d] Angola was listed as a 47th full participant at Cairo.

[e] Indonesia withdrew from the U.N. in the 20th Session and in the table is included with those not independent, because much of the data was on the U.N.

[f] Tanganyika, later Tanzania after the merger with Zanibar, became independent and joined the U.N. very late in the session

Latin American participation

Until 1970 only Cuba was a full participant. In 1973 Argentina, Chile and Peru were also at Algiers. In 1976, Argentina, Panama and Peru were full participants. In addition, observers from Latin America numbered 3 in 1961, 7 in 1964, 8 in 1970, 7 in 1973 and 7 in 1976.

Guests at the conferences

The category of 'Guests' was first introduced for 8 liberation movements at Lusaka in 1970. At Algiers the movements were upgraded to Observer status and at Colombo the PLO became a full participant, while the African movements remained Observers.

At Algiers in 1973 Austria, Finland and Sweden were Guests, whereas the first two had previously been Observers. Four international organisations were also Guests. The peripheral status of this category is shown by the addition of four bloc members, Australia, Philippines, Portugal and Romania, as Guests at the 1975 Lima Foreign Ministers Conference. The later three plus Switzerland were Guests again at Colombo.

TABLE A4.3   COUNTRIES NOT INCLUDED IN THE STUDY

| | | Non-Aligned Summits | |
| | Date of | 1973 | 1976 |
New U.N. Members	Joining U.N.	Algiers	Colombo
Bahrain	21/ 9/71	A	A
Bhutan	21/ 9/71	A	A
Qatar	21/ 9/71	A	A
Oman	7/10/71	A	A
United Arab Emirates	9/12/71	A	A
Bahamas	18/ 9/73	N	N
East Germany	18/ 9/73	Eastern Bloc	
West Germany	18/ 9/73	Western Bloc	
Bangladesh	17/ 9/74	A	A
Grenada	17/ 9/74	—	(N)
Guinea-Bissau	17/ 9/74	—	A
Cape Verde	16/ 9/75	—	A
Mozambique	16/ 9/75	—	A
Sao Tome and Principe	16/ 9/75	—	A
Papau New Guinea	10/10/75	—	N
Comoros	12/11/75	—	A
Surinam	4/12/75	—	N
Seychelles	21/ 9/76	—	A
Angola	1/12/76	—	A
Samoa	15/12/76	N	N
Djibouti	20/ 9/77	—	—
Vietnam	20/ 9/77	—	A

TABLE A4.3   CONTINUED

Other Countries/Groups		1973 Algiers	1976 Colombo
North Korea	. . .	N	A
South Korea	. . .	N	N
Palestine Liberation O.	. . .	(N)	A
Switzerland	. . .	N	G
North Vietnam	. . .	N	—
South Vietnam Saigon	. . .	N	—
South Vietnam P.R.G.	. . .	A	—

Key to Tables A4.1 and A4.3

A	Attended as full participants
N	Did not attend
(N)	Observers
G	Guests
—	Not independent at the time

TABLE A4.4   SUMMARY OF THE ATTENDANCE AT NON-ALIGNED SUMMITS

Countries	1961 Belgrade	1964 Cairo	1970 Lusaka	1973 Algiers	1976 Colombo
Full Members	25[a]	47[b]	53	75[ce]	85[d]
Observers	3	10	12[c]	9[d]	9
Guests	—	—	1[d]	3	7
Others					
African Lib. Movements	—	—	7 Guests	14 Obs.	6 Obs.
U.N.	—	—	—	Guest	Obs.
O.A.U.	—	Obs.	Obs.	Guest	Obs.
Arab League	—	Obs.	—	Guest	Obs.
Other Intergov. Organisations	—	—	—	1 Guest	2 Obs.
Puerto Rico Socialists	—	—	—	Obs.	Obs.

Notes: (a) Including Algerian provisional government, (b) Including representatives from Angola, (c) Including South Vietnam P.R.G., (d) Including Palestine Liberation Organisation, (e) Including a representative of Prince Sihanouk's Cambodian government in exile.

TABLE A4.5.   CHANGES IN THE NAMES OF COUNTRIES

Benin was Dahomey until 2/12/75.

Central African Empire was Central African Republic until 4/12/76.

Congo (Brazzaville) became the Congo People's Republic and is now known simply as the Congo. See also Zaïre.

Egypt formed the United Arab Republic with Syria on 21/2/58 until 13/10/61 when Syria became independent again. Egypt kept the name U.A.R. until 2/9/71 when it became Egypt again.

Kampuchea was known as Cambodia under Prince Sihanouk until 1970, and as the Khmer Republic under General Lon Nol until April 1975.

Samoa was formerly Western Samoa.

South Yemen combines the former territories of Aden and the South Arabia Federation, became successively South Yemen and the Yemen People's Republic and is now officially known as Democratic Yemen.

Sri Lanka was Ceylon until 22/5/72.

Zaïre was originally known as Congo (Leopoldville), then as Congo (Kinshasa), then Congo Democratic Republic. See also Congo.

Cluster-Bloc Analysis and Statistical Inference*

Introduction

The analysis of legislative voting and judicial decisions has long been regarded as a proper domain of study for the political scientist. But, because of the vast amount of work involved, few systematic studies have emerged. In addition the prospective researcher must choose from at least five methodological approaches: (a) the construction of indices of cohesion for particular groups, (b) cluster-bloc analysis, (c) Guttmann scaling, (d) factor analysis, and (e) 'complete analysis'. The main use of all the methods is to provide a description of the structure of the various groups in the legislature, Guttmann scaling is the only method in which the voting groups must be described with reference to a particular issue set of related roll-calls; the other methods may be used with either a set of related roll-calls or with *all* the issues on which votes were taken.[1]

Hovet has examined the voting records of the United Nations General Assembly and its main committees for the first sixteen U.N. Sessions.[2] He was concerned to discover how cohesive the various groups, that meet behind the scenes in caucus, actually are in their roll-call voting. For each group he constructed percentage indices of identical voting, 'solidarity' voting (when the dissenting members abstain rather than vote against the group), and divided voting. Lijphart has shown that these indices are not sound for comparing groups of ten or less members.[3] Lijphart also suggested that we can understand the voting structure of the U.N. much better when we empirically determine the voting blocs than when we examine the record of pre-determined groupings. Lijphart suggested that cluster-bloc analysis, as developed by Beyle in 1931

*Reprinted from the *American Political Science Review*, Vol. LXVI, June 1972, pp. 569–82. One change has been made. Table A5.6 below has been substantially extended.

from earlier work by Rice in the 1920s, was a more satisfactory methodology.

The three other alternative methods also allow the groups to emerge empirically from the voting records. Guttmann scaling is well known and is conceptually simple to understand. But for the analysis of U.N. voting, which is the author's main interest, it has only been used to examine one U.N. Session,[4] although it has been used more extensively to study other bodies. Guttmann scaling is not necessarily an alternative to cluster-bloc analysis but can serve as a useful complement to it. Once blocs have been discovered, we can then see whether they can be described in terms of the issues which unite them. We can ask if the bloc has a low variance in its scores on a Guttmann scale.

The two remaining methods, factor analysis[5] and 'complete analysis',[6] have the advantage that they are firmly based on well-developed statistical methods. Many political scientists, however, remain sceptical about applying such high-powered methods to simple YES, NO, ABSTAIN data.[7] What is substantively more important is that, although these methods may successfully discover voting blocs, they tell us very little about the relationships *between* blocs. As Truman puts it, cluster-bloc analysis 'has the considerable advantages of keeping close to the data and of requiring few assumptions in manipulating them'.[8] For his study of the 81st Congress, Truman observed that the method offered other advantages. 'Given the availability of the paired agreement scores, it was possible to perform a number of specialised analyses for particular subgroups within the parties . . . such as the seniority leaders, the elective leaders, the policy committees and the like'.[9] Truman comments that in using this method 'one is obliged to pay a price, namely foregoing most of the refined techniques of statistical inference that are at least theoretically possible with more elaborate methods'.[10] The aim of this paper is to show that it is not necessary to pay such a price. The cluster-blocs need only show paired agreement scores that are statistically acceptable at a stipulated level of significance.

The concept of random voting

The first step in cluster-bloc analysis is to calculate an agreement score for every possible pair of members of the legislative body. Then these scores must be scanned to see whether they qualify for inclusion in a table or a matrix or a diagram (depending on the researcher's preference), to illustrate those groups of members that together form a cluster-bloc. The resulting bloc is thus a subgroup of the legislature that shows greater than average cohesion. Every member of the bloc is in high agreement with every other member of the bloc. The problem is what constitutes 'high agreement'? The following quotations (with italics added) show how this problem has worried all those who have used cluster-bloc analysis. Truman in his study, *The Congressional Party* said that,

The choice of this cut-off point is an *arbitrary one*. . . . Nevertheless, the choice need not be haphazard. If it is set high the blocs will be relatively small. . . . But the number of votes on which all members of the bloc are agreed will be relatively high. If it is set low, the blocs will be larger . . . but the number of unanimous votes within the blocs will be smaller. . . . In the Senate sets [of roll-calls] agreements on more than half of the roll-calls were considered.[11]

Lijphart faced the problem in studying U.N. voting:

The figure can be *arbitrarily set* at 95, 90, or 80 per cent for instance . . . it is preferable to analyse the Indices of Agreement at successively lower levels, beginning with Indices of 100 per cent, in order to discover the exact level at which the blocs emerged.[12]

Schubert was concerned with the analysis of judicial decisions:

On the basis of limited empirical application . . . for the tables of overall inter-agreement, which are expressed in percentages, the average of the ratios of the included pairs can be used as an Index of Inter-Agreement, with ·70 or better considered high, ·60; to ·69 moderate and less than ·60 low.[13]

As long ago as 1931, Beyle tried to tackle this problem of determining a significant level of agreement. He started by considering what would happen if the legislators were voting purely at random and pointed out that

If only chance factors were operative, there would be a 50–50 chance of a legislator voting on one side of a question, one-half of unity. Similarly, the change of a second legislator so voting would be also one-half of unity. The chance that both legislators would so vote, and thus be in agreement, would be one-half times one-half, or one-fourth of unity.

Up to this point Beyle is entirely correct in his reasoning. He goes on:

Given 8 votes . . . their chance agreement on a given side of the questions would be one-fourth of eight or two agreements. [An index may be constructed such that] the numbers between two and eight would be represented by proportionate degrees between zero and 100. Thus, the index number representing the significance of three agreements would be 16·6; the index number for four agreements would be 33·3; for 5, 50·0; for 6, 66·6; and for 7, 83·3. Index numbers for 33·3 may be taken to be particularly significant as indicating cohesion equal to, or greater than two times chance.[14]

Hayes pointed out in 1938 that this index has no meaning or value.

'The *degree* of relationship and the *probability* of relationship are not at all the same thing. Degree of relationship is independent of the size of the sample involved, while probability is directly affected by the size of the sample.'[15] Beyle is right that one would expect by chance to get two agreements on one side, out of eight roll-calls, but he is wrong to say that twice the expected result is significant. Significance is not determined by the result being two, three, or any multiple of the expected value of a sampling distribution but by the result being so many standard deviations from the expected value (assuming normality).

Unfortunately, Hayes himself then pursued a completely fallacious argument; he attacked Beyle's assumption that random voting was the proper standard of comparison, claiming that for two legislators

the probability of their agreements being within the possible range of chance factors depends upon the frequency with which each of them votes 'aye' and 'nay'. . . . Only when given those frequencies can one calculate the probability of their agreeing with each other. For instance if two legislators each voted 'aye' on every bill that came up, of course they would *agree* on every bill. However, that would be no indication that they were significantly related (in statistical terminology) to each other.[16]

Intuitively this conclusion makes no sense. If two legislators are in 100% agreement on enough roll-calls, there *must* be common political factors at work. Either they co-operate, or they are both loyal to the majority leader, or they both believe in following a Congressional consensus, or some other political process is operating. No person can be regarded as having an innate probability of voting 'aye' of anything other than 0·5, unless he is motivated by some factor such as a desire to follow the consensus. Such a discovery would be in itself of interest and be significant.

As a result, Beyle's basis tenet must be upheld: an agreement score must be regarded as significantly high if it is larger than any value that would be likely to occur with random voting. Beyle was only concerned with agreement occurring on one side of a question. Most people now use indices of identical voting that count joint agreement either for *or* against the question; such indices will be discussed in the remainder of this paper.

If two legislators A and B, both vote at random on a roll-call, there are four possible outcomes to the voting:

A's vote	B's vote	
(1) Yes	Yes	Identical voting
(2) No	No	
(3) Yes	No	Disagreement
(4) No	Yes	

With the probability of voting Yes equal to the probability of voting No and both equal to $0\cdot5$, the probability of each result is $0\cdot5 \times 0\cdot5 = 0\cdot25$. The probability of agreement is then the probability of occurrence of either the first outcome or the second outcome, i.e. $0\cdot25 + 0\cdot25 = 0\cdot5$. Similarly the probability of disagreement is $0\cdot5$, for any one roll-call. Having started by considering just one legislator voting Yes or No, we have now moved one step further and derived the probability of agreement for a pair of legislators jointly voting on the same roll-call. The symbols p_f will be used to signify the probability of agreement and p_d the probability of disagreement. Although the original assumption of random voting with $P(\text{Yes}) = P(\text{No}) = 0\cdot5$ leads to a conclusion with a similar result, namely $p_f = p_d = 0\cdot5$, it must be remembered that we are now dealing with the joint behaviour of a pair of legislators and not with an individual legislator.

What happens if the two legislators each vote on eight separate roll-calls? There are nine possible *agreement* patterns. The two legislators may fail to agree on any of the eight roll-calls, or they may agree on $1, 2, 3, \ldots$ or even all eight roll-calls. This gives nine possible agreement scores, ranging from 0% to 100%. The probability of each score's occurring by random voting can be calculated using the general laws of probabilities and the binominal distribution.[17]

$P(r$ agreements in N roll-calls$)$
= No. of ways of getting r agreements times
    Probability for each way.
$= C_r^N p_f{}^r p_d{}^{N-r}$

As emphasised above, the 'number of ways of getting r agreements' concerns the joint behaviour of two legislators. Thus there is only 'one way' of getting no agreements at all: they are opposed to each other on every one of the eight roll-calls.[18]

The probability equations for eight roll-calls have been set up in column 3 of Table A5.1. The C_r^N term is evaluated according to the formula:

$$C_r^N = \frac{N!}{r!(N-r)!}$$

We have already seen that $p_f = 0\cdot5$ and also that $p_d = 0\cdot5$. When these values are substituted in the expressions given in column 3 of Table A5.1, the results obtained are in column 4. When the probabilities for the nine possible agreement scores are summed, the total comes, as it always must, to $1\cdot0$. Figure A5.1 shows that, even in voting on as few as eight roll-calls, the sampling distribution approaches a normal curve.

TABLE A5.1   PROBABILITY OF OBTAINING EACH AGREEMENT
SCORE, WITH EIGHT ROLL-CALLS

1	2	3			4	5	6
No. of Agree-ments	%Score	*Probability of each Score*				*Cumulated Probabilities*	
0	0%	C_0^8	p_f^0	p_d^8	0·00391	0·00391	1·00000
1	12·5%	C_1^8	p_f^1	p_d^7	0·03125	0·03516	0·99609
2	25·0%	C_2^8	p_f^2	p_d^6	0·10937	0·14453	0·96484
3	37·5%	C_3^8	p_f^3	p_d^5	0·21875	0·36328	0·85547
4	50·0%	C_4^8	p_f^4	p_d^4	0·27344	0·63672	0·63672
5	62·5%	C_5^8	p_f^5	p_d^3	0·21875	0·85547	0·36328
6	75·0%	C_6^8	p_f^6	p_d^2	0·10937	0·96484	0·14453
7	87·5%	C_7^8	p_f^7	p_d^1	0·03125	0·99609	0·03516
8	100·0%	C_8^8	p_f^8	p_d^0	0·00391	1·00000	0·00391

FIG. A5.1   SAMPLING DISTRIBUTION FOR RANDOM VOTING.
8 ROLL-CALLS, SIMPLE PERCENTAGE INDEX OF AGREEMENT.

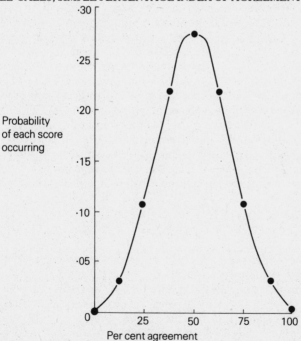

The values of the agreement scores, that are significantly
different from the 'expected' mean value 50%, are found by

examining the tails of the sampling distributions. At the 0·001 level of significance, with eight roll-calls no score is significant. Even 100% agreement could occur by chance as often as four times in a thousand. But, using a single-tail test, 100% is significant at the 0·01 level. When we move up to the 0·025 level of significance 100% is still the only significant score. By the time we consider a 0·05 level of significance and are prepared to take the greater risk of being wrong in our inference, a score of 87·5% agreement may also be considered significant. Thus in performing cluster-bloc analysis on eight roll-calls the cut-off points for forming blocs should be either 87·5% or 100%, depending on the level of significance at which the researcher wishes to operate.

As the sampling distribution is completely symmetrical we can also consider the second tail of the distribution and find scores so low that they represent *significant disagreement*. Thus, on eight roll-calls, 0% is significant at the 0·01 or 0·025 level, and 12·5% or less is significant at the 0·05 level. To the author's knowledge no other researchers have considered particularly low scores in their analyses of voting patterns. In any large assembly it is difficult enough to handle all the information generated about high agreement, and in any case most assemblies have enough consensus operating that scores below 30% or so would be unusual. If, however, an assembly were found to be divided into two or more distinct cluster-blocs, it would be well worth considering whether the divisions are so deep that there is also significant disagreement between the blocs or between some of their members.

So far the discussion has only considered voting on eight roll-calls. If a different number of roll-calls were under consideration, then the whole argument must be repeated to find the cut-off points for the agreement scores on N roll-calls. The general formula is that J or less agreements will occur on N roll-calls with a probability of

$$P = \sum_{I=0}^{I=J} C_I^N \cdot p_f^I \cdot p_d^{N-I}$$

Fortunately this expression can be evaluated by computer. The results, for random voting on up to 250 roll-calls, are given in Table A5.2. After 30 roll-calls the results are only given for every 10, and after 80 roll-calls for every 20, since the differences in cut-off points become very slight. To err on the side of caution, one should use the cut-off points higher in the table.[19] Thus, if 57 roll-calls were being considered the 0·05 level of significance were adopted, one should use the figure given for 50 roll-calls (cut-off = 64·0% rather than that for 60 roll-calls (cut-off = 61·7%).

TABLE A5.2 PERCENTAGE CUT-OFF POINTS FOR CLUSTER-BLOC
ANALYSIS: SIMPLE INDICES OF INDENTICAL VOTING*

Significance Levels for Single-Tailed Tests

No. of Roll-calls	Disagreement				Agreement			
	0·001	0·01	0·025	0·05	0·05	0·025	0·01	0·001
4	—	—	—	—	—	—	—	—
5	—	—	—	0·0	100·0	—	—	—
6	—	—	0·0	0·0	100·0	100·0	—	—
7	—	0·0	0·0	0·0	100·0	100·0	100·0	—
8	—	0·0	0·0	12·5	87·5	100·0	100·0	—
9	—	0·0	11·1	11·1	88·9	88·9	100·0	—
10	0·0	0·0	10·0	10·0	90·0	90·0	100·0	100·0
11	0·0	9·1	9·1	18·2	81·8	90·9	90·9	100·0
12	0·0	8·3	16·7	16·7	83·3	83·3	91·7	100·0
13	0·0	7·7	15·4	23·1	76·9	84·6	92·3	100·0
14	7·1	14·3	14·3	21·4	78·6	85·7	85·7	92·9
15	6·7	13·3	20·0	20·0	80·0	80·0	86·7	93·3
16	6·3	12·5	18·8	25·0	75·0	81·3	87·5	93·8
17	5·9	17·7	23·5	23·5	76·5	76·5	82·4	94·1
18	11·1	16·7	22·2	27·8	72·2	77·8	83·3	88·9
19	10·5	21·1	21·1	26·3	73·7	79·0	79·0	89·5
20	10·0	20·0	25·0	25·0	75·0	75·0	80·0	90·0
21	14·3	19·1	23·8	28·6	71·4	76·2	81·0	85·7
22	13·6	22·7	22·7	27·3	72·7	77·3	77·3	86·4
23	13·0	21·7	26·1	30·4	69·6	73·9	78·3	87·0
24	16·7	20·8	25·0	29·2	70·8	75·0	79·2	83·3
25	16·0	24·0	28·0	28·0	72·0	72·0	76·0	84·0
26	15·4	23·1	26·9	30·8	69·2	73·1	76·9	84·6
27	18·5	25·9	25·9	29·6	70·4	74·1	74·1	81·5
28	17·9	25·0	28·6	32·1	67·9	71·4	75·0	82·1
29	17·2	24·1	27·6	31·0	69·0	72·4	75·9	82·8
30	20·0	26·7	30·0	33·3	66·7	70·0	73·3	80·0
40	22·5	30·0	32·5	35·0	65·0	67·5	70·0	75·5
50	26·0	32·0	34·0	36·0	64·0	66·0	68·0	74·0
60	28·3	33·3	35·0	38·3	61·7	65·0	66·7	71·7
80	31·3	36·3	37·5	40·0	60·0	62·5	63·8	68·8
100	34·0	37·0	39·0	41·0	59·0	61·0	63·0	66·0
120	35·0	38·3	40·0	41·7	58·3	60·0	61·7	65·0
140	36·4	39·3	40·7	42·1	57·9	59·3	60·7	63·6
160	37·5	40·0	41·9	43·1	56·9	58·1	60·0	62·5
180	37·8	40·6	42·2	43·3	56·7	57·8	59·4	62·2
200	38·5	41·5	42·5	43·5	56·5	57·5	58·5	61·5
250	40·0	42·4	43·6	44·4	55·6	56·4	57·6	60·0

*Probability of Agreement = 0·5; Probability of Disagreement = 0·5.

The definition of indices

We must now examine more carefully the assumption that random voting is the proper standard of comparison for deciding which scores are significantly high. Surely it will be possible, in a legislature or assembly that operates by achieving high consensus and avoiding roll-calls on divisive issues, to obtain the result that every member of the legislature is in significant agreement with every other member of the legislature? Of course this is true, but it would be a major finding about the behaviour of the legislature. We would not have discovered any cluster-blocs within the legislature but we would have firmly established that such divisions as there were either were very weak or were not expressed in the roll-calls. Therefore, the first examination of the scores should always be against the null hypothesis of random voting. Indeed we now have for any legislature of M members an Index of Agreement, I_α, that is statistically based.

$$I_\alpha = \frac{\text{Number of pairs of members in significant agreement}}{\text{Total possible number of pairs of members}}$$

$$= \frac{\text{Number of pairs in significant agreement}}{M\,(M{-}1)/2}$$

Similarly, for a legislature that has deep divisions, we have an Index of Significant Disagreement, I_β,

$$I_\beta = \frac{\text{Number of pairs in significant disagreement}}{M\,(M{-}1)/2}$$

The two give an overall Index of Cohesion, $I_\gamma = I_\alpha - I_\beta$

In theory it will be possible for I_γ to obtain a negative value by the number of pairs in disagreement being higher than the number of pairs in agreement, but this is not very likely to occur in practice. I_γ should not be reported without the corresponding values of I_α and I_β, and all three should be given at the chosen level of significance. This is because both I_α and I_β may become higher at a lower level of significance.

Just as these three indices may be used to examine the cohesion of the whole legislature they may also be used to examine specified subgroups. The following results, for example, were obtained in a study of behaviour of the African Group in the United Nations General Assembly.[20]

When the internal cohesion of specified groups is under consideration it may also be of interest to know how strong is the relationship *between* the groups. For example, are the Africans closer to the NATO or to the Warsaw Pact powers? Since the first

TABLE A5.3   COHESION OF THE AFRICAN GROUP IN THE U.N.

| Session | $p \leq \cdot001$ | | | $p \leq \cdot05$ | | |
	I_α	I_β	I_γ	I_α	I_β	I_γ
15th	56·0%	0%	56·0%	72·7%	1·0%	71·7%
16th	90·8%	0%	90·8%	100·0%	0%	100·0%
17th	77·1%	0%	77·1%	96·2%	0%	96·2%
18th	89·5%	0%	89·5%	99·6%	0%	99·6%
20th	100·0%	0%	100·0%	100·0%	0%	100·0%

step in cluster-bloc analysis would be to calculate agreement scores for every state with every other state, we may examine the level of agreement between every member of NATO and every member of the African group. For example, if the agreement score between France and Madagascar were found to be significantly high, this would constitute a 'link' between the two groups. In general if the groups are of size M_1 and M_2 we may define the following indices to examine the relationship between the groups:

Inter-group agreement

$$IG_\alpha = \frac{\text{No. of significant links between the groups}}{\text{Total possible no. of links between the groups}}$$

$$= \frac{\text{No. of significant links}}{M_1 \times M_2}$$

Inter-group disagreement

$$IG_\beta = \frac{\text{No. of significant disagreements between the 2 groups}}{M_1 \times M_2}$$

Inter-group adhesion

$$IG_\gamma = IG_\alpha - IG_\beta$$

We have already seen in Table A5.3 that the African Group was relatively disunited in the United Nations 15th Session, but in subsequent sessions it became more united until in the 20th Session I_α attained 100% at the 0·001 significance level. The earlier lack of unity might be explained by the fact that during 1960 the African states formed two rival groups that met regularly outside the United Nations. They became known as the Casablanca and Brazzaville groups. The Inter-Group Indices may be used to examine whether or not the differences within the African group in the U.N. were an expression of the split between these two rival groups.[21]

TABLE A5.4   CASABLANCA-BRAZZAVILLE INTER-GROUP AGREEMENT

| | $p \leq \cdot 001$ | | | | $p \leq \cdot 05$ | |
Session	IG_α	IG_β	IG_γ	IG_α	IG_β	IG_γ
15th	1·8%	0%	1·8%	12·7%	5·4%	7·3%
16th	45·0%	0%	45·0%	100·0%	0%	100·0%
17th	48·6%	0%	48·6%	100·0%	0%	100·0%
18th	73·6%	0%	73·6%	98·6%	0%	98·6%
20th	100·0%	0%	100·0%	100·0%	0%	100·0%

The indices in Table A5.4 clearly show a split in the 15th Session and a rapid change in subsequent sessions; by the 20th Session, the two groups show no significant differences at all. The increase in cohesion of the African group as a whole was mainly due to the decrease in hostility between the two rival subgroups. Several explanations of such patterns of change are possible. In this case the increased adhesion is due not so much to *rapprochement* of the two groups as to the resolution or dimunition of the four main disputes that originally led to the formation of the groups: Mauritania gained admission to the U.N.; Algeria gained its independence from France; the bitterness of the disputes in the Congo were somewhat eased; and Nkrumah had to accept failure for his own militant brand of Pan-Africanism.

One of the original reasons for suggesting that cluster-bloc analysis was a more useful methodology was the advantage it offered of permitting empirical determination of the voting groups. But by using the voting agreement scores and the above indices we can also examine *any* specified group that is of interest. The indices are statistically based and are simple to comprehend. They have the same meaning when groups of different sizes are compared. By contrast, if Hovet tells us that a group is divided 50% of the time, we do not know whether there is just one deviant member (in which case I_α would remain quite high) or whether the group is regularly split into two different factions, (in which case I_α would be low and I_β might be high).

Significant relative agreement

As suggested earlier, a group might achieve such a high consensus that every member was in significant agreement with every other member. Also we have seen that this extreme result did occur for the African group in the United Nations 20th Session. Knowing this does not mean that one cannot say anything about the structure of such a group. It simply means that the group is homogenous and united as compared to any model of random voting.

In any one session of a legislature or assembly, however, the issues on which the members are called upon to vote do not present a random stimulus. One session may produce a very high consensus simply because no controversial issues arise or lead to roll-calls during the period that it is meeting. In this situation we may take the total votes on any one roll-call as an approximate measure of the stimulus provided by the roll-call. Thus if the U.S. Senate votes 63–37 in favour of a bill, we may say for any individual Senator the probability of voting 'aye' was 0·63 and the probability of voting 'nay' was 0·37. The resulting probability that any two Senators will agree is

$p_f = 0 \cdot 63^2 + 0 \cdot 37^2 = 0 \cdot 534$ and the probability that they will disagree is

$p_d = 2 \times 0 \cdot 63 \times 0 \cdot 37 = 0 \cdot 466$

If such a calculation is made for each roll-call during the session, the average probability of agreement for the session can be obtained. Then, by substituting these new values of p_f and p_d in the equations given earlier, a different sampling distribution is generated. Since random voting, with an average 50–50 split on all roll-calls, represents the maximum possible division within a legislature, any values of p_f calculated empirically from the voting marginal totals are likely to be higher than 0·5. The sampling distribution could then no longer be normal but would be skewed towards 100%. As the argument has not rested on the assumption of normality, the skew does not mean we cannot obtain significant cut-off points. In fact, the exact probability for every point on the sampling distribution can be calculated. Therefore we still obtain exact significance levels from the tails of the distribution. To distinguish these cut-off points from the ones obtained by comparison to random voting we may term them the levels of significant *relative* agreement. They may only be used in a particular assembly to examine alignments on a set of roll-calls.[22]

Judicial decisions

Very often in the study of judicial decisions, a large number of cases are summarised by using cluster-bloc analysis. Indeed, in many ways this is an ideal use of the methodology, because it is possible to gain a better understanding of all the inter-relationships in a small body such as a court. Courts may operate, however, with a high degree of unanimity and therefore, against the null hypothesis of random voting, the court may appear to be completely united, with every judge in significant agreement with every other judge. One response to such a situation is to regard it as essential rather than optional to study significant *relative* agreement. An alternative response is to eliminate from the study the unanimous decisions and perhaps those with only a single dissenter. Schubert has analysed split decisions and has even constructed matrices of agreement scores solely for marginal decisions of the U.S. Supreme Court.[23] Russell in analysing the Canadian Supreme Court has to omit as many as 70% of the decisions because they were unanimous.[24] Such omissions are perfectly acceptable so long as the focus of analysis is the nature of the divisions within a court. But if we wish to study whether division is increasing or decreasing over time, then unanimous decisions cannot be ignored.

Because of the special nature of a dissenting legal opinion, several authors have taken to studying agreement in assent and agreement in dissent separately from the overall pattern of agreement.[25] When this is done, we are reverting to Beyle's preoccupation with agreement on one side of an issue. The null hypothesis of random voting then gives a probability of agreement of 0·25 (derived from either Yes/Yes pairs or No/No pairs on their own, according to whether agreement in assent or agreement in dissent is taken). This probability value makes the cut-off points much lower (table available on request). Even though the cut-off points are low, joint dissent is likely to be so infrequent that no bloc structure is revealed amongst the agreement-in-dissent scores. This is not so likely to occur when the agreement-in-assent scores are examined.[26] If we use the *relative* probability of agreement in dissent, it is likely to be much lower even than 0·25, and the *relative* probability of agreement in assent will be much higher.

It frequently happens in a court that there is only one voice in dissent. This is in contrast to a legislative body, where one person will probably avoid being seen in such isolation. In legislatures, the dissenter may either be absent for the vote or a roll-call may be avoided and thought unnecessary by the majority. In the courts, when there is only one dissenter, he obviously cannot be in agreement with anyone else. This means that such decisions cannot be taken into account in calculating the average probability of agreement in dissent, though they *can* be used in calculating the average probability of agreement in assent. Given this problem, it is not possible to approximate to the average probability of dissent by simply taking (total number of dissents)/(total possibilities for dissent). If there is a large number of decisions with single dissenters, the average probability of agreement in dissent will be *very* low and it may not be possible to find significant pairs.

United Nations voting

When we wish to study voting in the United Nations, the problem is complicated by abstentions. The General Assembly accepts this as a recognised form of voting that is entered into the Official Records along with the details of those voting Yes or No. It is not equivalent to a state being absent and is used to express limited opposition to a proposal. Both Reiselbach and Meyers took this into account by including joint abstentions in their indices of identical voting for pairs of states.[27] On the other hand Lijphart went further and suggested that allowance should also be made for the fact that Yes-Abstain or a No-Abstain pairs are in 'partial agreement', he defined an Index of Agreement:

$$I_A = \frac{(f + \frac{1}{2}g)}{t} \times 100,$$

Where f = the number of identical roll-calls, for the two states
g = the number in which the states showed partial agreement
t = the number that both states participated in.[28]

The assumption of random voting in the U.N. would require: $P(\text{Yes}) = P(\text{No}) = P(\text{Abstain}) = 1/3$. There are then nine possible outcomes, when two states vote, and each has a probability of $1/3 \times 1/3 = 1/9$.

	A's vote	*B's vote*	
(1)	Yes	Yes	
(2)	No	No	Agreement
(3)	Abstain	Abstain	
(4)	Yes	Abstain	
(5)	Abstain	Yes	Partial
(6)	No	Abstain	Agreement
(7)	Abstain	No	
(8)	Yes	No	Disagreement
(9)	No	Yes	

Using the same symbols, p_f = probability of agreement, and p_d = probability of disagreement, with the new symbol p_g = probability of partial agreement, we have:

$$p_f = 1/3, p_g = 4/9, \quad p_d = 2/9 \quad \text{and} \quad p_f + p_g + p_d = 1\cdot 0$$

For those such as Reiselbach and Meyers, who use simple indices of identical voting to study the U.N., the argument given above still applies. The same table may be used as for any other legislature, such as the Congress, which uses simple Yes-No voting. The only difference is that random voting would not give $p_f = 0.5$, but $p_f = 0.3333$ and as partial agreement is ignored $p_d = 0.6666$. The levels of significant *relative* agreement are found as before by calculating the average empirical value of p_f.[29] For N roll-calls:

$$p_f = \Sigma \frac{(P(\text{Yes})^2 + P(\text{No})^2 + P(\text{Abstain})^2)}{N}$$

For those who wish to use Lijphart's Index of Agreement, the situation is a little more complicated. Not only does the use of partial agreements give more discreet values that the index may assume, but it also means that the same value of the index may be produced by different voting patterns. For example when votes are taken on 6 roll-calls, there are not seven but thirteen possible scores, which may be formed from twenty-eight possible voting patterns, as given in Table A5.5.

The probability equations are also more complicated, as multinominal distributions are generated for each agreement score, e.g.

$$
\begin{aligned}
P(I_A = 50.0\%) &= C_3^6 \cdot p_f{}^3 \cdot C_3^3 \cdot p_g{}^0 \cdot p_d{}^3 \\
&\quad + C_2^6 \cdot p_f{}^2 \cdot C_2^4 \cdot p_g{}^2 \cdot p_d{}^2 \\
&\quad + C_1^6 \cdot p_f{}^1 \cdot C_4^5 \cdot p_g{}^4 \cdot p_d{}^1 \\
&\quad + C_0^6 \cdot p_f{}^0 \cdot C_6^6 \cdot p_g{}^6 \cdot p_d{}^0 \\
&= 20 \left(\frac{1}{3}\right)^3 \left(\frac{2}{9}\right)^3 \\
&\quad + 90 \left(\frac{1}{3}\right)^2 \left(\frac{4}{9}\right)^2 \left(\frac{2}{9}\right)^2 \\
&\quad + 30 \cdot \frac{1}{3}\left(\frac{4}{9}\right)^4 \cdot \frac{2}{9} \\
&\quad + \left(\frac{4}{9}\right)^6 \\
&= 0.2001
\end{aligned}
$$

Even on random voting the distributions are not normal but slightly skewed towards 100%. Although the procedure is more complicated, the probability of each point on the distribution can still be

TABLE A5.5   ALL POSSIBLE OUTCOMES WHEN TWO STATES
VOTE IN THE U.N. ON SIX ROLL-CALLS

Structure of the Voting pattern

	$f+\frac{1}{2}g$	$I_A(\%)$	Agreement	Partial Agreement	Disagreement
(1)	6·0	100·0	6	0	0
(2)	5·5	91·7	5	1	0
(3)	5·0	83·3	5	0	1
(4)	5·0	83·3	4	2	0
(5)	4·5	75·0	4	1	1
(6)	4·5	75·0	3	3	0
(7)	4·0	66·7	4	0	2
(8)	4·0	66·7	3	2	1
(9)	4·0	66·7	2	4	0
(10)	3·5	58·3	3	1	2
(11)	3·5	58·3	2	3	1
(12)	3·5	58·3	1	5	0
(13)	3·0	50·0	3	0	3
(14)	3·0	50·0	2	2	2
(15)	3·0	50·0	1	4	1
(16)	3·0	50·0	0	6	0
(17)	2·5	41·7	2	1	3
(18)	2·5	41·7	1	3	2
(19)	2·5	41·7	0	5	1
(20)	2·0	33·3	2	0	4
(21)	2·0	33·3	1	2	3
(22)	2·0	33·3	0	4	2
(23)	1·5	25·0	1	1	4
(24)	1·5	25·0	0	3	3
(25)	1·0	16·7	1	0	5
(26)	1·0	16·7	0	2	4
(27)	0·5	8·3	0	1	5
(28)	0·0	0	0	0	6

calculated, and the cut-off points for significant agreement or for
significant disagreement are found at the tails of the distribution.
The results for varying numbers of roll-calls, with the assumption of
random voting, are given in Table A5.6.

When Lijphart studied 44 roll-calls on colonial issues in the 11th
and 12th Sessions of the General Assembly, he used cut-off points

of 95·5% and 87·5% to produce two diagrams of the cluster blocs. At the 95·5% level, he found one bloc consisting of the communist states, three small blocs of Western states, and an Arab bloc. Twelve other states had one or two isolated links but did not form a bloc. At the 87·5% level the communist and Arab blocs merged and were highly intermeshed with the other Afro-Asians; the Western states and some of the Latin Americans also formed another large bloc, and the remainder of the Latin Americans had some links with the Afro-Asians. By using these high cut-off points Lijphart did find the core of the bloc structure but he also overemphasised the divisions within the Assembly. At the $p \le 0.001$ level of significance, which is a high level of significance to use, it is necessary to go down to a cut-off point of 73·0%, for 44 roll calls. This would be almost certain to reveal a continuous structure of overlapping blocs, with the Latin Americans acting as a crucial group in the middle, having links with both sides. Thus the choice of cut-off points is not without substantive significance. By taking them too high one may overemphasise the splits in the Assembly.

Yet again it is possible to use cut-off points to indicate significant *relative* agreement for United Nations voting. But as there are three variables, p_f, p_g, and p_d to take into account, there will be a greater variability in the reference tables.[30] The values of the relative probabilities of agreement, partial agreement and disagreement may be calculated as follows:

$$p_f = \frac{\Sigma [P(\text{Yes})^2 + P(\text{No})^2 + P(\text{Abstain})^2]}{N}$$

$$p_g = \frac{\Sigma 2[P(\text{Yes}) + P(\text{No})] \cdot P(\text{Abstain})}{N}$$

$$p_d = \frac{\Sigma [2P(\text{Yes}) \cdot P(\text{No})]}{N} = 1 - p_f - p_g$$

It is also possible to use the Indices I_α, I_β, and I_γ to examine the cohesion of groups in the U.N. and the Indices IG_α, IG_β, and IG_γ to examine the adhesion between groups in the U.N. Indeed the earlier examples of the use of these indices were taken from data on voting in the General Assembly.

The investigation of issue dimensions

In factor analysis the votes on various roll-calls may be regarded as observations about the individual legislators (or states) and the factors generated represent blocs that vote in a similar way. Alternatively the votes by various assembly members may be

TABLE A5.6   PERCENTAGE CUT-OFF POINTS FOR CLUSTER-BLOC
ANALYSIS. LIJPHART INDEX OF AGREEMENT FOR U.N. VOTING

NO. OF ROLL-CALLS	SIGNIFICANCE LEVELS FOR SINGLE TAILED TESTS							
	DISAGREEMENT				AGREEMENT			
	.001	.010	.025	.050	.050	.025	.010	.001
1	-	-	-	-	-	-	-	-
2	-	-	-	0.00	0.00	-	-	-
3	-	-	0.00	0.00	100.00	-	-	-
4	-	0.00	12.50	12.50	100.00	100.00	-	-
5	0.00	10.00	10.00	20.00	90.00	100.00	100.00	-
6	0.00	16.67	16.67	25.00	91.67	91.67	100.00	-
7	7.14	14.29	21.43	28.57	85.71	85.71	92.86	100.00
8	12.50	18.75	25.00	25.00	81.25	87.50	93.75	100.00
9	11.11	22.22	27.78	27.78	83.33	83.33	88.89	94.44
10	15.00	25.00	30.00	30.00	80.00	85.00	85.00	95.00
11	18.18	27.27	27.27	31.82	77.27	81.82	86.36	90.91
12	20.83	25.00	29.17	33.33	75.00	79.17	83.33	91.67
13	19.23	26.92	30.77	34.62	76.92	80.77	80.77	88.46
14	21.43	28.57	32.14	35.71	75.00	78.57	82.14	89.29
15	23.33	30.00	33.33	36.67	73.33	76.67	80.00	86.67
16	25.00	31.25	34.37	37.50	75.00	75.00	78.13	84.37
17	26.47	32.35	35.29	38.24	73.53	76.47	79.41	85.29
18	25.00	33.33	36.11	38.89	72.22	75.00	77.78	83.33
19	26.32	34.21	36.84	39.47	71.05	73.68	76.32	84.21
20	27.50	35.00	37.50	40.00	72.50	75.00	77.50	82.50
21	28.57	33.33	38.10	40.48	71.43	73.81	76.19	80.95
22	29.55	34.09	38.64	40.91	70.45	72.73	75.00	81.82
23	30.43	34.78	39.13	41.30	69.57	71.74	76.09	80.43
24	31.25	35.42	39.58	41.67	70.83	72.92	75.00	79.17
25	30.00	36.00	40.00	42.00	70.00	72.00	74.00	80.00
26	30.77	36.54	38.46	42.31	69.23	71.15	73.08	78.85
27	31.48	37.04	38.89	42.59	68.52	70.37	74.07	77.78
28	32.14	37.50	39.29	42.86	67.86	71.43	73.21	78.57
29	32.76	37.93	39.66	43.10	68.97	70.69	72.41	77.59
30	33.33	38.33	40.00	43.33	68.33	70.00	73.33	76.67
31	33.87	38.71	40.32	43.55	67.74	69.35	72.58	77.42
32	34.37	39.06	40.62	43.75	67.19	70.31	71.87	76.56
33	34.85	39.39	40.91	43.94	68.18	69.70	71.21	75.76
34	33.82	39.71	41.18	44.12	67.65	69.12	72.06	76.47
35	34.29	40.00	41.43	44.29	67.14	68.57	71.43	75.71
36	34.72	40.28	41.67	44.44	66.67	69.44	70.83	75.00
37	35.14	40.54	41.89	44.59	66.22	68.92	70.27	75.00
38	35.53	40.79	42.11	44.74	67.11	68.42	71.05	75.00
39	35.90	41.03	42.31	44.87	66.67	67.95	70.51	74.36
40	36.25	41.25	42.50	45.00	66.25	67.50	70.00	75.00
41	36.59	41.46	42.68	45.12	65.85	68.29	69.51	74.39
42	36.90	41.67	42.86	45.24	65.48	67.86	70.24	73.81
43	37.21	40.70	43.02	45.35	66.28	67.44	69.77	73.26
44	37.50	40.91	43.18	45.45	65.91	67.05	69.32	73.86
45	37.78	41.11	43.33	45.56	65.56	67.78	68.89	73.33
46	38.04	41.30	43.48	45.65	65.22	67.39	69.57	72.83
47	38.30	41.49	43.62	45.74	64.89	67.02	69.15	73.40
48	37.50	41.67	43.75	45.83	65.62	66.67	68.75	72.92
49	37.76	41.84	43.88	45.92	65.31	66.33	68.37	72.45
50	38.00	42.00	44.00	46.00	65.00	67.00	69.00	72.00

TABLE A5.6 CONTINUED

PERCENTAGE CUT-OFF POINTS FOR CLUSTER-BLOC ANALYSIS
WITH THE PROBABILITY OF AGREEMENT = 0.333
OF PARTIAL AGREEMENT = 0.444
OF DISAGREEMENT = 0.222

NO. OF ROLL-CALLS	SIGNIFICANCE LEVELS FOR SINGLE TAILED TESTS							
	DISAGREEMENT				AGREEMENT			
	.001	.010	.025	.050	.050	.025	.010	.001
51	38.24	42.16	44.12	46.08	64.71	66.67	68.63	72.55
52	38.46	42.31	44.23	46.15	64.42	66.35	68.27	72.12
53	38.68	42.45	44.34	46.23	65.09	66.04	67.92	71.70
54	38.89	42.59	44.44	46.30	64.81	66.67	67.59	71.30
55	39.09	42.73	44.55	46.36	64.55	66.36	68.18	71.82
56	39.29	42.86	44.64	46.43	64.29	66.07	67.86	71.43
57	39.47	42.98	44.74	46.49	64.04	65.79	67.54	71.05
58	39.66	43.10	44.83	46.55	64.66	65.52	67.24	70.69
59	39.83	43.22	44.92	46.61	64.41	66.10	67.80	71.19
60	40.00	43.33	45.00	46.67	64.17	65.83	67.50	70.83
61	40.16	43.44	45.08	46.72	63.93	65.57	67.21	70.49
62	40.32	43.55	45.16	46.77	63.71	65.32	66.94	70.97
63	40.48	43.65	45.24	46.83	64.29	65.08	66.67	70.63
64	40.62	43.75	46.09	46.88	64.06	65.62	67.19	70.31
65	40.77	43.85	46.15	46.92	63.85	65.38	66.92	70.00
66	40.91	43.94	46.21	46.97	63.64	65.15	66.67	70.45
67	41.04	44.03	46.27	47.01	63.43	64.93	66.42	70.15
68	41.18	44.12	46.32	47.79	63.97	64.71	66.91	69.85
69	41.30	44.20	46.38	47.83	63.77	65.22	66.67	69.57
70	41.43	44.29	46.43	47.86	63.57	65.00	66.43	70.00
71	41.55	44.37	46.48	47.89	63.38	64.79	66.20	69.72
72	41.67	44.44	46.53	47.92	63.19	64.58	65.97	69.44
73	41.78	44.52	46.58	47.95	63.01	64.38	66.44	69.18
74	41.89	44.59	46.62	47.97	63.51	64.86	66.22	69.59
75	42.00	44.67	46.67	48.00	63.33	64.67	66.00	69.33
76	42.11	44.74	46.71	48.03	63.16	64.47	65.79	69.08
77	41.56	44.81	46.75	48.05	62.99	64.29	65.58	68.83
78	41.67	44.87	46.79	48.08	62.82	64.10	66.03	68.59
79	41.77	44.94	46.84	48.10	63.29	64.56	65.82	68.99
80	41.87	45.00	46.88	48.12	63.12	64.37	65.62	68.75
81	41.98	45.68	46.91	48.15	62.96	64.20	65.43	68.52
82	42.07	45.73	46.95	48.17	62.80	64.02	65.85	68.29
83	42.17	45.78	46.99	48.19	62.65	63.86	65.66	68.67
84	42.26	45.83	47.02	48.21	62.50	63.69	65.48	68.45
85	42.35	45.88	47.06	48.24	62.94	64.12	65.29	68.24
86	42.44	45.93	47.09	48.26	62.79	63.95	65.12	68.02
87	42.53	45.98	47.13	48.28	62.64	63.79	65.52	68.39
88	42.61	46.02	47.16	48.30	62.50	63.64	65.34	68.18
89	42.70	46.07	47.19	48.31	62.36	63.48	65.17	67.98
90	42.78	46.11	47.22	48.33	62.22	63.89	65.00	67.78
91	42.86	46.15	47.25	48.90	62.64	63.74	64.84	68.13
92	42.93	46.20	47.28	48.91	62.50	63.59	65.22	67.93
93	43.01	46.24	47.31	48.92	62.37	63.44	65.05	67.74
94	43.09	46.28	47.34	48.94	62.23	63.30	64.89	67.55
95	43.16	46.32	47.37	48.95	62.11	63.68	64.74	67.37
96	43.23	46.35	47.40	48.96	61.98	63.54	64.58	67.71
97	43.30	46.39	47.94	48.97	62.37	63.40	64.95	67.53
98	43.37	46.43	47.96	48.98	62.24	63.27	64.80	67.35
99	43.43	46.46	47.98	48.99	62.12	63.13	64.65	67.17
100	43.50	46.50	48.00	49.00	62.00	63.00	64.50	67.50

TABLE A5.6 CONTINUED

PERCENTAGE CUT-OFF POINTS FOR CLUSTER-BLOC ANALYSIS
WITH THE PROBABILITY OF AGREEMENT = 0.333
OF PARTIAL AGREEMENT = 0.444
OF DISAGREEMENT = 0.222

	SIGNIFICANCE LEVELS FOR SINGLE TAILED TESTS							
NO. OF	DISAGREEMENT				AGREEMENT			
ROLL-CALLS	.001	.010	.025	.050	.050	.025	.010	.001
101	43.56	46.53	48.02	49.01	61.88	63.37	64.36	67.33
102	43.63	46.57	48.04	49.02	62.25	63.24	64.71	67.16
103	43.69	46.60	48.06	49.03	62.14	63.11	64.56	66.99
104	43.75	46.63	48.08	49.04	62.02	62.98	64.42	67.31
105	43.81	46.67	48.10	49.05	61.90	62.86	64.29	67.14
106	43.87	46.70	48.11	49.06	61.79	63.21	64.15	66.98
107	43.93	46.73	48.13	49.07	61.68	63.08	64.02	66.82
108	43.98	46.76	48.15	49.07	62.04	62.96	64.35	66.67
109	44.04	46.79	48.17	49.08	61.93	62.84	64.22	66.97
110	44.09	46.82	48.18	49.09	61.82	62.73	64.09	66.82
111	44.14	46.85	48.20	49.55	61.71	62.61	63.96	66.67
112	44.20	46.88	48.21	49.55	61.61	62.95	63.84	66.52
113	44.25	46.90	48.23	49.56	61.50	62.83	64.16	66.37
114	44.30	46.93	48.25	49.56	61.84	62.72	64.04	66.67
115	44.35	46.96	48.26	49.57	61.74	62.61	63.91	66.52
116	44.40	46.98	48.28	49.57	61.64	62.50	63.79	66.38
117	44.44	47.01	48.29	49.57	61.54	62.82	63.68	66.24
118	44.49	47.03	48.31	49.58	61.44	62.71	63.98	66.53
119	44.54	47.06	48.32	49.58	61.34	62.61	63.87	66.39
120	44.58	47.08	48.33	49.58	61.67	62.50	63.75	66.25
121	44.63	47.52	48.76	49.59	61.57	62.40	63.64	66.12
122	44.67	47.54	48.77	49.59	61.48	62.30	63.52	65.98
123	44.72	47.56	48.78	49.59	61.38	62.60	63.82	66.26
124	44.76	47.58	48.79	49.60	61.29	62.50	63.71	66.13
125	44.80	47.60	48.80	49.60	61.20	62.40	63.60	66.00
126	44.84	47.62	48.81	49.60	61.51	62.30	63.49	65.87
127	44.88	47.64	48.82	49.61	61.42	62.20	63.39	66.14
128	44.92	47.66	48.83	49.61	61.33	62.11	63.28	66.02
129	44.96	47.67	48.84	50.00	61.24	62.40	63.57	65.89
130	45.00	47.69	48.85	50.00	61.15	62.31	63.46	65.77
131	45.04	47.71	48.85	50.00	61.07	62.21	63.36	65.65
132	45.08	47.73	48.86	50.00	61.36	62.12	63.26	65.91
133	45.11	47.74	48.87	50.00	61.28	62.03	63.16	65.79
134	45.15	47.76	48.88	50.00	61.19	62.31	63.43	65.67
135	45.19	47.78	48.89	50.00	61.11	62.22	63.33	65.56
136	45.22	47.79	48.90	50.00	61.03	62.13	63.24	65.44
137	45.26	47.81	48.91	50.00	60.95	62.04	63.14	65.69
138	45.29	47.83	48.91	50.00	61.23	61.96	63.04	65.58
139	45.32	47.84	48.92	50.00	61.15	61.87	63.31	65.47
140	45.36	47.86	48.93	50.00	61.07	62.14	63.21	65.36
141	45.74	47.87	48.94	50.00	60.99	62.06	63.12	65.25
142	45.77	47.89	49.30	50.00	60.92	61.97	63.03	65.49
143	45.80	47.90	49.30	50.00	60.84	61.89	62.94	65.38
144	45.83	47.92	49.31	50.00	61.11	61.81	62.85	65.28
145	45.86	47.93	49.31	50.00	61.03	81.72	63.10	65.17
146	45.89	47.95	49.32	50.34	60.96	61.99	63.01	65.07
147	45.92	47.96	49.32	50.34	60.88	61.90	62.93	65.31
148	45.95	48.31	49.32	50.34	60.81	61.82	62.84	65.20
149	45.97	48.32	49.33	50.34	60.74	61.74	62.75	65.10
150	46.00	48.33	49.33	50.33	60.67	61.67	63.00	65.00

TABLE A5.6

PERCENTAGE CUT-OFF POINTS FOR CLUSTER-BLOC ANALYSIS
WITH THE PROBABILITY OF AGREEMENT = 0.333
OF PARTIAL AGREEMENT = 0.444
OF DISAGREEMENT = 0.222

| | SIGNIFICANCE LEVELS FOR SINGLE TAILED TESTS | | | | | | | |
| NO. OF | DISAGREEMENT | | | | AGREEMENT | | | |
ROLL-CALLS	.001	.010	.025	.050	.050	.025	.010	.001
151	46.03	48.34	49.34	50.33	60.93	61.59	62.91	65.23
152	46.05	48.36	49.34	50.33	60.86	61.84	62.83	65.13
153	46.08	48.37	49.35	50.33	60.78	61.76	62.75	65.03
154	46.10	48.38	49.35	50.32	60.71	61.69	62.66	64.94
155	46.13	48.39	49.35	50.32	60.65	61.61	62.58	64.84
156	46.15	48.40	49.36	50.32	60.58	61.54	62.82	65.06
157	46.18	48.41	49.36	50.32	60.83	61.46	62.74	64.97
158	46.20	48.42	49.37	50.32	60.76	61.71	62.66	64.87
159	46.23	48.43	49.37	50.31	60.69	61.64	62.58	64.78
160	46.25	48.44	49.37	50.31	60.62	61.56	62.50	64.69
161	46.27	48.45	49.69	50.31	60.56	61.49	62.73	64.91
162	46.30	48.46	49.69	50.62	60.49	61.42	62.65	64.81
163	46.32	48.47	49.69	50.61	60.74	61.35	62.58	64.72
164	46.34	48.48	49.70	50.61	60.67	61.59	62.50	64.63
165	46.36	48.48	49.70	50.61	60.61	61.52	62.42	64.55
166	46.39	48.49	49.70	50.60	60.54	61.45	62.35	64.76
167	46.41	48.50	49.70	50.60	60.48	61.38	62.57	64.67
168	46.43	48.51	49.70	50.60	60.42	61.31	62.50	64.58
169	46.45	48.52	49.70	50.59	60.36	61.24	62.43	64.50
170	46.47	48.53	49.71	50.59	60.59	61.47	62.35	64.41
171	46.49	48.83	49.71	50.58	60.53	61.40	62.28	64.62
172	46.51	48.84	49.71	50.58	60.47	61.34	62.21	64.53
173	46.53	48.84	49.71	50.58	60.40	61.27	62.43	64.45
174	46.55	48.85	49.71	50.57	60.34	61.21	62.36	64.37
175	46.57	48.86	49.71	50.57	60.29	61.14	62.29	64.29
176	46.59	48.86	49.72	50.57	60.51	61.36	62.22	64.49
177	46.61	48.87	49.72	50.85	60.45	61.30	62.15	64.41
178	46.63	48.88	49.72	50.84	60.39	61.24	62.36	64.33
179	46.65	48.88	50.00	50.84	60.34	61.17	62.29	64.25
180	46.67	48.89	50.00	50.83	60.28	61.11	62.22	64.17
181	46.69	48.90	50.00	50.83	60.22	61.05	62.15	64.09
182	46.70	48.90	50.00	50.82	60.44	61.26	62.09	64.29
183	46.72	48.91	50.00	50.82	60.38	61.20	62.02	64.21
184	46.74	48.91	50.00	50.82	60.33	61.14	62.23	64.13
185	46.76	48.92	50.00	50.81	60.27	61.08	62.16	64.05
186	46.77	48.92	50.00	50.81	60.22	61.02	62.10	63.98
187	47.06	48.93	50.00	50.80	60.16	60.96	62.03	64.17
188	47.07	48.94	50.00	50.80	60.11	61.17	61.97	64.10
189	47.09	48.94	50.00	50.79	60.32	61.11	61.90	64.02
190	47.11	48.95	50.00	50.79	60.26	61.05	62.11	63.95
191	47.12	48.95	50.00	50.79	60.21	60.99	62.04	63.87
192	47.14	49.22	50.00	51.04	60.16	60.94	61.98	64.06
193	47.15	49.22	50.00	51.04	60.10	60.88	61.92	63.99
194	47.16	49.23	50.00	51.03	60.05	61.08	61.86	63.92
195	47.18	49.23	50.00	51.03	60.26	61.03	61.79	63.85
196	47.19	49.23	50.26	51.02	60.20	60.97	61.99	63.78
197	47.21	49.24	50.25	51.02	60.15	60.91	61.93	63.96
198	47.22	49.24	50.25	51.01	60.10	60.86	61.87	63.89
199	47.24	49.25	50.25	51.01	60.05	60.80	61.81	63.82
200	47.25	49.25	50.25	51.00	60.00	61.00	61.75	63.75

regarded as observations on the nature of the roll-calls. Then the factors represent groups of roll-calls that reflect a common issue dimension. Nobody has yet attempted such an approach with cluster-bloc analysis, but it can in fact be used in the two comparable ways. The technique need not be limited to the investigation of the voting blocs among assembly members but can also be used to investigate whether there are any *issue-sets* that evoke a common response.

To discover issue-sets it is first necessary to construct agreement scores for every possible pair of the roll-calls. If just identical voting is considered, then Issue Similarity,

$$I_s = \frac{\text{No. of Assembly Members casting Identical Votes}}{\text{Total No. of members voting on both roll-calls}} \times 100$$

Or if it is decided to allow for abstentions in United Nations voting, then Issue Similarity,

$$I_s = \left(\frac{i + \frac{1}{2}h}{s}\right) . 100,$$

where i = No. of states that cast identical notes on the two roll-calls;

h = No. of states partially agreed on similarity of the roll-calls, i.e. voting Abstain on one and Yes or No on the other;

s = Total No. of states that vote on both roll-calls.

Once the Issue Similarity scores have been calculated we wish to know which scores are high enough to give pairs of significantly similar roll-calls. Two new symbols may be used.

p_i = probability of identical voting on the roll-calls;

p_o = probability of opposite voting on the roll-calls;

With a simple index which ignores abstentions, a legislator may vote in one of only four different ways on two roll-calls (1) Yes/Yes, (2) No/No, (3) Yes/No and (4) No/Yes. With random voting each has a probability of one in four, and thus $p_i = 0.5$ and $p_o = 0.5$. The equations for Issue Similarity scores will be the same as those for voting agreement between legislators. Therefore Table A5.2 gives the same cut-off points for significantly similar roll-calls.

If a group of roll-calls form a set in which every roll-call is significantly similar to every other roll-call in the set, then we may take it that the roll-calls all represent different aspects of a common underlying issue dimension. But according to the logic it is also possible to find pairs of roll-calls that are significantly dissimilar. In this case, we would also conclude that the two roll-calls represent the *same* dimension. Very often in roll-call voting there is a switch in the way those with the same attitudes must vote in order to express that attitude, e.g. a conservative American Senator who considers that India is becoming socialist might vote *in favour* of an amendment to the Foreign Aid Bill to deny all aid to India, and then when the amendment fails would vote *against* the Bill as a whole. Such a pair of roll-calls would then have a high dissimilarity and should be part of the same issue-set. There must of course be a congruent pattern to any sets made up from roll-calls that are significantly similar to some roll-calls while being significantly dissimilar to others in the set. In general if A and B are similar while A and C are dissimilar, then B and C must be dissimilar as well, in order to make A, B, and C form a set.

If Issue Similarity scores are calculated for United Nations roll-calls including Abstain/Abstain pairs but ignoring partial similarity pairs, then $p_i = 0.3333$ and $p_o = 0.6667$. If partial similarity is included in the Index, then the probability of identical voting $p_i = 0.333$, of opposite responses $p_o = 0.2222$, and of partially similar responses $p_h = 0.4444$, and the cut-off points are the same as those in Table A5.6.

Just as we may study the significant relative agreement of legislators in relation to a particular set of roll-calls, it is also possible to study the *significant relative similarity* among issues. In other words, identical motions or bills formulated in an identical way may produce different results in different legislatures or even in the same legislature at a different time. Therefore, by analogous reasoning to that given earlier, values of p_i, p_o and, if necessary, p_h may be determined empirically, and the appropriate significance tables may be calculated.

Conclusions

In order to avoid being mesmerised by figures, one must reiterate the limitations that are inherent in all methods of legislative roll-call analysis. In the first place, the data consists solely of the recorded votes. While each legislator is thus making a conscious and deliberate public commitment, his recorded vote is still only a partial manifestation of the legislator's attitude. It has already been well established that in elections the individual citizen voter casts his vote on the basis of long-established party loyalties or on just the broad outlines of the issues. Similarly, legislators usually vote on the broad principles of a bill, the technicalities or legal points usually being disposed of in committees. Thus roll-calls do provide a coherent set of data that indicate alignments on the main issues. Judicial decision-making should perhaps be treated with more caution. The strictest interpretation of the role of a judge asserts that neither political nor moral attitudes should have any effect on judicial decisions. Although in America, at least, it is well established that the attitudes of judges are reflected in their decisions, they are certainly not the only determinant factors.

Secondly, while the establishment of statistical significance is of great value it is not an end in itself. It does not *eliminate* the risk of error but just gives us a *known* risk of error: for example, in the U.N. 20th Session there were 117 states, which gives 6786 possible pairs of states. At the $p \leqslant 0.001$ level of significance we would expect to be wrong 7 out of 6786 times in assigning agreement or lack of agreement to a pair of states and at the $p \leqslant 0.05$ level we would expect to be wrong with as many as 34 pairs. It may be stating the obvious, but it is necessary to stress that any voting pattern discovered on the basis of statistical significance is not necessarily one that is *substantively* significant.

Thirdly, cluster-bloc analysis is a purely descriptive technique. It does not in itself provide any explanation of political processes. Very often we may wish to use it for simple exploration, asking such questions as, What blocs exist? How stable are they over time? The results may then suggest theories or may be used to support theories, but are not a substitute for theory. Indeed with the average legislature so much data will be generated that the researcher will be lost unless he knows beforehand exactly what he is looking for. There will probably be several hundred issue similarity scores and several thousand legislator agreement scores. Even very simple propositions will help in handling this amount of data.

Cluster-bloc analysis has long been established as one of the main methods available for legislative roll-call analysis. It can now become *the* main method, especially since the widespread use of computers in the social sciences means that the vast amount of labour formerly required should no longer be a hindrance to its use. Now that the method can be shown to have a sound statistical base, there is no longer any reason for the researcher to be forced to take arbitrary decisions that may greatly affect the results. The methodology is much strengthened. The use of summary indices that give limited information about predetermined groups is no longer necessary. The data itself can be used to discover empirically what are the voting blocs, but it can also be used to study any specified group. Factor analysis need no longer be considered a superior methodology, since it requires some substantial manipulation of the data and dubious assumptions about the level of measurement and normality.[31] Cluster-bloc analysis does not require this, and it allows the researcher to remain closely in touch with his data. Useful indices of cohesion within a group and adhesion between groups may be derived from the agreement scores.[32] Finally the methodology can also be adapted to find issue-sets that indicate underlying issue dimensions. If the cluster-blocs are then examined on each of the issue-sets, we have a very powerful method of analysis.

References

1. In everyday use the words 'vote', 'roll-call' and 'issue' may be used with a high degree of interchangeability. To avoid confusion in this article, the use of the nouns will be restricted as follows: 'vote' – one decision of Yes/No/Abstain by one individual; 'roll-call' – the aggregate result of all the members publicly voting on one resolution, bill, amendment, case or procedural question; 'issue' – an underlying dimension that is common to a set of related roll-calls.

2. Thomas Hovet, *Bloc Politics in the United Nations* (Cambridge, Mass.: Harvard University Press, 1960). Thomas Hovet, *Africa in the United Nations* (Evanston, Ill.: Northwestern University Press, 1963).

3. Arend Lijphart, 'The Analysis of Bloc Voting in the General Assembly: A Critique and a Proposal', *American Political Science Review*, 57 (December 1963), 902–17.

4. Leroy N. Reiselbach, 'Quantitative Techniques for Studying Voting Behaviour in the U.N. General Assembly', *International Organization*, 14 (Spring 1960), 291–306.

5. On U.N. voting, Hayward R. Alker and Bruce M. Russett, *World Politics in The General Assembly* (New Haven: Yale University Press, 1965), used factor analysis to discover issue dimensions and described states in terms of factor scores. Bruce M. Russett, in 'Discovering Voting Groups in the United Nations', *American Political Science Review*, 60 (June 1966), 327–39, used the alternative Q-type factor analysis.

6. Keith Hope, 'Complete Analysis: A Method of Interpreting Multivariate Data', *Journal of Market Research Society* (U.K.) 2 (1969), 267–84. The example given in this article used data from the 17th Session of the UN.

7. John E. Mueller, 'Some Comments on Russett's "Discovering voting Groups in the United Nations" ', *American Political Science Review*, 51 (March 1967), 146–8. Oran R. Young, 'Professor Russett: Industrious Tailor to a Naked Emperor', *World Politics*, 21 (April 1969), 486–95. Robert E. Riggs, Karen F. Hanson, Mary Neinz,

Barry B. Hughes and Thomas J. Volgy, 'Behavioralism in the study of The United Nations', *World Politics*, 22 (January 1970), 192–326, see especially page 211.

8. David Truman, *The Congressional Party* (Wiley, New York, 1959), p. 329.

9. Truman, p. 326.

10. Truman, pp. 321–2.

11. Truman, p. 324.

12. Arend Lijphart, 'Analysis of Bloc Voting. . .', p. 913.

13. Glendon A. Schubert, 'The Study of Judicial Decision-Making as an Aspect of Political Behavior', *American Political Science Review*, 52 (December 1958), 1007–25: quotation from pages 1012–13. (There is actually a substantial text covered by the ellipsis dots, but Schubert's meaning is not violated.)

14. Herman C. Beyle, *Identification and Analysis of Attribute-Cluster-Blocs* (University of Chicago Press, 1931), pp. 29–31.

15. Samuel P. Hayes, 'Probability and Beyle's "Index of Cohesion" ', *Journal of Social Psychology*, 9 (1939), 161–7; quotation from page 161, italics in the original.

16. Hayes, p. 163, italics in the original.

17. A discussion of probability theory and the binominal distribution is given in most statistical textbooks. See for example Blalock, *Social Statistics* (New York, McGraw-Hill, 1960) for a particularly clear exposition. The argument at this stage is identical to the conventional discussion of how many heads will be expected in N tosses of a coin.

18. This result could occur if legislator A voted Yes on all roll-calls and B voted No on all roll-calls; or the reverse could occur; or A could vote Yes on the first four and No on the second four, with B voting the reverse way, etc., etc. These variations which all produce the same agreement score of 0% have already been taken into account by derivation of p_f and p_d from the four original Yes-No voting patterns.

19. This is not always true as there are some discontinuities in the results due to percentaging on a relatively low base, e.g. at the 0·05 level, the cut-off for 110 roll-calls is 59·1% which is higher than that for 100 roll-calls. More detailed results are available on request.

20. Peter Willetts, *The Behaviour of the African Group in the UN General Assembly* (unpublished M.Sc. Dissertation, University of Strathclyde, Scotland).

21. Willetts, Chapter 4. Both Tables A5.3 and A5.4 are based on the use of Lijphart's Index of Agreement for U.N. votes, discussed later in this paper.

22. Details of the computer programme for those that need to calculate cut-off points for significant relative agreement are available on request. Tables for values of p_f = 0·6, 0·7, 0·8, and 0·9 have already been computed and are also available.

23. Glendon A. Schubert, *Quantitative Analysis of Judicial Behavior* (Glencoe, Illinois, Free Press 1959). Unanimous decisions constituted about 30% of all cases (p. 81). For marginal decisions matrices see p. 117 and pp. 149–53.

24. Peter Russell, *The Supreme Court of Canada as a Bilingual and Bicultural Institution* (Ottowa: Queen's Printer, 1969), 127.

25. C. Herman Pritchett, *Civil Liberties and the Vinson Court* (Chicago: University of Chicago Press, 1954). C. Herman Pritchett, *The Roosevelt Court: A Study in Judicial Politics and Values* (New York: MacMillam, 1948). See also Schubert, *Quantitative Analysis. . . .*; and Russell *The Supreme Court of Canada. . . .*

26. For example, on page 132 of Russell the two joint dissent matrices only yield one pair of judges in significant agreement, whereas on page 133 the joint assent matrices clearly show a bloc structure.

27. Reiselbach, 'Quantitative Techniques . . .', pp. 292–3. Benjamin D. Meyers, 'African Voting in the United Nations General Assembly', *Journal of Modern African Studies*, 4 (1966), 213–27.

28. Lijphart, *Analysis of Bloc Voting . . .*, p. 910.

29. Tables with p_f = 0·333, 0·4, 0·5, 0·6, 0·7, 0·8, 0·9 or details of computer programme available on request.

30. More detailed computations against the null hypothesis of random voting or for other specified values of p_f, p_g, and p_d will be undertaken on request.

31. See for example Alker and Russett, *World Politics . . .* p. 30, which uses a complicated process of 'standardization' of U.N. voting data. See also the references in note 7, for other authors that share my unease with factor analysis.

32. For example, by taking agreement scores between the U.S.A. and all small states on East/West issues in the U.N. and using the cut-off points given in Table A5.6, it was possible to determine for each state whether it was significantly aligned or not: H. Hveem and P. Willetts, *The Practice of Non-Alignment: on the present and the future of an international movement*, paper to the Universities of East Africa Social Science Conference, Dar es Salaam, December 1970. With factor analysis a Western Bloc would be found, but there is no way of determining whether the loading on this factor for a particular state is statistically significant or not.

Identifying the Group Structure in a Complex Sociomatrix *

One of the disadvantages of academics being divided into separate disciplines is that researchers can easily be working on similar problems without being aware that they could be of assistance to each other. In political science one of the techniques of roll-call analysis, which is used to analyse the decisions of courts, legislatures and the United Nations, is known as cluster-bloc analysis. This is just another name for a particular form of sociometry, in which the data is concerned with political distance rather than status ranking, information flows or friendship choices. The techniques have not made a great deal of progress, yet there appears to have been no attempt to draw on the literature of sociometry.

In a legislature the starting point is with the voting records of each of its members. From this data can be calculated for each pair of legislators the percentage of the roll-calls, that they both attended, in which they voted in agreement with each other, either by jointly agreeing with or by jointly opposing the motion. The result for a legislature of n members is a symmetric, square n by n matrix containing values in the range 0 to 100%. The diagonal cells can contain either 100% signifying that each legislator is in complete agreement with himself or, following the usual sociometric convention, zero percent if self-agreement is not considered meaningful. Use of the binominal distribution makes it possible to test these agreement scores for statistical significance against the null hypothesis of random voting.[1] If +1 is used to indicate significantly high agreement, 0 for medium levels of agreement and −1 significant disagreement, then we have another example of the standard sociomatrix. A cluster-bloc is defined as a group of

*The derivation of the matrix algebra to solve this problem and its expression as a programme was done by John Ford of the Department of Computer Science, University of Essex.

members, everyone of which is in significant agreement with every other. The sociologist will recognise this as a clique. The results would not be particularly interesting for a highly disciplined system such as the United Kingdom House of Commons, but they are of interest for the United States Congress[2] or European multi-party systems. Provided a computer is used, the Harary and Ross algorithm should be efficient in identifying the cluster-blocs.[3]

When voting in the United Nations is under study, 'Abstain' has to be treated as a conscious political choice, which is distinct from a state's delegates being absent from the vote. Allowance is made for this by introducing the concept of 'partial agreement', when one state votes for or against a resolution and another state abstains rather than vote in complete disagreement.[4] Nevertheless, it is still possible to test the agreement between a pair of states for statistical significance, by calculating a multi-nominal distribution for three-way random voting.[5] However, the Harary and Ross algorithm would not provide useful summary information on the cluster-blocs in most sessions of the United Nations General Assembly. The method yields a list of the members of each of the cluster-blocs, but in the fluid, non-party U.N. situation there is a continuous, complicated structure of overlapping blocs. From the 104 states voting in the 16th Session, one would have a list of at least 50 blocs with 20 to 35 members plus many more smaller blocs. The result gives no reduction in the volume of information that has to be comprehended.

One answer to this problem is to return to the approach suggested by Forsyth and Katz of displaying the whole group matrix. They proposed a method of 're-arranging the rows and columns in a systematic manner to produce a new matrix which exhibits the group structure'.[6] However, their procedures did not offer unambiguous rules to produce a unique solution, though 'the process has the obvious advantage that different investigators will tend to produce the same or very similar matrices'.[7] Curiously enough Festinger in a subsequent article quite erroneously said that Forsyth and Katz suggested 're-arranging the order of the rows and columns so as to minimise the square of the perpendicular deviations of the numbers from the diagonal of the matrix'.[8] but in so doing he offered a criterion for a unique solution. Unfortunately the idea was not taken up because, before the advent of computers, it involved too much work.

In complex situations, such as the analysis of U.N. voting, rather than trying to identify cliques, the aim can be to identify the overall group structure displayed in the matrix. The structure is most clearly visible when those members that have a high antimetry[9] towards each other are placed close together. Then the fundamental problem is to re-order the rows of a given matrix A (with N rows and N columns) and re-order the columns, in the same manner, so that as far as possible the largest elements of A are on or near the main diagonal. This general formulation meets the suggestion that we should handle 'valued graphs', because to reduce the data to zero/one dichotomies and to present the 'choice in all or nothing terms leads to the loss of potentially available information'.[10] But the algorithm given below is more satisfactory than Doreian's answer, which is to identify the cliques at different levels of the values in the matrix. The information is more fully used, if simultaneous account is taken of all the different values. In legislative roll-call analysis the values in the matrix can be the values of the index of voting agreement, though problems of different levels of absenteeism or the desire to make comparisons across different numbers of roll-calls at different time periods may mean that it is preferable solely to consider the results of the significance tests. A matrix that only contains ones and zeroes is merely a special case of a valued graph.

An algorithm that aims to put the larger elements of the matrix near the main diagonal can also handle negative values. They will be moved as far away from the diagonal as possible. Thus, in U.N. voting, pairs of states that are in significant disagreement with each other can be signified with -1 and the algorithm follows Forsyth and Katz's rule that we should 'Re-arrange the order of the groups so that the two groups having the greatest mutual rejection, as measured by the proportion of minus signs, are at the extreme ends of the principal diagonal and the others appear inside in order of diminishing amounts of rejection.'[11]

We may measure the distance of a matrix element A_{ij} from the main diagonal by the quantity $(i-j)^2$. Given an arbitrary NxN matrix B, then, we may assess how close it is to the desired situation by examining the quantity

$$\sum_{i=1}^{N} \sum_{j=1}^{N} \left[B_{ij} \times (i-j)^2 \right]$$

Suppose that the rows of A are re-ordered so that the i th original row is now the α_i th row. Then the i th original column is now the α_i th column. Hence, we can assess the usefulness of this particular re-ordering by examining the quantity

$$\sum_{i=1}^{N} \sum_{j=1}^{N} \left[A_{\underset{i}{\alpha}\underset{j}{\alpha}} \times (i-j)^2 \right] \quad ,$$

where $(\alpha_1, \alpha_2, \ldots, \alpha_N)$ is some permutation of the set $(1, 2, \ldots, N)$. (Subsequently, we shall refer to such a vector $\underline{\alpha}$ as a P-vector.) Thus, our basic criterion will be to minimise

$$f(\underline{\alpha}) = \sum_{i=1}^{N} \sum_{j=1}^{N} \left[A_{\underset{i}{\alpha}\underset{j}{\alpha}} \times (i-j)^2 \right]$$

over all possible P-vectors $\underline{\alpha}$, since, hopefully, this will force the largest elements of A to be close to the main diagonal.

We now consider under what circumstances 'f' may be reduced. Let $\underline{\beta}$ be another P-vector which is identical to $\underline{\alpha}$ except for two interchanged elements.

Thus,

$$\beta_i = \alpha_i, \quad i = 1(1)N, \quad i \neq m,n,$$

$$\beta_m = \alpha_n,$$

$$\beta_n = \alpha_m, \quad m \neq n.$$

Then,

$$f(\underline{\beta}) = \sum_{i=1}^{N} \sum_{j=1}^{N} \{ A_{\beta_i \beta_j} \times (i-j)^2 \}$$

$$= \sum_{\substack{i=1 \\ i \neq m \\ i \neq n}}^{N} \left\{ \sum_{\substack{j=1 \\ j \neq m \\ j \neq n}}^{N} [A_{\beta_i \beta_j} \times (i-j)^2] + A_{\beta_i \beta_m} \times (i-m)^2 + A_{\beta_i \beta_n} \times (i-n)^2 \right\}$$

$$+ \left\{ \sum_{\substack{j=1 \\ j \neq m \\ j \neq n}}^{N} [A_{\beta_m \beta_j} \times (m-j)^2] + A_{\beta_m \beta_m} \times (m-m)^2 + A_{\beta_m \beta_n} \times (m-n)^2 \right\}$$

$$+ \{ \sum_{\substack{j=1 \\ j\neq m \\ j\neq n}}^{N} [A_{\beta_n \beta_j} \times (n-j)^2] + A_{\beta_n \beta_m} \times (n-m)^2 + A_{\beta_n \beta_n} \times (n-n)^2 \}$$

$$= \sum_{\substack{i=1 \\ i\neq m \\ i\neq n}}^{N} \{ \sum_{\substack{j=1 \\ j\neq m \\ j\neq n}}^{N} [A_{\alpha_i \alpha_j} \times (i-j)^2] + A_{\alpha_i \alpha_n} \times (i-m)^2 + A_{\alpha_i \alpha_m} \times (i-n)^2 \}$$

$$+ \{ \sum_{\substack{j=1 \\ j\neq m \\ j\neq n}}^{N} [A_{\alpha_n \alpha_j} \times (m-j)^2] + A_{\alpha_n \alpha_m} \times (m-n)^2 \}$$

$$+ \{ \sum_{\substack{j=1 \\ j\neq m \\ j\neq n}}^{N} [A_{\alpha_m \alpha_j} \times (n-j)^2] + A_{\alpha_m \alpha_n} \times (n-m)^2 \}.$$

Thus, using the known expression for $f(\underline{\alpha})$, we obtain

$$f(\underline{\beta}) - f(\underline{\alpha}) = \sum_{\substack{i=1 \\ i\neq m \\ i\neq n}}^{N} \{ [A_{\alpha_i \alpha_m} - A_{\alpha_i \alpha_n}] \times [(i-n)^2 - (i-m)^2] \}$$

$$+ \sum_{\substack{j=1 \\ j\neq m \\ j\neq n}}^{N} \{ [A_{\alpha_m \alpha_j} - A_{\alpha_n \alpha_j}] \times [(n-j)^2 - (m-j)^2] \} \quad (1)$$

Recalling that A is symmetric, so that $A_{\alpha_m \alpha_j} = A_{\alpha_j \alpha_m}$, etc., we have, on simplifying,

$$f(\underline{\beta}) - f(\underline{\alpha}) = 2(m-n) \sum_{\substack{i=1 \\ i\neq m \\ i\neq n}}^{N} \{ (A_{\alpha_i \alpha_m} - A_{\alpha_i \alpha_n}) \times (2i-m-n) \} \quad (2)$$

The algorithm which has been devised is, therefore, to examine the expression on the right-hand side of equation (2) for various choices of the pair of integers 'm' and 'n'. If a pair (m, n) is found such that the expression is negative, so that $f(\underline{\beta}) < f(\underline{\alpha})$, α_m and α_n are interchanged to give the new P-vector $\underline{\beta}$. Starting again with $\underline{\beta}$, we search for a new pair of integers, and so on. When a P-vector $\underline{\alpha}$ is found for which no pair of integers gives a reduction in 'f', the algorithm terminates.

As was mentioned above, the algorithm is general in that it will accept either interval or nominal data and both positive or negative values. Non-symmetric matrices may also be handled by using equation (1) rather than equation (2). Some results for the U.N. 16th, 20th and 25th Sessions are given in Chapters 3–5. It is suggested that results from a valued matrix may be printed in the same way using + and – signs. The matrix could be printed several times, each time using the same order of the rows and the columns produced by the algorithm, but changing the levels at which a + or a – sign would appear. Thus within the same overall structure different levels of cohesion would be successively displayed.

It is possible that on some occasions the vector $\underline{\alpha}$ that is found may not be the desired global minimum of 'f', but it can be proved that $\underline{\alpha}$ is certainly a local minimum of 'f'. In practice it appears that inspection will usually determine whether, in fact, a global minimum has been found. When Salazar's Portugal is found amongst the communist states, the answer is clearly to move Portugal to the other extreme of the matrix and apply the algorithm again to the new configuration. Local minima seem most likely to occur, in the standard sociograms, when a near isolate cannot be moved without disturbing the ordering of medium to large sized cliques. An additional safeguard in case of doubt would be to apply the algorithm to different initial orderings of A. If all tests yield the same final ordering, then it may be viewed with a fair degree of confidence.

Figure 3.1 shows an initial configuration, for finding U.N. cluster-blocs, with the states given in alphabetical order, and Figure 3.2 shows the results of re-ordering the matrix. The main cliques can be readily seen and have been identified by drawing lines round the groups of states. Once one is no longer concerned solely with perfect cliques, there is no satisfactory answer as to where the lines should be drawn. Jordan may be considered a member of the first clique, despite its failure to reach significant agreement with Mongolia; similarly the Ivory Coast was included in the second clique, but should the Central African Republic have been included as well?

The group in the middle presents a complex picture that cannot be clearly defined. But this is not a problem with the method, so much as a reflection of the fact that real world situations can often be complex. When the data does contain a clear set of perfect overlapping cliques or of distinct cliques, then the algorithm will identify them.

In addition to the possibility of local minima, there are several ways in which the matrix may be printed in different orderings that are in fact equivalent to each other. If they are not eliminated from the analysis beforehand, complete isolates may appear in any position that separates them from the distinct cliques. They may appear at either end of the matrix or in between cliques. Secondly if more than one member of the group has an identical pattern of relationships with the rest of the group, then these identical members will appear together but their relative ordering is of no significance, being dependent upon the initial configuration of the matrix. Thus in Figure 3.2 there is no significance to the ordering of the first eight communist states nor to the ordering of Indonesia, Mali, Guinea. Lastly, there is no unique solution to the ordering of separate cliques (or separate sets of overlapping cliques), that have no links across the clique boundaries, except that the order may be determined by a pattern of antagonisms between the cliques. The order within each clique may be determined, without there being a unique order for the whole cliques relative to each other.

As the number of members in the group and the complexity of their relations increases, the computing time required for the algorithm increases dramatically. There appear to be no problems involved in starting the programme with an approximate guess as to the final ordering of the matrix, in order to save computer time. Another approach might be to use the first few stages of the Harary and Ross algorithm as a preliminary to the use of the algorithm given above. Without any attempt having been made to prove the idea, the algorithm appears to operate more efficiently, if it is slightly modified for computing purposes. The basic structure of the group of N members may be first obtained by only inter-changing elements m and n when

$$f(\underline{\beta}) - f(\underline{\alpha}) < -N^2$$

Then further refinement is obtained by making changes when

$$f(\underline{\beta}) - f(\underline{\alpha}) < -N^2/10$$

The process is repeated, reducing the order of magnitude of the threshold level for making changes, until zero is reached.

References

1. See Appendix 5.

2. D. Truman, *The Congressional Party* (Wiley, New York, 1959).

3. F. Harary and I. C. Ross, 'A Procedure for Clique Detection Using the Group Matrix', *Sociometry*, Vol. 20, September 1957, pp. 205–15.

4. A. Lijphart, 'The Analysis of Bloc Voting in the General Assembly: A Critique and a Proposal', *American Political Science Review*, Vol. LVII, December 1963, pp. 902–17.

5. See Appendix 5.

6. E. Forsyth and L. Katz, 'A Matrix Approach to the Analysis of Sociometric Data: Preliminary Report', *Sociometry*, Vol. 9, December 1946, pp. 340–7. Quote from page 341.

7. *Ibid.*, p. 346.

8. L. Festinger, 'The Analysis of Sociograms using Matrix Algebra', *Human Relations*, Vol. 2, 1949, pp. 153–8. Quote from page 154.

9. This is the term used by R. D. Luce in 'Connectivity and Generalised Cliques in Sociometrix Group Structure', *Psychometrika*, Vol. 15, June 1950, pp. 169–90.

10. P. Doreian, 'A Note on the Detection of Cliques in Valued Graphs', *Sociometry*, Vol. 32, June 1969, pp. 237–42. Quote from pages 237–8.

11. Forsyth and Katz, *op. cit.*, p. 343.

Bibliography

1. Documents on non-alignment in chronological order

(a)   *Select Documents on Asian Affairs. India 1947–50, Vol. 2 External Affairs*, Ed. by S. L. Poplai (Oxford University Press for the Indian Council of World Affairs, 1959).

(b)   *Panchsheel: Its Meaning and History* (Lok Sabha Secretariat, New Delhi, 1958).

(c)   'Final Communiqué of the Bandung Conference, 24 April 1955', pp. 429–36 of N. Frankland and P. Woodcock (Eds.) *Documents on International Affairs 1955* (Royal Institute of International Affairs and Oxford University Press, London, 1958).

(d)   *Foreign Policy of India: Texts of Documents, 1947–59* (Lok Sabha Secretariat, New Delhi, 1959).

(e)   *Belgrade Conference of Heads of State or Government of Non-Aligned Countries* (Jugoslavija Publishing House, Belgrade, 1961 and second undated edition).

(f)   *Nasser Speaks. Basic Documents*. Translated by E. S. Farag (The Morssett Press, London, 1972), contains 'The Philosophy of the Revolution' and 'The Charter'.

(g)   Charter of the Organisation of African Unity' (General Secretariat of the O.A.U., Addis Ababa, 1965). Reprinted in Z. Cervenka, *The Organisation of African Unity and Its Charter* (C. Hurst and Co., London, 1969).

(h)   *The U.A.R. and the Policy of Non-Alignment* (Ministry of National Guidance, Cairo, undated, presumed to be 1964), contains some information on the Colombo preparatory meeting.

(i) *Synopsis of the Second Conference of Non-Aligned Countries* (Information Department, Cairo, undated, presumed to be 1964).

(j) *Conference of Heads of State and Governments of Non-Aligned Countries, Cairo, October 5–10, 1964* (Ministry of National Guidance, Information Administration, Cairo, undated).

(k) *Consultative Meeting of Special Government Representatives of Non-Aligned Countries, Belgrade, July 8–12, 1969* (Medunarodna Politika, Belgrade, 1970).

(l) *Documents. Activity of Non-Aligned Countries* (circulated at the Lusaka Conference, no publishing information included, appears to be Medjunarodna Politika, Belgrade), contents include 'Communiqué of Ministers Meeting in New York 27 September 1969' and 'Final Communiqué of the Preparatory Meeting of Non-Aligned Countries, Dar es Salaam, 13–17 April 1970'.

(m) 'Third Conference of Non-Aligned Countries in Lusaka, September 8–10, 1970', in *Review of International Affairs*, No. 491 and No. 492, Belgrade, 1970.

(n) *Lusaka Declaration on Peace, Independence, Development, Co-operation and Democratisation of International Relations and Resolutions of the Third Conference of Heads of State or Government of Non-Aligned Countries* (U.N. note verbale NV/209, 12th November 1970).

(o) 'Non-Aligned Countries Communiqué September 1971', in *Review of International Affairs*, No. 516, Belgrade, 1971, pp. 15–18. Other sources date this communiqué 1/10/71.

(p) 'Guyana and the Non-Aligned Movement', *Guyana Journal*, December 1971, Vol. 1, No. 5 (Ministry of External Affairs, Georgetown), pp. 41–7. This contains some notes on the Lusaka summit and the New York meeting, including the members of the Preparatory Committee omitted from (o) above.

(q) *The Thrust of Non-Alignment* (Ministry of External Affairs, Georgetown, July 1972), contains notes on the Preparatory Committee meetings.

(r) *The Georgetown Declaration. The Action Programme for Economic Co-operation and Related Documents* (Ministry of External Affairs, Georgetown, publication undated).

(s)   'Meeting of the Preparatory Committee of Non-Aligned Countries in Kabul', *Review of International Affairs*, No. 556, Belgrade, 1973, pp. 17–18.

(t)   *Fundamental Texts, Fourth Conference of Heads of State or Government of Non-Aligned Countries* (no publication details given, but produced by the Algerian Government). Almost all the contents are in *United Nations Document A/9330*.

(u)   'Declaration of the Non-Aligned on the Middle East', *Review of International Affairs*, No. 565, Belgrade, 1973, p. 15.

(v)   'Meeting of the Co-ordinating Bureau of the Non-Aligned, Algiers 19–21 March 1974', *Review of International Affairs*, No. 576, Belgrade, 1974, pp. 17–21.

(w)   'Conference of Developing Countries on Raw Materials, Dakar, 3rd to 8th February 1975', *United Nations Document E/AC.62/6*.

(x)   'Ministerial Meeting of the Co-ordination Bureau of the Non-Aligned Countries, Havana, March 1975', *United Nations Document NV/463*.

(y)   'Conference of Ministers for Foreign Affairs of Non-Aligned Countries, Lima 25 to 30 August 1975', *United Nations Document A/10217*.

(z)   'Documents of the Fifth Conference of Heads of State or Government of Non-Aligned Countries', *United Nations Document A/31/197*.

(A)   'Ministerial Meeting of the Bureau of Non-Aligned Countries Algiers, May 30–June 2, 1976', *United Nations Document A/31/110*.

(B)   'Documents of the Conference of Foreign Ministers of the Co-ordinating Bureau of Non-Aligned Countries', Delhi, April 1977, *United Nations Document A/32/74*.

(C)   O. Jankowtsch and K. P. Sauvant (Eds.), *The Third World Without Superpowers: The Collected Documents of the Non-Aligned Countries* (Oceana Publications, Dobbs Ferry, first of four volumes due out in 1978).

2. Articles and short studies

(a)   C. F. Alger and S. J. Brams, 'Patterns of Representation in National Capitals and Inter-governmental Organisation', *World Politics*, Vol. 19, July 1967, pp. 646–63.

(b)   H. Alker, 'Dimensions of Conflict in the General Assembly', *American Political Science Review*, Vol. LVIII, 1964, pp. 642–57.

(c)   S. N. Anabtawi, 'Neutralists and Neutralism', *Journal of Politics*, Vol. 27, May 1965, pp. 351–61.

(d)   J. C. Charlesworth (Ed.), 'Is International Communism Winning?', *Annals of the American Academy of Political and Social Science*, Vol. 336, July 1961, pp. 75–97.

(e)   N. Choucri, 'The Non-Alignment of Afro-Asian States: Policy Perception and Behaviour', *Canadian Journal of Political Science*, Vol. 2, 1969, pp. 1–17.

(f)   N. Choucri, 'The Perceptual base of Non-Alignment', *Journal of Conflict Resolution*, Vol. XIII, March 1969, pp. 57–74.

(g)   C. V. Crabb, 'American diplomatic practices and neutralism', *Political Science Quarterly*, Vol. 78, September 1963, pp. 418–43.

(h)   C. V. Crabb (Ed.) 'Non-Alignment in Foreign Affairs', *Annals of the American Academy of Political and Social Science*, Vol. 362, November 1965, pp. 1–128.

(i)   M. A. East, *Some Observations on Foreign Policy-Making in the Ugandan Ministry of Foreign Affairs*, Seminar Paper, Department of Political Science and Public Administration, Makerere University, September 1972.

(j)   P. J. Eldridge, 'India's "non-alignment" policy reviewed', *Australia Outlook*, Vol. 19, August 1965, pp. 146–57.

(k)   R. Gott, 'The Decline of Neutralism, The Belgrade Conference and After' in *Survey of International Affairs 1961* (Royal Institute of International Affairs and Oxford University Press, London, 1965).

(l)   F. L. Hadsel, 'Africa and the world: nonalignment reconsidered', *Annals of the American Academy of Political and Social Science*, Vol. 372, July 1967, pp. 93–104.

(m)   H. Hveem and P. Willetts, 'The Practice of Non-Alignment', paper to the *Universities of East Africa Social Science Conference*, Dar es Salaam, December 1970.

(n)   B. Korany and N. Tawfik, 'Nonalignment: Its Conflict-Reducing Function in the International System', *Annals of International Studies*, Graduate Institute of International Studies 1972, pp. 47–84.

(o)   A. Lijphart, 'The Analysis of Bloc Voting in the General Assembly: A Critique and a Proposal', *American Political Science Review*, Vol. LVII, December 1963, pp. 902–17.

(p)   F. Low-Beer, 'The concept of neutralism', *American Political Science Review*, Vol. LVIII, June 1964, pp. 383–91.

(q)   P. Lyon, 'Neutrality and the Emergence of the Concept of Neutralism', *Review of Politics*, Vol. 22, April 1960, pp. 255–68.

(r)   L. Mates, 'Nonalignment and the Great Powers', *Foreign Affairs*, 1970, pp. 525–36.

(s)   P. J. McGowan, 'Africa & Non-Alignment: A Comparative Study of Foreign Policy', *International Studies Quarterly*, Vol. 12, September 1968, pp. 262–95.

(t)   A. P. Rana, 'The intellectual dimensions of India's nonalignment', *Journal of Asian Studies*, Vol. 28, February 1969, pp. 279–312.

(u)   L. H. Reiselbach, 'Quantitative Techniques for Studying Voting Behaviour in the U.N. General Assembly', *International Organisation*, Vol. 14, Spring 1960, pp. 291–306.

(v)   R. L. Rothstein, 'Foreign Policy and Development Policy: From Nonalignment to International Class War', *International Affairs* (Chatham House, London), Vol. 52, No. 4, October 1976, pp. 598–616.

(w)   B. Russett, 'Discovering Voting Groups in the United Nations', *American Political Science Review*, Vol. LX, June 1966, pp. 327–39.

(x)   'Southern African Customs Union Agreement', *Standard Bank Review*, July 1970.

(y)   H. Teune and S. Synnestvedt, 'Measuring International Alignment', *Orbis*, Vol. 9, 1965, pp. 171–89.

(z)   P. Willetts, 'The Behaviour of the African Group in the General Assembly' (M.Sc. dissertation, University of Strathclyde, 1970 unpublished).

(A)   P. Willetts, 'Towards a Theory of the Phenomenon of Non-Alignment', paper to the E.C.P.R. *Workshop on Models of International Relations*, Mannheim, April 1973.

3. Books on non-alignment

(a)   L. Acimovic (Ed.), *Non-Alignment in the World of Today* (Institute of International Politics and Economics, Belgrade, 1969).

(b)   J. W. Burton, *Non-Alignment* (André Deutsch, London, 1966).

(c)   J. W. Burton, *International Relations: A General Theory* (Cambridge University Press, London, 1967).

(d)   C. V. D. Crabb, *The Elephants & The Grass: a study of non-alignment*, (Praeger, New York, 1965).

(e)   Y. Etinger and O. Metikyan, *The Policy of Non-Alignment* (Progress Publishers, Moscow, 1966).

(f)   G. H. Jansen, *Afro-Asia and Non-Alignment* (Faber and Faber, London, 1966).

(g)   K. P. Karunakaran, *Outside the Contest* (Peoples Publishing House, New Delhi, 1963).

(h)   B. Korany, *Social Change, Charisma and International Behaviour: Toward a Theory of Foreign Policy Making in the Third World* (Sijthoff, Leiden, 1976).

(i)   K. London, *New Nations in a Divided World; the international relations of the Afro-Asian states* (Praeger, New York, 1964).

(j)   P. Lyon, *Neutralism* (Leicester University Press, Leicester, 1963).

(k)   L. W. Martin (Ed.) *Neutralism & Nonalignment: The new States in world affairs* (Praeger, New York, 1962).

(l)   L. Mates, *Nonalignment—Theory and Current Policy* (Oceana Publications, Dobbs Ferry, New York, 1972).

(m)   P. F. Power, *Neutralism & Disengagement* (Scribner Research Anthologies, New York, 1964).

(n)   A. Z. Rubinstein, *Yugoslavia and the Nonaligned World* (Princeton University Press, New Jersey, 1970).

(o)   F. A. Sayegh, *The Dynamics of Neutralism in the Arab World* (Chandler, San Francisco, 1964).

(p)   B. Sen, *Against the Cold War* (Asia Publishing House, Bombay, 1962).

Other books to which reference has been made

(a)   H. Alker and B. Russett, *World Politics in the General Assembly* (Yale University Press, New Haven, 1965).

(b)   M. Barratt-Brown, *After Imperialism* (Merlin Press, London, revised edition, 1970).

(c)   M. Barratt-Brown, *The Economics of Imperialism* (Penguin Modern Economics Texts, London, 1974).

(d)   J. W. Burton, A. J. R. Groom, C. R. Mitchell and A. V. de Reuck, *The Study of World Society: A London Perspective* (International Studies Association, Occasional Paper Number 1, University of Pittsburgh, 1974).

(e)   Z. Cervenka, *The Unfinished Quest for Unity. Africa and the O.A.U.* (Julian Friedmann, London, 1977).

(f)   Committee on Foreign Affairs Personnel, *Personnel for the New Diplomacy* (Taplinger Publishing, New York, 1963).

(g)   J. Dugard, *The South West Africa/Namibia Dispute* University of California Press, Berkeley and London, 1973).

(h)   A. G. Frank, *Capitalism and Underdevelopment in Latin America* (Monthly Review Press, New York and London, 1969).

(i)   J. Frankel, *National Interest* (Macmillan, Key Concepts in Political Science Series, London, 1970).

(j)   T. Hovet, *Bloc Politics in the United Nations* (Harvard University Press, Cambridge, Mass., 1960).

(k)   I.S.S. *The Military Balance 1970–71* (The Institute for Strategic Studies, London, 1970).

(l)   Keesings, *Treaties and Alliances of the World* (Keesings Publications Ltd., London, 1968).

(m)   M. J. Kerbec, *Legally Available U.S. Government Information* (Output Systems Corporation, Virginia, 1970).

(n)   T. Lie, *In the Cause of Peace* (Macmillan, New York, 1954).

(o)   G. Liska, *Nations in Alliance. The Limits of Interdependence* (John Hopkins Press, Baltimore, 1968).

(p)   A. A. Mazrui, *On Heroes and Uhuru-Worship* (Longman, London, 1967).

(q)   H. J. Morgenthau, *Politics Among Nations* (A. A. Knopf, New York, third edition, 1962).

(r)   G. A. Nasser, *On Consolidation of the Cause of World Peace* (U.A.R. State Information Service, Cairo, 1966).

(s)   K. Nkrumah, *Neo-Colonialism: The Last Stage of Imperialism* (Heinemann African Writers Series, London, 1965).

(t)   M. S. Rajan, *India in World Affairs 1954–56* (Asia Publishing House, New Delhi, 1964).

(u)   R. Rose, *Politics in England Today* (Faber and Faber, London, 1974).

(v)   G. Rosner, *The United Nations Emergency Force* (Columbia University Press, New York and London, 1963).

(w)   Stockholm International Peace Research Institute, *The Arms Trade with the Third World* (Almqvist and Wiksell, Stockholm and Humanities Press, New York, 1971).

(x)   C. L. Taylor and M. C. Hudson, *World Handbook of Political and Social Indicators. Second Edition* (Yale University Press, New Haven and London, 1972).

(y)   F. O. Wilcox and C. M. Marcy, *Proposals for Change in the United Nations* (Brookins Institution, Washington D.C., 1955).

(z)   J. Woddis, *An Introduction to Neo-Colonialism* (International Publishers, New York, 1967).

Index

303